THE PROUD DECADES

THE PROUD DECADES

America in War and in Peace

1941 ◁◁◁ 1960

JOHN PATRICK DIGGINS

W · W · NORTON & COMPANY · NEW YORK · LONDON

Since this page cannot legibly accommodate all the permissions and credits, pages 366–67 constitute an extension of the copyright page.

Copyright © 1988 by John Patrick Diggins

All rights reserved.

Published simultaneously in Canada by Penguin Books Canada Ltd., 2801 John Street, Markham, Ontario L3R 1B4.

Printed in the United States of America.

The text of this book is composed in Linotype Walbaum, with display type set in Walbaum.
Composition and Manufacturing by The Maple-Vail Book Manufacturing Group.
Book design by Antonina Krass

Library of Congress Cataloging-in-Publication Data
Diggins, John P.
 The proud decades: America in war and in peace, 1941–1960 / John Patrick Diggins.
 p. cm.
 Bibliography: p.
 Includes index.
 1. United States—Civilization—1945–   2. United States—Civilization—1918–1945. I. Title.
E169.12.D56   1988
973.9—dc19   87-24182

ISBN 0-393-02548-9

W. W. Norton & Company, Inc., 500 Fifth Avenue, New York, N.Y. 10110
W. W. Norton & Company Ltd., 37 Great Russell Street, London WC1B 3NU

FOR JOAN

Contents

When an epoch is closed, the following epoch is not generous, or even just, to it. What it achieved is taken for granted; what it failed to do is the outstanding and irritating fact.

JOHN DEWEY

Introduction

"There are in history no beginnings and no endings," wrote R. G. Collingwood in 1939, the momentous year World War II broke out and changed the world forever. "History books begin and end, but the events they describe do not."

This book begins and ends in full knowledge that history neither starts nor stops for the historian. While covering the period 1941 to 1960, opening with Pearl Harbor and concluding with the election of John F. Kennedy, many events depicted here had their origins in earlier years, and many developments of the period still affect our generations. In reexperiencing the past we may learn some things about today's world, proving the philosopher Søren Kierkegaard's maxim that although life must be lived forward, it can only be understood backwards.

Of the forties and fifties it may be said that no such previous decades have been so important in creating the conditions that govern our lives. Thus, the book seeks to explore a series of themes: the cold war and the question of its inevitability; domestic politics and the successes and failures of the Democratic and Republican parties; the changing nature of American society as a result of economic growth and post-World War II abundance; popular culture and the enduring idols of Americans young and old; higher culture and the influence of European refugee intellectuals; and the early civil rights movement and the first stirrings of feminism.

Difficult to classify politically, the forties and fifties represented neither reform nor reaction, neither liberal activism in the name of social justice nor conservative consolidation and a return to the old order. Yet it would be wrong to claim, as some writers have, that the era was merely a period of passivity and postponement, as though nothing important happened until the radical sixties came along to awaken America from its ideological slumbers. The view put forth here suggests that the sixties were the aberration and that the forties and fifties are decades that tell Americans more about themselves.

But this book is an overall survey, not a sustained argument. It attempts to recount, and sometimes reinterpret, American politics, diplomacy, society, and culture in order to appreciate what the country was up against and what the people believed in and lived for. Almost equal attention is given to different aspects of American life. Perhaps the book's dimensions are similar to those some wit once suggested for the "miniskirt" that began coming into vogue at the end of the fifties: short enough to arouse interest and long enough to cover the matter.

In recent times historians have demanded a new "synthesis" to interpret American history, and in France the call is for *histoire en totalité,* a genre of scholarship that purports to connect each discrete event and episode to an overarching interpretive scheme. Clearly there is a deep human need to see history as a whole, to find meaning in it. And no doubt there are obvious interpretive themes that the historian can discern in, if not impose upon, the forties and fifties. But to emphasize, for example, the conventional interpretation of consensus and conformity would force a selective focus on politics and society to the neglect of poetry, philosophy, and the fine arts, creative activities throbbing with restlessness and dissonance during the period. A study of the wider panorama of the two decades brings forth their richer variety and ambiguity—the tension, for instance, between the mood of moderation in national politics and the daring innovation that exploded in cultural modernism.

Some events and episodes of the forties and fifties may leave the reader, as they did the author, with a sense of shame and sorrow. The fire-bombings of Dresden and Tokyo, Hiroshima and Nagasaki; the Holocaust and America's indifference to the plight of European Jews; the internment of Japanese-Americans; the race riots of the war years; the Port Chicago mutiny trial; McCarthyism and the Red Scare; the quiz-show scandals and their mindless audience; the unabashed materialism, spiritual shallowness, and banal "togetherness" of the era; and the government's refusal to work fully and systematically toward the international control of atomic energy—all are chapters of American history that must be confronted honestly. Against the tragic mistakes of the past, history must strengthen a nation's memory, of the bad as well as the good.

But the same decades offer Americans much to be proud of, both then and now. World War II was a great and good war, fought courageously by young Americans who had to win back on the battlefield what statesmen had lost in the conference room. After the war former enemies became America's friends. Nations such as Germany, Italy, and Japan thrived under democratic political institutions once thought alien to their cultures. The Marshall Plan for Western Europe and the Point Four program for aid to the underdeveloped world were deeds of unprecedented generosity. Postwar America witnessed a number of breakthroughs in science and medicine, from penicillin to the polio vaccine. Fields of learning advanced enormously. Public education became available to millions of college students, most of whom easily moved beyond the professional and economic status of their proud parents. The same decades enjoyed remarkable economic growth and, after the Korean War, solid years of peace and prosperity. Politically this era witnessed something unique in the twentieth century: two sucessive presidents, Harry S. Truman and Dwight D. Eisenhower, each representing a different party and each fulfilling two terms of office. Both leaders demonstrated the responsibilities and virtues of the Oval Office and not its abuses and vulnerabilities. Under Truman and Eisenhower Americans experienced some bitter political controversies but they never lost faith in government.

Thus, if the forties and fifties may seem the worst of times, they were also in part the best of times. To emphasize one side of the story to the exclusion of the other would be misleading. Likewise with the expression of pride. After World War II, for example, nationalistic pride led Americans to want to see their political values and institutions adopted abroad. To the extent they were not, a kind of overweening pride, or hubris, could release frustrations born of vanity as well as fear when the world refused to conform to America's will—or what publisher Henry Luce called "the American experience" and, even more boldly, "The American Century." But it was also racial pride—the demand for human dignity—that motivated black civil rights activists in the forties and fifties; and social pride—the demand for conspicuous possessions—that fueled the economy.

Pride, of course, is an ambiguous human attribute. For centuries moralists have warned against it as the sin of arrogance that destroys civilizations; some have indicted it as a conceit we admire in ourselves but not in others, the nemesis of narcissism that leads to self-idolatry rather than humility. The dialectic between pride and shame should thus counterbalance each emotion. A capacity for both is essential to keeping history honest. The sorrow and the glory in this period of America's past are inseparable. To be worthy of truth, history must make us shudder as well as smile.

ACKNOWLEDGMENTS

The author is indebted to John Morton Blum, David Kennedy, William E. Leuchtenberg, and Ronald Steel for reading a first-draft manuscript of the present book. Their careful criticisms saved me from several potential errors of fact, interpretation, and misplaced emphasis. A word of appreciation is also due to Patty Peltekos for her thorough copy-editing and fact-checking, and to Ed Barber for his thoughtful editorial suggestions. I am also grateful to Carolyn Gee and Elizabeth Ruyle for typing the manuscript into a computer, and to Ruth Mandel for tracking down the illustrations. Finally, the book is dedicated to Joan, who endured it all and who, like the author, is a proud product of "the proud decades."

PART ONE

From Pearl Harbor to Hiroshima

"Tora! Tora! Tora!"

On the afternoon of Sunday, December 7, 1941, the nation's radio broadcasts and professional football games were interrupted. That morning, at 7:55 A.M. Hawaiian time, the Japanese navy inflicted a surprise attack on Pearl Harbor, home of America's Pacific fleet. Most Americans, sensing that their lives would be changed by the shocking event, would remember exactly where they were that afternoon. President Franklin D. Roosevelt called December 7 "a date which will live in infamy." He knew better, however, than to say, as he had done when he took office eight years earlier, that "there is nothing to fear but fear itself." This time the enemy was real, as real as the anger and hatred that swept America.

On the West Coast airwaves buzzed with stories of approaching Japanese submarines and planes. People stacked sandbags against public buildings to prepare for an aerial attack and glued blackout paper to the windows of their homes in case of night raids. In Los Angeles and San Francisco civil defense wardens enforced curfews and police followed up rumors of spy networks in Japanese neighborhoods, while at night cars crept without lights along coastal highways. For weeks up and down the coast, schools closed as frequent air-raid alarms sounded and students were ordered home to seek shelter. A few of the more adventurous grabbed their .22s and BB guns and headed to the beach to await the invasion. Sport and hardware stores immediately ran out of ammunition, flashlights, and binoculars. One student, then sixteen,

In San Francisco six months after Pearl Harbor, air raid wardens enforcing dimout regulations.

recalled many years later that he and his friends did "the only thing we knew how: take a gun and defend our land." On bluffs and ocean-front rooftops people vigilantly tried to sight the enemy. Except for incendiary bombs dropped in Oregon—they failed to set off expected forest fires—and later some light shelling of Santa Barbara's oil fields, Japanese military power never touched American shores.

Yet the attack on Pearl Harbor had been brilliantly conceived and executed. Not only did the Japanese demonstrate the striking capacity of the new aircraft carrier, they also employed fighter planes armed with shallow-water torpedoes, high-level precision bombers, and two-man midget submarines. Japanese officers feared that their armada would be discovered in the weeks it took to cross the Pacific or that American naval vessels would have left the area. But as the first for-mation of planes hurtled down the Pearl Harbor corridor and pilots saw within their view the United States Pacific Fleet, the signal went out "Tora! Tora! Tora!" ("Tiger! Tiger! Tiger!"), code words informing the Japanese navy that the enemy had been caught unawares. Pearl Harbor fires raged for a week after the bombing, and when the smoke had cleared the damage seemed staggering. Twenty-four hundred Americans had been lost, 68 of them civilians. Eight battleships, three light cruisers, three destroyers, and four auxiliary craft were either sunk or capsized. Forty-two bombers were either destroyed or damaged on the ground, as were dozens of fighter planes. All but ignored in the helpless feeling that swept Americans was one large consolation—it could have been much worse.

Not only did the attack miss those American aircraft carriers which fortunately were at sea, it also failed to knock out repair shops and fuel-storage facilities. Destruction of these vital logistical resources would have forced the Pacific Fleet to operate from the West Coast. In addition, the twenty-year-old battleships at Pearl Harbor were regarded as nearly obsolete; although several would be repaired and see action within a year, more than three hundred new warships were under construction at the time of the attack. Within months, moreover, American industry would be producing more planes per day than were lost at Pearl Harbor. Above all, the sneak attack, launched without a declaration of war, united Americans and enabled the country to enter the war to vindicate its honor. In the long run, these unintended results turned Japan's first-strike strategy from triumph to disaster.

What were Japan's intentions? Although some Japanese hotheads believed America could be defeated, the major objective at Pearl Harbor was to cripple the United States Pacific Fleet so that Japan could expand unhindered into Southeast Asia. Ironically, the theoretical

Pearl Harbor's "Battleship Row" after the Japanese attack.

rationale Japan relied upon for Pearl Harbor came from an American. In the early part of the twentieth century Captain Alfred Thayer Mahan insisted that the country which commanded the seas would enjoy superior power. That position, Mahan held, could be achieved by a single, decisive naval battle, such as Japan had won against Russia in 1904. In the 1930s worldwide depression reinforced the conviction among Japanese military officers that only overseas expansion could solve the country's economic problems. But how to do this? Japan scarcely concealed its intention to penetrate China for reasons of historical rivalry and countries like Java and Malaya for natural resources and markets. American public opinion resented such imperialistic aims, and in 1940 Congress began to impose embargoes on various strategic exports to Japan. The following year when Japan announced a protectorate over the entire French Indochina (now Cambodia, Laos, and Vietnam), President Roosevelt responded by freezing Japanese assets in the United States. When it became clear to Japanese military leaders that American retaliation would restrict Japanese access to fuel and other vital materials and that the United States would never allow a free hand in China, war became inevitable. For six months before Pearl Harbor the Japanese premier, Prince Fumimaro Konoye, tried to negotiate an agreement, but General Hideki Tojo refused to agree with the State Department's demand that Japan withdraw some troops from China. Even while discussions continued, the die had been cast.

Pearl Harbor has been the subject of considerable "revisionist" history, a school of thought expounded shortly after the war that tends to shift the blame for events from foreign powers to American herself. Thus President Roosevelt has been charged by a few journalists and historians either with mistaking Japan's aims or deliberately setting up Pearl Harbor as a means of getting America into World War II. Believing it inexplicable that Roosevelt would have the whole fleet at Pearl Harbor, and aware that cryptologists had cracked Japan's secret code, these revisionists insist that he must have known in advance of the attack.

To be sure, Roosevelt and his advisors recognized that the Imperial Navy and the entire Japanese economy depended on raw materials from the United States. Thus the banning of shipments made war imminent if not inevitable: the question was not so much *when* but *where*. The reading of the coded messages and other intelligence reports seemed to confirm the feeling that Hawaii would be immune from attack not only because of its distance but also because the reports pointed toward a Japanese move against British and Dutch possessions in Southeast Asia and specifically against the Philippines. Roosevelt's willingness to continue discussions with Japan even in the light of imminent war was not meant to mislead the American people; on the contrary, he desired to postpone as long as possible a war in the Pacific while America marshaled the resources it would need to join the war already taking place in Europe. Here Western European democracies had been waging what appeared to be a losing battle against Adolf Hitler and the Third Reich.

When Hitler was elected chancellor of Germany in 1933, most Americans expressed no great alarm. To many Americans Hitler and his National Socialist movement represented a legitimate effort to correct the injustices of the World War I Versailles settlement, curb the growing influence of communism, and address economic problems caused by the world-wide depression. Although the militaristic and racist ideology of Nazism seemed excessive, the sober German people themselves would surely prove too civilized to succumb to it. Some American diplomats, notably Joseph P. Kennedy and William C. Bullitt, would come to believe that the Soviet Union posed a greater threat than Nazi Germany.

But American attitudes changed as Nazism revealed its brutally aggressive character. Public opinion grew more apprehensive with each advance of the German war machine: the occupation of the Rhineland (1936), the *Anschluss* ("union") with Austria (1938), and the seizure of Czechoslovakia (1939). By 1939 it seemed clear that England's "appeasement" policy of conceding to Hitler's territorial demands had been a tragic error, and when Hitler ordered the invasion of Poland in September, the British Foreign Office and Parliament declared war on Germany. There followed an eerie quiet period, "the phony war," in which Russia remained neutral in accordance with a nonaggression pact with Germany and Hitler hesitated in launching an attack in the West. Before the end of 1940, however, German tanks and paratroopers stuck out in a blitzkrieg that brought down France, Holland, Belgium, Denmark, and Norway. Then the Luftwaffe went to work on England with round-the-clock aerial assaults and England reeled. This last remaining democratic power in Europe had an army in disarray, thousands of whom had barely escaped the Nazi noose in the "miracle of Dunkirk." Nor were its navy and air force fully equipped to face the most fearsome fighting machine in world history. England now battled for her life.

As the situation grew increasingly desperate in Europe, Americans were divided. Although the great majority desired the defeat of Hitler, they also hoped that the Allies could hold out without American participation in the war. Such attitudes handicapped the Roosevelt administration's efforts to revise the Neutrality Act of 1937, one of a series of congressional moves to ensure that the United States did not repeat the diplomatic policies that led to intervention in 1917. But the sentiment behind neutrality and noninvolvement went deeper than the lessons of the First World War and President Wilson's unfulfilled hopes for the League of Nations. In truth, America has always vacillated between desiring to protect its political ideals from the rest of the world and desiring to see those ideals prevail in the world.

The doctrine of nonintervention has a long, honored tradition in American history, going as far back as President George Washington's Farewell Address in the late eighteenth century. Sharing a widespread conviction that the Old World was corrupt and in decline, Washington advised future generations to beware of "entangling alliances." The principle of nonintervention in the affairs of other nations was also invoked by President Abraham Lincoln to condemn America's war with Mexico and Czarist Russia's occupation of Hungary. In the early twentieth century the principle took on a double meaning, dividing those who wanted America to remain aloof from the entire world and those who supported intervention in Asia only. One the eve of 1941, President Roosevelt felt the urgency to challenge all noninterventionist traditions when he called upon America to help the world realize the four vital freedoms—freedom of speech, freedom of worship, freedom from want, and freedom from fear. But his eloquent appeal failed to change the sentiments of the numerous and disparate but adamant noninterventionists.

First were the isolationists, those who distrusted *any* American involvement in the affairs of Europe. Motivated by a mixture of Anglophobia, hatred of Roosevelt, or genuine pacifist sympathies, the isolationists organized around the America First Committee and the leadership of Charles A. Lindbergh, the famous aviator who admired the Luftwaffe. For Lindbergh, German efficiency had rendered the Third Reich unbeatable. The America First movement was strong in the Midwest and the Mountain states, from which Idaho's Senator William E. Borah thundered that "all this hysteria is manufactured and artificial." Basically, the isolationists assumed that Hitler posed no threat to America's security and that England was fighting not for democracy but merely to save its empire.

A second group was the guilt-stricken liberals. These progressive intellectuals had earlier supported America's entry into World War I and then became bitterly disillusioned with President Woodrow Wilson's messianic promise to "make the world safe for democracy." Much of this disillusionment flowed from the liberals shock at discovering Wilson's Fourteen Points being violated in the Versailles peace settlement in 1919, when victorious England and France imposed reparations upon Germany and various European peoples were denied the right to national self-determination. In the twenties the impression grew that America had been seduced into the war by bankers, munitions producers, and British propaganda. American boys who died for their country, protested the poet Ezra Pound, died for the profiteers and their botched civilization, "an old bitch gone in the teeth." In the thirties a Senate investigating committee issued a report that allegedly documented a conspiracy between the munitions industry and Wall Street. Thus when war broke out in Europe in 1939, many writers remained convinced America must heed the lessons of the past. "No matter what happens," declared the eminent philosopher and educator, John Dewey, "stay out." That rationale had been expressed a year earlier in a celebrated article in the liberal *New Republic.* "I remember vividly the days before 1917," editor Bruce Bliven explained, "when a country that did not want to go to war was tricked and bullied and persuaded into doing so. . . . I feel, as I watch the motion picture of events unreeling on the screen of time, that I have seen it all before. This is where I came in." Other intellectuals like the poet Archibald MacLeish and the essayist Lewis Mumford challenged such liberal attitudes, claiming that Dewey's "progressive" philosophy left America innocent of the reality of "evil" and thus unprepared for Hitler.

Other groups, smaller in number but louder in clamor, also opposed intervention. Followers of the right-wing Father Charles Coughlin were pro-fascist and looked favorably upon Italy's dictator, Benito Mussolini, and the German-American Bund, which attracted about 25,000 members, supported Hitler's anti-Semitism. The radical Left also had its reasons for advocating nonintervention. Communists, whether one of the 60,000 members of the Communist party or of the fellow travelers sympathetic to Russia, believed that America must follow the Soviet Union's example and remain neutral. This attitude quickly reversed itself when Hitler marched into Russia in June 1941, and the American Communist party immediately came out for intervention. On the other hand, its rival, the Trotskyist Socialist Workers party, opposed collaboration with the Russian dictator Joseph Stalin even in an united front against Hitler. Some members of American ethnic groups also opposed intervention. Polish-Americans distrusted American aid of the

Soviet Union, Irish-Americans felt much the same toward aiding England, and Americans of Italian and German descent feared a war against their home countries.

President Roosevelt had also helped create the noninterventionist mood when campaigning for reelection in 1940. Again and again he reminded audiences of how much he and his wife hated war and assured them that no American boys would be sacrificed on the field of battle. But Roosevelt was basically an internationalist who valued the League of Nations and world cooperation. Thus the string of sudden Nazi conquests and Britain's precarious fate forced him into action, but through means of indirect intervention. Most Americans favored these early efforts to support the Allies and prepare our country to be the "arsenal of democracy." In 1940 America enacted the first peacetime draft in history; the following year it was renewed by only one vote in the House. Roosevelt also dispatched by executive order fifty destroyers to Britain, and steered through Congress the Lend-Lease Act enabling him to transfer American military supplies to Britain without payment. Two-thirds of Americans favored lend-lease, though only for a limited period. Thus, even as German U-boats (submarines) sank American vessels and Congress responded by authorizing the arming of merchant freighters, America was not quite ready to contemplate a clear and deliberate declaration of war.

One reason for this reluctance was a conviction that domestic issues needed to be faced before America could turn to international problems. America had yet to win her own war against the Great Depression, and a sizable number of Americans remained convinced that they could simply fight fascism abroad by perfecting democracy at home. Even those of this view, however, were divided over the New Deal, Roosevelt's vast program of social reform and economic regulation that ushered in what came to be known as the "welfare state." Some thought the New Deal had fallen short of its goal. Others argued that it had gone too far and that the goals had been misconceived to the point of jeopardizing individual liberty. Some Americans loved Roosevelt for what he had done *for* them, others hated him for what he was doing *to* them.

FDR AND THE FATE OF THE NEW DEAL

No other American president has so deeply touched the lives of the American people as Franklin Delano Roosevelt. A man of enormous

President Franklin D. Roosevelt, symbol of hope and confidence during the depression and war years.

energy and captivating charm, Roosevelt's impact on America's political culture was so great that many subsequent presidents, even Republicans, would strive to walk in his shadow. A handsome, broad-shouldered man who waved a flamboyant cigarette holder while beaming a jovial grin, Roosevelt had been crippled by polio and was confined to a wheelchair. Nevertheless he had a joyous lust for life and a compassionate desire to see progress everywhere. No sooner had he seen the Sahara than he wanted to irrigate it. Born and bred an aristocrat, Roosevelt identified with the plight of the common folk, so much so that some wealthy Americans called him a traitor to his class. In the 1940 election he won an unprecedented third term, promising to see America through the war years with the same buoyant confidence that he brought to domestic problems during the depression. Yet some of those problems persisted. By 1941 the New Deal was at an impasse.

In the forties memories of the depression still haunted the American conscience—the breadlines, the jobless hovering around a fire seeking warmth, the homeless who lived in tents, their skinny and ragged children, migrant workers making their way across the country in broken-down jalopies, college graduates selling apples on a street corner. Some of these conditions had been improved. When Roosevelt took office in the depths of the depression in 1933, 25.2 percent of the American work force was unemployed. By 1940 that figure had been reduced to 9.3 percent, and the following year the jobless rate dropped considerably further due to the war in Europe and the demand for American supplies. Still, five and one-half million adults lacked work, and many of those lucky jobholders could barely make ends meet.

The New Deal had made a brave attempt to fight the depression on all fronts: numerous measures had been introduced to bring immediate relief to the unemployed through government work projects; banks and stock market institutions had been reformed through federal regulatory agencies; farmers assisted through subsidies and price supports; labor conditions had improved now that unions held the right to collective bargaining; and the sinking morale of thousands of young Americans had been raised by involving them in conservation and forestry projects. Social security for the elderly and unemployment insurance for those out of work had been enacted into law. Housing was now available to the poor through government-sponsored slum-clearing programs, and home ownership was considerably more accessible to the middle class through the guaranteed-mortgage loans of banks and other lending institutions. Many of these programs proved successful, and many who benefited from them praised Roosevelt and became part of his vast electoral coalition: farmers (especially small farmers), industrial workers, the poor and the aged, and lower-middle class ethnic groups (Jews, Irish, Poles, Italians, Germans, and Slavic Americans). Although New Deal liberals made every effort to include the hitherto excluded, some groups were left out, namely migrant workers, domestic servants, and masses of unorganized workers without union affiliation.

The famous Roosevelt coalition also included black Americans grateful for the small relief they received from the New Deal's public work projects. But the Roosevelt administration had postponed facing a problem that lay ahead of America for years to come—the problem of racism. In the North, labor unions showed little interest in opening their ranks to black workers; in the solidly Democratic South, programs designed to help blacks floundered on one white attitude: "Jeezus Christ, you ain't goin' to pay no nigger sixteen bucks a week, are you?"

Opposition to the New Deal grew throughout the thirties and peaked in the 1940 presidential election. The Republican candidate Wendell Willkie appealed to businessmen and middle-class white Americans who saw themselves as victims of the New Deal's progressive taxes and government regulations. Republicans accused the New Deal of swelling the size of government with unnecessary agencies, preferring the safety of economic security to the risks of entrepreneurial opportunity, and destroying the confidence of the business community. Even so, Roosevelt easily won the election over Willkie, and it is worth noting that the Republicans did not repudiate all of the New Deal. Willkie attacked public-power projects like the Tennessee Valley Authority (TVA) but not social security, aid to farmers, or trade-union bargaining power. Thus, on the eve of America's entry into World War II, the Republican party remained ambivalent about the New Deal, as did many southern Democrats. Years earlier Roosevelt had failed to persuade Congress to pass further progressive legislation. Yet many of the New Deal programs became part of a common heritage shared by both parties. Where the Republicans and Democrats would differ most acutely in future years was over fiscal policy.

Much of the New Deal fiscal policy was derived from the ideas of Sir John Maynard Keynes, a British economist. Keynes questioned an older classical school of economists who assumed that free-market forces could operate on their own in response to the principle of supply and demand. According to Keynes, such self-regulating mechanisms broke down when business income declined in periods of recession or depression and brought on unemployment. In such situations, he argued, the government must intervene to create aggregate demand by increasing consumer power. This demand would stimulate production in the private sector. And the government could at least temporarily stimulate the economy by spending more than it would receive from taxes. After 1937 the New Deal experimented only fitfully with Keynesian economics, for Roosevelt remained nervous with the prospect of unbalanced budgets and an increasing national debt. While national income and industrial production increased markedly in the mid-thirties, growth in both areas began to drop toward the end of the decade when Roosevelt cut back on spending from fear of growing deficits. The result was the recession of 1937–38. Only when war preparations required increasing national defense expenditures in the early forties did income and production once again rise, but this situation forced itself upon the Roosevelt administration. Meanwhile, the Republicans had argued all along that the New Deal had retarded economic recovery. If the federal budget were balanced by cutting expenses, they insisted, then business would revive sufficiently to absorb the unemployed and make relief spending unnecessary.

This debate between liberal Democrats and conservative Republicans, between those who believed in government spending to bring about recovery and those who looked to private enterprise, was never resolved. When America entered World War II fiscal policy had more to do with military victory than economic recovery. In truth, America never committed itself to the full implications of Keynesianism. While Keynes advocated heavy government spending in periods of depression, he also advocated heavy government taxation in periods of prosperity in order to constrain consumer demand and thereby prevent inflation and reduce the national debt. Herein lies the enduring dilemma for the American politician: would future generations willingly be taxed to pay off debts incurred for programs that benefited others? Would they even be willing to pay for programs that had once benefited themselves or their parents and relatives? The irony of the New Deal is that the more economic conditions improved, the less people felt they needed it.

Just prior to America's entry into the war, the nation was profoundly divided more by class than by generational conflicts. With massive unemployment and millions still on relief, many insecure Americans continued to blame the nation's economic problems on government interference, deficit spending, labor unions, and lazy workers. The South still resisted social welfare programs that touched the sensitive subject of race relations. Thus Roosevelt, a savior to some Americans, became a scourge to others, "that man in the White House." With the shock of Pearl Harbor, however, political recriminations and class divisions yielded momentarily to the cold fact that America was at war. Even isolationists and reactionaries who weeks earlier had attacked Roosevelt as a war-monger now cheered him as the nation's leader. Jaded college students found themselves rising to sing "The Star-Spangled Banner." The outward display of Americanism was "something that I always sneered at, but we all stood and we all tingled. So the fervor started right off the bat," recalls one member of the Pearl Harbor generation. The surge of patriotism that swept the country made Americans more interested in producing bullets and tanks than debating budgets and taxes. Never before in its history, and never again in its immediate future, would America enjoy such unity in time of war.

THE HOME FRONT

World War II was the most popular war in American history. Outraged by the attack on Pearl Harbor, fearful of Hitler's conquest of Europe, people everywhere wanted to do what they could. High school seniors looked forward to graduation day, after which they could enlist in one of the armed services. Coeds received instruction in first aid to help the Red Cross. Citizens undertook scrap drives, collecting tin cans, paper, metal junk, and used shoes. Old tires, floor mats, and even balloons were stockpiled on the assumption that Japan would control all rubber resources, and milk-weed pods were picked as a substitute for silk in parachute production. Housewives brought jars of fat to butcher shops so that the glycerin extracted could be used in making bullets. To ease the shortage of vegetables, lawns blossomed into victory gardens. A call for civilian defense workers yielded twelve million volunteers. Five million young men volunteered for military service (ten million more would be inducted by 1944), and more than one hundred thousand nurses joined the WACS, WAVES, and SPARS, the women's branches of the army, navy, and coast guard. Other Americans donated blood, bought war bonds, and worked overtime in shipyards and aircraft plants. Mothers took turns at child-care centers while others served as airplane spotters. Many Americans accepted the rationing of gasoline, tires, meat, and butter, and even children understood why there were no Hershey bars. It was truly a people's war.

At least at first. After the initial flush of patriotism, the world of politics, government, and business returned to more familiar ways. Roosevelt had created a series of agencies to coordinate economic mobilization for war production. But throughout 1942 civil administrators, old New Dealers, military officers, and politicians bickered with one another over government contracts and scarce resources. Liberals charged that big business intended to continue profiting from consumer sales instead of shifting to all-out military production. The economist Keynes urged Roosevelt to speed conversion of the country to a full war economy. Nothing less would overcome shortages in munitions, shipping, aircraft, and trained military personnel.

The American work force mobilized for the war effort. In 1942 throngs of men and women flocked to war plants and trade-union leaders accepted a no-strike pledge for the duration of the war. The United Auto Workers' vice-president Walter P. Reuther showed how part of the battle for Europe could be won on the assembly lines of Detroit by promising the production of five hundred planes a day. Unemployment dropped continuously, reaching a record low of 1.2 percent in 1944. Enjoying high wages for the first time in their lives, workers felt the hard times of the depression were over. Yet many believed there would be a postwar depression, and soon more immediate grievances developed. The Roosevelt administration imposed a wage ceiling, some

In order to enlist the support of the entire population, the US government had artists depict the war as a battle for production on the home front.

employers violated child-labor laws in order to hire high-school drop-outs at low pay, and United States Steel and other big industries were challenging union membership by calling for an open shop. Fearing the gains of the New Deal were being undermined, some union men began grumbling about a strike. When a wildcat strike erupted in the San Francisco shipyards, troops in armored cars with machine guns moved in to crush it. Faced with growing worker unrest, Roosevelt established a National War Labor Board (NWLB) that would mediate among labor, management, and the public interest.

Roosevelt also had to deal with John L. Lewis, the beetle-browed, barrel-chested head of the United Mine Workers who spent his weekends reading Shakespeare and the classics. Stubborn, intelligent, once a hero to the liberal Democrats, Lewis fell into disfavor when he threatened to withdraw coal from war industries. And Lewis's men did engage in work-stoppages throughout the war as did some railroad and steel workers. But working with the NWLB, Roosevelt persuaded miners to accept an older formula for tying wage increases and fringe benefits to the cost-of-living index. Congress, more reflective of the public's critical mood, enacted legislation imposing on workers a thirty-day "cooling off" period of discussion prior to striking, after which the president was authorized to seize striking plants and order strikers back to work. Often wartime labor felt it was being ignored by the Roosevelt administration, particularly when rumors spread that troublemakers would be ordered fired by the government or drafted into the army. But even so, American workers came through. Although there was talk of absenteeism in the early years of the war, the great majority of workers sweated for long hours, accepting overtime and swing shifts and putting some of their time and a half paychecks into war bonds.

During World War II American farmers made enormous gains. Unlike the depression era, with its dust bowls and floods, the early forties enjoyed excellent weather. Farmers also benefited from a guaranteed market in feeding the military services and from new agricultural machinery and planting methods. Crop production increased by 50 percent and farm income soared 200 percent until the government imposed ceilings on agricultural prices. Before the end of the war many farmers had paid off their mortgages. Lands once ravaged by drought and soil erosion were now becoming the "breadbasket of the world."

As with workers, however, farmers recognized that the sudden prosperity resulted from a war economy that would soon end, and thus they too looked forward with apprehension. Farmers also had immediate grievances. The scarcity of field hands and spare machinery parts was a source of frustration. More controversial were disputes over parity (the equivalence between current purchasing power and that previously established by the government), incentives to be used to increase production, and the government's price stabilization policies. Such issues divided the poor and the relatively well-off small farmers from rich growers and huge agro-corporate enterprises. Agricultural organizations engaged in bitter rivalry with other institutions. The American Farm Bureau represented the interests of large producers and the Farm Security Administration (FSA) those of small family farms. The Farm Bureau pushed through Congress legislation allowing ceilings only after prices had reached 110 percent of their prewar levels. At the same time the bureau tried to undermine health care and other antipoverty welfare measures the FSA had sponsored to improve the plight of small, independent farmers. The bureau also made every effort to weaken both the New Deal's Agricultural Adjustment Administration and the Department of Agriculture and to set for itself parity levels. Roosevelt, convinced that uncontrolled farm prices would further exacerbate inflation, was able to hold agricultural producers in line during the war. But increasingly American farmers of all stripe and size grew resentful at the suggestion of any system of price controls. Having benefited from the New Deal years earlier, farmers were the first large constituency to become estranged from the Roosevelt coalition. They would not be the last.

By the end of the 1930s the business community had little use for Roosevelt and the New Deal. During the war, however, it developed a new appreciation for the role of government. Spurred by lucrative contracts as well as patriotic duty, the Ford and General Motors companies converted to military production in early 1942; soon new aviation companies like Martin and Grumman were mass-producing army bombers and naval fighter planes. The collaboration of business and government would be praised by administrators and technocrats who took pride in such wartime inventions as synthetic rubber, frozen foods, and prefabricated housing. But contract scandals and rumors of shoddy production of military hardware troubled liberal Democrats. Builder Henry J. Kaiser used lobbies to secure government loans in order to rush into production a fleet of untested "Liberty" freighters; and at Curtiss-Wright plane engines were reported to be substandard. Harry S. Truman, Democratic senator from Missouri, organized a committee to investigate war production and became a hero for keeping a close surveillance on quality control and excess war profits. The Roosevelt administration tried to bring some measure of rational coordination by establishing the War Production Board (WPB), headed by Donald Nelson of the Sears, Roebuck Company. With the approval of liberals, Nelson eliminated competitive bidding to give small business a piece of the action in war production. But the WPB, staffed by corporate executives who accepted the government's "dollar-a-year" gesture stipend while maintaining their own private salaries, proved incapable of curbing the influence of big business and coordinating allocations and priorities. When Roosevelt later replaced Nelson with Charles E. Wilson of the General Electric Company, small businesses saw even less chance of obtaining defense contracts.

If there appeared little equality of opportunity in profits from production, neither did there appear much "equality of sacrifice" in income after taxation. Sharply increased taxes, facilitated by the introduction of payroll withholding, was sufficient to finance only about half of the war's cost. In 1943 Roosevelt wanted to increase income taxes further to bring annual revenues to $16 billion; he also advocated increased levies on stocks, bonds, and other investments. But Congress voted only $2.2 billion, leaving corporate wealth safe, and Congress made its bill law by overriding the president's veto. Nevertheless, during the war years there occurred a greater redistribution of income, particularly from the upper to the middle class, than during any similar time span in the twentieth century. Although the president could never convince Congress of the need for a progressive tax policy, personal income soared mainly because workers were fully employed and many were even working overtime and the United States was spending over three hundred million dollars a day on the war. In order to fight the war, America was now doing what Keynes had urged to fight the depression.

Without an effective tax-savings policy to curb the war's inflationary pressures only two other mechanisms remained—price control and rationing, the chief responsibility of the Office of Price Administration (OPA). During the early war years Americans had an unprecedented amount of money in their pockets. Yet except for a haircut or a movie, it was difficult to spend money when stores stood half-empty. Economists assumed that a situation of growing demand in decreasing supply would fuel inflation by driving prices sky-high, and thus OPA aimed to establish price levels for goods like butter and meat and ration their allocation by means of stamps and coupons. Some OPA regulations proved easy to circumvent. A liquor store, for example, would compensate for the regulated price on a bottle of scotch by requiring the customer to buy a case of beer along with it. In Oklahoma City a car dealer only sold an automobile if the buyer also agreed to purchase his dog for $400; once off the lot, the dog would find its way home. Those who headed OPA, young New Deal intellectuals like John Kenneth Galbraith and Leon Henderson, might be amused by such cleverness, but they resented pressures by business to receive exemptions from price controls. Businessmen also complained about an endless stream of government paperwork and some tried unsuccessfully to pressure Congress into cutting OPA's appropriations. Yet on the whole OPA succeeded in bringing inflation under control and the public supported its regulations. When the advertising executive Chester Bowles took over OPA, he identified price controls with patriotism in a successful public relations campaign. Leggy Hollywood starlets joined the campaign by denouncing the black market and giving up nylon stockings.

The patriotic elan of the war years helped the President but not necessarily his party or what remained of the New Deal. After Pearl Harbor Roosevelt called for an adjournment of party politics for the duration of the war, and in the congressional elections of 1942 he deliberately avoiding campaigning to help Democrats. A low voter turnout, due to

wartime preoccupations and the many Democratic workers and soldiers migrating, resulted in a Republican gain of forty-seven seats in
the House and ten in the Senate. Now on the defensive, Democrats
spent the next two years justifying old New Deal agencies like TVA
and FSA, advocating the extension of social security and support to
agriculture to preserve the family farm, and protecting the rights of
labor and racial minorities. Such sentiments did not sit well with the
southern wing of the Democratic party, which had been aligning with
Republicans on several issues.

Thus by 1944 Roosevelt faced a party divided against itself. With
government agencies headed by businessmen, liberal Democrats looked
to Vice-President Henry A. Wallace to sustain the reform legacy.
Something of a populist, Wallace regarded the struggle against fascism
as "a people's revolution," the final effort to make the world safe for
the "common man" by means of economic planning and agricultural
abundance. Earlier Wallace had created a bitter controversy when he
charged Jesse Jones, the Texas banker who headed the Reconstruction
Finance Corporation, with hamstringing military production. Pleading
the need for unity, Roosevelt removed Wallace from his administration
and later dropped him as vice-president and chose Harry Truman to
run on the presidential ticket. Truman's candidacy had to overcome
the opposition of Wallace supporters before he won approval on the
third ballot at the national convention. Following his reelection, Roosevelt, to close ranks and heal wounds, appointed Wallace as secretary
of commerce.

The Republican party nominated New York governor Thomas E.
Dewey, who had earlier made a name as a vigorous prosecutor of rack-
eteers. In doing so Republicans passed over Wendell Willkie, the 1940
candidate who had been advocating international obligations to preserve peace and a strong central government to control business, stances
anathema to isolationist and conservative Republicans. Roosevelt tried
to woo Willkie and independent liberal Republicans into the Democratic campaign. But Willkie's refusal to commit himself until after the
election, and then his sudden death in October at the age of fifty-two,
precluded any possibility of an ideological realignment of the two parties.

In the early stages of the campaign Republicans acted cocky. Many
important newspapers and even the eminent columnist Walter
Lippmann predicted Dewey's victory. The New Deal was no longer
"new" and many people no longer feared unemployment in the prosperous war years. Yet Dewey was careful only to indict the unfulfilled

promises of the New Deal, not its essential welfare and regulatory policies. The Republicans concentrated instead on Roosevelt's age and failing health, a sensitive issue exploited only at the risk of backfiring in charges of bad taste. Still, the issue could hardly be pushed aside. Although the president's physician pronounced him "perfectly O.K.," those who attended his campaign speeches in early fall saw a gaunt figure who lacked the spark and wit that had enlivened his earlier press conferences and the warm intimacy that had characterized his "fireside chats." Even though the press remained discreet, some of Roosevelt's associates, aware of his earlier bouts with influenza, bronchitis, fevers, headaches, high blood pressure, and moments of absent-mindedness, wondered if he would die before election day.

But a month before the election Roosevelt came out in full swing, leaving no doubt who was the champion campaigner. Standing in drenching rain, riding in long, open-car motorcades, FDR seemed the soul of vitality. In contrast to Dewey's banal and serious style, the president's robust humor also won the day. When a columnist rumored that the president had ordered a destroyer to the Aleutian Islands to bring back his pet dog, which he allegedly left behind, Roosevelt replied: "These Republican leaders have not been content with attacks on me, or my wife, or my sons . . . they now include my little dog Fala." Then Roosevelt joked that he would not put up with "libelous statements about my dog," leaving a radio audience of millions roaring with laughter.

During the campaign Roosevelt never lost sight of the future needs of America for postwar reconstruction and the immediate needs of his party for ideological unity. Earlier, in a State of the Union address, he called for a "second Bill of Rights" that should be as "self-evident" as the truths enunciated at the Constitutional Convention in Philadelphia in 1787. The original Bill of Rights was designed to protect people from the abuses of tyrannical government. Roosevelt would now use the resources of government to protect people from the tyranny of hunger and fear that had paved the way for the dictatorships of the twentieth century. Thus to the eighteenth-century principles of life, liberty, and property Roosevelt in his 1944 speech added a new "economic bill of rights" that promised security, opportunity, and hope:

> The right to a useful and remunerative job in the industries or shops or farms or mines of the nation.
> The right to earn enough to provide adequate food and clothing and recreation.

The right of farmers to raise and sell their products at a return which will give them and their family a decent living.

The right of every businessman, large and small, to trade in an atmosphere of freedom from unfair competition and domination by monopolies at home or abroad.

The right of every family to a decent home.

The right to adequate medical care and the opportunity to achieve and enjoy good health.

The right to adequate protection from the economic fears of old age, and sickness and accident and unemployment.

And finally the right to a good education.

Although Roosevelt would not live to see America at peace, no doubt he looked forward to reinvoking the New Deal after the war and possibly even using Keynesian economics to promote full employment. A cynic might conclude that FDR was simply promising something for everyone. Actually he was seeking to reformulate the very meaning of liberalism. The older classical notion that liberty and government were incompatible made sense when individual natural rights were essential to resisting the power of monarchy. In modern democratic society, however, the preservation of freedom would depend upon the security and well-being of the people. Their welfare could be achieved through a government accountable to the electorate.

Roosevelt comfortably won the 1944 election with 54 percent of the vote to Dewey's 46 percent. Democrats interpreted the victory as an endorsement of postwar internationalism and Roosevelt's pledge of a full employment program. Thanks to the help of Sidney Hillman and a new Congress of Industrial Organizations (CIO) political action committee, which turned out six million workers at the polls, Roosevelt won the big industrial cities and the urban black vote. Even though John L. Lewis endorsed Dewey, his mine workers went for Roosevelt. The president also brought in on his coattails William Fulbright of Arkansas to the Senate and Helen Gahagan Douglas of California and Adam Clayton Powell, Jr., of New York's Harlem to the House. But during the war years changes taking place in society were more important than politics and elections. So were the conditions that failed to change.

YEARS OF OPPORTUNITY, YEARS OF SHAME

World War II disrupted the rhythm and fabric of American society. During the hard times of the Great Depression people generally could cling together traditionally as neighbors, friends, and relatives. At first, World War II reinforced this togetherness, uniting people emotionally, but then driving them apart geographically. Many Americans found themselves confused and disoriented in strange surroundings. Young soldiers who had known little temptation as teenagers returned on leave with drinking problems or venereal disease. A few GIs, fearing the scream of shells, and not realizing others were as scared as they were, had to be committed to mental hospitals. Even the young and the brave, feeling the first throbs of romance, knew war as the wounds of the heart:

> I left my heart
>   at the Stage Door Canteen
> I left it there with
>   a girl named Eileen.

The prospect of losing a close friend or family member also took its toll on American nerves. As it turned out, American casualties in World War II were relatively slight. Some 400,000 died in battle, another 670,000 were wounded. In Europe, where war preyed upon civilians and soldiers alike, some thirty-five million lost their lives: an estimated twenty million Russians, five million Germans, 1.5 million Yugoslavs, and six million Jews throughout Central and Eastern Europe. Still, America mourned its own; the early death of so many young Americans and the sight of returning wounded with mangled limbs weighed upon the nation's conscience. The mailman became a harbinger of terrible pain: "Dear _____, It is my sad duty to inform you . . ." Gold stars, symbol of a family member dead or missing in action, hung in homes throughout America.

For many Americans the intimacy of friends and neighborhoods became a casualty of the war. The early forties witnessed one of the great internal migrations in American history. Not only were eleven million young servicemen and women uprooted and sent to every part of the globe, civilian populations also picked up and moved to war industry locations. This huge demographic shift represented the beginning of a long trend. Substantial population gains occurred in Connecticut, Delaware, Maryland, Michigan, and Florida, and particularly the states on or near the Pacific coast. In California the increase amounted to over one million new inhabitants or 14.5 percent from 1941 to 1944. In Virginia and the District of Columbia, larger increases took place: a massive 27.5 percent that stemmed from the upsurge in government personnel. Rural states, especially in the Midwest, experienced high losses. So did New York, where more than a half million people left to relocate in areas of greater war activity. Few who migrated chose to come home again after the war.

In the early forties the American family experienced stresses and dislocations unknown since the Civil War. With fathers in the armed services, children were reared by mothers alone. Many children even felt deserted after being dropped off at a stranger's house as their mothers went to a USO agency to serve coffee and doughnuts to GIs. Many teenagers without parents at home drifted into juvenile delinquency. Single women suffered from confused standards. While prostitution flourished in big cities and seaports, 1940s morality forbade "good" women from sleeping around or living with a man. Many felt pressured into marrying a soldier they had known for only a few weeks; weddings frequently took place on a two-day pass followed by a honeymoon in some drab hotel. Often the hurried marriages were followed by a quick divorce initiated by a "Dear John" letter, the one letter from home a GI felt too depressed and embarrassed to share with his buddies. Women also sensed the meaning of shame. Some whose lovers or fiances had been overseas for years suddenly found themselves pregnant, community outcasts. Homes for unwed mothers grew to a thriving business.

A painful farewell to a GI
about to go overseas.

*A sample of the six million American women who left their traditional roles
to enter the industrial work force during the war.*

For the majority of women, however, the war brought historic
opportunities. Across the country day-care centers opened, enabling
mothers to work outside the home. For the first time in their lives many
women came to feel the power of unsuspected abilities and resources.
Liberated from domestic drudgery, women began to talk about tools
and production quotas rather than meals and diapers. Yet it is doubtful
that World War II witnessed among American women what feminists
would later call "consciousness raising." Most American women,
especially working-class women, experienced their war roles as almost
normal; many middle-class women saw them as temporary; and others
who did desire change ran up against stubborn attitudes and obstacles
from both sexes. In 1943 a poll asked a national cross section of women
living within twenty-five miles of a war plant: "If you were offered a
job in a war plant today, would you take it?" Twenty-eight percent
answered yes and 51 percent no. Had American women not been
ambivalent about donning overalls there would have been no need for
the myth of Rosie the Riveter. Had there been a strong feminist movement in the forties, like the one that spirited the Greenwich Village
rebellion in the World War I era, women might have used their status
as productive workers to seek new identities. Actually, the percentage
of women to men in the professions declined after 1945.

The six million women who entered the war plants and the one hundred thousand or so who joined the armed services did so for a variety of reasons: out of patriotic spirit; because their men were serving; to improve their economic situation; to flee from a boring job or family difficulties. To a woman who had previously been a waitress, hotel maid, laundress, or domestic servant, defense work offered considerably better pay and more challenging tasks, and to black women and the daughters of recent immigrants such work was a godsend. But to educated middle-class women who wanted rewards commensurate with their abilities, military service and factory work could be frustrating. Traditional job classifications relegated women to the tedium of clerical work and the mindless monotony of the assembly line. Although federal policy stated that women should be paid the same as men for doing the same job, the policy was seldom implemented. Labor unions saw women as a threat to traditional male occupations. In shipyards men earned three times more than women. Only in the private sector, in such nonunionized fields as publishing and journalism, did women enjoy meaningful work with the promise of advancement.

Yet when the war came to an end women faced a cruel dilemma. Those who now appreciated a new sense of independence or had families relying on their weekly paycheck were reluctant to give up their jobs. But most others, even if they no longer believed that a woman's place is in the home, still felt that they must step aside so that, as one woman put it, man's place would not be out on the street without a job. Thus the same patriotic duty that drove women into the work force later compelled them to withdraw and make way for the returning heroes. A year after the war ended a cross section of the American people were asked: "On the whole, who do you think has the most interesting time, the woman who is holding a full-time job, or the woman who is running a home?"

	Women with full-time job	Women running a home	No difference	Don't know
Men	27.1%	49.2%	8.4%	15.3%
Women	32.0%	49.7%	7.8%	10.5%

Polls conducted after the war indicate that some attitudes had changed, particularly in regards to equal pay for women, which 76 percent of Americans approved of with only slight differences between men and women. But such polls miss the deeper psychological significance of the war for male and female alike. Feeling the anxiety of separation, what Americans experienced was not so much aspiration as deprivation. GIs overseas and their wives and sweethearts at home desperately missed one another. The soldier might visit a brothel and his fiancée might have an occasional date, but what remained on their minds was the photo in the purse and the long-awaited letter. Americans were, in truth, lonely and filled with desire born of an unquenchable nostalgia for intimacy. Small wonder that so many of the World War II generation were eager to settle down, marry, and have children.

White Americans may have longed for an end to the war and a return to the comforts of normal life, but for black Americans such a return could hardly be contemplated. To many blacks the past meant the depression, unemployment, poverty, racial oppression, and the Ku Klux Klan and its blazing cross—some homecoming! During the First World War black leaders patiently suspended pressing their grievances for the duration of the war. One leader who learned not to repeat the mistakes of the past was A. Philip Randolph of the Brotherhood of Sleeping Car Porters. A leader of courage, militancy, and great personal integrity, Randolph was considered "the Gandhi of the Negroes" because of his effective use of passive resistance tactics. In the spring of 1941 he called for a march of 100,000 orderly demonstrators down the streets of Washington, D.C., to protest the exclusion of blacks from employment in the defense industry. In June, before the mass demonstration

Black Americans protesting racist segregation in the armed services.

Black officers and pilots had their own air squadron, which saw combat in the invasion of Italy.

took place, Roosevelt issued a presidential declaration, the momentous Executive Order 8802, banning racial discrimination in industry and government and establishing a Fair Employment Practice Committee (FEPC) to investigate such abuses. The FEPC hearings confirmed what blacks knew all along. In Los Angeles Douglas Aircraft employed 33,000 workers. All but ten of them were white. North American Aviation had hired eight blacks—all janitors. Seattle's Boeing Aircraft had 41,000 workers and no blacks. Such revelations brought pressure on industry to hire blacks and to redefine job classifications. In factories and shipyards across the country racial barriers had been broken even though unions resisted upgrading jobs for blacks. By the end of the war civil rights organizations would demand that the FEPC become a permanent government agency.

Although thirteen million blacks comprised 10 percent of the population, they numbered 16 percent of Americans enlisted in the armed services. Here, too, racism had to be fought if America were to make the war against Nazism meaningful. At the outset of the war the various branches had all been segregated. The army had separate camps and refused to train blacks as officer candidates; the air force denied them flight training; the navy wanted them to remain as mess attendants; and all branches opposed the enlistment of black women. Gradually, under pressure from the government, the racial barriers came down and blacks were allowed to advance as combat personnel. Some black pilots, trained with the 369th Air Squadron at Tuskegee Institute, Alabama, saw action in the invasion of Sicily. Still, most of the training camps were in the South where Jim Crow sentiment remained as strong as ever. Black soldiers suffered insults at the hands of sheriffs, police, bus drivers, shopkeepers, and, to a lesser extent, white commanding officers. In Beaumont, Texas, and in Little Rock, Arkansas, two black servicemen were arrested and shot for sitting in the wrong section of a bus. Other killings of black soldiers were reported in cities in Texas, Alabama, and South Carolina. Threats of black uprisings were rumored throughout the South. The uprisings actually came, however, in the North.

In August 1943, in New York's Harlem section, the bitter, smoldering resentment against the mistreatment of black soldiers exploded into a bloody race riot. In a hotel lobby a black MP asked his mother to wait while he tried to help a Negro woman who was in an altercation with a white policeman. After a heated exchange, the MP struck the policeman and then turned away, refusing to obey the order to halt. The policeman drew his revolver and shot the MP in the shoulder. Instantly the story spread throughout Harlem that a black soldier had been shot in the back and killed by a white man as his mother looked on in horror. Rage swept the neighborhood, leaving it a rubble of broken glass and burnt-out buildings. Five people were killed, 367 injured, and damages came to more than $5 million.

An earlier race riot that erupted in Detroit left even deeper scars. During the war many southern blacks had moved north to Michigan seeking work in the defense industry. Before long, tensions arose as blacks and whites competed for jobs, limited housing, and ration stamps. In February 1942 clashes broke out when white neighbors tried to prevent blacks from moving into the Sojourner Truth war housing project. Then on one hot summer day the following year, black and white youths taunted one another at a beach. A melee broke out and rumors spread like wildfire. White sailors joined the fray and blacks from the inner city, enraged by the story that a coloured woman and her baby had been tossed off a bridge, rushed to the beach with clubs and chains. The riot, one of the ugliest in American history, raged out of control for three days until Roosevelt declared a national emergency and dispatched six thousand federal troops to the city. Thirty-four people were killed (twenty-five blacks and nine whites), and more than seven hundred

Detroit during the race riots in the summer of 1943.

injured. Property damage exceeded $2 million and one million man-hours were lost in war production. Equally devastating was the lingering racial bitterness. Detroit's white mayor warned ominously: "We'll know what to do next time." As for blacks, they had flocked to Detroit seeking the opportunity denied them in the South. "There ain't no North no more," wept an old black woman. "Everything now is South."

In 1944 the Swedish-born economist Gunnar Myrdal published *An American Dilemma,* a study of racism in light of America's democratic principles. In World War II America's racial dilemma became a moral embarrassment that had to be faced. The massive entry of blacks into industry, government, and the military helped to begin the process of integration. In politics blacks felt a new sense of pride as they watched A. Philip Randolph win labor struggles and the dashing Adam Clayton Powell, Jr., move toward political power, and the NAACP substantially increased the number of black registered voters in the Southeast. In cultural areas racist sentiment had also been challenged. Just before the war the popular Hollywood movie *Gone with the Wind* depicted blacks as childlike and helpless. During the war the film *This Is Our Life* dramatized a black law student struggling against discrimination, and on Broadway Paul Robeson starred in *Othello* to standing ovations. Before the war the Daughters of the American Revolution (DAR) refused to allow singer Marian Anderson to perform in Constitution Hall; in 1943 she sang there before an integrated audience in a war-relief fund raiser. Still, many patterns of racism persisted, even at America's oldest and most elite institutions. One black high-school senior wrote an open letter to the students of Princeton University in 1943, which admitted no blacks:

> If you discriminate against me because I am uncouth, I can become mannerly. If you ostracize me because I am unclean, I can cleanse myself. If you segregate me because I lack knowledge, I can become educated. But if you discriminate against me because of my color, I can do nothing. God gave me my color. I have no possible protection against race prejudice but to take refuge in cynicism, bitterness, and hatred.
> Think on these things.

Other ethnic minorities also had reason to seek refuge in cynicism during the war years. Racial hatred erupted in Los Angeles when the mayor and some city officials blamed the Mexican-American community for crime and gang warfare. The Hearst press drummed up fear of the "pachucos," tough male youths who wore broad-brimmed hats, tight pants, long hair waved in the back, and draped coats that fell to their knees. The city made it a crime to wear a zoot suit, and police patrolled the East Los Angeles barrio, often making mass arrests. Many gang members were prosecuted on the scantiest of evidence; twenty-two were convicted of murder and sentenced to life in San Quentin (a sentence later reversed); and a sheriff issued a report purporting to prove that Mexican-Americans had a "biological" predisposition to crime. Then in the summer of 1943 a vicious riot erupted, prompted by a newspaper story that a gang of pachucos had beaten up a sailor. By evening thousands of sailors and soldiers were forcing their way into movie houses and cafes, grabbing all zoot-suiters in sight, ripping their clothes and punching them to the ground as civilians applauded.

During the war, racial and ethnic tensions that exploded in New York, Detroit, and Los Angeles made urban Americans afraid and suspicious. Prejudice and intolerance seemed to spew forth everywhere, as though patriotism required hatred as a moral duty. Editors of *Life* concluded that bigotry was "America's No. 1 social problem," and the black newspaper, *The Pittsburgh Courier,* condemned what it called "Hitlerism at Home." Eleanor Roosevelt wondered how a war could be successfully fought in the name of political freedom when the civil rights of minorities were being violated in the United States.

The record of civil liberties fared reasonably well compared to the First World War's patriotic hysteria and red scare. There was no systematic government harassment of communists or fascists even though the country was at war with fascist regimes. In the first year of the war Italian-American and German-American aliens were subjected to restrictions such as curfews, entering strategic areas, carrying cameras and shortwave receivers, and other measures taken for reasons of military security. Such precautions were soon lifted, however, and all fears of a "fifth column" of spies and traitors consisting of "enemy aliens" of European descent subsided. Even if an improvement on the past, civil liberties proved spotty at best. Both a right-wing and a left-wing journal were suppressed for antiwar utterances. Numerous pacifists and conscientious objectors, some of whom were members of the Jehovah's Witnesses or the Black Muslims, were prosecuted. As many as six thousand went to jail. But the greatest violation of civil liberties involved Japanese-Americans, a people at once loyal, patriotic, and as willing to serve their country as their sons had been willing to fight by enlisting in the armed services.

In the spring of 1942 the United States government rounded up and shipped off to relocation camps 112,000 men, women, and children— the Japanese population of California, Oregon, and Washington. Some were Issei, Japanese immigrants who clung to Japanese customs and communities; many more were Nisei, American citizens born in this country to Issei parents whose language and traditions were left behind as they learned English and became assimilated; and a few were Kibei, American-born Japanese who had studied in Japan. The government made little distinction among these groups, many of whom were American citizens and entitled to all the legal rights of citizenship. After the air attack on Pearl Harbor, those rights were infringed one by one as the emotional winds of hatred and revenge swept through California. Within days Japanese-Americans were fired from their civil service jobs; their licenses to practice law and medicine were revoked, their insurance policies canceled, their businesses boycotted and fishing boats confiscated. Eventually their constitutional rights to due process were suspended.

"The only good Jap is a dead Jap," shouted a California congressman on the floor of the House. "Japs live like rats, breed like rats, and act like rats," Idaho's governor, Chase Clark, informed the press. Cartoonists joined politicians in fomenting anti-Japanese hysteria by drawing sketches showing how to distinguish "Nips" from other Asians in order to remind Americans that the "Chinese and Koreans hate the Japanese more than we do." Racial hatred clearly contributed to the tragic fate that befell the Japanese-Americans. It is not, however, a sufficient explanation. Prior to Pearl Harbor, growers, nurserymen, and produce-market dealers in southern California had resented the competition of the hard-working Japanese-Americans. After December 7, two other factors suddenly had to be faced: military security and public safety. The first problem proved baseless when officials such as J. Edgar Hoover of the FBI recognized that Japanese-Americans were not hanging out laundry to send signals to submarines or photographing the Golden Gate Bridge for an attack on San Francisco. The second problem concerned even civic leaders who spoke out in behalf of their Japanese neighbors and bore witness to their loyalty. They feared that in the likelihood of another air attack on Hawaii, or even the sporadic bombing of the West Coast from a sub, Japanese-Americans would be vulnerable to mob violence (as indeed some were when they returned from the relocation camps to rural areas of California where they had no support networks). Thus for their own protection, so the reasoning went in the months following Pearl Harbor, all Japanese, alien and citizen alike, must be rounded up and moved to what one California congressman called "inland concentration camps."

West-coast relocation of Japanese-Americans in 1942.

The decision to intern young Nisei and their parents had the support of many liberal public figures, from California's Attorney General Earl Warren to columnist Walter Lippmann. President Roosevelt left the decision to authorities on the West Coast who in turn worked with the War Department to develop an evacuation plan. Even though FBI Director J. Edgar Hoover reported no evidence of espionage among Japanese-Americans and the U.S. attorney general, Francis Biddle, urged caution, Governor Culbert Olson of California and General John DeWitt of the United States Army had considerable support on the entire West Coast when they obtained from Roosevelt an executive order empowering the military to carry out the evacuation. The United States Supreme Court upheld the legality of excluding Japanese-Americans from the Pacific coastal region. In *Korematsu v. United States* (1944), the Court ruled that Japanese-Americans were not being denied their constitutional rights because of racial discrimination but because of the requirements of military security. Three justices, however, dissented, issuing a vigorous statement criticizing a detention program that violated due process of law on the basis of an "erroneous assumption of racial guilt" that should be settled in the courts and not by "military judgment" alone.

Under the War Relocation Authority posters were pasted on the doors of Japanese-Americans ordering them to report to evacuation centers. Children too young to know English were tagged and herded with their families onto trucks. Some families were first housed in race-track horse stalls before being deposited in camps in the remotest and most barren regions of various western states. Living in one-room barracks with no privacy, unable to forget that their crops, farms, and bank accounts had been confiscated, many adults survived the war in silent and apathetic depression, proud mothers and fathers reduced to humiliation and shame. The younger and angrier Nisei clashed among themselves. Some refused to sign a loyalty oath and thus renounced their American citizenship; others volunteered to serve in the military. Thirty-three thousand Nisei did wear American uniforms in World War II. By the end of the war the highly selective, elite 442nd Division was the most decorated combat force in the army. It was, ironically, a segregated unit.

THE WAR, THE HOLOCAUST, AND THE BOMB

The shock of Pearl Harbor created an impression that Japan and Germany had been united in their military objectives. Actually Hitler wanted

Japan to attack Russia and leave America alone. Now the outcome of the Second World War depended upon two factors without which an Allied victory would not have been possible: America's entrance and Russia's resistance.

A bleak situation faced the Allies in the spring of 1942. Although Germany was now fighting a war on two fronts, having failed to win Britain's surrender before turning on Russia, Nazism was triumphant in Western Europe, from Scandinavia to the Mediterranean. Germany had access to Mideastern petroleum and Swedish iron ore on which her war effort depended. The Fascist powers of Germany, Italy, and Japan had been preparing for war since the 1930s and their armies had already had valuable combat experience in Spain and Ethiopia. Germany and Japan could also draw upon millions of conquered people in Eastern Europe and in Asia for forced labor. Both countries, moreover, could boast of their far-reaching striking power. Within months after Pearl Harbor German submarine "wolf packs" were sinking scores of American merchant ships off the coast of Florida, New York, and Cape Cod. The torpedoing of freighters and tankers continued in the Atlantic and Caribbean for nearly two years, until the United States developed a convoy escort system to feed the vital lifeline to Britain.

The Allies—Britain and her dominions, Russia, the United States, and China—had certain advantages that in the end proved decisive. The Allies had clear numerical superiority, a unified military command structure in Western Europe directed by General Dwight D. Eisenhower, almost unlimited natural resources and industrial capacity in America and Canada immune to bombardment, and the inspirational leadership of President Roosevelt and Winston Churchill, England's indomitable prime minister, who made clear his determination to fight the war until Nazism was wiped from the face of the earth. The Allies also enjoyed a distinct psychological advantage. In Western Europe and Asia they would arrive as liberators rather than as conquerors. In contrast to the Germans and Italians, who made enemies with every conquest and had to contend with an antifascist underground, and to the Japanese, whose imperialism proved even more brutal than western colonialism, the Allies did not have to face the hatred of the European, Chinese, and Indonesian people; nor did they have to worry about uprisings and sabotage raids. In several instances the Office of Strategic Services (OSS) worked with the French and Italian resistance in preparation for paratroop landings. Except for France's unreliable Vichy government, set up by Germany, and the equally undependable Italian dictator Benito Mussolini, Hitler had no one to work with. After July 1944, when Hitler barely escaped an assassination attempt, he could not even trust his own generals.

Even though America had been brought into the war by the attack on Hawaii, Roosevelt agreed with Churchill that the Axis strength in the European theater of war warranted greater urgency than the Pacific. The first great struggle was to secure the North Atlantic. America had not only to continue lend-lease shipments to England but also find a way to get supplies to a Russia now cut off from the West and in desperate need of food and munitions. There was no alternative. American ships headed into the North Sea, infested with German submarines, and along the Norwegian coast, where German destroyers and cruisers awaited them in the fjords. So great were the casualties—on one voyage, twenty-two out of thirty-three merchant ships were sunk—that sailing to Russia became known as "the suicide run to Murmansk." And German subs continued to bring down ships throughout the Atlantic from Iceland to the Bay of Biscay. For two years the war hung in balance. Until the German wolf-pack menace was overcome, America could not ship to England the men and materials needed to stage an invasion of occupied Europe. As Germany launched more and better equipped subs, England and America quadrupled the production of ships and planes designed to deal with them, as well as electronic equipment necessary to intercept German communications. Finally huge convoys with as many as one hundred freighters and tankers were organized and escorted by destroyers, Coast Guard cutters, slow-flying bombers, and blimps armed with sonar and depth-charges. By the end of 1943 the war against the U-boat had been won due to superior Allied productive capacity and coordination of sea and air power.

But in the Pacific events proceeded like one continuous catastrophe. Shortly after Pearl Harbor the Japanese landed on Wake Island and Guam and secured control of communications across the central Pacific. Having captured the Malay Peninsula and driven the British out of Singapore and Hong Kong, Japan launched an amphibious assault on the Philippines. After a valiant defense of the nearby island of Corregidor, President Roosevelt ordered General Douglas MacArthur to evacuate. He left behind 12,500 American and 60,000 Filipino troops who had no choice but to surrender. The press reported the infamous "death march" from Bataan to the prison camps in which thousands of Americans, Australians, and Filipinos lost their lives from wounds and disease. Japan had also taken Sumatra and Java and their vital oil deposits and rubber plantations; with the capture of Rangoon, Japan controlled the Burma Road and had China isolated. The colonial territories of the French, English, Dutch, and Americans had all fallen to Japan and her new empire, "The Rising Sun."

The strategy of the American navy, under Admiral Chester W. Nimitz, was to play a waiting game until new ships and more troops arrived. Meanwhile, American carriers conducted nuisance sorties over Wake, the Marshalls, and other Japanese-held islands; and General James H. Doolittle led an air attack over Tokyo that did little damage but much to lift American morale. Japan had no intention of engaging in a land war with the United States. But Admiral Isoroku Yamamoto wanted to engage the American navy in full battle, assuming that a few more disastrous defeats like Pearl Harbor would persuade Americans and their government to withdraw from the South Pacific, leaving Japan to her conquests. In the summer of 1942 a reinforced American navy fought off Japanese battleships at Midway and the Coral Sea and turned back attempted landing invasions on New Guinea and on several tiny atolls in the mid-Pacific. At the battle of Midway America lost the carrier *Yorktown;* Japan lost four carriers and their air squadrons. The tide had turned.

Naval combat in the Pacific was unique in the history of warfare. The battle of Coral Sea was fought entirely by carrier-launched aircraft, with neither American nor Japanese ships coming within sight of one another. Even more unique was the war carried on beneath the oceans by submarine. Two percent of America's naval personnel accounted for 55 percent of Japanese losses at sea, including numerous merchant ships as well as carriers and cruisers. But the price was high: 22 percent of American submariners lost their lives, the highest casualty rate amongst any branch of the armed services.

The battle of Leyte Gulf, fought off the Philippines in the fall of 1944 in preparation for an invasion of the Japanese-occupied mainland, was decisive. Recognizing the strategic importance of the Philippines as a stepping-stone for America's advance into Asia, the Japanese planned an attack on small-armed naval vessels guarding troopships and landing craft. Admirals Thomas C. Kinkaid and William F. "Bull" Halsey directed their fast-carrier task forces in a bloody three-day naval campaign in which the Japanese lost three battleships, four carriers, six cruisers, and more than a dozen destroyers. Off the Philippine coast seven hundred Allied troops and cargo ships stretched to the horizon awaiting the invasion. Leyte Gulf was the greatest naval engagement in world history and the final fleet battle of World War II.

In Europe an unprecedented development in modern military theory

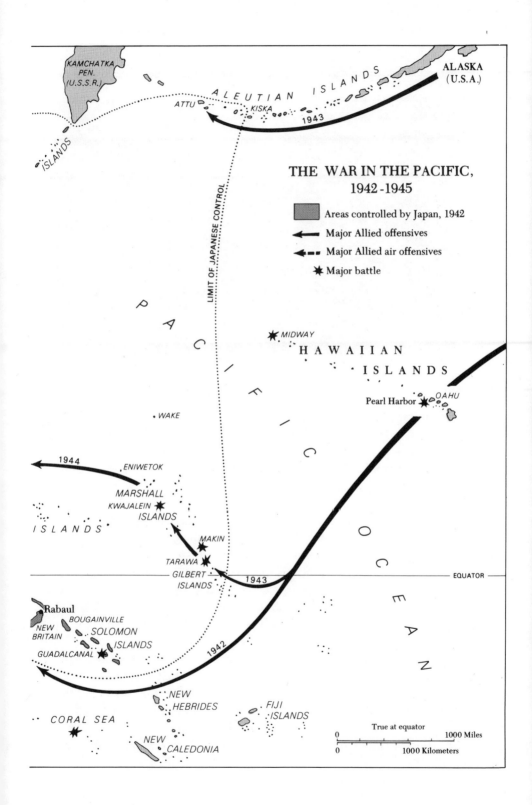

KAMCHATKA
PEN.
(U.S.S.R.)

ALEUTIAN ISLANDS

ALASKA
(U.S.A.)

ATTU

KISKA

1943

ISLANDS

LIMIT OF JAPANESE CONTROL

THE WAR IN THE PACIFIC,
1942-1945

Areas controlled by Japan, 1942

Major Allied offensives

Major Allied air offensives

Major battle

P

A

C

I

F

I

C

MIDWAY

HAWAIIAN

ISLANDS

WAKE

Pearl Harbor OAHU

1944

ENIWETOK

MARSHALL

KWAJALEIN

ISLANDS

MAKIN

ISLANDS

O

TARAWA

GILBERT

ISLANDS

1943

EQUATOR

C

E

Rabaul

BOUGAINVILLE

NEW
BRITAIN

SOLOMON

GUADALCANAL

ISLANDS

1942

A

N

NEW
HEBRIDES

FIJI
ISLANDS

CORAL SEA

True at equator

0

1000 Miles

NEW

0

1000 Kilometers

CALEDONIA

Ruins from the bombing of Dresden during World War II.

was taking place: the doctrine of strategic air offensive, which was designed to level cities as well as factories in order to weaken the morale of the civilian populations. Beginning in 1943 the American and Royal Air Forces conducted a sustained bombardment of the industrial Ruhr Valley and seaports like Hamburg and Bremen. Later, when the war was drawing to a close, the city of Dresden was targeted with incendiary bombs that killed more than 100,000 civilians. Since Hitler had deployed a similar air-bombing strategy to attack the people of London, and since the bombing of German industrial targets seemed to relieve pressure on Russia, this massive saturation bombing had popular support. But after the war, a United States Air Force study revealed that the obliteration bombing offensive, which cost the lives of 160,000 American and British airmen, had not substantially hindered German war production.

Bombing itself would not bring victory. The Allies realized that Hitler would not surrender unconditionally unless the German army, the Wehrmacht, was defeated, and this required a colossal invasion of the continent. In 1942 the American command had planned a cross-channel operation to secure a beachhead in France in preparation for a full invasion the following year. The British wanted to wait until the Allies had overwhelming ground and air forces. Churchill, aware of the sacrifices Russia was making, opposed a cross-channel invasion but favored a lesser operation that would divert enough German troops from the Russian front so that the Red Army would not have to bear the brunt of the war. The Americans and British compromised on Operation Torch, and in fall 1942 the Allies landed in North Africa. There American and British tank commanders, Generals George S. Patton Sr., and Sir Harold Alexander and Field Marshall Sir Bernard L. Montgomery, drove through mountain and desert in pursuit of the brilliant Field Marshall Erwin Rommel (the "desert fox") and his powerful Panzer divisions. With Rommel's Afrika Korps defeated, the Allies then staged an invasion of Sicily and Italy.

The campaigns in North Africa and Italy destroyed the myth of Germany's invincibility, and with Russia's great victory at the battle of Stalingrad in spring 1943, Nazism was in retreat everywhere. Nevertheless, German soldiers fought tenaciously as they pulled back; Hitler would hardly contemplate surrender; Rommel, who had relinquished his command in North Africa, was back in Berlin regrouping his forces; and German industry was increasing not only its production of tanks, subs, and aircraft but also beginning to develop rockets, jet-propelled fighter planes, and possibly an atomic bomb. It became clearer than ever that the Continent needed to be invaded. Germany must be attacked, her army destroyed, and Berlin captured.

Operation Overlord, the June 6, 1944, invasion of Normandy, was the greatest amphibious assault recorded in history. Allied forces assembled in England consisted of French, Polish, Belgian, Norwegian, and Czech troops, as well as American, British, and Canadian. Almost three million men waited to cross the English Channel, supported by millions of tons of equipment and thousands of airplanes and naval vessels ranging from battleships and cruisers to troop transports and landing barges. Although the Allied air forces had been knocking out bridges and roads in northern France weeks before the invasion, the Normandy coast remained well fortified with German artillery emplacements, underwater and land mines, pillboxes and concrete blockhouses connected by underground tunnels, and fields of wire entanglement. Some German officers thought the landing would be at Calais because of its docking facilities and closer distance to Paris. But that seaport had been made virtually impregnable. Eisenhower and his advisors, deciding that docks and oil pipelines could be constructed after the invasion, chose the Normandy coastline.

Under cover of naval gunfire and air bombardment, six American, British, and Canadian divisions landed on the beaches. The first wave

WAR IN EUROPE AND AFRICA,
1942-1945

Axis Powers at outbreak of war

Maximum extent of Axis military power

Allies

Neutral countries

Allied offensives

Heaviest Allied aerial bombing

Inside limit of German U-boat operations

of troops had to disembark from their boats in water up to their waists and sometimes deeper, then crawl through minefields while gunfire poured down from the bluffs above. "D-Day" had its share of disaster. Some parachute drops behind the lines missed their targets, several landing craft capsized in the surf, and a crack American Ranger squadron suffered heavy casualties as it worked its way up the face of cliffs to capture German strongholds. But on the whole, the invasion went well. After eight hours of fierce fighting the cliffs had been overtaken. Soon roads were cleared and tanks and heavy artillery were moving inland to support advanced troops. The outnumbered Germans fought bravely, but one by one small towns were captured in the battles of Saint-Lô, Caen, and Cherbourg. Within weeks Allied armament divisions were moving rapidly through France toward Paris. The liberation was coming! As American soldiers advanced with the Eiffel Tower in sight, Parisians rose up against the hated Nazis. On August 25, 1944, Paris was freed and General Charles de Gaulle triumphantly entered the city. Then GIs in tanks, trucks, and jeeps poured into Paris, welcomed with tears of joy, hugs, tiny American flags, flowers, wine, and cognac.

Until Allied troops entered Germany, few Americans thought of the war as an ideological struggle against the forces of fascism. Most soldiers wanted to come home as soon as possible, and to do so they knew

French women welcoming the Allied liberators after enduring the humiliation of the German occupation.

they must kill or capture the enemy until he laid down his arms. With such sentiments members of the twenty-eighth Infantry and 101st Airborne divisions held their position valiantly in the winter of 1944–45, finally turning back a last desperate German counter offensive in the famous Battle of the Bulge, which sealed Hitler's fate.

Then came the horror. Not until American troops crossed the Rhine and began liberating concentration camps did they understand the meaning of the dreaded Gestapo, the "final solution," the Waffen-SS and the SS-Totenkopfverbande (Death's Head Units). With the gates of Auschwitz and Dachau opened to the eyes of the world, western civilization recoiled in anguish. So monstrous was the sight of charred skeletons in the ovens and living corpses with shaved heads staring from the barracks that some soldiers shot SS officers on the spot. The world had always known "sin," the author and political scientist Hannah Arendt would write of the camps, but "radical evil" on this ghastly scale was so new that one no longer knew how to punish or forgive. "Just as the victims in the death factories or the holes of oblivion are no longer 'human' in the eyes of their executioners, so this newest species of criminals is beyond the pale even of solidarity in human sinfulness."

In the camps in Germany, Poland, and Hungary, six million Jews lost their lives along with three million Russians, Poles, Slavs, and Gypsies. While this mass execution was taking place, Catholic and Protestant organizations in the Western world remained almost indifferent. Not until 214 Polish priests were executed did the Vatican issue a formal protest, without any effect on the Catholic hierarchy in Germany. As to America, a 1944 November Gallup poll indicated that 76 percent of the public believed "that the Germans have murdered many people in the concentration camps." Only a few Americans who read a liberal or radical journal or several Jewish publications knew it was worse than murder: the mass extermination of men, women, and children who died by gassing after being ordered into rooms disguised as shower baths. The media—the popular press, radio, and newsreels—gave the story little coverage. The influential *New York Times* relegated it to the back pages, and other papers reported the deaths as due to war-time deprivations instead of anti-Semitic insanity.

Several relief agencies, including the "Emergency Committee to Save the Jewish People of Europe" organized in the spring of 1944, made every effort to publicize the exterminations and to persuade the United States government to undertake rescue missions. Several proposals were put forth: a request that the United Nations threaten retribution to those

American army officers force German civilians to see the horrifying reality of the Landsberg concentration camp.

guilty of genocide; to call upon neutral European countries to temporarily accept refugees and guarantee that food, medicine, and clothing would be sent; to ask England to revise its 1939 policy restricting Jewish immigration to Palestine; and to have the United States open its doors to Jewish war refugees and other displaced persons. Later, as the war drew to an end and the exterminations continued with diabolical efficiency, it was suggested that the Allied air forces bomb the railroads leading to the camps. Few of these proposals became policy, and the Allies continued to bomb Dresden, not Dachau.

The Holocaust torments the conscience of those willing to remember the horrors of the past in order not to see them repeated. Before the war 94 percent of the American people denounced the *Kristallnacht*, the "Night of Broken Glass" (November 9, 1938), when German storm troopers smashed the windows of Jewish shopkeepers, looted their homes, and terrorized their neighborhoods. Yet more than 60 percent of Americans desired to keep Jewish refugees, even displaced children, out of the United States, and this sentiment remained unchanged during the war. In 1942, when news filtered out of Poland about the plight of Jews, a United Nations conference convened at Bermuda to take up the refugee problem. But the White House, State

Department, and Congress all feared an inundation of permanent Jewish settlers, as did some members of the Jewish community who were wary that such a massive influx could increase anti-Semitic feelings. Eleanor Roosevelt prevailed on the State Department to allow five thousand Jewish children to enter the United States, an effort eviscerated by bureaucratic red tape and deliberate stalling on the part of anti-Semitic civil servants. Roosevelt himself was at first kept insulated from the problem by advisors concerned about the political implications of the refugee issue. Finally, Treasury Secretary Henry Morgenthau, Jr., got through to the president and with the War Refugee Board, established in 1944, the United States helped save 200,000 Jews in Europe and gave sanctuary to another 100,000 who had managed to escape the death camps. Much more could have been done, as demonstrated by the heroic accomplishments of a single individual in Hungary, the Swedish diplomat Raoul Wallenberg, who risked his life rescuing thousands of Jews. That more was not done must be regarded as the great moral failure in modern history.

Roosevelt and most of the American people believed that the best way to aid European Jews was to defeat Nazi Germany as quickly as possible. In spring 1945 Germany was caught in a gigantic pincer, with a Russian offensive blitzing through Poland and Allied divisions racing across the Rhine and into the Ruhr Valley. By April the German resistance had collapsed and Italian partisans had captured and hanged dictator Benito Mussolini. On May 1 Hitler committed suicide and six days later Germany signed an unconditional surrender.

But the good news from the western front did little to ease the grief that Americans had felt three weeks earlier. On April 12, Roosevelt died, and when the world learned the electrifying news, people everywhere mourned. To many Americans Roosevelt's passing was like a death in the family. The most inspiring figure of the depression and war years, a symbol of hope and freedom to millions, he was suddenly gone. No one knew what to expect from the new man in the White House who had been overshadowed in FDR's illustrious presence. "Is there anything I can do for you?" Vice-President Harry S. Truman asked Eleanor Roosevelt when he heard the news. "Is there anything *we* can do for *you?*" she replied. "You are the one in trouble now."

Two vexing decisions faced Truman: how to deal with the Soviet Union, truculent now in regards to postwar Eastern Europe, and how to defeat Japan. The second issue involved some unexpected developments that had tragic consequences. In the Pacific, American strategy originally aimed to advance upon Japan through Burma and with the support of China and her teeming population. But as an ally China turned out to be weaker than expected and her leader, Chiang Kai-shek (Jiang Jieshi), seemed more interested in propping up his corrupt regime than in fighting the Japanese. Thus, shortly before his death, Roosevelt accepted General MacArthur's advice to retake the Philippines as a springboard for an assault on the Japanese mainland. MacArthur returned to the Philippines as he had earlier vowed, and after ferocious battles featuring kamikaze planes, the strategic islands of Iwo Jima and Okinawa fell to the United States Navy and marines between March and June 1945. American forces had been staging light attacks on the Japanese homeland from the islands of Guam and Saipan. But the character of the attacks now changed. Assuming that Japan could be bombed into submission, military strategists ordered raids on crowded cities using incendiary and napalm bombs. The destruction was horrifying. Large parts of Kobe and Tokyo and other industrial cities were devastated by fire storms. Eight million wooden homes were destroyed and more than 300,000 people killed. Japan was in flames, yet she still refused to surrender.

While the air force had been furiously bombing Japan, scientists at Los Alamos, New Mexico, were completing the Manhattan Project—the testing of the first atomic bomb, which was made possible by the recent discovery of fissionable plutonium and uranium-235. On July 16, 1945, the bomb was exploded at Alamogordo, New Mexico; a quiet white flash followed by the roar of a shaking desert, and then a mushroom cloud soaring seven miles high. A week later at the Potsdam Conference, Japan was presented an ultimatum: surrender or suffer "prompt and utter destruction." Although the Japanese emperor may have wanted to capitulate, as did most Japanese, some military officers thought surrender dishonorable, and government officials ignored the Potsdam ultimatum while making peace overtures to Switzerland and Russia. At the orders of President Truman, on August 6, a single B-29 dropped an atomic bomb on Hiroshima, and three days later a second bomb fell on Nagasaki. The crew on the Hiroshima raid felt the painful flash of light and the shock wave of air turbulence, and then they saw a towering mushroom of fire and smoke that rose 10,000 feet per minute. No one wanted to imagine the inferno below. Most of the city vanished and close to 100,000 people died instantly.

Truman's decision to use the atomic bomb has been the subject of intense and endless controversy. Truman himself, noting that Japan called for a cease-fire a week after Hiroshima (an official surrender was signed in September), defended his decision on the grounds that

*Casualties and survivors the
day after the bombing of
Nagasaki, August 10, 1945.*

it saved the lives of half a million American soldiers who would have
been killed in the invasion of the mainland. Every GI in the Pacific
was relieved to hear about the bomb, now knowing the war would end
and that they had survived it. Because of the heavy resistance with
which Japan defended Iwo Jima, Okinawa, and Tarawa, battles in which
some 50,000 American soldiers died, it seems likely that an invasion
would have meant a prolonged and bloody war in which the Japanese
and Americans would have suffered far more casualties than the lives
lost at Hiroshima. The kamikaze attacks had impressed upon Americans an image of Japanese soldiers as death-defying fanatics; it could
not be ignored that less than five percent of Japanese fighting men had
ever surrendered in any one battle. Military experts estimated that an
invasion of Japan would be more risky and dangerous than the Normandy landing.

Still, was there no alternative? Critics argued that Truman should
have ordered a demonstration explosion off the coast of Japan. That
proposal was rejected on the grounds that a dud bomb may have only

*The sky over Hiroshima min-
utes after the atomic bomb
exploded on August 6, 1945.*

stiffened Japan's resistance, or that the plane carrying the bomb could easily be shot down, or that Japanese militarists who wanted to pursue the war would suppress news of the bomb. Some critics also argue that the dropping of a second bomb on Nagasaki was unnecessary since the two days that had passed did not allow the Japanese government time to reach a decision. But later, a close study of Japan's chiefs of staff and war minister revealed that following Hiroshima they were already speculating that America had only one bomb and thus the war could continue. Any prospect of a negotiated peace acceptable to Japan had been precluded by the American policy, adopted earlier against Germany, of unconditional surrender.

Many scientists who built the bomb did not anticipate its use against Japan. Most of the physicists who worked on the Manhattan Project, many of whom were refugees who had fled European fascism, assumed that they were in a race with Hitler, as did Albert Einstein when he informed President Roosevelt that Germany was developing an atom bomb. When England proved helpless to defend herself against the Third Reich's V-2 rockets, American scientists grew more apprehensive about the possibility of German scientists developing supersonic weapons with nuclear warheads. After Germany had been invaded and her scientific laboratories examined, investigators concluded that there was no evidence that the Nazis had successfully developed the bomb (although they would have, if some German physicists had not obstructed the effort and who were later appalled to read that America would use such a weapon). With the defeat of Germany there was no military need to continue developing the bomb, but the momentum and intellectual excitement of cracking the secrets of nature compelled American physicists to proceed. What scientists discover can seldom be ignored. Once international scientific circles learned that the power locked in an atom equals its mass multiplied by the speed of light squared, the genie was out of the bottle. After the Los Alamos explosion a private poll was conducted of the scientists who had worked on the bomb at the Chicago-based Manhattan Project. Forty-six percent supported a proposal for a demonstration explosion off the waters of Japan, and another 23 percent favored a demonstration in the United States in the presence of Japanese observers. A number of scientists also sent a petition to President Truman warning against using the bomb until Japan had sufficient time to surrender. Yet some of the leading scientists close to the president, such as James B. Conant and Vannevar Bush, approved of Hiroshima as a target, as did J. Robert Oppenheimer, the director of the Manhattan Project, who soon afterwards anguished about his decision, reminding his colleagues that physicists now had to recognize that they "have known sin."

Then, as now, some believed that the bomb was immoral because of the vast death and suffering it wrought, and there are those who, pointing to the even greater devastation of Tokyo and Dresden, insist that mass terror of civilian populations was a foregone conclusion. If a few Americans felt guilt, many more felt revenge, arguing that without Pearl Harbor there would have been no Hiroshima. According to the polls, 75 percent of Americans approved of Truman's decision, seeing the bomb as the bringer of peace. Some realized the implications of the weapon and felt the primal fear of annihilation. Soon, with the outbreak of the cold war, the bomb became the possible instrument of universal extinction and Americans wondered how they would live with it, as though civilization had inherited an incurable disease.

But the victorious ending of the Second World War resulted more in joyous celebration than somber reflection. On V-J Day, August 14, 1945, America turned into a saturnalia. In cities across the nation traffic came to a halt as people danced in the streets. Strangers toasted one another and, to the delightful roar of crowds, sailors grabbed and kissed passing and willing young women. Americans had good reason to rejoice.

The famous Life *photographer Alfred Eisenstaedt captured the festive joy that swept America on V-J day, August 14, 1945.*

Instantaneous joy overcame American sailors upon hearing that the Japanese had surrendered.

In the years since Pearl Harbor the United States had overcome the greatest crisis facing the country since the Civil War. A war that most Americans originally did not want to fight turned into one of the proudest triumphs in the history of the Republic. Yet the war had no happy ending. With the forces of fascism defeated, Americans began to read and hear about "communism," and the Soviet Union, recently regarded as an old ally, emerged as a new enemy. Once again Americans felt, as they had in 1919, that they had won the war but lost the peace. This time the feeling was worse, for there could be no postwar retreat into isolationism. In 1945, America achieved victory but not security. What had eluded the country at the end of the war was precisely what FDR had promised at its beginning—"freedom from fear."

2

The Cold War

LENIN'S LEGACY

The war was over; now, how to make the peace? Earlier, President Harry Truman had his own ideas when conferring in Washington with Russian foreign minister V. M. Molotov. In April 1945, Truman warned him that Stalin had made certain agreements in regard to postwar Poland. There was nothing further to be said, Truman insisted firmly, other than to instruct "'Marshal Stalin to carry out that agreement in accordance with his word." The stunned Molotov was aware of what happened to anyone who tried to give advice to Stalin, the bloody dictator who presided over the execution of millions of his own people. Lamely he replied: "I've never been talked to like that in my life." "Carry out your agreements," Truman snapped back, "and you won't get talked to like that." What would soon come to be known as the "cold war" was now front-page headlines.

The cold war can be viewed simplistically in a number of ways—as a conflict between communism and capitalism, totalitarianism and democracy, even atheism and religion. Such antinomies, while in part true, are often intended to win political allegiance rather than to engage in the harder task of historical analysis.

First, the cold war is not a war at all, but rather a description of a state of affairs in which the United States and the USSR are neither in combat nor at peace but in a situation of undeclared hostility, an "armed truce." And while the cold war has deep roots, its flowering was sudden, erupting in the spring of 1945 as World War II drew to a close. In this respect the cold war might be seen as the natural outcome of "bipolarity" with the United States and the USSR emerging as the two new superpowers contending for influence and hegemony. Yet much in this was not new. Hostility between America and Russia had waxed and waned since the Bolshevik Revolution of 1917, when Czar Nicholas II fell from power. At that time, President Woodrow Wilson hoped that Russia and its new provisional government would stay in the First World War and keep up the eastern front against Germany. The Wilson administration also hoped, as did the rest of America, that with the end of Czarist despotism, Russia would transform itself into a genuine democracy and become part of the liberal West that had a common heritage in the eighteenth-century Enlightenment.

Few Americans were aware that V. I. Lenin, the brilliant Bolshevik leader who was conspiring against Russia's liberal provisional government, had assumed that the Russian Revolution would be the spark to ignite revolutions throughout the industrial world. Nor did many Americans fully understand that the communists had now distinguished themselves from their social democratic opponents by claiming that a revolution could achieve the goals of Karl Marx only by dispensing with parliaments, constitutions, rival political parties, and just about everything else associated with western "bourgeois" liberalism. From the Leninist point of view, revolutionary communism and democratic liberalism are incompatible because all capitalist regimes continue the institutions of oppression and exploitation—private property and the profit system. Ignorant of all this and of Bolshevik determination to negotiate an immediate settlement with Germany in 1917, some American liberals believed that the United States and Soviet Russia could possibly work together to defeat Germany and to reconstruct the postwar world. These same hopes characterized President Roosevelt's attitudes toward Stalin's Russia a quarter-century later. In both cases they led to the same sense of disillusionment and betrayal.

The first disillusionment had less to do with ideology than diplomacy and military necessity. It came with the Treaty of Brest-Litovsk in 1918, whereby Russia withdrew from the war after having embarrassed western governments by exposing their secret plans for postwar settlements. Criticizing the separate peace as well as bolshevism's undemocratic methods, Wilson now called Russia "a Judas among nations." He ordered American troops to enter the northern port cities of Murmansk and Archangel, in part to reconstitute the eastern front and in part to help the Czech-Slovak troops escape from Russia. It remains debatable what America's participation in the Allied interven-

tion meant—was it really to aid the antibolshevik counterrevolutionaries and thereby subvert the new Soviet state? But the intervention,
accompanied by other interventions by the British and Japanese and
coming in the midst of a fierce Russian civil war, only confirmed the
Bolshevik suspicions: the Western world was bent on destroying the
revolution and restoring the property and privileges of the old order.
This view was also shared by the American John Reed, romantic hero
of the October Revolution, friend of Lenin, and founder of the American Communist party. But, except among Reed and his small band of
followers, the Bolshevik cause had little support in America. Indeed,
the American press predicted again and again the collapse of Communist Russia. When instead the Red Army vanquished all competition for Russian power, Wilson refused diplomatic recognition of the
new Soviet regime. And America's government embarked upon its first
antibolshevik "red scare," which drove the Communist party underground and hounded radicals of all persuasions. Thus the seeds of the
cold war were sown long before Russia emerged as the leading European power.

In the 1920s American attitudes toward the Soviet Union softened
for several reasons. For one thing, Lenin began to have second thoughts
about the prospect of world revolution and called upon communists in
the Western world to give up their "infantile" notions about the collapse of capitalism and to enter the trade union movement and participate in electoral politics. When Joseph Stalin succeeded Lenin in 1924,
Russia seemed to be abandoning Leon Trotsky's program for "permanent revolutionary struggle" in favor of building "socialism in one
country." Moreover, American business began to eye Russia as a
potential market, and industrialists and financiers like Henry Ford and
J. P. Morgan urged the government to extend diplomatic recognition
to the USSR. Recognition was bestowed by FDR in 1933, at a time
when Russia's "five-year plans" seemed to offer an immediate answer
to the crisis of world depression. The following year, when Russia
adopted "the popular front" and called upon all political groups to join
together in opposing Hitler and the menace of Nazism, the Soviet
Union's image in America became even more favorable. The Communist party now championed such virtues as patriotism and the family. While few college students and intellectuals joined the CP, many
became "fellow travelers," those who believed that communism was
the proper solution to Russia's backwardness. Others accepted the
popular front rationale that the Soviet Union remained the only "bul-
wark" against the Third Reich.

In the latter half of the 1930s, however, sinister developments in Europe cast three shadows on American opinion. During the Spanish Civil War (1936–39), Spanish Communist party leaders, aided by Russian military advisers, carried out Stalin's order to execute Spanish anarchists who were resisting domination from the Kremlin. The Moscow Trials (1936–38) enabled Stalin to purge all opposition elements within Russia. American reporters, observing the fate of the heroes of the October Revolution, listened incredulously as they were told that former leaders put to trial and executed were counterrevolutionaries and even spies for Nazi Germany. The Soviets justified these "show" trials on the grounds that Russia must eliminate all dissent in preparation for the conflict with Hitler. In August 1939, however, the world was again stunned when the Soviet Union negotiated a nonaggression pact with Germany, a move that allowed Hitler to plan his invasion of Poland without fearing a Russian counteroffensive on the eastern front.

This nonaggression pact was the last straw for some. Certainly, the pact shattered the illusions of the popular front. But some die-hard American Stalinists were quick to offer justification—the Soviet Union had not been invited to participate in the earlier Munich Conference (1938). With the Nazi's brutal "rape of Prague" in 1939 what was Russia to think, except that the West would stand idly if Hitler intended to move eastward and conquer Czechoslovakia and Poland as a means of advancing upon Russia. Having failed to promote collective security alliances with France and England, in 1939 Russia found herself desperately isolated and, following Lenin's example of 1918 in the Brest-Litovsk treaty, Stalin too warded off the Germans by trading space for time. So went the rationale. After Hitler's June 1941 declaration of war on Russia, and following Japan's attack on Pearl Harbor, the Soviet Union and the United States found themselves unexpectedly in bed together, aligned against a common enemy. Thus the "Grand Alliance," as British Prime Minister Churchill would call the three allied powers, was really a coalition of convenience rather than conviction, a war alliance forged out of immediate military necessity by powers that had their own objectives.

THE GRAND ALLIANCE AND YALTA

Would Russia withdraw from the Second World War as it had from the First? According to George F. Kennan, who served in the American Embassy in Moscow before and after the war, such a thought could

not be ruled out. Especially so since Russia and the western democracies felt no obligation toward one another. Each would follow its own
interest as circumstances dictated. But in 1941, Russia needed the West,
for Germany had driven hundreds of miles into Russia, threatening its
heartland.

With Russia in the war, circumstances in 1941 dictated that Britain
and the United States extend aid to her, and Churchill and later Roosevelt made the case to their countries. But war material seemed slow
to arrive to the eastern front, and Stalin complained when the allies
suspended some convoy runs to Archangel, owing to heavy losses from
submarine attacks.

Even more exacerbating was the issue of the second front, the opening of a new theater of war in France so as to force Germany to withdraw some of its divisions from Eastern Europe. The long battle for
Stalingrad—a crucial yet indecisive struggle in which Russians and
German troops took, lost, and retook houses and city blocks in hand-
to-hand street fighting—began in the fall of 1942. Since the entire fate
of the war turned on Russia's ability to withstand the German offensive, Stalin wanted to see a second front opened before the end of the
year, and had he gotten his way this would have been planned for
1943. Roosevelt agreed. But Churchill, recalling the bloody price the
British paid for the mass offensives of the First World War, proposed
that a cross-channel invasion be postponed until the trans-Atlantic
movement of American troops and supplies was safe enough to ensure
the Allies overwhelming superiority. When Churchill tried to spell out
this rationale in Moscow and insisted that the Allies undertake only
wider Mediterranean operations, Stalin became surly and suspicious.
He welcomed the air raids on Germany and the invasion of North Africa.
But why could not the Anglo-American command cross the channel
into France and make up for its lack of numerical strength by sheer
aggressive spirit? Even if a raid on the French coast proved unsuccessful and cost thousands of lives, it would be a legitimate price to pay to
divert the German army, catch Hitler in a pincer on two fronts, and
thus turn the tide of the war. Why should Russia sacrifice ten thousand
men a day when America and England were afraid to attack the Germans?

An Allied incapacity to launch a major offensive in the West precluded the possibility that the Allies could make a second front dependent upon good Soviet political behavior in the East. In this respect the
geographical configurations of the future cold war had already been
determined in the early years of World War II. The Allies wanted Sta-

lin to defeat Hitler's armies on the eastern front without collecting the fruits of victory. As an editorial in the liberal *New Republic* noted, the Allies were asking for the impossible—"the victory of communism over fascism without the spread of communism." The full implication of that rare perception had been obscured by the changing image of communism during the war. In parts of the media the Red Army was depicted as fighting not for the cause of Soviet communism but for the deeper traditions of "Mother Russia" and Peter the Great. Some columnists who had never taken Marxism seriously were happy to report that the Russian people had ceased doing so as well. Few considered the possibility that Stalin took himself seriously and that he had created a totalitarian system that would be impermeable to western appeals based on democratic ideals. Thus, during the war, it was tempting to see the advances of the Red Army as possibly bringing liberation and freedom and not, as it would turn out, domination and tyranny.

In the spring of 1943 Russia emerged victorious in the glorious battle for Stalingrad, and in the following summer the second front opened with the D-Day invasion of Normandy. It was during this period that American opinion soared with admiration for the brave and hardworking Russian people. In March 1943, *Life* magazine devoted a special issue to the Soviet Union and hailed Stalin as a great nationalist leader. At the same time several liberal writers, with little knowledge of the subject, published articles and books in an attempt to convince Americans that Russian communism and Western democracy contained elements of compatibility that could lead from a military alliance during the war to a political and moral friendship afterwards. The USSR did much to foster this impression by downplaying communism and emphasizing traditional patriotism. During this period, fear of "capitalist encirclement" was seldom invoked and the Comintern, the international organization to which communist parties of various countries belonged and served as obedient instruments of Soviet foreign policy, was abandoned.

In view of such amiable developments, a sunny prospect loomed when the Big Three—Roosevelt, Churchill, and Stalin—met at Teheran in November 1943. Much of the discussion turned on military concerns such as the state of the Russian front and the forthcoming invasion of France. But matters pertaining to postwar settlements came to have far greater consequence. How would eastern Europe be reconstituted and how would Russia protect herself after the war? Stalin flatly rejected any suggestion that an international organization like the United Nations could guarantee Russia's security. He made it clear that the Soviet

The "Big Three"—Stalin, Roosevelt, and Churchill—at the historic Teheran Conference, November 28 to December 1, 1943.

Union must have hegemony over the Baltic states of Latvia, Estonia, and Lithuania. Roosevelt explained that American public opinion would not tolerate anything less than "the right of self-determination." Stalin countered that the Baltic republics would have an opportunity for popular expression but not under any system of international control. Stalin also insisted that the Russian-Polish border be redrawn to the 1939 line formed by the nonaggression pact with Germany, and he asked that East Prussia be incorporated into the USSR. Churchill approved of these realignments. Roosevelt, pressured by the exiled Polish government in London to resist such demands, could only express frustration. "Do you expect us and Great Britain to declare war on Joe Stalin if they cross your previous frontier? Even if we wanted to, Russia can still field an army twice our combined strength, and we would just have no say in the matter at all. What is more . . . I'm not sure that a fair plebiscite if there ever was such a thing would not show that those eastern provinces would not prefer to go back to Russia." Although impatient with the Polish exiles, Roosevelt reminded Stalin that America would not lose sight of Polish interests and national sovereignty, and Churchill reinforced the point by noting that England had gone to war with Germany to defend Poland.

At the Yalta Conference (February 1945) Roosevelt hoped to lay the foundations for world peace and order. Here the Big Three hammered out resolutions on the organizational structure of the United Nations. The United States and Britain won a place for France on the Security Council and Russia secured the same veto power insisted upon by the United States Senate. They also dealt with the postwar dismemberment of Germany and the establishment of occupational zones. On the issue of Poland, however, no clear agreement could be reached. Russia now occupied Poland and had in place a hand-picked government, called the Lublin Poles. Roosevelt wanted the Polish exiles in London, as well as other "democratic elements" broadly representative of the Polish nation, to be part of the new government. Stalin objected, arguing that any future Polish government must be "friendly" to the USSR. Roosevelt recognized that trouble lay ahead, but he could not openly acknowledge it for fear America would repeat the tragedy of 1919 and refuse to join the UN, heir to Woodrow Wilson's unrealized dream of the League of Nations. In the spring Roosevelt considered applying economic pressure by stalling on Russia's request for further lend-lease commitments. But he also felt that Stalin, who was accusing the United States of using the German surrender in Italy as a means of negotiating a separate peace between Nazi Germany and the West, would only grow more suspicious at such an act. Uncomfortable with the brute realities of power politics, Roosevelt went to his death in April still hoping that the Grand Alliance could be held together by good will.

When Truman assumed the presidency, the American and British armies were moving eastward through Germany with unexpected momentum and speed. After they had advanced beyond the occupation lines agreed upon with the Russians, Truman had to decide how far the Allied armies should be allowed to go. Churchill wanted them to move as far east as possible before the war ended, to be withdrawn whenever Russia fulfilled its promises of democratic government in Poland. He particularly wanted the Allies to liberate the historic cities of Berlin and Prague. Truman, however, yielded to the advice of Eisenhower and the Joint Chiefs of Staff that such cities were not important military objectives. To General Patton's chagrin, American tank divisions were ordered to hold back or pursue retreating German armies southward while Russian forces entered Prague and Berlin.

Thus, at the Potsdam Conference in July 1945, one of the first paradoxes of power in the cold war emerges. Although the United States now had the atomic bomb, Russia, by virtue of conventional weapons, occupied every capital city in Eastern Europe except Athens and Belgrade. The Big Three discussed German reparations and the denazification of German society, Russia's entry into the war against Japan, and her demands for access to the Mediterranean by way of the Turkish straits. Again, no agreement could be reached on free elections in Poland or on the nature of other East European governments. Truman left the conference reasonably confident that he, like FDR, could hold his own in a dialogue with Stalin. But what he wrote in his Potsdam diary in the evenings indicates what held his mind: "We have discovered the most terrible bomb in the history of the world. It may be the fire destruction prophesized in the Euphrates Valley Era, after Noah and his fabulous Ark."

The explosions at Hiroshima and Nagasaki, and afterwards the atomic tests on the Bikini atolls, made it clear that the development of such weapons threatened to condemn the world to extinction. In September Secretary of War Henry L. Stimson recommended to the president that the United States share its atomic secrets with the Russians and approach them with a proposal to cooperate in development of atomic energy under the jurisdiction of the UN. Truman at first hesitated, in part because the recommendation departed from Roosevelt's policy of restricting information on the bomb, an attitude shared by 71 percent of the American people. But the need for some system of international regulation prompted him to appoint Undersecretary of State Dean G. Acheson and former TVA Director David E. Lilenthal to develop a plan. They proposed the creation of an international Atomic Development Authority that would control all raw materials used in developing atomic weapons, including those in the Soviet Union, and would outlaw the making of new atomic bombs while allowing the United States to keep its small stockpile. In all likelihood the Soviet Union had no intention of agreeing to a proposal that would have prevented its own development of an atomic arsenal. But Truman made that possibility a certainty when he appointed Bernard M. Baruch to present the plan to the UN. A financier known to be a staunch anticommunist, Baruch revised the Acheson-Lilenthal proposal to include sanctions against violators and, more seriously, to suspend a nation's right to use the UN Security Council's veto power to avoid punishment for such violations.

A UN Commission endorsed the Baruch plan 10–0, with Russia and Poland abstaining. Soviet Ambassador Andrei Gromyko agreed to the principle of international control but insisted that inspection would invade national sovereignty and that the provision for suspending the

Security Council's veto power on matters pertaining to atomic energy violated the agreement with which Russia had joined the UN. Thus the arms race began with the same impasse that would propel it for decades to come: control, yes; inspections, no. Peace would become dependent on a balance of terror.

With the Red Army enjoying overwhelming numerical superiority, the Truman administration was in no position to relinquish America's atomic advantage. Nor would the American people have allowed it. When Baruch presented his plan to the UN in June 1946, the cold war had escalated beyond expectations. The Soviets remained entrenched in Eastern Europe, had occupied northern Iran, and were threatening Turkey's precarious status in order to secure long-sought military footholds on the Bosporus and Dardanelles. At the same time Stalin was predicting the collapse of Western capitalism. Meanwhile, negotiations for a United States loan to Russia collapsed and American naval vessels were dispatched to the Mediterranean. A few months before the UN conference Churchill, in a speech delivered in Fulton, Missouri, described what had been taking place. "From Stettin in the Baltic to Trieste in the Adriatic an iron curtain has descended upon the Continent."

In May 1946, Russia withdrew from Iran, perhaps the only instance when Soviet foreign policy seemed responsive to American pressure (later Russia would withdraw from Austria for different reasons). In Eastern Europe the Soviets had set up communist governments in every country except Austria and Czechoslovakia. Some of these countries— Austria, Rumania, Bulgaria, and Hungary—had fought with Hitler; others—Czechoslovakia, Yugoslavia, and Poland—had allied with the West in underground resistance. The fate of Poland and the promise of free elections remained the most volatile issue in the first years of the cold war. Why had Stalin agreed to free elections at Yalta? One possible explanation, according to W. Averell Harriman, then America's ambassador in Moscow, is that Stalin had been misinformed about the popularity of the Communist party in Poland. After the war there was little chance that he would allow elections to take place for he now knew the communists would lose.

What had happened in Eastern Europe had no precedent in either Russian history or in Marxist theory. The czars had not forced their neighbors to become exact models of Russian monarchy, and Karl Marx had assumed that communist revolutions would be democratic since they would be forged by the working masses. Stalinism, in contrast, now meant the deliberate capture of state power in order to impose "revolution" from above. Each satellite country was to be a replica of Russian's totalitarian system. With the Communist party in control of the organs of central and local government, the armed forces, the security police, the schools and the press, the satellite regimes were "people's republics" in name only.

When the full reality of the Yalta violations sank in, Truman was put on the defensive as the cold war entered domestic politics. Worsening relations with the Soviet Union, together with revelations of a communist spy ring in Canada and America, led to fear and suspicion. "What is Russia up to?" shouted the normally mild Arthur H. Vandenberg in the Senate. "We ask it in Manchuria. We ask it in eastern Europe and the Dardanelles. . . . We ask it in the Baltic and the Balkans. We ask it in Poland. . . . We ask it sometimes even in connection with events in our United States. What is Russia up to now?" No one could say for sure, but no politician would admit it. When Russia published the hitherto secret agreements made at Yalta, conservative Republicans were aghast. Charging that Roosevelt and Truman had "sold out" Eastern Europe to communist totalitarianism, Republicans turned Yalta into a symbol of shame, another instance of the liberals' fondness for appeasement. Conservative isolationists who opposed America's entry into the war now felt vindicated in warning that communism, not Nazism, was the real enemy. Democrats tried to defend themselves. Roosevelt, they pointed out, had conceded no area to the Soviet Union not already being occupied by the Red Army. A few Democrats turned the Republican attack around and argued that America, instead of failing to have done anything to save Eastern Europe, was now doing too much to antagonize Russia. In a speech at Madison Square Garden, Commerce Secretary Henry Wallace insisted that Russia's control of Eastern Europe was a necessary precaution against the threat of a revived Germany, and that Stalin was only bringing the benefits of "socialism" to his war-starved neighbors. Although he did not hesitate to criticize Stalin's totalitarian state, Wallace insisted that England and the US were "ganging up" against Russia, and such a "get tough" policy would only provoke Stalin to respond in kind. Wallace and his followers also believed that Eastern Europe was part of Russia's sphere of influence. The lost friendship between America and the Soviet Union could be regained by resuming aid and free trade. Wallace's speech infuriated Secretary of State James F. Byrnes, who threatened to resign unless Truman called for Wallace's resignation, which Truman, equally angry, did.

Americans were also angry. Public opinion had turned sharply against

DENMARK SWEDEN U.S.S.R.

NORTH
SEA

BALTIC SEA

Hamburg

EAST
Bremen

Berlin

ANNEXED
BY
POLAND

ACCESS
CORRIDOR

JOINT OCCUPATION
BY FOUR POWERS

GERMANY

WEST

Bonn

BEL.

LUX.

SAAR

GERMANY

FRANCE

Frankfurt

IRON CURTAIN

Munich

AUSTRIA

SWITZERLAND

ITALY YUGOSLAVIA

Danzig

EAST PRUSSIA

TO
U.S.S.R.

TO
POLAND

Warsaw

POLAND

Lublin

Oder R.

Neisse R.

CZECHOSLOVAKIA

Vienna

HUNGARY

0 100 Miles
0 100 Kilometers

OCCUPATION OF GERMANY AND AUSTRIA

French zone British zone U.S. zone Soviet zone

Russia. Although 60 percent of Americans rejected Churchill's proposal for a joint military alliance against the Soviet Union, and only 17
percent advocated going to war, close to 75 percent of the people believed
that America must strengthen itself militarily. If Americans had any
hope for peace, it was gloomy regarding the short run. Possibly in the
long run an economically recovered Russia would come to identify with
the affluent, bourgeois Western world and lose its revolutionary zeal.

In intellectual circles, that hope came to be known as the theory of
"convergence," the notion that eventually the heightened tensions of
the Stalinist regime must begin to normalize. Simultaneously, western
democracies must begin to accept the legitimacy of the Soviet Union
and its satellites. But among intellectuals there was little consensus on
this theory. The conservative Right and the radical Left were polarized:
the former believed that the Soviets were intent on conquering the world,

the latter that they were devoted to peace and security. James Burnham, an ex-Trotskyist and author of *The Struggle for the World* (1947),
became the leading theoretician of the right-wing perspective. The left-
wing case found a platform in the communist press and in the writings
of a few liberal columnists in *The Nation* and *New Republic*. But the
position of the liberal Democrats was best reflected in the thoughts of
Walter Lippmann and George Kennan, two highly intelligent writers
who disagreed about the proper approach to the Soviet Union.

Lippmann had reached his conclusion before the cold war was reality. As early as 1943 in *U.S. Foreign Policy: Shield of the Republic*,
Lippmann argued that "to encourage the nations of Central and Eastern Europe to organize themselves as a barrier against Russia would
be to make a commitment that the United States could not carry out."
The overwhelming preponderance of Soviet military force in Eastern
Europe at the conclusion of the war would determine the fate of that
region, and the most Lippmann hoped for was that Russia might allow
countries like Poland to exist as neutral states. After the war Lippmann
took a position critical of both Wallace and Truman. He observed that
Wallace suffered from the pacifist delusion that peace automatically
follows from disarmament and good will. Truman sensed the dangerous realities of Soviet Russia but focused on the wrong place. Stalin's
control of Eastern Europe was essentially defensive, and England and
America's efforts to dislodge the Soviets could only convince the Russians that "a coalition is being organized to destroy them." This conviction could be exploited by party leaders to tighten their totalitarian
grip. If Eastern Europe were lost, elsewhere in the world—Japan, the
Mediterranean, Western Europe, southern Asia, part of China, half of
Germany, all of Africa—Britain and the United States still reigned
supreme. In light of such hegemony throughout the world, and in view
of America's newly found atomic weapon, was it not reasonable that
Russia feared the West and clung to Eastern Europe?

What seemed reasonable to Lippmann seemed questionable to Kennan. In an eight-thousand word telegram sent from the Moscow
Embassy to the State Department, Kennan wrote that Soviet leaders
labored under a "neurotic view" of the West. Their attitude was shaped
from fears of securing their borders against attack, an attitude carried
over from the age when Russians on the plains and steppes were
defenseless against warring nomadic tribes. The Soviet mentality also
derived from an ideological fanaticism that conceived world politics in
terms of heightening crises and inevitable confrontations. In fact, the
Soviets followed the czars in using the presence of a hostile environ-

ment to justify their despotic rule. Thus the cold war could not be mitigated by concessions. When and if the Soviet Union sought to expand its influence in any vulnerable area outside its perimeters, United States foreign policy must be firm and grounded in the realities of power politics rather than the illusions of good faith.

Kennan's telegram, distributed throughout the State Department, served as the intellectual rationale for the Truman administration's increasingly hard-line policy toward Russia. The opposing Lippmann-Kennan positions posed a question that has continued to provoke controversy in what is known as "revisionist" history. Was the cold war avoidable or was it inevitable?

REVISIONIST ARGUMENTS

Much revisionist historiography, written while the Vietnam War was raging in the 1960s, follows the reasoning of Henry Wallace in the 1940s in attributing responsibility for the emergence of the cold war to America. Assuming that a confrontation with the Soviet Union could have been avoided by American action, the revisionists argue as follows: (1) America, whether intentionally or otherwise, aroused Soviet suspicions by failing to open a second front early in the war and by cutting off lend-lease to Russia at the close of the war; (2) Truman's ordering of the bombing of Hiroshima made the Soviets even more fearful since "atomic diplomacy" came to be seen as a strategic instrument in America's policy; (3) America's ultimate aim was to extend her economic power over conquered Europe as a means of sustaining an inherently unstable capitalist system; and (4) Soviet motivation was essentially defensive and cautious in nature rather than radical and expansionist, and Stalin's seizure of power in Poland and elsewhere was a result of America's increasingly hard-line stand, especially after Truman succeeded Roosevelt. These arguments need to be scrutinized one by one.

A cross-channel attack on Normandy would have opened a second front, but such an assault was logistically impossible when Stalin demanded it in 1942. It was not until May 1943 that the Atlantic was made safe from U-boat attacks and sufficient landing craft had arrived in Britain. The Allies could have risked a landing earlier than June 1944 and suffered great casualties. But no evidence tells us that an earlier assault would have influenced postwar territorial agreements. Nor would it have alleviated Stalin's suspicion that the Allies were dal-

lying so that Hitler could fight the "menace" of communism for them—
an old suspicion predating even the 1939 nonaggression pact. Stalin's
distrust was not allayed even when the Allied armies held back and
allowed Russian tanks to enter Prague and Berlin first.

Stalin's suspicious nature was inherent, not contingent, indeed so
paranoiac that he feared everyone, even his own people. A man who
ordered the execution of millions of loyal Bolsheviks during the purges,
had his leading generals shot just before the outbreak of war, and
arranged the murder of Leon Trotsky in Mexico was a man patholog-
ically determined to see conspiracy everywhere. "Stalin was a very distrustful man, sickly suspicious," wrote Nikita Khrushchev in his secret
report to the Twentieth Party Congress in 1956. "We knew this from
our work with him. He could look at a man and say: 'Why are your
eyes so shifty today' or 'Why are you turning so much today and avoiding to look at me in the eyes?' The sickly suspicion created in him a
general distrust even toward eminent party workers he had known for
years. Everywhere and in everything he saw 'enemies,' 'two-facers' and
'spies.'"

Roosevelt referred to Stalin as "Uncle Joe" and Truman first likened
him to Tom Pendergast, a Missouri political boss. Small wonder they
were quickly disillusioned. "A man who had subjected all activities in
his own country to his views and to his personality, Stalin could not
behave differently outside," observed Yugoslav communist Milovan
Djilas. "Having identified domestic progress and freedom with the
interests and privileges of a political party, he could not act in foreign
affairs other than as a hegemonist." On the eve of World War II Franz
Borkenau anticipated what Roosevelt and Truman would be up against
in 1945. "Stalin, the man who could not allow a single one of his old
companions to live, is the last man to believe in the possibility of sin-
cere collaboration in the international field. A man such as Stalin cannot be brought to reason by argument."

As for lend-lease, no doubt Russia resented its cancellation in May
1945. But Truman had no choice. When the bill had first passed four
years earlier, Congress legislated its demise at the war's end. The same
cut-off applied to England. That Truman hastily reversed the policy
and continued aid to Russia without conditions also suggests that neither he nor his advisors considered using economic assistance as a lever
to force concessions from the Soviets.

The thesis that America's "atomic diplomacy" was responsible for
the cold war holds that Truman postponed the Potsdam Conference
until after the bombing of Hiroshima so as to have a bargaining chip

with Stalin, a way of forcing Russian concessions in Eastern Europe. Yet Russia did not protest the dropping of the bomb; in fact, the American Communist party regarded Hiroshima as "right, justified, and necessary." Nor did Truman flaunt the bomb at Potsdam. Rather he recognized the communist-installed Polish government; in doing so, he was carrying out Roosevelt's earlier policies and not, as the revisionists argue, departing from them. Actually the position of Molotov and other diplomats hardened after the bomb was dropped, perhaps because they knew what Secretary of State Byrnes was slow to grasp: the bomb meant little as a bargaining instrument in diplomacy because Truman and his advisors had no intention of using it in Europe. Indeed no American leader then dared to suggest, as did the British philosopher Bertrand Russell, that it be used in a preemptive strike against Russia. Faced with "the impotence of omnipotence," Truman resorted to traditional statecraft. If his position on Eastern Europe grew tougher, the new hard line had less to do with the bomb than with his disillusionment over Soviet conduct.

In the economic interpretations of the cold war American foreign policy is not seen as reacting to developments in the Soviet Union but as reflecting the nature of capitalism and its need to have access to and control of overseas markets and foreign investments. This Marxist interpretation rests on the assumption that America's economic system is inherently imperialistic and exploitive; it also posits that big business, or "corporate capitalism," holds such sway in the White House and State Department that, finally, the interests of private enterprise prevail over all other considerations. No doubt the Roosevelt and Truman administrations, worried about the possibility of a postwar depression, pressured England to reduce its Commonwealth trade restrictions in order to open up new markets for American business. But revisionists also insist that American business pressured government to oppose Soviet occupation of Eastern Europe so that countries like Poland, Rumania, and Bulgaria would be open to investment opportunities. Not only is there scant evidence for such an interpretation but in reality the situation may have been just the opposite: trade with Eastern Europe was essential if American influence was to be effective for political, and not necessarily economic, purposes. The conclusion of "Reconstruction of Poland and the Balkans," a briefing paper prepared for the Yalta Conference, was that the Soviet Union would inevitably have the dominant influence in these areas. "While this government probably would not want to oppose itself to such a political configuration, neither would it desire to see American influ-

ence in this part of the world completely nullified. In the situation of
Poland and the Balkan states after the war the United States can hope
to make its influence felt only if some degree of equal opportunity in
trade, investment and access to sources of information is preserved."

It is hardly surprising to find the United States using economic pressure to influence its political objectives; nor is it shocking to discover
that the Soviet Union had used political, even military, pressure to
achieve its economic ends, even the ends of imperialism. Thus Stalin
agreed to withdraw Russian troops from the Mideast only after Iran
granted oil concessions to the Soviet Union. The bottom line is this—
both America and Russia emerged from World War II as superpowers.
Both countries would use whatever means, be it trade or tanks, to promote their respective interests, whatever their economic systems.

Part of the complexity of the cold war stems from America's percep-
tions of Soviet intentions. Revisionists are right to believe that Russia
displayed considerable restraint in its stance toward the West and was
by no means embarking upon revolutionary adventurism. In China Stalin
supported the nationalist Chiang, to the distress of the communist Mao.
In the Aegean he refused to aid the Greek communists in their revolution and pressured Yugoslavian leader Marshal Josip Tito into calling off a planned attack on Trieste; in Italy he recognized the rightist
General Pietro Badoglio and in France the conservative General De
Gaulle. By taking such stances Stalin, essentially a conservative
bureaucrat, had reached an understanding with Churchill whereby
Poland would be considered within the suzerainty of Russia and the
Mediterranean that of England. In contrast to Churchill, Roosevelt and
Truman refused to think in terms of imperial power politics. As Arthur
M. Schlesinger, Jr., has observed, American leaders saw the sphere-
of-interest diplomacy as a violation of all the principles the war was
supposedly being fought for as spelled out in Roosevelt's Four Freedoms, the Atlantic Charter between the United States and Britain, and
the Declaration of the United Nations. As politicians they also realized
that abandoning the fate of Eastern Europe would arouse the wrath of
the electorate. In 1945 American public opinion had rapidly turned
against Russia and no politician wanted to be identified with Yalta.
Given the constraints of American political realities, the sphere-of-
interest policy could hardly be contemplated as an option to the East-
West confrontation.

Yet the view that Russia acted for reasons of national security and
then moved to control her bordering states only after United States
policy became hostile needs to be scrutinized. For that impression, in

addition to showing indifference to the equally legitimate security needs of smaller countries, ignored the possibility that much of Russia's insecurity derived less from her sense of isolation than from her internal political system. The insecurity was bred of a suspicion toward opposition of any kind, a conviction that goes back to the Leninist dogma that revolutionary communism and democratic socialism are incompatible and that therefore power, by definition, cannot be shared. Stalin carried this conviction further, making all government subordinate not only to a single party but to his personal police state. After the war East European governments would be doomed to the same fate that befell all those who, in Stalin's mind, might pose an opposition to his monomaniacal rule. Thus Hungary remained relatively independent until 1947, when the Soviet Union moved in to reverse an election return and smashed the resistance of the Smallholders' Party by arresting its courageous leader, Béla Kováks. Whether Russia was reacting to the Truman Doctrine (discussed shortly), we simply cannot document since Soviet diplomatic archives remain closed. But the possibility of genuine democracies thriving on Russia's borders were as threatening ideologically to Stalinism as America might be politically and militarily. Even Czechoslovakia, which historically had looked to Russia as her savior from Prussian expansionism, and whose leader Eduard Beneš was fully committed to cooperating with the Soviet Union, fell behind the iron curtain in 1948.

The Stalinization of much of Eastern Europe began long before the cold war and it was not, as the revisionists maintain, simply a response to Truman's diplomacy. In all probability, Poland's future had been determined during the war by the same Stalinist mentality that would not tolerate opposition wherever it could be crushed. In 1943 news reached the West that the Soviet Union had executed the Polish Jewish leaders Victor Ehrlich and Henryk Alter. Four years earlier, when Russia marched into eastern Poland during "the phony war," Soviet troops arrested fifteen-thousand Polish military officers. When Germany invaded Poland the following year, the bodies of thousands of officers were discovered in what is now known as the Katyn Forest massacre. In 1945, as the Polish underground came out of hiding to fight the Nazis on the streets of Warsaw, Stalin ordered his tanks to remain on the outskirts of the city, thereby assuring that the brave uprising would be crushed by the retreating Germany army. After betraying the Polish resistance to its enemies, Stalin showed that he would settle for nothing less than total domination of Russia's neighbors by whatever means.

Such Stalinist behavior may not mean that the Soviet Union was mobilizing to indefinitely expand its power throughout the world. In the United States certain writers, now bitterly disillusioned with the "dream" of communism, began to argue that Stalin and Hitler were of the same ilk. To them, communist Russia aimed at world conquest as had Nazi Germany, and Yalta proved again what American should have learned from Munich: the enemy must be fought, never appeased. Yet Stalin always put the interests of Russia ahead of the interests of international communism. He opposed revolutionary uprisings in Greece, for example, because of an agreement with Churchill on spheres of interest, and in China out of fear that a successful victory would endanger the right of the Kremlin to remain the supreme symbol of world communism.

Nevertheless, no one could know for sure what Stalin was up to, not even communists in Western countries. In April 1945, the French communist Jacques Duclos conveyed the new Moscow line when he denounced the American Communist party leader Earl Browder for advocating "peaceful coexistence." According to a former CP member, Browder's replacement by William Z. Foster signaled that a "polarization" between the Soviet Union and its Western allies was inevitable and would "dominate" postwar relations.

WHY THE COLD WAR? ITS IDEOLOGICAL DIMENSIONS

In the end the cold war could best be seen as ideological in character, and this description cuts both ways. The Soviets, interpreting events through Marxist-Leninist ideology, tended to see any stable situation as inherently contradictory and thus pregnant with the seeds of inevitable conflict between communism and capitalism. The Americans, drawing from Wilsonian assumptions, believed that national self-determination, representative government, free enterprise, and free elections have universal relevance. The Truman administration wanted to see such institutions springing to life in Poland and elsewhere. But this liberal perspective ignored the fact that free elections did not prevent Hitler from coming to power and that representative government did not prevent much of southern and eastern Europe from succumbing to fascism before the war. From the Soviet point of view it seemed pernicious that the United States, which had murmured no protest of the Polish dictator Józef Piłsudski in the early thirties, now cried foul about a communist dictatorship in Poland in the late forties. From the American point of view, the Soviets were betraying the ideal for which the war had been fought, ideals spelled out in the Atlantic Charter and implied, however vaguely, in the Yalta settlement. But Stalinist Russia could hardly abide by such liberal ideals, and the American people were not prepared to face that harsh fact. Nor was the Truman administration, which had assumed that the communists would behave like any other party and run for office and participate in coalition governments. But a Stalinist party brooks no sharing of power and aims at nothing less than total control. In 1945 the United States and USSR were speaking past one another.

To locate the origins of the cold war in ideology is not to suggest that ideology explains the cold war when it is used merely as propaganda, that is, when each side made claims that hardly squared with reality. The Soviet line of portraying the world as ridden with conflict between socialism and capitalism cannot begin to explain the deeper conflicts that would develop among the communist countries themselves. The American characterization of the cold war as a matter of democracy versus totalitarianism may have been accurate in 1945–46. But in the second phase of the East-West confrontation in 1947–49, the United States found itself aligning with countries that were neither liberal nor democratic but simply anticommunist. America would now see itself as defending the "free world" while Russia claimed to be defending "socialism."

Such claims obscure the deeper historical and cultural issues. Both superpowers viewed the world not as it was but as they wished it to be. In addition, their respective world views had been shaped by profoundly different histories. Modern Russia emerged from czarist despotism and aristocracy, where private property was regarded as an inherited privilege by the rich and the cause of scarcity and famine by the poor. It was natural, therefore, that Soviet leaders would embrace Marxism, see conflict and class struggle everywhere, and regard the private ownership of property not as a natural right originating in labor and promoting liberty but as the source of oppression and exploitation that must be extirpated. American history was innocent of such conditions. Unacquainted with feudalism and aristocracy, Americans valued liberty and property. America's leaders saw consensus and social harmony everywhere. Thus, at the end of the Second World War, it was understandable that Americans, now experiencing unprecedented power and prestige, expected their way of life to prevail and believed that other countries would eagerly desire to become like the United States. The influential publisher Henry R. Luce coined the expression "The American Century" to capture this ethos. "American experience is the key to the future," he pronounced in 1945. "America must be the elder brother of the nations in the brotherhood of man."

Pride in the "American experience" was precisely the problem. A country that had achieved freedom without having to overcome poverty, had won power and then succeeded in controlling it in a revolution that was truly unique in not devouring its own children, a country whose people were "born equal" (Tocqueville's expression) and did not have to struggle against reactionary class forces to become so— such a country could scarcely constitute a model for the rest of the world.

That America could be a model for the world was implicit in Roosevelt's economic plans for the postwar era. Some of those policies emerged from the Bretton Woods Conference held in New Hampshire in 1944 and attended by representatives from forty nations, including the Soviet Union. Haunted by the anarchic conditions of the world economy in the post-World War I era and again during the depression, American and British specialists wanted to see national monetary systems brought under international control. These new policies would ease balance-of-payment difficulties and stabilize exchange rates in order to achieve postwar reconstruction by means of cooperative world trade. In some respects the hopes that inspired such proposals derived from the century-old Anglo-American assumption that flourishing international trade would render war obsolete as nations became interdependent. Some of the institutions that evolved from Bretton Woods, especially the World Bank, the International Monetary Fund (IMF), and the Export-Import Bank, succeeded in overcoming the restrictions that had previously hindered world trade. But Treasury Secretary Henry Morgenthau and others who had planned Bretton Woods believed that future world peace depended on their success in winning the cooperation of the Soviet Union. The Soviets, however, refused to sign the Bretton Woods agreement. Why? First, they wished to guard their data on foreign-exchange balances. And they feared opening up Eastern Europe to Western influences, suspecting that political strings would be attached to loans from the World Bank. Many Soviet "experts" also believed that the American-fed Western economy was about to undergo another depression and possibly, as Marx had predicted of advanced capitalism, a complete collapse.

John Maynard Keynes knew how tenacious Marxist ideology was from his debates with communists at Cambridge University. He had warned Americans at Bretton Woods not to expect Soviet cooperation. But American hopes persisted. Perhaps nowhere was the ideological dimension of the cold war better manifested than in the proud assumption that American consumerism would undermine Soviet communism. Sewell Avery of Montgomery Ward recommended shipping millions of mail-order catalogs to the Russian people and the sociologist David Riesman suggested parachute-dropping nylon stockings. Whet the appetite of the Russians and they may come to appreciate how capitalism has succeeded in overcoming backwardness and scarcity. Ever since the eighteenth century the philosophers of liberal capitalism had insisted that only private property and the pleasures of consumption could provide the incentives for work, innovation, progress, and freedom. But in the following century Karl Marx offered a different message: progress, freedom, and human happiness have nothing to do with material possessions. Thus, to the Soviet Marxist of the twentieth century, Western liberalism did not mean natural right and political representation but private property and economic exploitation.

The decisions made at Yalta and Potsdam were symptoms rather than causes of an ideological impasse. The cold war would escalate on the basis of conventional power politics, but its origins lie in ideas and doctrines that evolved from different historical experiences. What happens in history is determined by what is thought and felt. The minds of the United States and Russia were too profoundly different to share a view of the future.

"I want this election in Poland to be the first one beyond question," Roosevelt remarked to Stalin at Yalta. "It should be like Caesar's wife. I did not know her but they said she was pure."

"They said that about her," Stalin replied, "but in fact she had her sins."

THE TRUMAN DOCTRINE AND THE MARSHALL PLAN

The formation of the United Nations offered a great hope for peace in 1945. During World War II popular sentiment had shifted on the League of Nations. Several wartime books lamented America's failure to enter the League and Hollywood produced a popular movie dramatizing Woodrow Wilson as a saintly prophet scorned by a reactionary Senate. Would America repeat its mistakes of the past? When the Senate debated ratification of the UN Charter in 1945, even the isolationist Republican Arthur Vandenberg and opponent of lend-lease, came out in support of the bill. Before a hushed gallery packed with reporters, Vandenberg spoke of how Pearl Harbor and the development of new weaponry had driven him to change his life-long belief in American self-reliance. In the new world no nation "can immunize itself by its own exclusive action. . . . I want maximum American cooperation. . . . I want a new dignity and a new authority for international law. I think self-interest requires it." Senators of both parties rose to give Vandenberg a standing ovation. The press hailed his speech as the turning point in history at which America had joined the world.

On Friday, February 21, 1947, the British ambassador in Washington telephoned the State Department seeking an emergency meeting with General George C. Marshall, who had recently replaced James Byrnes as secretary of state. As Marshall was away for the weekend, sessions were arranged with lower-level officials and it soon became clear why the matter was so urgent. England was asking America to shoulder a part of her burden, to assume responsibility for defending the British sphere-of-interest in the Mediterranean.

Specifically, the British pointed to Greece and Turkey. Greece was in the midst of a civil war with communist guerillas. Turkey was weak and tottering, a temptation to meddlers. Both needed over $400,000,000 in immediate aid, which Britain could not afford. Truman and Marshall understood the frustration felt by Churchill and De Gaulle when lend-lease was terminated at war's end. On the other hand, they also knew that the American people, worried about a postwar depression, were in no mood to play the role of rich uncle forever. Nor was the Republican party, which was demanding tax cuts and reduction in government spending. Even so, Truman plunged ahead. Before Truman went to Congress to make his plea for aid, Acheson and Vandenberg advised him to dramatize the situation in Greece not simply as a civil war but as a Soviet attempt to penetrate the Aegean and establish control in the Middle East. There was little truth to that advice since Stalin did not intend to get involved in the Greek civil war. Truman's cataclysmic rhetoric did indeed "scare hell," in Vandenberg's phrase, out of Congress and the public. What might have been defined as a local struggle now took on global implications.

Truman used another arrow as well, formulating the struggle in democratic terms. "I believe that it must be the policy of the United States to support free peoples who are resisting attempted subjugation by armed minorities or by outside pressures." The Greek-Turkish aid bill rode this crest of rhetoric to Senate approval by a vote of 67–23 and in the House by 287–107. The idea that the United States would come to the assistance of any country struggling against the forces of communism became known as the Truman Doctrine.

The doctrine was not without its opponents in Congress, the State Department, and the press. Some critics pointed out that Greece was plainly undemocratic and reactionary. Others wondered why the fate of Greece and Turkey was not a matter for the UN. Ohio's Senator Robert A. Taft argued that the bill would exacerbate the East-West conflict and Henry Wallace predicted that it would bring "a century of fear." George Kennan, George Marshall, and the diplomat Charles E. Bohlen favored economic rather than military aid and worried that the "flamboyant anticommunism" in Truman's speech was too provocative. Others like Lippmann believed that with the Truman Doctrine American foreign policy was becoming dangerously universalistic and overburdened. Yet during the congressional debates Representative Walter Judd, once a medical missionary to China, asked a telling question: why was the United States rushing to oppose communism in Greece and at the same time urging communists in China to cooperate with Chiang's nationalist government? In his reply, Acheson tried to differentiate the two areas, implying that China was simply too large a country to be supported by the United States. In 1947 the cold war still meant that only events in Europe would be regarded as within America's defense perimeter.

The decision to focus on Europe also underscored what came to be known as the Marshall Plan. At the time of the Truman Doctrine, Kennan, Marshall, and others had reached gloomy conclusions—the Chinese civil war was hopeless; Chiang's regime was so corrupt that American aid would probably end up in communist hands; and, most importantly, China was too underdeveloped to become a major industrial power. At the same time much of Western Europe lay in ruins. Its industries had been heavily damaged by the war. Massive unemployment was evident everywhere, and millions of displaced persons roamed homeless. According to a report by former president Herbert C. Hoover, the children of Europe lived on the edge of starvation. "The seeds of totalitarianism," Truman had warned in his speech to Congress, "are nurtured by misery and want." To revive Europe, Kennan and his staff developed a program for economic recovery that was presented in a speech by Secretary of State Marshall at Harvard University in June 1947. The program called upon European nations to cooperate in a plan of mutual assistance to the best of their ability, and pledged the United States to contribute substantially to whatever remaining aid was necessary, which was estimated to be roughly seventeen billion dollars.

The Marshall Plan realized its two objectives of integration and restoration. Such experiments as the Organization of European Eco-

Secretary of State George C. Marshall receiving an honorary degree at Harvard University, just prior to delivering his "Marshall Plan" address.

nomic Cooperation laid the basis for what would later become the Common Market. Marshall Plan aid also paid for 25 percent of Europe's total imports between 1947 and 1950, added nearly 10 percent to Europe's resources, and played a vital role in accelerating investment, increasing consumption, creating employment, and expanding industrial output 40 percent above output in 1938. Above all, the Marshall Plan realized its political objectives. In facilitating industrial recovery, it reduced the danger that prolonged economic chaos would undermine democratic governments in Western Europe.

Although the Marshall Plan would eventually prove a smashing success, Congress debated for six months before approving it. Some Republican critics saw it as little more than "New Dealism" in Europe and the "China first" members of Congress demanded and got a further appropriation for Chiang's government. Henry Wallace had mixed feelings. He first admired the spirit of American noblesse oblige; then, thinking of how it might affect Russian-American relations, concluded it was really a flagrant "Martial Plan."

The Soviet Union and its satellites were invited to participate in the

Marshall Plan. Some historians regard this decision to include Russia as a "gamble," taken in part because the Truman administration did not want to be seen as polarizing the cold war, but also with the expectation that Russian acceptance was improbable owing to the stipulation that each participating country must open its economic records. Bringing a team of eighty-nine technical specialists, Soviet Foreign Minister Molotov attended the Paris meeting and showed interest in the American offer. But after being handed a telegram from Moscow, he walked out and denounced the Marshall Plan. The Soviet Union then ordered the satellite countries to rescind their applications.

Why this Soviet advance and quick retreat? The Soviets may have assumed that the Marshall Plan would be another lend-lease arrangement whereby Russia could simply request aid without economic supervision; or possibly they feared that economic recovery fueled by America would rejuvenate Germany; perhaps the precarious situation of Russia vis-à-vis her satellites compelled the Soviets at least to show up at the Paris conference in expectation of getting in on the give-away before the full implications of the plan were understood. Still another possibility was that Stalin saw the huge transfer of American aid as a danger to the "socialist" bloc because it would whet the appetites of the satellites for the capitalist system—as indeed Truman had hoped. Curiously, events proved both Truman and Stalin wrong. When Yugoslavia broke from the Soviet orbit in 1948, Marshal Tito accepted Western aid and yet continued his socialist economy.

While the Marshall Plan helped stabilize Western Europe, the situation in Eastern Europe worsened. A week before Marshall's address at Harvard, Hungarian communists staged a coup d'etat in Budapest. In other Eastern countries all non-Stalinist socialists were driven from power as the Soviet Union set up the Cominform (successor to the Comintern) to coordinate Communist party activities within and outside the Eastern bloc. At the same time the Soviets were pressuring Finland to join a military alliance.

Most shocking was the news from Prague. In February 1948, Czech communist leaders, possibly worried about their own fading popularity as a minority party and the danger of the nation being lured into the West by the temptations of Marshall aid, seized control of the government by manipulating a cabinet crisis. This event evoked images of the earlier "rape of Prague" by Hitler in 1939. Czechoslovakia represented the last remnant of democracy behind the iron curtain. The communist takeover traumatized the West and led to the death, whether by suicide or murder, of Jan Masaryk, the beloved leader and son of Tomáš Masaryk, founder of the Czechoslovak republic and devoted scholar of Russian history.

In April, the United States enjoyed some relief from cold war strains when the Italian Communist party lost its bid for electoral power. This communist setback was aided by American money covertly funneled to the opposition parties. At the same time relations between Yugoslavia and Russia had so deteriorated that some commentators saw Stalin losing his grip on the satellite system. But in June 1948 the psychological tide turned against the West as newspapers throughout the world blared headlines of a military showdown with Russia in Berlin.

Germany had been partitioned into Allied occupation zones after the war. The Soviet policy was to keep West Germany as well as its own eastern zone economically weak and dependent. England, France, and the United States, however, wanted to see West Germany a viable part of noncommunist Western Europe. As a means of rejuvenating West Germany and coordinating its economic development with that of other nations, a currency reform was proposed, which meant the end of the four-power accords and the first step in setting up West Germany independent from the three western zones. The Soviets claimed the new economic policy violated Potsdam agreements stipulating four-power deliberations in all German affairs. And the Russians did more than complain. They acted first by interfering with Allied military trains headed for West Berlin and then by halting all ground traffic. Berlin was now blockaded, isolated within the eastern orbit, and the Truman administration was completely surprised.

Truman and his advisors failed to anticipate the blockade because they regarded such a move not simply as a tactical maneuver to force some concession but as a high-risk adventure related to the overall struggle for Europe. With West Berlin now cut off and her population without supplies, Truman had a decision to make—should he break the blockade and possibly bring on war with Russia or should he relinquish the besieged city as an indefensible outpost? While the issue was being debated in the UN, Truman and General Curtis E. LeMay decided on a middle course—to use aerial transport to bring fuel and food to the desperate Berliners. In a matter of weeks more than five thousand tons were flown in the dramatic airlift that had C-54 cargo planes taking off every minute from the airports at Wiesbaden, Rhein-Main, and Frankfurt and landing with amazing safety and efficiency at Berlin's Tempelhof Airport. Many doubted that Berlin could be sustained through the cold winter. But thousands of pilots were called back into service or taken from their desk jobs to assure the success of "Operation Vittles." The blockade and airlift ended in May 1949. Ironically, the image of Berlin, once the stronghold of militarist Prussia and Nazism, was transformed and morally rehabilitated. "Russian folly," observed the historian Arnold J. Toynbee, "has turned Berlin into the heroic symbol of liberty."

Still another irony further compounded the unintended consequences of Russian policy. Soviet actions taken in the East for security reasons in fact had the opposite effect, rendering Russia more insecure by uniting Western nations against her. As a result, America returned to a policy abjured since the eighteenth century: it entered a diplomatic alliance with foreign powers for reasons of mutual protection. In 1949 the United States created the North Atlantic Treaty Organization (NATO), which included Great Britain, Canada, Iceland, Norway, France, Italy, Portugal, the Netherlands, and Luxembourg. Greece and Turkey were added in 1952 and West Germany in 1955. The decision to form NATO came in the aftermath of Russian subjugation of Czechoslovakia and the Berlin blockade. These events convinced most in the West that Russia would expand and control wherever possible. Thus, NATO would serve as a buffer, and the treaty signatories agreed that an act of aggression against one member would be considered an attack upon all, to be answered by individual or collective resistance. Only by banding together could Western Europe hope to begin to match the numerically superior Red Army. By joining NATO the United States was committed to stop Soviet military forces from advancing beyond the territories occupied in 1947. In short, America committed itself to containing the Soviet Union. Behind this policy lay the theoretical formulations of George F. Kennan.

THE KENNAN-LIPPMANN DEBATE

A man of wide learning and deep reflection, Kennan had studied literature, religion, and politics at Princeton. He would go on to serve for twenty-one years in the Foreign Service, an experience that reinforced his conviction that international relations was a field of inevitable conflict requiring intelligent control. His conviction about the ineluctability of power had also been influenced by the theologian Reinhold Niebuhr, whose neo-orthodox Protestantism revived the old idea of original sin that modern liberalism had once eliminated from political philosophy. Kennan's momentous article signed simply "X," appeared

The meditative George F. Kennan, who first formulated the theory of containment and later criticized its misuses.

in *Foreign Affairs* in 1947. He used the term "messianic," as had Niebuhr, to describe the "political personality" of the Soviet regime and to suggest that the communists had "found in Marxist theory a highly convenient rationalization for their own instinctive desires." Although the Soviets had no fixed blueprint or hurried timetable, they would continue to increase pressure and push their influence outward until they were "contained by the adroit and vigilant application of counterforce at a series of constantly shifting geographical and political points." This counterforce, Kennan hoped, would eventually produce such Russian "frustration" that containment would lead to "either the breakup or gradual mellowing of Soviet power."

Kennan's analysis did much to shape Truman's cold-war diplomacy. There were dissenters, to be sure, most notably Walter Lippmann, who subjected the "Mr. X" article to a searching critique in *The Cold War: A Study in U.S. Foreign Policy* (1947). Lippmann dismissed ideology in favor of a nationalistic interpretation, arguing that Stalin was behaving much as Peter the Great and Ivan the Terrible had in centuries past. He averred that Russia had occupied Eastern Europe not out of expansionist designs but simply because World War II had left her terribly insecure. Lippmann also regarded the prescription of containment as a "strategic monstrosity." He saw America aligning with a series of questionable and unreliable puppet regimes, stretching her military resources to every corner of the globe, including Asia. As a means of allaying Soviet fears, he proposed that the United States recommend a mutual withdrawal of Soviet and American troops in Germany under strict guarantees of demilitarizing Russia's historic enemy.

Ironically, Kennan would come around to Lippman's view when he saw his doctrine of containment leading to a call for indiscriminate intervention wherever and whenever communists threatened to come to power. Both writers had doubts about the Truman Doctrine; and both noticed that if American aid had succored Greece, its fate had also been helped by Tito's break with the Cominform, which closed the border between Yugoslavia and Greece and deprived Greek communists of sanctuary. Kennan would also agree with Lippmann that NATO posed an obstacle to the neutralization of central Europe by threatening to rearm Germany.

But Kennan's unfettered ideas suited the times. Cold War tensions were on the rise in America and McCarthyism was rising with them.

The eminent columnist Walter Lippmann, the first major nonradical writer to criticize America's confrontation with the Soviet Union.

As an anticommunist scare gripped the country in the late forties and fifties, formulation of American diplomatic policy passed to the hands of Dean Acheson, who replaced Marshall as secretary of state in 1949. Acheson's view of cold war policy was embodied in a top secret document he obtained from the National Security Council and titled NSC–68. The NSC had been established in July 1947 to coordinate the military services and to advise the president. Predicting "the polarization of power that inescapably confronts the slave society with the free," NSC–68 described the Soviets as desiring to impose their authority everywhere. To that end their efforts "are now directed toward the domination of the Euroasian land mass." Kennan strongly objected to NSC–68. He argued that Stalin had no grand scheme for world conquest, that the Soviet sphere of influence lay in Eastern Europe, and that American diplomacy was already too rigid and militaristic. But Acheson and Truman were watching the home front too. Wary of domestic rumblings over apparent Soviet successes, they overrode Kennan's objections and used NSC–68 to quadruple defense spending and accelerate United States military build-up, including development of the hydrogen bomb. NSC–68, a durable document, lived on to become the rationale for America's intervention in the Korean War.

Scholars who have assessed the Kennan-Lippmann debate largely judge Lippmann's position more intelligent to the extent that Kennan had to repudiate the misuses of his own containment policy. Yet both analyses, in retrospect, appear flawed. Lippmann's interpretation of Soviet communism as an extension of Russia's monarchial past is valid in respect to the persistence of the autocratic state. It is questionable, however, as an explanation of Soviet diplomatic behavior. Among other omissions, it ignored the cordial relations some czars enjoyed with liberal England and France while fretting about the Ottoman Empire. In this respect, bolshevism and Stalinism broke with Western values, and Lippmann's refusal to take them seriously as different led him into illusions. The Russians "can't be such fools as to talk about democracy in Poland and Italy and elsewhere unless they intend to have a good deal of it at home," he wrote privately to a friend in 1944. The following year Lippmann informed a correspondent that the United States and England would be allowed to supervise elections in Poland in accordance with the Yalta agreement. Curiously, years earlier in *The Good Society* (1937), Lippmann had written that collectivized economies were incompatible with human freedom. Now he assumed that democracy—meaning free elections and national self-determination—

could evolve from an ideological system that had all along repudiated a political road to freedom.

If Lippman proved too hopeful about the evolution of democracy in Eastern Europe, Kennan proved too hopeful about the collapse of communism within the Soviet Union. Kennan believed that a steady application of "counterforce" would lead to "either the break up or the gradual mellowing" of the Soviet state. His argument rested on the assumption that the Soviet Union would be incapable of enduring its own stresses and contradictions. But to see Stalin's Russia as a contradiction of Western values, as did Kennan when he drew upon the German novelist Thomas Mann to uphold liberalism and reason, is to misperceive it as Stalin intended it to be. Like Lippmann, Kennan ignored totalitarianism as a theoretical challenge, the emergence of a new type of social formation in which all power had been collectivized and all opposition abolished. In contrast to European refugee intellectuals, neither Kennan nor Lippman paid much attention to Soviet Russia as a totalitarian system capable of resisting outside pressures and incapable of reforming itself from within. As the émigré scholar Hannah Arendt pointed out, Western thinkers had nothing to fall back upon to grasp the overwhelming reality of totalitarianism—its "horrible originality."

Kennan's containment policy proved quite successful in the short run. West Germany revived while Italy, France, Austria, Greece, and Yugoslavia remained independent. The expansion of Soviet influence and power beyond the iron curtain had been effectively arrested. Whether this stalemate flowed from America's display of counterforce or from the possibility that Stalin never intended to export revolution is difficult to ascertain.

Although successful in the short run, containment failed the long-term test, the mellowing of the Soviet state. Soviet totalitarianism and its denial of human rights remained completely unaffected by American diplomacy. Popular pressure for change never amounted to much in Russia. To deter aggression and to promote democracy are two entirely different propositions, it turned out, and the Kremlin's leaders viewed it as far safer to have Russia contained than to have Russia democratized. Whatever the success of Western "counterforce," the ideological nature of the cold war ran on its tragic course.

Kennan's doctrine of containment assumed that the "strong light" of the Kremlin was flickering out as a beacon of hope to certain countries in the Western world. Curiously, the Kremlin's candle had guttered in Asia twenty years before containment. In 1927 Chinese communists, led by the brilliant theoretician Mao Tse-tung (Mao Zedong), moved toward power not by following Stalin's advice but by defying it. When Mao led the communists to victory after World War II, the theoretical assumptions of the cold war had to be reconsidered by both super powers. In essence, Mao had demonstrated that communist movements can act independently of Moscow; despite what Marx, Lenin, Trotsky, and Stalin had claimed, peasants can win revolutionary struggles on their own without the support of urban workers; and China would advance toward a communist society without succumbing to the bureaucratization of life that made the Soviet Union an ideological disgrace. The beacon of hope for the Third World would now shine brightest in China's red star.

The Fall of Nationalist China and the Korean War

China had long hovered gigantically in the Western imagination. In May 1949, when the American people learned that the great land mass of China had been overrun by communism, it seemed that Napoleon's nightmare had come true: the "sleeping giant" would one day awake and dominate the world. The communist world of the USSR and China now consisted of between 13 and 14 million square miles (excluding Antarctica, one-fourth of the globe's land) and more than 750,000,000 people (one-third of the world's population). Shocked, angry, and frightened, Americans wanted an explanation. Dean Acheson and the State Department came forward with a White Paper that laid the blame squarely on Chiang Kai-shek and his inefficient and corrupt regime. Since the end of the war the United States had given Chiang more than two billion dollars in loans in addition to one billion dollars in war-surplus materials. "The unfortunate but inescapable fact," Acheson announced, "is that the ominous result of the civil war in China was beyond the control of the government of the United States. Nothing that this country did or could have done within reasonable limits of its capabilities could have changed the result. . . . It was the product of internal Chinese forces, forces which this country tried to influence but could not." Military advisors had also warned against the dangers of direct American intervention in a conventional land war in Asia, and generals testified that the well-supplied Nationalist Army had all that it needed except one thing—the will to fight. As China specialist John

Mao Tse-tung, in northern Shensi in 1947; the first communist leader to prove that underdeveloped countries did not have to wait for an industrial proletariat to make a revolution.

K. Fairbank put it, "The United States Government has done practically everything possible to save Chiang Kai-shek except actually shoot Chinese for him."

Many Americans remained unconvinced. Acheson depicted Chiang's regime as irresponsible and indulgent and China as ripe for communism. Yet opinion polls during the war indicated that Americans admired the Chinese as hard-working, intelligent, brave, religious, honest, practical, and completely indifferent to "radicalism," not to mention revolutionary communism. The American image of China had conjured up pictures of rice fields, pigtails, pagodas, the Great Wall, and benevolent American missionaries. In so far as the image was "ours," how did "we lose" China and who was responsible for it? An explosive question, particularly when raised by politicians who refused to accept a no-fault diplomacy.

In contrast to Eastern Europe, the communist triumph in China came as no surprise to the State Department. China experts had known throughout the forties that there was no easy solution in sight. After the war General Marshall had gone to China fruitlessly seeking a truce between the communists and nationalists and urging on them a coalition government. Stalin had been advocating the same course for China for twenty years. According to André Malraux, Mao even suspected Stalin of wanting to see the Chinese communist movement destroyed. Mao could hardly forget that when he took Stalin's advice in 1927, Chiang drove the communists out of the proposed coalition government and declared that he and his Kuomintang alone represented China's nationhood.

After the war, with the Japanese menace eliminated, Chiang made a feeble effort to carry out the early nationalist leader Sun Yat-sen's promise of land reform along with political democracy. It was too late. Reform faded as the communists gained power among the peasantry in the countryside, offering communal landholding to men and to women the promise of no more wife-beating. Ironically, General MacArthur was carrying out in occupied Japan a number of progressive ideals that Mao wanted for China and that Chiang had lowered in priority. The Japanese were given a new and democratic constitution. It eliminated the secret police and promoted the formation of unions and women's rights. It broke up the *Zaibatsu* system of cartels, and distributed over 4.5 million acres to the peasants. Through all of this critical period, Chiang was blind to social reform in China, and thus ignored Machiavelli's dictum that while it is "safer to be feared than to be loved," a political leader must strive to be both. But Chiang was, in Truman's words, "an old-fashioned warlord, and, as with the warlords, there was no love for him among the people."

When the communists came to power in China, Chiang gathered his forces, which had at one time outnumbered Mao's army by four to one, and retreated to the off-shore island of Formosa. In October 1949, Mao declared the formation of the People's Republic of China and sought diplomatic recognition. Many Western nations immediately granted it. The United States announced it would continue to recognize Nationalist China, now the great cause of conservative Republicans who saw Chiang as a true patriot who would someday cross the Formosa Strait to redeem his country as George Washington had once crossed the Delaware. As to Red China, the Truman administration had originally hoped to have friendly relations with Mao, seeing him as a possible Tito, fiercely independent of the Soviet bloc. Mao saw things differently. To the disappointment of the liberals, he sided with the Soviet Union. Denouncing American imperialism, he trumpeted China as the model for the conquest of power in colonial and semicolonial countries.

The cold war in Asia had begun. In early 1950 the United States ended its neutrality in the Indochinese war between the French and the Vietnamese rebels, led by Ho Chi Minh. Worried that Ho's insurgent Vietminh might be directed by China or Russia, the United States recognized the French-controlled states of Vietnam, Cambodia, and Laos. Soon American aid arrived to supplant that of the French and support their puppet ruler, Bao Dai, a chief of state who spent more time in Paris and on the Riviera than in Saigon. With such alignments, the moral suasion of the Truman Doctrine eroded away. In 1947 that doctrine had implied that America would come to the aid of "free" nations trying to determine their own destiny. By 1950 a country's political character mattered less than its strategic position.

Such was the situation on June 24, 1950, a quiet Saturday in Washington, when the State Department received a cablegram reporting that North Korea employed over seven divisions and 150 tanks to attack South Korea. Unlike the fall of China, the communist invasion of the Republic of Korea caught American diplomats by surprise.

At the conclusion of World War II, Korea was divided across the middle at the 38th parallel, with Russians in control of the north and Americans the south. The United States and the UN recognized President Syngman Rhee's nationalist regime as the legitimate government. Concurrently, both pressed for elections that might unite the country as specified in the Potsdam agreements. Russia vetoed UN efforts toward that goal. Meanwhile, Acheson and the State Department announced that America's defensive perimeter in Asia included Japan, Okinawa, Formosa, and the Philippines, implying that South Korea was on its own. In fact, the United States had been withdrawing American troops from the area. Presumably American diplomats believed that the next phase of the cold war, when and if it occurred, would be global in scope, a massive offensive against which the United States could defend such vital areas as the Philippines with superior air and naval power. A limited land war in a divided Asian country was precisely what America wanted to avoid. But if the State Department was caught off-guard by the North Korean invasion, the communists also miscalculated. Truman immediately interpreted the invasion as an act of aggression that must be resisted. Unless resisted, other communist leaders might be emboldened to undertake similar actions that could trigger World War III. Since the invasion was massive and obvious, and not the covert maneuver of internal subversion characteristic of cold-war politics in Eastern Europe, the integrity of the UN was at stake in its pledge to resist aggression. So too was Truman's presidency and the future of the Democratic party. Alleged to have "sold out"

Eastern Europe and "lost" China, Truman had to take a stand in Korea.

Within two days Truman announced to the nation that the United States was pledged to the defense of South Korea. He ordered the Seventh Fleet to the Formosa Strait and assigned General MacArthur to prepare his air and naval units for action. Two-thirds of the nation supported the president. Although Truman at first was careful not to link Russia to the invasion, according to the polls, Korea was viewed as evidence that Russia must be stopped, even if it meant the possibility of a third world war. The press, even some opposition papers, joined in hailing Truman's "magnificent courage and terse decision." Only Taft and a few other members of Congress questioned Truman's authority to act without congressional approval. The majority of the members broke into applause after the president delivered his message. The UN's Security Council, with the Russian delegate absent, condemned the invasion and called upon the world to assist South Korea. Several nations eventually did send combat divisions, including the British Commonwealth countries, France, Greece, Turkey, Belgium, the Netherlands, the Philippines, and Thailand. The Korean War was the first in cold-war history to be fought collectively, bringing the forces of the noncommunist and communist worlds into direct, full-scale conflict. But the alignment was misleading. Some countries sent only a token force. Nor had the objectives of the UN forces been specifically defined. Eventually this prolonged conflict in Korea would be the first

American soldiers recapturing Seoul during the Korean War in September 1950.

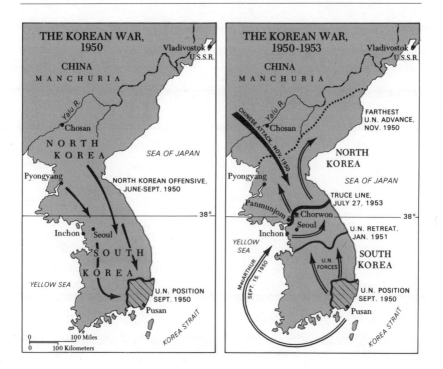

modern war America failed to win (or even to declare), concluding after four years in stalemate and armistice.

If the Korean War ended in frustration, it began in desperation. Within a week South Korea's capital, Seoul, had fallen and her ill-trained army was fleeing on all fronts. It now became clear that America's tactical support from air and naval units would be inadequate. At MacArthur's recommendation, the United States committed massive ground combat forces. But before they could be readied the communists overtook most of the Korean peninsula. In September MacArthur conceived a counteroffensive that involved an amphibious landing at Inchon that would cut-off communist troops in South Korea. Although the Joint Chiefs of Staff were skeptical, the invasion succeeded brilliantly. By October the North Korean army had been all but destroyed and UN forces possessed the entire region south of the 38th parallel. Unfortunately, the masterful victory served only to convince MacArthur of his infallibility. Now the general wanted to push beyond the 38th parallel in order to reunite Korea. Truman and the State Department hesitated, for the Chinese had made clear through diplomatic channels their determination to intervene if UN troops neared China's borders.

MacArthur reassured the president that the chances of China doing so were "very little," arguing that her army could not cross the Yalu River, North Korea's boundary with Manchuria, in time to halt a quick offensive. MacArthur's intelligence sources erred on the side of confidence. The Chinese had already been slipping across the Yalu at night and hiding their troops and armor before daylight in the rugged hillsides. Truman, impressed by MacArthur's military genius, assented to his demand to take the North Korean capital of Pyongyang. But Mac-Arthur exceeded his orders and began to advance toward the Yalu. When South Korean and American forces engaged in limited skirmishes with the Chinese, the undaunted MacArthur assured Truman that a full American offensive would make short shrift of the communists and that American boys would be home by Christmas. Instead, Mao's 200,000 soldiers, fighting ferociously through mountain passes and valleys in heavy snow and bitter cold, drove the UN troops back into South Korea. Eventually the UN forces regrouped and fought their way back to the 38th parallel, precisely where the war had begun.

With the war at an impasse in December 1950, the Russian ambassador to the UN proposed a truce, but MacArthur remained convinced that the war could be won. How? By bombing the Yalu bridges and Chinese installations beyond it, blockading China's entire coast, and bringing Chiang's army from Formosa as reinforcement for the invasion of China. Several UN members, especially Britain, feared that such an escalation could bring on a full-scale war, pairing Russia with China and perhaps bringing into play Russia's newly developed atomic bombs. Sharing such fears, Truman and the State Department began to speak of Korea as a "limited" war for a limited objective—the containment of communism in Korea, not its extermination in China. The military, including General Eisenhower, voiced doubts about Mac-Arthur's plan to invade China. General Omar N. Bradley would later express the views of the Joint Chiefs of Staff when he told Congress that MacArthur had proposed "the wrong war, at the wrong place and at the wrong time, and with the wrong enemy."

MacArthur, a soldier of the old school, believed that "in war, there is no substitute for victory." Any strategy of limited war that allowed the enemy to survive was not strategy at all. He began to speak out publicly on how American troops could move across the Yalu and doom China to such a threat of immediate military collapse that the communists would be forced to surrender. Korea would then be united. But when Senator Lyndon B. Johnson asked MacArthur why the Chinese could not simply retreat beyond the Yalu and refuse to surrender, MacArthur could only reply that such a question was "a hypothetical query." Where Truman believed that containment must remain limited and selective, MacArthur wanted to make it unlimited and massive, and hence he informed the press and Republican Congressman Joseph W. Martin, Speaker of the House, that Korea was the vital spot that would decide the war for global supremacy. Such pronouncements flouted an earlier directive by Truman that as president he was in charge of military as well as foreign policy. MacArthur was to make no policy statements without Truman's permission. When MacArthur continued to speak out, Truman consulted his military and State Department advisors. All agreed that the general must be relieved of command.

On April 12, 1951, when Truman announced that MacArthur had been dismissed, the president's critics growled and his enemies screamed. Most Americans, to be sure, wanted to win the war, but not by widening it. No one wished to risk a possible nuclear showdown between the superpowers. Yet American frustrations could easily be exploited by right-wing hawks convinced that the Korean campaign was being sabotaged by left-wing doves. Senator William Jenner of Indiana claimed that America "is in the hands of a secret inner coterie which is directed by the Soviet Union." Senator Joseph McCarthy, the Wisconsin Republican who would make a career out of sowing the same suspicions, called Truman a "son of a bitch." The White House was flooded with close to thirty thousand telegrams, almost all conveying the same message: "Impeach the little ward politician from Kansas City"; "Impeach the Judas in the White House"; "Impeach the B who calls himself President." A Gallup poll reported that the public supported the general against the president 69 to 29, and a young congressman from California, Richard M. Nixon, demanded MacArthur's immediate reappointment.

How had American politics come to such a mean and vicious state of mind? The emotional stresses of the cold war offer only a partial explanation. Equally important was the political situation facing America during the Truman years. The 1952 elections were approaching. The Republicans had not elected a president since 1928. For twenty years they had stood by, frustrated, watching Democrats run the country from the White House. In the 1948 election Republicans had been absolutely sure of victory in the race against Harry Truman. FDR was fortunate to be in office during a depression which the country looked to him to solve, and he was sustained in office by the patriotic war against Hitler. His charismatic charm and undoubted ability made his popularity understandable. And on FDR's death the Democrats had been lucky again, as the seemingly obscure and mediocre Truman became America's leader without facing a national election. Now standing in the way of dismantling the New Deal and turning government back to business was this stubborn man from Missouri. To make matters worse, the Korean War broke out not long after Truman took office following his stunning upset of Dewey. If Republicans felt vindicated by Truman's purported mishandling of the war, political victory had still eluded them and left the GOP in a state of confusion and frustration. The source of their problem was the new president whom some called both "cocky" and "half-cocked."

3

Truman, McCarthyism, and the Ordeal of Liberalism

THE MAN NOBODY KNEW: HARRY S. TRUMAN

Most Americans knew very little about Harry S. Truman when he assumed the presidency upon Roosevelt's death. Even the chief justice of the United States, when swearing in the thirty-third president, was unaware that he had no middle name, simply an initial. Yet before long Americans would know Truman just as he was: a blunt, outspoken man, at once determined, feisty, and courageous. With his thick, prissy glasses, patted-down hair, and ordinary vested suits, Truman lacked a media "image" to project. He simply spoke his mind regardless of the consequences; and his mind, while scarcely profound in any philosophical sense, displayed a down-home folk wisdom about the essential truths of life.

Truman never lost sight of his roots. After taking the oath of office, he immediately telephoned his ninety-one-year-old mother in Grandview, Missouri. "Mama, I'm terribly busy," he explained as if the president had to justify the duties that would change his life. "You probably won't hear from me for some time." When a music critic wrote an unflattering review of his daughter's debut as a soprano, Truman rushed off a letter to the *Washington Post*, calling the reviewer a "frustrated old man" and threatening to blacken his eyes and "kick his butt." Americans may have felt it undignified for the president of the United States to behave like a street-brawler, but they also admired a loving father who defended his daughter. They also knew that Truman himself could take criticism and ridicule. His inner convictions fortified him against the slurs of the press, and he disdained those who would cater to the vicissitudes of public opinion. "I wonder how far Moses would have gone if he'd taken a poll of Egypt?" Truman once wrote in a memo. "What would Jesus Christ have preached if he'd taken a poll in Israel? . . . It isn't polls or public opinion of the moment that counts. It is right and wrong and leadership."

Born in 1884, Truman was raised on several farms in western Missouri before his family settled in Independence, a small town in Jackson County near Kansas City. His boyhood desire to become a great soldier was frustrated when poor eyesight ruled out West Point, and his father's financial losses forced him to abandon his dream of a college education. His mother stimulated his interest in music and books. Young Truman practiced the piano daily and became a voracious reader of military history and the literature of classical antiquity. An admirer of the ancient republican ideals of citizenship, Truman would later single out three heroes to be emulated: Cincinnatus, the Roman warrior who saved the republic and then laid down his arms; Cato, the statesman who taught the virtues of austerity and sacrifice for the public good; and George Washington, the founder who established America on the right basis of patriotism and duty while shunning the temptations of power.

The ancient ideals of austerity and simplicity well-suited the small-town habits and values that Truman brought with him to Washington. But he also knew that the classical vision of citizens devoting their time and money to the public good was a boyhood fantasy. Truman's America was now a nation of consumers impatient with patriotic sacrifices so freely offered during the war. The challenge facing Truman was more mundane—to convince Americans that taxes were necessary to defray the national debt amassed during the war. "Nobody likes to pay taxes," he observed in an unsent letter to Stanley Marcus of the Nieman-Marcus Company. "A man will cry his head off over paying $100 taxes on his income but he will go and throw away $500 or $1,000 on a poker game and say nothing about it. I guess that is the way the human animal is made."

Truman's understanding of the human animal had been formed by the bourbon-and-poker ambience of Missouri politics and a life of hard knocks. After serving as a captain in World War I, Truman entered the men's clothing business, only to go bankrupt when a postwar recession plunged the economy in 1921, leaving him with debts that took years to pay. All but down and out, Truman sought the help of Tom Pendergast and his corrupt Kansas City political machine and won election as a county administrator. He was on his way politically, at a certain cost. Even so, he would distribute patronage for the Pendergast machine while keeping himself clear of graft and bribes. Gradually, he established a reputation for honesty and a style of "plain speaking" so candid that he did not hesitate to describe the Ku Klux Klan for what it was, "a bunch of damn cowards hiding behind bedsheets."

In 1934 Truman was elected to the United States Senate, winning a close Democratic primary race organized by the Kansas City machine. In Washington, Truman supported the New Deal but his connection with the shady Pendergast kept him estranged from Roosevelt. By 1940 Pendergast was in jail on tax evasion and Truman fought for reelection on his own, winning a narrow victory with the support of labor and blacks. During the war years Truman gained national stature as head of a special investigation committee to uncover waste and cheating in military procurement. When Roosevelt picked Truman to run with him as vice-president in 1944, the decision was hailed by all but the Wallace Democrats. His half-year as vice-president turned the man from Independence into a jaunty folk-hero many celebrities wanted to meet,

Little did Vice-President Harry S. Truman know that two months after he entertained actress Lauren Bacall he would be president of the United States.

including the film star Lauren Bacall, who perched on top of a piano and dangled her lovely legs while Truman, beaming from ear to ear, pounded out "The Missouri Waltz." But the day Truman was notified of Roosevelt's death, the imponderables of power suddenly fell upon him. Roosevelt had not included his vice-president in cabinet decisions. Hence Truman knew little of recent political and diplomatic developments, a situation he immediately corrected by avidly reading the cables and minutes. The day after he took the oath of office Truman stated to a group of reporters: "Boys, if you ever pray, pray for me now."

Comparisons made between FDR and Truman did little to enhance the status of the new president in his first months in office. Where Roosevelt had been gracious and dignified, Truman seemed coarse and impetuous. Roosevelt approached politics as a patrician of vision and obligation; Truman and his Missouri cronies seemed parochial and mediocre, people who lived not so much "for" politics as "off" it. And the president's proximity to such rascals would tarnish his administration. Later, as historians came to appraise Truman, they admired the way he faced problems directly, whereas Roosevelt tended to avoid confrontations. But in immediate images Roosevelt projected the profile of an aristocratic statesman; Truman behaved like a small-town merchant. These distinctions troubled Roosevelt's former disciples, who wondered whether Truman had what it takes to be a good president, not to mention a great one. But Harry Vaughn, an old National Guard buddy from Missouri, believed that as a "common man" Truman was closer to the norm. Assessing the early Truman presidency vis-à-vis Roosevelt, Vaughn observed that "after a diet of caviar, you like to get back to ham and eggs."

RECONVERSION AND LABOR UNREST

Aside from foreign affairs, the most troubling issue facing Truman after the Japanese surrender was reconversion, the process of readjusting a war economy to the normal operations of a country now at peace. Reconversion involved, first of all, the return of fifteen million men and women who had served in the armed forces. No politician dared oppose the public's demand to "bring the boys home" immediately, and Truman and Congress called for rapid demobilization. (Russia, having lost twenty million soldiers and civilians in the war, needed to bring her men home quickly to help with economic reconstruction, but

Stalin kept demobilization a secret.) Within a year and a half the armed services had been reduced to little over a million men. The millions of other servicemen returned to their hometowns and became absorbed into civilian life, a transition facilitated by new laws providing termination pay, unemployment compensation for one year, job reinstatement and seniority rights, insurance benefits, and various loans to veterans for houses, farms, and businesses. A little more than half of the returning soldiers, about 7,800,000 veterans, attended colleges and technical schools through generous subsidies provided by the GI Bill of Rights (1944), which cost the government $14.5 billion by the time it ended in 1956.

The GI Bill proved to have far-reaching implications. It made a college degree within the reach of millions who otherwise would have gone straight into blue-collar jobs or stayed on the farm. It expanded the entire system of higher education, creating new community and state colleges. It brought onto campuses a new type of student: older, serious, ambitious, eager to make up for lost time, and wondering if he had any appeal to coeds several years younger and fewer in number. An Educational Testing Service study also revealed an interesting aspect of the postwar veteran students. Despite their seriousness, they were less interested in knowledge than in graduation and moving on to a high-paying job. Education became more a matter of training than learning. The veteran student felt he had a right to ask of any subject: "What good will it do me?"

Many Americans were asking similar questions of government in general. In the postwar years national income and production continued to increase, but the lingering gap between rapidly rising demand and limited supply created inflationary tendencies that required price controls. Manufacturers and farmers, however, wanted an end to wartime regulations. They specifically sought to weaken the Office of Price Administration in order to profit from wartime savings that consumers were now anxious to spend. Under such pressure, Congress passed a weak price control bill that Truman vetoed. Not until prices soared and inflation reached a skyrocketing 35 percent did Congress respond with another bill that still proved too feeble to be effective. Prices continued to rise and the blackmarket thrived until early 1949, when production caught up to demand for most commodities. The national debt burgeoned as well, but here there was no end in sight. Except for the single year 1948, the rise in federal spending led to unbalanced budgets while political pressures led to slight reductions in income and excise taxes. In resorting to deficit financing, the richest nation in the world would continue to spend more than it made. No politician dared to ask Americans to pay for the services of government.

The problem was that, except for military defense, most services benefited specific pressure groups, especially the voting blocs of the Democratic party. Postwar housing was in acute supply. Many people who had worked in war industry, especially blacks and women, had been laid off, and returning veterans threatened to flood the labor market. To meet these problems, Truman proposed subsidies for public and private housing, extension of the Federal Employment Practice Committee, unemployment insurance, increases in social security and the minimum wage, support for farmers, a national health insurance system, and a federal policy committed to full employment. All such programs represented a resurgence of the New Deal, but Congress was not in a New Deal mode and Truman was not Roosevelt. While Congress did grant small amounts of aid for veterans' housing, it allowed the FEPC to expire, and it turned down Truman's other proposals. Social experiments would no longer be tolerated.

Passage of the Employment Act of 1946 suggests the extent to which New Deal liberalism had reached an impasse. The Employment Act committed the government to obtain "maximum employment, production, and purchasing power." Both the president and Congress were to review annually the state of the economy and the programs of government in light of the Act's objectives. In addition, the newly created three-member Council of Economic Advisors enabled Truman to draw upon academic experts like Leon Keyserling, who wanted to use economics not only to allocate scarce resources but to augment them. Much of the rationale behind the act derived from the Keynesian notion that the government would be "the lender of the last resort" and step in with appropriations to create a full employment economy. But neither Congress nor the public had reached a consensus on how this goal could be achieved, and opponents believed that full employment and optimum use of productive capacity would take place naturally through the unplanned operation of market forces.

The immediate postwar years reflected the country's stress and frustration. There were shortages of housing and consumer goods, cold-war tensions, overcrowded schools and classrooms, and disillusionment on the part of some soldiers who had returned to a country that seemed far removed from the dreams that comforted them during their lonely years overseas, an emotion documented in the 1946 Academy-Award winning film with the bitterly ironic title, *The Best Years of Our Lives.*

Even more stressful were the massive labor strikes that threatened to disrupt the economy. During the war workers benefited from full employment, high wages, and overtime pay. But the soaring inflation that followed the war eroded many of labor's gains. Many labor leaders no longer felt bound by the no-strike pledge honored during the war. In 1946 America witnessed one of the most severe periods of unrest in American labor history. Strikes broke out in almost every industry: steel, coal, electrical, lumber, shipping, railroads. Over four and a half million workers were associated with nearly five thousand labor disputes representing a loss of 116 million days of employment and production. When John L. Lewis's 400,000 soft-coal miners walked off the job, not only the economy but the whole program for European recovery became endangered. People began to hoard food and gasoline as the government warned that hundreds of thousands of Europeans would starve if shipments of grain and meat did not reach them within weeks.

The Truman administration tried to mediate between labor and management by approving a 15 percent wage increase. The unions held out for a 30 percent raise to make up for lost overtime pay and the rising cost of living. When mediation failed, Truman ordered the government to seize the railroads and he lashed out at union leaders for putting their own interests ahead of the nation's welfare. He also sought authority from Congress to draft workers and to use the army to run the railroads, a threat that forced union leaders to capitulate. An angry Congress now granted the president the right to seek court injunctions compelling workers to remain on the job, a measure he used to take over the coal mines when Lewis refused to order his men back to work. A federal court also fined the United Mine Workers $3,500,000, which, though later reduced, forced Lewis to back down.

Republicans in Congress enjoyed the spectacle of a Democratic president using government resources to move against labor and Senator Robert Taft spoke out eloquently against such action. Actually, Truman was looking for a way that mediating agencies of government could iron out labor-management conflicts. But in Congress Senator Taft turned the country's anti-labor mood into an assault on the union movement. In 1947 Congress passed the Taft-Hartley Act, which outlawed the closed shop and secondary boycotts, held unions liable for breach of contract and damages due to jurisdictional strikes between rival unions vying to represent a specific group of workers, legalized injunctions against strikes that endangered national health and safety, compelled workers about to strike to obey a sixty-day cooling off period, and required union leaders to take a non-communist oath. Truman vetoed the bill in a vigorous speech. Although the veto was overridden by overwhelming majorities in both houses of Congress, his opposition regained the support of labor for the Democratic party.

Nonetheless, public opinion had been turning against Truman. More and more people began to doubt his ability to master the office of the presidency. Soon he became the butt of jokes. "To err is Truman." "Don't shoot the piano player; he's trying hard." "He reminds me of an uncle who played the piano in a whorehouse two years before he found out was goin' on upstairs." "Who is the power behind the drone?" The future of the Democratic party looked bleak, the fate of liberalism bleaker still.

THE GREAT UPSET: THE ELECTION OF 1948

In the summer of 1946 Karl Frost, a Massachusetts advertising executive, devised a campaign slogan for state Republicans. The first version read:

HAVE YOU HAD ENOUGH OF THE ALPHABET?

Frost aimed to indict the "alphabet soup" of government agencies and programs like OPA, FEPC, and TVA. Then the line was reduced to four words:

HAD ENOUGH?
VOTE REPUBLICAN!

The expression caught on in the fall congressional elections. The American people, impatient with postwar readjustments, high prices and shortages, cold-war insecurities, and the seeming incompetence of the president, turned to the Republican party for the first time since 1930. The newly elected Eightieth Congress had fifty-one Republicans and forty-five Democrats in the Senate and 246 Republicans and 188 Democrats in the House. With Truman's ratings dropping to an abysmal 32 percent approval and the GOP controlling both houses of Congress for the first time since 1928, Republicans were jubilant and interpreted the election as a repudiation of New Deal liberalism.

But against the Eightieth Congress Truman began defending the New Deal. In addition to attacking the Taft-Hartley law, Truman also opposed a Republican bill to reduce taxes in the upper-income brackets. He continued to persuade Congress to resume economic controls to fight inflation, and he proposed government assistance to low- and middle-income housing, a national medical insurance program, and federal aid to elementary and secondary schools. In some respects he pushed beyond the New Deal by tackling a sensitive issue that even FDR did not directly address: race.

Although Truman was too much a southerner to espouse social integration together with equal opportunity, he was also the first twentieth-century American president to identify himself with a systematic effort to eliminate racial discrimination. Responding to demands by black leaders that the government take a stand on racism in politics, employment, and segregated neighborhoods, Truman appointed a civil rights committee in 1946 and staffed it with distinguished liberals. They wrote the report *To Secure These Rights,* a condemnation of all forms of racism which the solicitor general used in cases coming up before the Supreme Court. Truman also directed the Justice Department to file an amicus curiae (friend of the court) brief in current constitutional cases involving restrictive housing covenants and other racial barriers. In 1948 he issued an executive order against segregation and inequality of opportunity and advancement in the armed forces. The order proved difficult to implement since there was no urgent time schedule, and thus, during the Korean War some combat units remained segregated. Yet the Truman administration had placed itself solidly behind the efforts of blacks to attain full citizenship by requesting that Congress pass a voting-rights act, an antilynching bill, and legislation to outlaw discrimination in interstate transportation and to establish the FEPC on a permanent basis. By 1952 the Truman administration supported the demands of blacks and white civil rights leaders to end segregation in elementary and secondary schools.

Truman's progressive stance, together with pressure from liberal Democrats to take a stronger stand on civil rights at the convention, assured the Democrats of the black vote as the 1948 election approached. But what other groups Truman could count upon remained uncertain. Aside from disgruntled labor leaders like Lewis, there were also rumbles of revolt from the right, the left, and the center of the Democratic party itself. Many southern Democrats had become thoroughly alienated by the government's position on civil rights. Those on the left who supported Henry Wallace's anti-cold war pronouncements felt bitter when Truman dismissed his commerce secretary. Even in the center former New Deal liberals complained of "the Missouri Gang," old cronies and World War I buddies Truman had brought to Washington. Some, like Clark M. Clifford, the special counsel to the president, were able and astute, even if he wished only to institutionalize the New Deal rather than expand it. Others, like Edwin Pauley, the California oil-man Truman appointed as undersecretary of the navy, seemed little more than wheeler-dealers. Pauley once suggested to Interior Secretary Harold L. Ickes that the Democratic party could raise several hundred thousand dollars if the government dropped its suit asking title to off-shore oil fields. Liberals complained that "fixers" like Pauley and Harry Vaughn had the president's ear while idealists like Ickes had left government service in disgust. Truman's gang, wrote the columnist I. F. Stone, "were not unusually corrupt or especially wicked— that would have made the capital a dramatic instead of a depressing experience for a reporter. They were just trying to get along. The Truman era was the era of the moocher. The place was full of Wimpys who could be had for a hamburger."

By the spring of 1948, a sizable "dump Truman" movement had grown among liberal Democrats, many of whom could agree with *Time* magazine's assessment of the president as "awkward, uninspired, and above all, mediocre." The *New Republic* assured its readers that Truman could not prevent depression, bring about recovery, save world peace, or lead his party to victory. The Americans for Democratic Action, a liberal anticommunist organization, wanted to see Dwight D. Eisenhower run as the Democratic candidate. At the convention in Philadelphia delegates sported buttons declaring "We're just Mild about Harry." Even Truman's mother-in-law thought it would be futile for Harry to seek reelection.

The mood at the convention remained gloomy. Eisenhower had declined to be considered a candidate, and a desperate revolt led by Congressman James Roosevelt, FDR's son, fizzled out. The Democrats had no one to turn to but Truman, who selected the esteemed Kentucky senator, Alben W. Barkley, to run as the vice-presidential candidate. The choice of Barkley was intended to appease the southern wing of the party. Earlier, delegates from Mississippi and Alabama had walked out of the convention and threatened to align themselves with the new "Dixiecrat" party formed in July, a states' rights party organized by southern conservatives in protest of Truman's civil rights program. The Dixiecrats' presidential nominee was Governor Strom Thurmond of South Carolina, who was determined to save the South from Truman "the carpetbagger" and, if we can believe his rationale, to preserve segregation as a matter of community, "otherwise there would be no Harlem in New York City, no Chinatown in San Francisco, no South Side in Chicago."

Henry Wallace's revolt splintered the Democratic party further. The former commerce secretary had continued to denounce the government's foreign policy after his dismissal in 1946, and when the Truman Doctrine was announced, he felt duty-bound to offer the American people an alternative. In early 1948 Wallace's Progressive party drew large audiences under the banners of peace and freedom. The Progressives responded to Wallace's desire to move America beyond the limits of interest-group liberalism, the broker-state politics left by the New Deal and inherited by Truman. Vaguely socialist, Wallace spoke of nationalizing coal mines and railroads and helping to redistribute wealth by challenging the "swollen profit structure." But as a symbol of hope and dissent, Wallace had even greater appeal to Americans growing fearful of cold war tensions, especially students, radical intellectuals, and Hollywood celebrities. At the same time, however, Wallace's sympathetic attitude toward Russia in the cold war, which included not only his acceptance of the Soviet thesis of "capitalist encirclement" but also the Progressives' proposal to hand over American atomic weapons to the UN, created a fierce reaction among anti-Stalinist writers and labor leaders. Former Trotskyist Dwight MacDonald ridiculed Wallace's naiveté and the Americans for Democratic Action denounced the Progressive party for forging a liberal-communist alliance. The United Auto Workers' Walter Reuther called Wallace a "lost soul. . . . Communists perform the most complete valet service in the world. They write your speeches, they do your thinking for you, they provide you with applause, and they inflate your ego."

Reuther may have been exaggerating, but Wallace refused to listen to any advice about repudiating publicly the support of the CP. Michael Straight, the *New Republic* editor (and, with Guy Burgess, who later defected to Russia, once an underground communist at Cambridge University), recalled in his memoirs the dilemma of Progressives associating with communists, who during 1947 and 1948 took the name Progressive Citizens of America (PCA).

"I had bound *The New Republic* to Henry Wallace," Straight reflected. "He, in turn, had allowed himself to be bound to the PCA. To whom was the PCA bound? I asked myself that question and I feared the answer." Straight recalled a PCA rally in Los Angeles in March 1947, where actress Katharine Hepburn made a militant speech to a crowd of twenty-eight thousand people. Wallace asked Straight what he thought of the event:

Former Secretary of Commerce Henry A. Wallace, attacking Wall Street and calling for support of the Soviet Union, before the Progressive Citizens of America at Madison Square Garden, September 11, 1946.

> "Once again," I said, "it was Communist-led."
> "Can you prove that?" Wallace asked.
> "No," I said, "I can't."
> "Then you shouldn't say it."

Straight, who by then had broken with the communists but chose to keep his past to himself, observed that Wallace "was heading for the land of illusions from which I had come. I knew from experience that collaboration with the Communist party would destroy Wallace, but I could not share my experience with him."

Many of Wallace's supporters dismissed the dangers of a liberal-communist alliance while the communists themselves saw it as an opportunity to revive the spirit of the Popular Front. Several reporters saw the Progressives as a growing populist movement and some predicted that they would pull as many as ten million protest votes. To vote for Wallace was to vote for peace.

But everyone predicted the Republicans would win. So confident was the GOP that it nominated Thomas Dewey, the man Roosevelt defeated in 1944. Dewey, assured of victory in November, did not so much run for the presidency as walk. Convinced that Truman had already committed political suicide by advocating progressive legislation that antagonized specific groups, Dewey assumed he could speak in vague generalities about "pride" and "unity." He never mentioned the New Deal, and his evasiveness on other issues inspired one reporter to call him "the Mr. Hush of politics." Still, Dewey's lead in the polls was staggering. Elmo Roper gave Dewey 44.2 percent, Truman 31.4, Thurmond 4.4, and Wallace 3.6. After September Roper continued polling but stopped reporting the results. "My silence on this point," he assured the public, "can be construed as an indication that Mr. Dewey is still so clearly ahead that we might just as well get ready to listen to his inaugural."

While the public awaited the inevitable, Truman never doubted he could do the impossible. The president called a special session of Congress to ask again for passage of housing and other progressive legislation. He expected the Republicans to refuse, and when they did he rebuked "that Republican Eightieth Congress, that do-nothing, good-for-nothing, worst Congress." Truman also took his message to the people, traveling thirty thousand miles on a "whistle stop" tour of the country and delivering several hundred speeches from the rear of a train. His peppery speeches attacking Congress and implying that the Republicans would dismantle the New Deal drew rousing applause and shouts of "Give em hell, Harry!" Dewey's advisors became somewhat concerned as they noticed Truman's crowds growing in size and enthusiasm. Still, the polls had Dewey far ahead as late as the end of October and 70 percent of the press supported the Republican candidate. On election night the *Chicago Daily Tribune* issued an "Extra" optimistically announcing "DEWEY DEFEATS TRUMAN." The following day the returns confounded everyone. Truman won 24,200,000 votes, Dewey 22,000,000, Thurmond 1,200,000, and Wallace 1,100,000. Many Americans, even some Republicans, were delighted at seeing the experts look ridiculous. When Truman returned to the capital, the streets were lined with cheering crowds and the *Washington Post* hung a banner as his motorcade passed by:

MR. PRESIDENT, WE ARE READY TO EAT CROW
WHENEVER YOU ARE READY TO SERVE IT

What happened? For one thing, the polls completed their last survey on October 15, eighteen days before the election. Thus they failed to catch a last-minute shift to the Democrats. The midwestern farm vote,

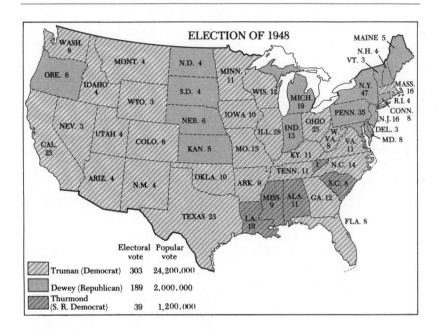

traditionally a Republican stronghold, went Democrat due to both a mid-October break in grain prices and to Truman's claim that the postwar prosperity growers were enjoying would be jeopardized under a Republican administration. Truman also picked up millions of Wallace supporters who feared a Dewey victory more than they hated the president. Truman carried the largest thirteen cities as workers remembered the President's opposition to the Taft-Hartley Act. The ethnic vote proved decisive. In some cities blacks gave Truman larger pluralities than Roosevelt had received in 1944. The German-American vote, which had drifted from Roosevelt in 1940 and 1944 because of the war, returned to the Democrats in 1948.

Although a stunning victory, at first glance the margin appeared narrow, and 1948 turned out to be the closest presidential election since 1916. Truman won by only a little more than two million votes, and the percentage of the popular vote was 49.5 to 45.1. Thurmond deprived Truman of four southern states and Wallace took New York and possibly New Jersey away from him. Dewey swept all the industrial Northeast except for Rhode Island and heavily Catholic Massachusetts. Yet the old New Deal coalition of labor, ethnics, and city bosses held fast. Had it not been for the Dixiecrats and Progressives draining votes from the Democrats, Truman would have beaten Dewey by a greater percentage than had Roosevelt in 1944.

Both diplomatic and domestic conditions contributed to Truman's victory. His response to the crises in Turkey and Greece showed that he had what it takes to confront problems rather than postpone them, and during the tense Berlin blockade he proved he could decide with conviction and act with caution. But in American politics domestic concerns are generally uppermost in the minds of voters, and ultimately Truman appealed to both lower-class Americans eager for housing and welfare legislation and to an emergent middle class still too insecure of its status to turn against the New Deal. "I own a nice house," a suburban resident stated when recalling how he had decided to vote. "I have a new car and am much better off than my parents were. Why change?"

Since Truman's victory also meant a new Democratic Congress, the future appeared bright for the new social programs. In the spring of 1949 Truman spelled out a comprehensive legislative agenda he called the "Fair Deal." It proposed a new farm policy, public housing projects, increased social security and expansion of its coverage, higher minimum wages, and programs for soil conservation, flood control, and public power.

The Brannan Plan, Truman's farm policy named after the agriculture secretary, never emerged from committee. It attempted to end the New Deal system of propping up farm income by restricting production (to the detriment of consumers, who had to pay higher prices). The new plan would allow the market to determine prices and growers would receive income subsidies if their total earnings fell below the parity level based on production costs, mortgage payments, and other outlays. But the large growers, represented by the American Farm Bureau, preferred the old system of price supports rather than direct payments, which had definitive limits and favored small family farms over agribusinesses. Republicans also opposed the Brannan Plan in an effort to win back the farm vote. Truman wanted full production and farm prosperity; farmers wanted high prices regardless of productive output. When prices surged upward during the Korean War and full production became a military necessity, farmers returned to the Republican party.

The Housing Act of 1949, which funded slum clearance projects and low-rent housing, represented an attempt to reverse the deterioration of the inner cities. Truman also had success in seeing Congress pass his programs for increasing social security levels and coverage and for raising the minimum wage to keep up with the cost of living. But others on his agenda—national health insurance, repeal of the Taft-Hartley Act, civil rights, and federal aid to education—were not enacted into law.

In the end, the Fair Deal's achievements were as modest as the nation's political mood. Much of Congress more than ever consisted of bipartisan conservative coalitions and the growing number of middle-class Americans were content with the status quo. Yet even the suburbanite who prized his new house and car could seldom listen to the evening news in peace and contentment. The cold war no longer meant Eastern Europe and Korea. It now meant Washington, the State Department, the press, Hollywood studios, college campuses, nuclear physics laboratories, the Unitarian Church, even the United States Army. The enemy, some were saying, was everywhere.

THE RED SCARE

The great fear of communism that gripped the United States in the postwar years came to be known as McCarthyism, after the Republican Senator from Wisconsin, Joseph McCarthy. The phenomenon of McCarthyism cannot be understood apart from the events that preceded his wretched entrance onto the political scene. Nor is it entirely accurate to dismiss McCarthyism as simply a "witch-hunt" or a characteristically American "paranoid style" of politics. For paranoia is by definition a type of psychosis in which the person experiences delusions of persecution and conspiracy when none actually exist in objective reality. Yet in all probability McCarthyism would not have been possible had it not been that some in the American Communist party conceived politics as a covert strategy of infiltration and subversion. Ironically, both McCarthyism and the American communists who became its victims mirrored one another in their images of conspiracy. McCarthy and his supporters saw America being subverted by the NKVD, the Soviet Union's secret police. Communists accused of spying saw themselves being victimized by the FBI and the Soviet Union being encircled by the forces of capitalism. Perhaps it was easier to view events as conspiratorial than for either side to admit that it could not exist without the other.

Although McCarthyism was a product of the cold war, the legal apparatus that facilitated the Red Scare had been established years earlier. In the 1930s un-American activities committees were formed in the Congress and in various state assemblies for investigating subversive organizations, fascist as well as communist. In 1940 Congress passed the Alien Registration Act (better known as the Smith Act), which made it illegal to advocate or to organize any group with the intent of overthrowing any government in the United States by force or violence. In July 1948, several months after the Truman Doctrine had brought the cold war into America's living rooms, the government initiated prosecutions of Communist party officials for organizing groups which, whether or not they actually conspired to overthrow government, had taught doctrines that advocated as much. In a split decision, the Supreme Court upheld the conviction of the communists, maintaining that government cannot wait until a "clear and present danger" presents itself, for then it may be too late to act.

Many liberals protested the decision. They insisted that any group or individual had a constitutional claim to the protection of the First Amendment and the Bill of Rights, regardless of political positions. The American Civil Liberties Union (ACLU) held that while any citizen can be required to register as an agent of a foreign government, he or she cannot be indicted for teaching and advocating the overthrow of government by force and violence. Otherwise Thomas Jefferson would have to be classified as "un-American" and the American Republic could have never been born. The cold war placed great strains upon the constitutional safeguard of liberties. As Justice Oliver Wendell Holmes once said, in regard to civil liberties, the Constitution must protect opinions we loathe as much as those we love. Yet the Truman Court had a point: the Communist party may exploit constitutional liberties to undermine constitutional government as an expression of the capitalist system.

Rumors of covert communist activity first surfaced in spring 1945 when federal agents raided the office of *Amerasia*, a radical journal of Asian affairs, and found classified documents that had been taken from the State Department. No evidence could be found that the editors intended to pass on the documents to a foreign power. But the following year the Canadian government announced the arrest of twenty-two persons charged with illegally passing information to Soviet officials and the probability that the NKVD had established espionage rings in Britain and the United States. Meanwhile, Congress's House Un-American Activities Committee (HUAC) had stepped up its investigation of subversive infiltration into government, industry, organized labor, the movie industry, and the universities. HUAC's interrogations created bitter controversy and divided Hollywood and the academic intellectuals.

The Truman administration, fearing that the Republicans would exploit the growing anticommunist scare, issued a loyalty order in March 1947, requiring FBI checks on all government workers. Sixteen thousand employees were investigated. Not one was found to be disloyal or a card-carrying communist. But two were dismissed as security risks; 202 who resigned were regarded as unsuitable for such "personal" reasons as homosexuality; and about one hundred others lost their jobs because of "reasonable grounds" to suspect possible disloyalty. Often the employees had no opportunity to confront their accusers or even to be informed of the nature of the accusations. Such trial by innuendo had a devastating effect upon the morale of government employees, especially in the State Department, where foreign affairs specialists were intimidated into acquiescing to cold war orthodoxy.

While the innocent felt pressured into conforming, the guilty felt pressured into informing. In the summer of 1948 Elizabeth Bentley and Whittaker Chambers testified before congressional committees that they had engaged in espionage for Soviet agents and that they were quite willing to name others who had done so. Bentley, described by one newspaper as the "Beautiful Blonde Spy Queen," decided to let it all out when her Russian lover jilted her. Actually, she was a rather frumpish and romantically insecure spinster. Whatever her motives, the rejected Miss Bentley reeled off a series of names, including Henry Dexter White, an assistant secretary of treasury and an important architect of postwar monetary policies conceived at the Bretton-Woods conference, and Lauchlin Currie, an economist who had served as a White House advisor to President Roosevelt. Although the FBI could never verify the charges, Currie's career was damaged and White suffered a fatal heart attack shortly after delivering an emphatic rebuttal.

Chambers testified to HUAC that Alger Hiss, a former State Department officer present at the Yalta Conference, had been a member of the CP during the Popular Front era of the 1930s. Instead of admitting that like many students in the 1930s, he had flirted with communism, Hiss denied the charges and sued Chambers for libel. The denial did not impress Congressman Richard M. Nixon, who sensed that if Hiss functioned as an implanted agent, as Chambers suggested, he need not have been a known CP member. Nixon offered his prosecutorial services to Chambers. He then surprised everyone by charging not merely that Hiss had been a party member but that he had been a communist spy and had copied State Department documents that Chambers had passed to the Russians. At first such charges seemed incredible to many Democrats. Truman and Acheson defended Hiss and dismissed the hearings as a "red herring." Liberals also tended to believe in Hiss's

Whittaker Chambers testifying that Alger Hiss was a communist spy.

innocence and claimed that Chambers, Nixon, and the FBI were merely Red-baiting. Yet Chambers dramatically produced—from of all places, a pumpkin on his farm—secret documents, some of which bore Hiss's handwriting and others copied from a typewriter that once belonged to Hiss. When this evidence emerged, a federal grand jury issued a perjury indictment against Hiss for denying Chambers' allegations. The first trial resulted in a hung jury; the second, in January 1950, in a conviction.

With the accusations and denials headlined daily in the press, the Hiss trial became one of the most sensational American political controversies of the twentieth century. The two figures stood as symbols of a cold war morality play. Chambers was a tortured ex-communist full of guilt and suicidal despair, but with a newly discovered religiosity that made him all too ready to atone for the sins of a whole generation. Hiss, the embodiment of the Ivy League, had offered his talents to the Roosevelt administration: composed, articulate, well-dressed, well-mannered, well-connected, and bookish. Most HUAC members, including Nixon, Karl Mundt, and Chairman J. Parnell Thomas, were anti-New Deal avengers out to discredit the whole program of liberalism. Before long the seed of suspicion had been planted: Hiss, the Har-

vard Law School graduate groomed for national leadership, the epitome
of the new elite ruling class, had been seduced to spying by a foreign
power. How many more Hisses were there among the wise and famous?

Probably not many, but the question haunted Americans in late 1949
and throughout the spring and summer of the following year. During
that period America experienced a series of shocking events and revelations: the fall of China; the uncovering of a spy ring in England headed
by Klaus Fuchs, a scientist who had worked on the Los Alamos Project; the alarming news that the Soviet Union had exploded an atom
bomb; the conviction of communist leaders under the Smith Act; and
the arrest of Ethel and Julius Rosenberg on espionage charges. All of
these events lay ready for someone audacious enough to link together
into a vast conspiratorial scheme, even if the scheme had to be invented.

When Joseph McCarthy made his now-famous speech to the
Republican Women's Club in Wheeling, West Virginia, on February
9, 1950, the gnawing impression that there were communists in high
places in government had been bandied about for some time. But
McCarthy was the first to cite names and numbers. Not only Hiss but
Dean Acheson, the "pompous diplomat in striped pants, with a phony
British accent." They were all of a type, "the bright young men who
are born with silver spoons in their mouths." It was not that our enemy

*Alger Hiss defending himself
against Chambers' accusa-
tions.*

is so powerful, McCarthy emphasized in explaining America's set-backs abroad, it was the "traitorous actions of those who have been treated so well by this Nation." McCarthy then told the startled ladies that while he did not have the time to go through all the names of CP members in the State Department, he had in his hand a list of 205. The whole show of waving a paper in his hand was an impulsive bluff. When the news soon blared through the press, reporters quizzed him on the precise number. McCarthy scaled it down from 205 to fifty-seven and then, two evenings later in Nevada, he screamed in a drunken stupor that newsmen had stolen the document with the figures. "He lost his list," one reporter recalled, "between his eighth and ninth bourbons." A week later journalists badgered him again at a luncheon. "Listen, you bastards," McCarthy shouted as he pounded his table. "I'm not going to tell you anything. I just want you to know I've got a pailful of shit, and I'm going to use it where it does me most good."

McCarthy never turned up a single communist not known to the FBI or other intelligence agencies. But from 1950 to 1954 he became a powerful force of intimidation and terror in American political life. In the Senate he had the support of Taft, Kenneth Wherry, and Styles Bridges. When a Senate committee headed by the Maryland Democrat Millard Tydings reported that McCarthy's accusations were unfounded, McCarthy circulated faked photos showing Tydings whispering to the head of the CP. Whether or not such tactics accounted for Tydings' failure to be reelected in 1950, other members of the Senate and House would think twice before speaking out against McCarthy. A consummate demagogue, McCarthy played upon cold war emotions and made charges so fantastic that frightened people believed the worst; for any accusation so sensational makes the truth seem a dull anticlimax. He was a master of the "pseudo-event," press conferences where he announced another round of charges with a mass of documents which, upon close inspection, turned out to prove little, but by then the news of who was named had made the headlines. Through McCarthy's accusations, outstanding intellectuals and distinguished diplomats such as the Asian specialist Owen Lattimore were driven out of the academic world and the foreign service.

Was Truman responsible for McCarthyism? No doubt his own loyalty program was hastily thrown together and probably did contribute to the confusions and insecurities of the era. And perhaps Truman should have listened to the advice of nuclear physicists and informed the public that the Soviets would be able to develop an atomic bomb within a short time. Still, Truman never confused Soviet aggression with domestic subversion. Even when he used the "scare hell" tactic on Congress and the public during the Greek-Turkish crisis of 1947, he did not suggest that communism was an internal threat. That impression grew only after the numerous espionage revelations, Russia's explosion of the bomb, and the fall of China in 1948–49.

But why McCarthyism? Some scholars argue that McCarthyism itself was a calculated movement on the part of big business interests to turn back the whole welfare state by likening liberalism to communism. No doubt some conservative capitalists exploited McCarthyism to that purpose, but they hardly created the emotional conditions that made McCarthyism possible in the first place. The thesis that McCarthyism represented a distinct class movement ignores the popularity of anti-communism among a variety of classes, ethnic groups, and geographical areas throughout the United States. Those who subscribe to the class thesis have emphasized that in Wisconsin McCarthy's support came mainly from the wealthier Republican districts. Yet it does not necessarily follow that because lower-class neighborhoods voted Democratic, McCarthy had little support among American workers. Actually, many workers, especially Irish-, Polish-, and German-Americans, and other ethnic groups, were staunchly anticommunist either because of their strong religious background or their concern for the fate of relatives in Eastern Europe. Such workers could vote Democratic, cheer on Truman's attack on business interests, and yet want to see communists eliminated from government and other institutions.

But anticommunism was not necessarily synonymous with McCarthyism. Many labor leaders and intellectuals shared a widespread conviction that McCarthy's vulgar anticommunism was opportunistic and aimed not at uncovering spies but simply winning publicity and harassing dissenters who spoke out against cold war orthodoxies. Legal scholars in particular saw McCarthyism as subversive of the principles upon which the Republic was founded. The Constitution had been drafted in 1787 to restrict the power of the state, and the framers were careful to emphasize that no acts can be regarded as treasonable other than those specified in the Constitution—levying war against the government or giving aid and comfort to the enemy, both of which required two witnesses to "the same overt act." The framers also insisted on specifying the kinds of proof necessary for conviction of treason and on "restraining the Congress, even in punishing it, from extending the consequences of guilt beyond the person of the author." McCarthy and his ilk were doing precisely what the framers had warned against when they compiled lists and subpoenaed witnesses on no more basis than rumor, innuendo, and other flimsy scraps of evidence that might prove "guilt by association." In order to make America safe from communism, McCarthy would destroy the safeguards guaranteed by the Constitution. Who was being "un-American"?

"HE DONE HIS DAMNEDEST"

The spirit of that question captured Truman's response to the anticommunist issue. In 1948 congressmen Richard Nixon and Karl Mundt sponsored a bill in the House requiring communists to register with the government. Two years later they supported Pat McCarran, a conservative Democratic senator from Nevada, in passing the Internal Security Act, better known as the McCarran Act. Voted into law shortly after the outbreak of the Korean War, the McCarran Act required that communist and communist-front organizations register with the Subversive Activities Control Board, which in addition would investigate any group reported to be ideologically suspect. It also empowered the federal government to order the arrest of persons suspected of subversive activity in times of national emergency. Truman and several congressmen denounced the McCarran Act as unconstitutional. Ironically, what came to trouble Truman was not so much the registration requirement but the possibility that the Subversive Activities Control Board could establish guilt solely by declaring an organization's position on any question parallel to that of the Communist party—the very argument his own attorney general had earlier made when the National Security Act was passed in 1947. To advocate recognition of Red China, for example, would be judged subversive because such a view happened to coincide with a similar view held by communists. Two decades later a sponsor of the McCarran Act, Richard Nixon, would call for recognition of communist China and travel there in the spirit of friendship and detente. But by then the Supreme Court had declared several of the McCarran Act's provisions unconstitutional. In 1950, however, Truman's veto of the bill was easily overridden in the House, 286 to 48, and in the Senate, 57 to 10. The McCarran Act represented, Truman protested in his veto message, "the greatest danger to freedom of press, speech, and assembly since the Sedition Act of 1798."

In 1952 Truman also attacked another bill cosponsored by McCarran, the Immigration and Nationality Act. Designed in part to establish immigration quotas, the bill set up complicated screening procedures to keep out "subversives" and aliens who had been associated with totalitarian states. In addition, it authorized the attorney general to deport immigrants affiliated with communist organizations even if they had received citizenship. The bill extended to the State Department's Passport Office nearly arbitrary power of deciding who could enter and leave the United States. This second "McCarron Act" proved even more embarrassing than the first. It denied Supreme Court Justice William O. Douglas permission to travel to China. Even more ironical, America soon discovered that those who fled totalitarian governments did so not to spread communism but to escape it. Truman predicted this in his veto message when he described the bill as an "absurdity" that reflected an iron-curtain mentality similar to the Soviet Union's. Once again Congress overrode the veto.

Truman's opposition to the McCarran Act, to HUAC, and to McCarthyism in general was courageous. Many politicians, even some liberal Democrats, feared taking on McCarthy. Truman did so fearlessly. Even in states like Massachusetts, where McCarthy had a strong following among Catholics, Truman lashed out at the shameless tactics of the Wisconsin demagogue. "The President of the United States," wrote columnist Murray Kempton, "is gambling that McCarthy is an overrated punk." While Republicans ducked the issue, the scrappy Truman defied his own Democratic advisors and kept up the counterattack. "Not even for campaign purposes would Harry Truman blanch or quail," Kempton continued. "Yesterday in Cumberland, Maryland, where McCarthy is generally credited with deciding the 1950 Senate election, the President called Joe 'a political gangster,' a denizen of the 'political underworld,' a dealer of the 'big lie.' His audience listened open-mouthed and then applauded."

Part of McCarthy's appeal was his reckless claim that America's diplomatic setbacks abroad could be attributed to internal conspiracies at home. The strategy struck an emotional response with the frustrations of the Korean War, which was beginning in 1950. Before Korea and the fall of China, the Truman administration's foreign policy enjoyed bipartisan support in Congress and among the public. The containment policy in Europe, the Marshall Plan, the Point Four Program extending economic aid to underdeveloped countries, and Truman's support of the State of Israel against the wishes of England and the Arab world had the backing of both parties. But on Asian issues in general and Korea in particular, bipartisanship broke down into rancor and suspicion.

When Truman dismissed General MacArthur in April 1951, the Republicans gained a hero and a martyr. In several towns across the nation flags were flown upside down or at half-mast and Truman and Acheson were hung in effigy. Republican congressional leaders invited MacArthur to address a joint session. When he arrived in San Francisco after being recalled from Korea, he was given a smashing welcome, and in New York the largest crowd ever assembled in Manhattan, possibly as many as seven million people, turned out to cheer his motorcade. No one doubted that if an election were held then and there the general would easily triumph over the president. But the MacArthur craze proved to be remarkably short-lived, and by 1952 the Republicans would be putting forth another military hero, Dwight D. Eisenhower.

The Korean War remained a problem without a solution because Truman chose neither to withdraw nor to escalate. By 1952 there was an armistice between North and South Korea, but fighting continued and American soldiers were still dying in the mud and snow. Negotiations bogged down over the issue of prisoner exchange and the right of UN inspectors to travel through North Korea as a guarantee against further aggression, a right the communists felt infringed upon territorial integrity. Thus the Democratic party had become identified with a war it could neither win nor end—always a bad sign.

The Truman administration faced other problems as well. Although the war in Korea fueled the economy and reduced unemployment, it also increased prices as Americans rushed to buy consumer items in expectation of scarcity and rationing. Truman established several government agencies to work with labor and management to control wages and prices. His anti-inflationary efforts were somewhat successful until the US Steel strike in the spring of 1952. Truman and the Office of Price Stabilization recommended increases in wages but not in prices since the steel companies' war-induced profits were already high enough. The recommendation was unacceptable to the companies and when the strike occurred in April, Truman, fearing the effects of a long halt in steel production on the Korean War effort, instructed his commerce secretary to take possession of the steel mills and operate them in the name of the United States Government under the authority of the president's war powers. The companies immediately challenged the legality of Truman's act in the federal courts and won a Supreme Court decision in what came to be known in constitutional history as *The Steel Seizure Case.*

Truman made the bold move assuming that prior legislation gave the president authority to order the take over of industries when they refused to give priority to defense production. In the case of the steel mills, however, production had been delayed because of labor disputes. Thus the Supreme Court ruled Truman's action unconstitutional as an usurpation of Congress's power as the law-making branch of government. Three justices wrote dissenting opinions, upholding the right of a president to invoke discretionary prerogative power in times of emergency. But the majority decision represented the first time in a dozen years that the Supreme Court opposed expansion of executive authority, a decision praised by many conservative congressmen.

Truman was a man of incorruptible integrity, but his administration had its share of graft, bribery, and corruption. In 1951 evidence began to emerge of pay-offs, leniency in tax collection, gifts in exchange for political favors, and other greasy dealings. The transactions were small stuff, ranging from a $520 deep-freeze to a $9,540 mink coat. Although the depth of corruption came nowhere near the Harding scandals of the 1920s, Republicans exploited it to the fullest, claiming that the Democratic party had opened the doors of government to new types of profiteers who enriched themselves at the federal trough. Truman did not help matters by appointing ineffectual investigators. Eventually nine Democrats went to prison. The "mess in Washington" became a hot campaign issue.

The 1952 national election was not, however, to have Truman as a target, except at a distance. He announced his decision not to seek reelection in March 1952. Although he later would be regarded as a plucky folk hero when many Americans were swept up by what *Time* magazine labeled "Trumania," his last years in office were tumultuous. Korea, communism, and corruption; MacArthur, McCarthyism, and mink coats—all saddled his administration with the stigma of incompetency, dishonesty, even treason in the State Department. Never a popular president when in office, Truman had an approval rating of around 32 percent in his last years and at times of only 23 percent. Only about one in four Americans supported him.

Americans had no doubt about the president's courage and honesty. Truman had defended Secretary of State Marshall when McCarthy charged him with "a conspiracy so immense and an infamy so black." Still, such efforts did little to restore confidence in his administration. Yet Truman left office an honorable man who knew in his heart that he had done his utmost to serve the country. At one of his last press conferences, in April 1952, he told reporters: "I have tried my best to give the nation everything I have in me. There are a great many people—I suppose a million in the country—who could have done the job better than I did it. But I had the job and I had to do it. I always quote an epitaph which is in the cemetery at Tombstone, Arizona. It says: 'Here lies Jack Williams. He done his damnedest.'"

Historians have judged Truman a "near-great" president, not in the class of Washington, Jefferson, Lincoln, or FDR, but close to Andrew Jackson and Theodore Roosevelt, leaders who were also resolute, forthright, and brave. Although Truman lacked charm, tact, and the ability to inspire, he always made clear where he stood and he assumed responsibility for his actions. In the early phase of the cold war in Europe, Americans admired Truman's decisiveness, but the stalemate of the Korean War made people weary of a "police action" that had no end in sight. In his domestic programs Truman was at least a decade ahead of the times. His plans for national health insurance met the opposition of the medical profession, and federal aid to education would have to wait until Russia's space program shocked America out of its complacency. His idea of the "Fair Deal" recognized that many Americans, especially ethnic Americans, were getting a raw deal. The presidential committee he organized and that issued the report *To Secure These Rights*, represented a historical turning point in attitudes within the government if not necessarily among the citizenry. The report called for eliminating racial barriers in education, housing, and employment; withdrawal of federal funds to institutions that practiced segregation; protecting the voting rights of minorities; establishing a permanent Commission on Civil Rights; and settling the evacuation claims of Japanese-Americans. It marked the first time the United States government had gone before the Supreme Court to condemn all forms of racial discrimination. The southern wing of the Democratic party made it impossible for such programs to be enacted into law, and Truman, it should be noted, did not push the racial issue. Truman also fought unsuccessfully to revise immigration laws to enable America to receive larger numbers of displaced persons, and he chastised Congress for writing a bill that discriminated against Catholic and Jewish refugees. Like Lincoln, Truman believed in equality as an ideal value, not as a fact that can be realized but as principle that can be approximated, and he drew upon America's best principles to fight its worst practices. Whether he won or lost, he did his damnedest.

4

Eisenhower and Dulles

THE GENERAL VERSUS THE EGGHEAD

Nineteen fifty-two was a rare year in American political history. The American people then watched what they have not seen since—a presidential campaign waged by two candidates who originally expressed no desire to run, even when asked to do so by the outgoing president. When Truman opted out in April, he realized that the Democratic chances depended on a popular, untarnished candidate. His first choice was former NATO commander, General Dwight D. Eisenhower, whom he had approached months earlier. Truman would "guarantee" Eisenhower the nomination at the Democratic convention and lend his full support. Eisenhower refused. He had been a Republican all his life. His differences with the Democrats on domestic issues were too great. Eisenhower also felt that as a military man he must stay above politics, and he longed to return to his roots in the neighborly small-town life of the Midwest.

Truman then turned to Adlai E. Stevenson, Democratic governor of Illinois. A complex, highly intelligent man, Stevenson was reluctant to run, perhaps sensing an inevitable Republican victory. He was not being coy. On the contrary, when his name was entered in the Oregon primary, Stevenson stated publicly that he wished he had the right to withdraw it. But a "draft Stevenson" movement emerged spontaneously throughout the country and gained momentum as the convention approached. Democratic party officials, anxious to put the Truman legacy behind them, needed a leader who could unite such disparate elements as farmers and laborers, southern Dixiecrats and northern blacks, big city bosses and liberal intellectuals. At the convention Stevenson was chosen over the southerners Senators Estes Kefauver and Richard Russell and the northern liberal W. Averell Harriman. Resigned to accepting the nomination, Stevenson would offer America something unseen in politics since the death of Abraham Lincoln: a leader who wrote many of his own speeches, turned easy platitudes into harder perplexities, asked people to "sacrifice," and reminded them that there were "no cheap and painless solutions."

While the Democratic party tried to overcome its divisions, the Republican tried to find its direction. For years the GOP had looked to Robert Taft as "Mr. Republican." A man of considerable knowledge and unyielding will, Taft wanted to scale down the scope of the federal government by reducing its regulatory agencies and turning over many of its welfare responsibilities to the states. Still, he often assumed stances that surprised both friend and opponent. He wrote the Taft-Hartley law; yet when Truman proposed drafting coal, steel, and railroad strikers in 1946, Taft protested that such an act "went farther toward Hitlerism, Stalinism, and totalitarianism than I have ever seen proposed in any labor strike." He supported McCarthy's anticommunist campaign and at the same time supported the right of communists to teach at his alma mater, Yale University. A critic of containment, he enjoyed

Democratic presidential candidate and Illinois governor Adlai Stevenson. The worn sole on his shoe seemed to some Americans further evidence of the absent-mindedness of "egghead" intellectuals.

the backing of neo-isolationists in arguing that America's first responsibility lay in protecting the western hemisphere from the corruptions of European power politics. Such a stance won the approval of writers like Lippmann who also wanted to make Americans aware of the limits of power. Taft warned against the dangers of government bureaucracy and socialism, yet he advocated modest programs of public housing, aid to education, medical care, and increases in the minimum wage and social security. He espoused private property and free enterprise, yet he had little regard for those who so admired businessmen and trusted them with the future of the Republic. "Eisenhower thinks that anyone who has made a lot money must be a good economist," he would later complain. "It's ridiculous. Just because someone can sell a lot of cars, it doesn't mean he can run a government department." Taft's positions on many issues were so balanced and thoughtful that even the liberal columnist Richard Rovere called him "a principled conservative." Yet Taft remained antistatist as well as antibusiness, and his support of McCarthy partook of the right-wing habit of identifying liberalism with complacency about communism and hence a danger to America's security.

Many eastern Republicans were anti-McCarthy. The eastern wing of the GOP supported the containment policy and looked forward to business determining the policies of the federal government rather than dismantling them. Taft was unacceptable to this group even though he had served well as Senate majority leader.

Far more attractive was General Eisenhower, who feared Taft's criticism of containment and his demand that American troops be withdrawn from Europe. But Eisenhower refused to announce his candidacy, even though his many supporters were intending to enter his name in the early primaries to prevent the neo-isolationists from capturing the GOP. In part Eisenhower's reluctance derived from a distaste for politics and politicians, which in turn derived from a long-held conviction that the president is not only the head of a party but the nation's commander in chief. What Eisenhower was holding out for, biographer Stephen E. Ambrose has pointed out, was not merely a draft but a nomination by acclamation so that he could arrive at the convention triumphantly, without grubbing for delegate votes. But to pursue such a course, friends informed Eisenhower, would simply allow Taft to gain momentum unopposed.

Finally, in February, Eisenhower agreed to run and returned from his NATO office in Europe. He easily defeated Taft in several early primaries. At the tumultuous convention in July, Eisenhower watched

General MacArthur deliver a bombastic, reactionary attack on the Democrats and Senator McCarthy moan about the betrayals of Yalta and communist conspiracies in government, while Illinois Senator Everett M. Dirksen denounced Dewey and the eastern wing of the party. The issue was never in doubt. Eisenhower won the nomination on the second ballot, but when a motion was made to make the choice unanimous, Taft's supporters cried "No!"

Eisenhower's nomination signified a victory for the eastern, internationalist wing of the Republican party represented by Dewey and Massachusetts Senator Henry Cabot Lodge. Yet Eisenhower believed in teamwork, and he ignored the advice of Easterners when he invited Taft to meetings to iron out differences on domestic issues. Earlier Eisenhower had also sought to conciliate Taft forces by suggesting as a possible running mate Richard M. Nixon, who had acquired a national reputation from his defense of Whittaker Chambers against Alger Hiss. The prospect of Nixon's place on the ticket assured California's large delegate vote on the first ballot. It also placated the McCarthyite Republicans wary of anyone without the instinct to make suspicion of communism the art of politics. Throughout the campaign Eisenhower, when pressed by reporters, refused to criticize McCarthy's reckless anticommunist campaign, and in the last weeks of the race he appeared with McCarthy in Wisconsin and provided symbolic support to McCarthy's own reelection. To Truman's dismay, Eisenhower would not even defend fellow general George Marshall when McCarthy claimed he was a danger to the country. Although a military hero, in politics Eisenhower had more cunning than courage. He deleted sentences praising Marshall from one of his speeches, then went on to say that to comment on McCarthy's accusations would simply be to indulge in personalities.

Eisenhower's campaign was, in fact, a masterpiece of evasion. The Republican platform had included statements attacking containment. It called for the liberation of the "captive peoples" of Eastern Europe. Even so, Eisenhower generally avoided foreign policy proposals other than to imply that the Democrats and their irresolution were to blame for America's setbacks abroad. A week before the election he announced he would "go to Korea," and his ratings increased even though he never mentioned what exactly he would do about the war itself. On domestic issues he was similarly vague. Before the campaign he compared the welfare state to the security of a prison; in his acceptance speech he promised a "program of progressive policies, drawn from our finest Republican traditions." He attacked the Truman administration for corruption, but when running mate Nixon was discovered to have been receiving secret political payments from a group of wealthy Californians, Eisenhower allowed himself to be outmaneuvered rather than immediately dropping Nixon from the ticket, as his advisors urged. The controversy over "the Nixon fund" provoked the famous "Checkers speech." Nixon, telecasting his teary-eyed apologies from Los Angeles, explained to Americans the difficulties of making ends meet. There were so many expenses—his mortgage payments, his wife's clothes, and his daughters' pet dog, Checkers, another gift from political donors so endearing that his family could never think of returning it. An Eisenhower advisor thought the speech "the corniest thing I ever heard," but he soon realized its effectiveness when he saw an elevator operator crying. By suggesting that it was not personal ambition but the material and emotional needs of his family that led him to accept financial gifts, Nixon shrewdly turned a political vice into the virtues of domestic responsibility and dog-devotion.

However desperate Nixon may have appeared to some journalists, candidate Eisenhower exuded a genial moral authority that won the hearts of Americans. The 1952 campaign was a contest of images. "Ike" had a soft and sunny demeanor, and a warm and winning smile. His dignified poise and personal charm easily compensated for the banal emptiness and homely cliches of his speeches. If he sought not to arouse the people to new political challenges, he was suited to reassure them that their elemental convictions were safe from doubt and confusion. He wisely avoided any open clash with the Democrats on specific domestic issues. Personality rather than ideology would determine the outcome of the election.

Democratic candidate Stevenson's personality would also prove crucial. No doubt the Democrats labored under stigmas of the Truman administration: Korea, communism, and corruption. These did not burden Stevenson much, for he disassociated himself from the Truman legacy, appearing to be as moderate as Eisenhower on domestic issues. He campaigned as a fiscal conservative dedicated to balanced budgets, and, to the distress of liberals, he downplayed the issue of race and civil rights. In foreign affairs he was equally committed to containment and defended the Korean war as a "crucial test in the struggle between the free world and communism." Unlike Eisenhower, he did speak out against McCarthy and the rabid anticommunists "who use 'patriotism' as a club for attacking other Americans." McCarthy counterattacked by referring to "Alger, I mean Adlai," thereby linking the Democratic candidate to the presumably traitorous Alger Hiss. But while

Stevenson displayed moral courage during the campaign, he was never able to reach the masses. Cab drivers and bartenders thought him too elitist because of his eloquence and intellect. Dubbed an "egghead," a term recently coined to describe bald professors who had more brains than hair, he was regarded as an intellectual who turned easy answers into harder questions. Democratic party bosses were frustrated with a candidate who, when asked to compromise on an issue to be assured of the votes from a specific constituency, replied: "I don't have to win." Yet Stevenson's urbanity and wit lifted the spirits of the liberal intellectuals. When Eisenhower criticized Stevenson for his humorous dismissal of charges made against the Truman administration, the latter responded that he worried less about his "funny bone" than the Republican's "backbone." Comparing Eisenhower's reported spiritual guru Norman Vincent Peale (author of *The Power of Positive Thinking*) to Saint Paul, Stevenson quipped: "Paul is appealing and Peale is appalling." But in the end Stevenson's gaiety and intellectual superiority were all that remained to console Democrats in the sorrows of defeat.

In contrast to 1948, the election return surprised no one, even though this time pollsters were reluctant to predict it. Eisenhower won every region except one border state and the deep South, which returned to the Democratic fold after its Dixiecrat fling in 1948. Eisenhower captured the popular vote 33,936,252 to 27,314,992 (47 percent to 40 percent). Republicans gained control of Congress, though only by a narrow margin, 48 to 47 in the Senate, 221 to 212 in the House. The Republicans had made inroads into traditional Democratic strongholds: lower-middle class blue-collar workers now enjoying the benefits of prosperity, Texans turning from cattle to oil, Irish and German Catholics worried about communism, and other old New Deal constituencies. Samuel Lubell described the election as "the revolt of the moderates."

Eisenhower's thirty-three million votes were the greatest number ever polled by an American. But 1952 was a record turnout, and Eisenhower fell well below FDR's 59 percent plurality in 1932 and 62 percent in 1936. Eisenhower's coattails proved strong in gubernatorial contests, in which the Republicans won twenty out of thirty elections, although Senate Republicans lost Wayne Morse, the progressive Oregonian who bolted the party during the campaign and announced himself an Independent. Also lost was Henry Cabot Lodge, who directed Eisenhower's campaign in the uncertain preconvention months and who fell in his bid for a fourth term in Massachusetts to John F. Kennedy. According to *Time*, the "poodle-haired, young (35) Representative" owed his victory to family wealth and the gatherings "given by his three beautiful sisters and his mother, where thousands of Massachusetts women sipped tea, ate cakes and were warmly greeted by the candidate."

Image was becoming important in national politics, often overshadowing issues. General Eisenhower embodied the military experience and expertise necessary to deal with the war in Korea; Stevenson, conversely, seemed an intellectual made to be burdened by anti-intellectual pejoratives—"longhairs," "do-gooders," "highbrows," "bleeding hearts." All of these suggested a wobbling leader who would rather write than fight. But was the general any more eager than the intellectual to wage a war to the bloody end? The Republicans opposed the Korean War because it was a limited engagement in which military action was taken to resist aggression, not necessarily to realize victory. And the American people, in choosing Eisenhower to resolve the frustrating stalemate in Korea, seemed to be questioning the doctrine of limited war. Whatever Eisenhower had in mind for the war, he could be trusted to do the right thing. Americans of the fifties saw in the new president an image of life as they wanted it to be.

THE POLITICS OF INERTIA:
EISENHOWER AND MODERN REPUBLICANISM

Most American writers and intellectuals, whether of the Democratic Left or Republican Right, looked upon Eisenhower as a decent but simple man—aptly nicknamed "Ike"—a man who enjoyed bridge and golf more than the challenges of government and the exercise of presidential power. Yet Ike's kindly image as the Boy Scout of American politics, or, as Lippmann put it, the "dream boy embodying all the unsatisfied wishes of all the people who are discontented with things as they are," suited perfectly the mood of the nation. The discontent and distrust bred by the cold war and McCarthyism would be eased by Eisenhower. The president would not embark upon new projects but end old problems or simply allow them to mend themselves. Like Calvin Coolidge, Eisenhower could do no wrong because he seldom tried to do anything at all. In recent years historians have shown Eisenhower as a much more able and forceful leader than previous generations had seen him. But while he was president, Eisenhower appeared the picture of repose. "The public loves Ike," observed the columnist Richard Strout in 1959. "The less he does the more they love him. That, prob-

*Ike made golf more popular
than ever in the fifties.*

ably, is the secret. Here is a man who doesn't rock the boat."

Eisenhower had been brought up to believe it was better to steer the boat than to rock it. Born in 1890, he was raised in Abilene, Kansas, by parents who might have been straight out of Grant Wood's painting *American Gothic*. His mother and father instilled the simple, time-honored values of work and accomplishment rather than curiosity and reflection. "They lived unquestioning lives, and they taught their sons to do the same," wrote one Eisenhower biographer, Stephen Ambrose. Education at West Point reinforced all that Eisenhower had learned at home about duty, service, and teamwork, as well as the necessity of rote learning and acceptance of authority. Such qualities could scarcely make Eisenhower an original thinker. Even so, they served him well in his slow rise up the military ranks until he finally emerged as supreme Allied commander in World War II. In that post, he proved his talents for organization and administration. He also showed a remarkable ability at sustaining a coalition alliance among arrogant European generals and statesmen who regarded any American as inferior. After a brief stint as president of Columbia University from 1948 to 1953, a service interrupted by a leave of absence when he headed NATO forces in 1951 and 1952, he entered politics and proved further his capacity for leadership as a soldier-president. Although occasionally inwardly troubled or angry, Eisenhower conveyed a sense of self-confidence born of strength rather than stubbornness. During his two administrations, journalists and intellectuals, offended by Eisenhower's grammatical infelicities and bland speeches, often ridiculed his verbal gaucheries and seemingly contradictory statements. But we know now that Eisenhower went to his press conferences intending to be vague and evasive as part of the game of politics. He was an avid reader of Eric Hoffer, author of *The True Believer*, who warned of the dangerous follies of intellectuals who wanted to impose their idea of truth. To Eisenhower politics meant not the pursuit of truth or justice but the art of conciliation and compromise, an art successfully practiced by a president of common sentiments and uncommon abilities.

To liberal Democrats, however, Eisenhower's cabinet selection was simply terrible—"eight millionaires and a plumber," quipped journalist Strout. The "plumber" was Martin P. Durkin, a union leader chosen as secretary of labor, who soon resigned. All other appointments reflected Eisenhower's unquestioned faith in successful businessmen like George M. Humphrey, a corporate banker who became treasury secretary, or Charles E. Wilson, a former General Motors executive who as defense secretary justified military spending by remarking that he had not come to Washington "to run a country store." Wilson also testified before Congress that "What was good for our country was good for General Motors, and vice versa," a gaffe that Democrats exploited time and again to imply that industry would run government for its own ends. Actually Wilson meant only to suggest that business and government were not at cross purposes, a view fully shared by Eisenhower. The Democrats believed that the New Deal and Fair Deal had set out to fulfill the goals of social justice. Conversely, Eisenhower became convinced that many liberal reforms resulted in organized special-interest politics that brought too much strain and conflict into the nation's social order. He conceived his administration as standing for the idea of disinterested public service that would inspire big business, labor, the professions, and government officials to work together toward resolving the nation's problems. As one historian has pointed out, Eisenhower detested "pressure groups" and other features of modern politics that would undermine "social harmony, self-discipline, limited government, and a depoliticized, administrative state."

If it is true that Eisenhower envisioned a "Corporate Commonwealth" for America, the vision implied a bold departure from Democratic and Republican traditions alike. Democratic President Truman saw no identity of interests among business, labor, and government. Thus, Truman took over the steel and coal industries and ordered companies to resume producing and workers back to their jobs. Nor had the Republican President Theodore Roosevelt seen any such identity, hence his older Progressive "Square Deal" demanded that business and labor be regulated, not integrated into a corporate system in which there would be no place for active citizen participation. Eisenhower, however, sought consensus. He saw no incompatibility between military virtues and business values, between pride, honor, and duty on the one hand and profit, greed, and opportunity on the other. Eisenhower looked to the business community for the source of responsible leadership, but he hardly invoked the notion of "commonwealth" as opposed to private wealth. Nor does the term "corporate" help explain Eisenhower's domestic policy, for that essentially European idea had been associated with big government, high taxes, and public spending—all anathema to the Republican party. In truth, Eisenhower's political stance deliberately shunned theoretical formulations: it was essentially middle-class economic liberalism without a lower-class social consciousness or constituency. For in the 1950s the classical notion of liberalism as the preservation of life and property simply became peace and prosperity for the majority.

Eisenhower had campaigned on a platform calling for a balanced budget and a reduced role for federal government; neither pledge could be fulfilled. Even after the Korean War both government spending and budget deficits rose, however moderately, as interest groups made demands upon the public sector. To the great relief of labor and liberals, Eisenhower accepted the welfare state, agreeing to modest expansion of social security, minimum wage, unemployment insurance, and public housing. The expression "modern Republicanism" caught on as both the president and his party came to recognize that the traditional conservative values of self-reliance and individualism were not necessarily jeopardized by a government that assumed responsibility for promoting economic prosperity and the welfare of the people.

Eisenhower would also tolerate an expanding role for government, especially if the nation's defense needs were involved. Thus he supported federal legislation for building 40,000 miles of highways and freeways to replace old, unsafe roads, and to facilitate military transportation. Conservative Republicans, fearing an increase in the national debt, first opposed the Federal Highway Act of 1956 until its financing was met by higher taxes on gasoline. The highway program would prove popular to Americans, who were rapidly exchanging city for suburb and experiencing a love affair with the automobile. Eisenhower also supported building a series of canals and locks to allow Atlantic merchant ships access to the Midwest through the Great Lakes. This project had long been opposed by New England railroad interests, utility companies, longshoremen, and coal miners, all fearing Canadian and midwestern competition. But the Saint Lawrence Seaway Act, dear to towns along the Great Lakes and to American steel companies desiring access to Canadian iron ore, became law in 1954. Its financing flowed from toll revenues.

In other areas Eisenhower favored a retrenchment of federal power, a rise in local state jurisdiction, and a greater role for private enterprise. Thus he allowed the Gulf states to take possession of off-shore tideland oils. This meant a loss of billions of dollars to the nation's treasury, as did continuation of the depletion allowances wherein oil companies deducted almost one third of their incomes from federal taxes. Eisenhower also wanted to see the TVA, his symbol of "creeping socialism," dismantled and reconceived on the basis of private enterprise. Bankers in his budget office urged that TVA's authority be restricted to flood control and its power-producing operations be increased. This power, they advocated, should be made available to a local Atomic Energy Commission (AEC) facility through a private utility company directed by Edgar H. Dixon and Eugene A. Yates. Democrats in Congress supported the TVA, pointing out that it could supply the power to the AEC at two-thirds the cost of the Dixon-Yates plan. Eisenhower nonetheless ordered the AEC to sign a contract with Dixon-Yates. Then it emerged that the government consultant who had recommended Dixon-Yates over other competitive bidders had been on a retainer from a Boston corporation that handled Dixon-Yates securities. Eisenhower had the federal contract cancelled and reluctantly acknowledged one of the first—but by no means the last—scandals of his administration.

Eisenhower's farm policy set out to break decisively with the New Deal. His secretary of agriculture, the devout Mormon Ezra Taft Benson, saw in the nation's farm programs many of the evils of socialism. Both Eisenhower and Benson wanted to get government out of agriculture; one way was through flexible parity rates that would decrease with production increases and vice versa. The aim was to lower governmental price supports so that market prices would be more responsive to supply and demand. But the attempt to overcome farm surpluses by encouraging growers to shift to scarcer crops had the effect of forcing small farmers out of business and favoring large farms with newer machinery needed to make such transitions. Benson wanted to eliminate all subsidies; the more politically astute Eisenhower continued government payments to sustain farm prices and even approved of the Democratic sponsored controversial soil-bank conservation program, which paid farmers who let portions of their land lie fallow. Eisenhower's agricultural program neither resolved the perennial problem of rising surpluses nor that of rising expenditures. From 1952 to the end of his two administrations, government agricultural spending increased from a little more than $1 billion to over $7 billion. Thus there was more continuity than change in the Republican and Democratic farm policies—to the extent that both efforts failed to bring supply in line with demand. Yet agricultural spending was now targeted differently. Eisenhower's program aimed not so much to rescue the poor farmer as to reward the successful producer.

Labor under the Republican administration was pretty much on its own. Eisenhower was more concerned about inflation than unemployment, which remained at about 5 to 6 percent in the mid-fifties. After the Korean War, as employment fell off in shipyards and aircraft factories, it picked up in highway and housing construction due in part to government programs. For the steadily employed, real family income increased by about $1,000, possibly as a result of Eisenhower's efforts to control inflation. Although the union movement benefited from the merger of the AFL and CIO in 1954, union membership, especially among auto, steel, and garment workers, declined throughout the fifties, partly as consequence of states passing right-to-work laws made possible by the Taft-Hartley Act. Perhaps the most important feature of the American work force in the Eisenhower years was not its political clout but its changing character and constituency.

The mid-fifties witnessed the emergence of what Daniel Bell has called "post-industrial society." Due to the "knowledge revolution" in technology in the postwar years, the occupational profile of America underwent profound change. Automation and other labor-saving devices meant fewer industrial workers on the assembly line and more clerical workers in the front office. By 1956 white-collar workers outnumbered blue-collar workers as new jobs opened up in sales, public relations, banking, government bureaucracies, service repair, public utilities, engineering, teaching, and secretarial work. Few of these workers belonged to unions; fewer still identified with the cause of labor. Most regarded themselves as upwardly mobile professionals. The remaining unionized industrial workers shared their aspirations, if not their achievements.

One study of a Ford Motor Company assembly plant found that, while most workers had few expectations of advancement other than minimal salary increments, they took pride in being able to maintain their families at a high level of consumption without having to work as hard as their fathers did. Nevertheless, although these workers appreciated the prosperity of the Eisenhower years and regarded themselves as middle-class, many fantasized about escaping the factory. Not one of them wanted his children to follow him into blue-collar work.

Such attitudes toward industrial work had political implications. Thus the alignment of the work force and the party system that had been forged during the New Deal showed signs of strain in the postwar era. The liberal wing of the Democratic party still identified with labor and social justice, while the Republican party represented business and white-collar professionals. Workers who wanted to see their college kids enjoy opportunity and mobility recognized their offspring may be lost to the Republican party. Liberal Democrats remained concerned about the old poor and deprived; Eisenhower Republicans reached out to the new rich and arrived.

Republican and Democratic leaders differed most sharply over economic policy. Still under the influence of Keynesianism, some Democrats believed that government could increase demand for goods and services with lower taxes and enough deficit spending to move the country toward a full-employment economy. Conversely, Eisenhower and his chief economic advisor, Arthur F. Burns, remained convinced that government spending had to be cut and taxes reduced. This conviction rested on a familiar Republican assumption—such a measure would stimulate private investment in productive enterprises and thereby create jobs and steady economic growth. The Republicans were right for the most part, though far from fully successful. American economic growth, while substantial, lagged behind that of West Germany and Japan, which had been rapidly closing the technological and productive gap after the war. Unemployment and deficits continued to rise. A mild recession occurred in 1953 and 1954, and two more would take place in the late fifties. But inflation became manageable after the Korean War, and what little existed was due in part to organized labor's ability to press for higher wages, which companies passed on to consumers in the form of higher prices. That more and more Americans could afford such prices indicated the arrival of a long-sought prosperity that had eluded the depression generation. In the Eisenhower years most Americans, perhaps as many as 80 percent, never had it so good. What of the remaining 20 percent?

In the fifties close to ten million Americans had an annual income of less than $2,000. These were the urban slum dwellers, the inhabitants of by-passed rural areas like Appalachia, migrant and dispersed agricultural workers, the minorities in their languishing ghettos, those receiving Aid to Families with Dependent Children (AFDC), and other bare survivors who made up the nation's forgotten 20 percent. Liberal Democratic organizations like Americans for Democratic Action (ADA) wanted government to address social problems through legislation dealing with medical care, public education, and racial discrimination. The Eisenhower administration was reluctant to do so.

In the postwar years soaring medical costs rose far above the reach of many lower-class Americans. President Truman advocated a program of national health insurance to be run much as social security. Preferring a voluntary to a compulsory plan, Eisenhower proposed a federal policy that would provide financial assistance to private health insurance companies. But the American Medical Association (AMA), not realizing, as it would two decades later, that such a policy would be a boon for doctors and hospitals, denounced it as "socialized medicine." Indeed, some Republicans were so fearful about the entry of government into health care that Eisenhower's first secretary of health, education, and welfare, the wealthy Texan Oveta Culp Hobby, opposed distributing the just-developed Salk polio vaccine to children. Already incensed by the attitudes of the medical profession, Eisenhower asked Mrs. Hobby to resign. Not until the end of the fifties, when Democrats called for medical care for the elderly and needy, did Eisenhower, after seven years in office, acknowledge the government's responsibility for the nation's health and physical welfare.

This same reluctance characterized Eisenhower's attitudes toward public education. The depression and war years had sharply curtailed local school budgets. After the war, with the "baby boom" flooding kindergarten and elementary grades, school buildings remained delapidated, instruction facilities inadequate, and teachers' salaries low and unattractive. Except in wealthy communities, standards deteriorated. In the late forties, for example, less than half of all public school teachers had a college degree. Truman had shown some interest in the growing demand for federal aid to education, but even the more supportive Senator Taft was unable to get a bill through Congress. Eisenhower responded by sponsoring a modest $2 billion appropriation that educators found hopelessly inadequate. Ironically, it was the Russians who would rescue America's school system in 1957, when they sent a satellite into space and awakened the country to its desperate need to teach math and science lest the cold war be lost in the classroom. But in the early and mid-fifties, proposals for federal aid to education also met ideological, religious, and racial opposition. Those who feared the power of the state believed financial aid would allow the government to control teachers and dictate curriculum. Catholics seeking aid for parochial schools aroused the ire of secularists who invoked the Constitution's First Amendment on separation of church and state. And Harlem Congressman Adam Clayton Powell aroused the opposition of the South when he insisted that no federal aid be extended to segregated school districts.

On issues such as education, poverty, and medical care, the Eisenhower administration saw no active role for government, and here it reflected the values of the era. More complacent than compassionate, the fifties generation pursued private interests and pleasure and remained almost indifferent to public responsibilities. If Americans looked up to any institution, it was business, not government. When Charles Wilson and his General Motors men arrived in Washington, Adlai Stevenson remarked that Americans had taken government away from the New Dealers and turned it over to car dealers. In electing Eisenhower president, Americans had also turned the country over to a general. Whether they wanted him to win the war in Korea or simply end it, few were exactly sure.

ENDING THE KOREAN WAR

When Captain James Jabara, the chief air officer of the United Nations forces in Korea, landed in the United States in 1951, he was welcomed by a reporter from his hometown of Wichita, Kansas. "Why are we fighting in Korea?" asked the reporter. "So that we won't have to fight in Wichita," answered Jabara.

The idea that America had to fight in remote parts of the world lest communist aggression threaten the nation's security was a conviction accepted by both parties. The fate of Korea seemed crucial to Indochina. How could those peoples stand up to communism unless assured that the United States would give complete and sustained support? A few years later Eisenhower coined a term to describe this mentality— "the 'falling domino' principle. You have a row of dominoes set up, you knock over the first one, and what will happen to the last one is certainly that it will go over very quickly." The domino metaphor assumed that communism represented an international, monolithic movement. The metaphor also assumed that communism as a political phenomenon moved with the chain-reaction logic of physical proper-ties. It was a facile metaphor that prevented Americans from seeing that insurgent communist movement in southeast Asia were too nationalistic and independent to follow predictable patterns of power. Later the domino theory could scarcely account for the growing rivalry between Moscow and Peking that, in retrospect, complicated the motives for the outbreak of the war. Did the Soviets really assume that the United States would withdraw from Asia and allow communism to overrun Korea? Or did they want to see their emerging antagonist, Red China, become involved in a conflict with the United States? Did China intervene in Korea because MacArthur's forces had threatened her borders or to assure that Korea would not become a Soviet satellite? Whatever the answers to these perplexing questions, the United States was more interested in getting out of Korea than in understanding the shifting power relations in Asia.

Although Eisenhower's election promised to offer a fresh approach to Korea, his stance differed little from Truman's. Eisenhower had avowed that the war could be won and that his personal intervention would bring about a "peace with honor." Until the cease fire in the summer of 1951, Truman's position was to continue the war without widening it on the hope that North Korea would accept peace terms on the basis of *status quo ante bellum*. When Eisenhower took office he faced essentially the same options that had stymied Truman: to find a military solution or to hold to the policy of limited engagement.

An immediate issue stalling peace talks at Panmunjom was prisoner exchange. The United States and the Republic of Korea (ROK) forces had taken 130,000 prisoners and the Democratic People's Republic of Korea 65,000. The communists insisted that all prisoners of war be repatriated, even the fourteen thousand Chinese soldiers who expressed no desire to be returned. To the distress of the American public, there were also a small number of American soldiers who succumbed to communist political "education" and collaborated with their captors. The Indian ambassador to the UN, recognizing the right of war pris-oners to remain where they chose, proposed that the issue of repatria-tion be postponed until after a peace settlement had been reached. Eisenhower was ready to seize any proposal that would hasten a solu-tion, but when both sides agreed to an exchange of sick and wounded prisoners, Syngman Rhee, head of the ROK, did everything he could to sabotage the plan.

Eisenhower also had to struggle against members of his own admin-istration. Secretary of State John Foster Dulles insisted that unless the peace settlement called for Korea's unification, the United States must break the armistice and resume fighting. The president adamantly opposed any suggestion of a military escalation, knowing full well that the American people would never stand for it. Some conservative Republicans also began to side with Rhee, who objected to any settlement that left Chinese communists in North Korea and Korea divided at the 38th parallel. Hard-line cold warriors muttered that negotiations at Panmunjom were another "Munich" that would only appease the aggressor; a few suggested that the whole war could be settled immediately if America had the "guts" to use atomic bombs.

The Eisenhower administration had considered the nuclear option. Chinese officials also knew that Eisenhower was under pressure to achieve a quick military solution and that atomic warheads were stocked on nearby Okinawa. In the spring of 1953 the possible use of atomic weapons was discussed at several meetings of the Joint Chiefs of Staff and Eisenhower's National Security Council. The president and his advisors weighed the advantages and disadvantages, but the imponderables caused them to hesitate. Dulles, recognizing that "world opinion" would be outraged by an atomic escalation, advised that "we should do everything to dissipate this feeling." Eisenhower believed that atomic air strikes should be a last resort, used only if fighting resumed and the war bogged down or spilled out beyond Korea. But Eisenhower also worried that the Soviet air force might retaliate and bomb the defenseless population centers of Japan. The Joint Chiefs of Staff reminded the president that United States Naval forces in Pusan Harbor would be a perfect target for a communist counter-strike. Field commanders pointed out that atomic bombs might prove of little use against a North Korean army widely dispersed in mountain territory, and diplomats feared the adverse reaction of Britain and other allies. Advisors also had to consider the possibility that the Soviets, instead of retaliating, would allow the United States to exhaust its limited supply of atomic bombs in Korea, so that they might later act with impunity in Europe if a crisis situation occurred. Nevertheless, Eisenhower let it be known, through India's Prime Minister Jawaharlal Nehru, that the United States might judge it necessary to "use atomic weapons if a truce could not be obtained."

A settlement was finally reached in July 1953. The decisive factor may have been Stalin's recent death. North Korea and China were uncertain of Russia's position should war resume. Thus, within six months Eisenhower had fulfilled his campaign promise.

No Korean peace treaty was ever written, which deprived Red China of an opportunity to make claims on Formosa and demand membership in the UN. What of Eisenhower's nuclear threat? "Perhaps," one historian has concluded, "the best testimony to the shrewdness of the president's policy is the impossibility of telling even now whether or not he was bluffing." A curious compliment. The doctrine of deterrence, the idea that the threat of nuclear retaliation would prevent aggression, had been conceived in response to possible actions taken by the USSR and its numerically superior conventional forces. To risk nuclear warfare and mass slaughter simply out of frustration with a small third world power such as Korea bespoke a policy less shrewd than weary.

America achieved its political objectives in Korea to the extent that intervention prevented a communist takeover. Even so, Korea was essentially a strategic defensive war which sapped the country's energies and emotions. The American people had little patience for a long, slow, grinding war that ended in a military stalemate on the battlefield. So did the congressmen who tried unsuccessfully to gain the votes to pass the Bricker Amendment, named after Republican Senator John W. Bricker of Ohio, which would have restricted presidential power in foreign policy. Whatever the complexities of the cold war, public attitudes pressed toward one conclusion: win or get out. The lesson seemed to be that limited wars are too costly and that the whole idea of containment by means of conventional weapons had to be reconsidered. Eisenhower, one of the most cost-conscious presidents in modern history, now sought to reformulate American foreign policy, both to distinguish it from Truman's and to make it positive rather than negative, a new military posture that would be assertive rather than simply defensive. For such a reformulation Eisenhower turned to his secretary of state, John Foster Dulles.

THE "NEW LOOK" IN AMERICAN FOREIGN POLICY

At a conference on Indochina in 1954, China's Defense Minister Chou En-lai (Zhou Enlai) approached Dulles with a smile and proffered handshake. Dulles crudely turned his back on Chou and hurried away. It was a gesture characteristic of Dulles, who saw the cold war as a moral struggle between the forces of good and the forces of evil. A Presbyterian trained as a lawyer, Dulles valued righteousness as much as realpolitik. He regarded China as "fanatically hostile to us and demonstrably aggressive and treacherous," and he urged Eisenhower

Secretary of State John Foster Dulles, at a press conference on January 11, 1956, rejecting a proposal to suspend testing of the H-bomb.

to "unleash" the Formosan nationalist forces against Asian communism. Dulles sincerely believed that the cold war represented the last desperate effort to preserve the free world from the enemies of democracy. But when Indian Prime Minister Nehru chose a neutral stance, desiring to remain anticolonialist as well as anticommunist, Dulles would shift America's allegiance to Pakistan, a dictatorial regime, which soon used American military aid to threaten India, the world's largest democracy.

Dulles was also instrumental in articulating the "New Look" in America's foreign policy. During the 1952 campaign the Republicans denounced containment as "immoral," and some cold warriors advocated a more aggressive policy that would help free people behind the iron curtain. Referred to as "liberation" or "rollback," the new diplomatic posture was also meant as a return to nuclear strategy rather than the continued reliance upon conventional weapons that seemed so inconclusive in Korea. "We have adopted a new principle," Vice-President Nixon informed the country in 1954. "Rather than let the communists nibble us to death all over the world in little wars, we will rely in future on massive mobile retaliatory powers." "Massive retaliation" also aimed at cutting the military budget, which consumed 70 percent of federal expenditures. The aim was to "get more bang for the buck," as Secretary of Defense Charles E. ("Engine Charlie") Wilson put it. The doctrine had its first visible manifestation when the United States exploded a large hydrogen bomb in the Pacific in March

1954. Dulles was convinced that the new policy would enable America to reduce local defense positions around the world because the nation now had the "great capacity to retaliate by means and at places of our own choosing."

Actually, the new diplomacy strengthened America's military power but weakened its posture by precluding all options other than resort to the dreaded bomb. Thus, when East German workers rose in rebellion in 1953, Eisenhower felt it necessary to announce to the world that the United States had no intention of intervening militarily. Dulles, however, continued to espouse massive retaliation and even to arouse the expectations of the oppressed peoples of Eastern Europe by implying that the United States would support their uprisings. This false message would lead to the Hungarian tragedy of 1956. Two years earlier the columnist James Reston perceived the dilemma of trying to convince an aggressor that it would face retaliation not necessarily confined to the point of attack. The new diplomacy, he wrote, creates the impression throughout the world that "in the event of another proxy or bushfire war in Korea, Indochina, Iran or anywhere else, the United States might retaliate instantly with atomic weapons against the USSR or Red China." Several other critics, among them Acheson, Rovere, and the young Harvard professor, Henry A. Kissinger, author of *Nuclear Weapons and Foreign Policy* (1954), also began to expose the fallacies of the new diplomacy. Instead of allowing America to take the initiative, they pointed out, retaliation was simply a response to the adversary's initiative, and its proposed massive nuclear dimension left the United States without real, usable power in situations that required deploying traditional ground forces.

Not exactly. The United States could still go underground and use the resources of the Central Intelligence Agency (CIA), a quasi-secret organization that had evolved from the Office of Strategic Services of World War II years and become formally established in the National Security Act of 1947. In the Eisenhower administration the size and reach of the CIA, now headed by Allen Dulles, brother of the secretary of state, increased enormously. Its first notable covert operation came with the Iranian crisis of 1953. Two years earlier an anti-colonial, nationalist movement, led by Mohammad Mosaddeq, challenged the power of the shah and took over the Anglo-Iranian Oil Company. The British government, which had been receiving a greater share of profits from the company than Iran had from her own natural resource, demanded compensation for its losses. When Mosaddeq refused, British Foreign Secretary Sir Anthony Eden turned to the Eisenhower administration for help. The British did not want the United States to intervene directly, fearing that American business interests would demand a share of Iranian oil. Thus a joint plot was devised, "Operation Ajax," whereby the CIA funneled millions of dollars into Iran to bribe army officers and hire a mob, including brawny weight lifters recruited from Teheran's athletic clubs, to overthrow Mosaddeq and return the shah, who had been deposed in a recent coup. Grateful to the United States, the shah did what the British feared and allowed their monopoly of Iranian oil to be broken. Gulf, Texaco, and Standard Oil of New Jersey obtained a piece of the action.

Unnoticed by most Americans, the CIA staged a repeat performance in Guatemala in 1954. A desperately poor country, Guatemala had been struggling toward economic development by means of labor and land reforms under the leadership of Colonel Jacobo Arbenz Guzmán, who had come to power through proper constitutional procedures in 1951. When Arbenz Guzmán confiscated the American-owned United Fruit Company, the State Department demanded payment and Dulles went before the Court of Arbitration at the Hague and claimed Guatemala was falling to "international communism." This charge seemed to have some validity when tons of military supplies began to reach Guatemala from Czechoslovakia. But it was also true that some members of the Eisenhower administration, including the two Dulles brothers, had a financial stake in the United Fruit Company. Possibly because of this embarrassing connection, all those involved were sworn to absolute secrecy when Eisenhower gave the CIA the go-ahead. The first covert strategy involved hiring the small, "ragtag" army of Castillo Armas, who had been personally suggested by CIA agent Howard Hunt. But Armas's invasion by way of Honduras failed to lead to a popular uprising. Only with the help of CIA pilots and aircraft supplied by Nicaraguan dictator Anastasio Somoza did the Arbenz Guzmán regime fall. The deposed leader then appealed to the UN, and the British and French were prepared to vote with Russia in the Security Council condemning American intervention until Eisenhower persuaded them to abstain. Dulles went so far as to insist that the United States had no intention of allowing the UN to interfere in matters pertaining to the Caribbean. In doing so, he echoed, if unconsciously, the Soviet's sphere-of-interest reasoning in Eastern Europe.

In Iran and Guatemala the president could instruct the CIA to do its undercover, countersubversion work while he looked the other way. In Southeast Asia, however, back-alley coups could seldom alter the course of events. After the Korean War the most critical spot in Asia was Vietnam, torn by eight bloody years (1946–54) of civil war between the communist and nationalist Vietminh and the French colonial army. By 1954, the American contribution had risen to as much as 70 percent of the French military budget, in addition to technical advisors and CIA pilots, money and skills Eisenhower preferred to direct to American troop involvement. When the fortress Dien Bien Phu was under seige by Ho Chi Minh and his communist guerrillas in March 1954, the French desperately urged United States intervention. Eisenhower had little sympathy with French efforts to retain its imperial colony. Yet it was at this juncture that the "domino" metaphor began to haunt him. He also realized privately that an atomic air strike, recommended by some American generals, was out of the question, both because of its technical uncertainty and the repercussions of world opinion. Memories of the Korean War, never forgotten by the president's trusted advisor General Matthew B. Ridgway, who felt America's first commitment was to the defense of Europe, could not be ignored. Neither could the reluctance of the British to support American intervention, nor the opposition in Congress to such action. All such considerations caused Eisenhower to waver on sending combat troops to Vietnam.

Meanwhile, in April 1954, the Russians proposed a four-power conference to be held in Geneva. Shortly afterwards a new French government, under President Pierre Mendès-France, pledged itself to securing peace in Indochina. Negotiations at Geneva between the French and Ho's forces led to the partition of Vietnam at the 17th parallel and to the agreement that both sides would participate in national elections to be held in 1956, supervised by a joint commission of India, Canada, and Poland. The referendum intended to reunify the country within two years. Eisenhower recognized that the popular Ho Chi Minh would easily win a national election. He also knew that the settlement banned the introduction of new military forces. Therefore, the United States never signed the Geneva accords, which involved only the communist insurgents and the French, not the shaky South Vietnamese government. Possibly because Eisenhower feared the charge of appeasement at Geneva by conservative Republicans, he then arranged for Ngo Dinh Diem, fiercely anticommunist and in self-imposed exile, to return from the United States to become the premier of South Vietnam. At the same time Dulles had been putting together the South East Asian Treaty Organization (SEATO), a mutual security alliance that first involved Britain, France, Australia, the Philippines, Thailand, and was extended to include South Vietnam, Laos, and Cambodia.

In many ways SEATO created as many problems as it solved. First,

it compromised the "new look" in Republican foreign policy by returning America to the same containment doctrine that the Eisenhower
administration had set out to repudiate. It also violated the Geneva
accords in two respects, even though the United States had not been a
signatory to them. The accords had stipulated that neither South nor
North Vietnam could join an alliance with foreign powers. By aligning
with South Vietnam as a sovereign state, the United States committed
itself to defending Diem, a dictator who had no intention of letting
democratic elections take place. The CIA had informed Eisenhower
that if elections were held, Ho Chi Minh would certainly win, perhaps
commanding as much as 80 percent of the vote. Eisenhower could no
more afford free elections in Vietnam in 1954 than Stalin could afford
them in Poland in 1945. The morality of the cold war had come full
circle, condemning in one part of the world what could be condoned
in another.

SEATO also aimed to isolate communist China, which the United
States refused to recognize, while continuing to treat Formosa as the
legitimate government for all 650 million Chinese. In response, the
Peking regime denounced the United States and Chiang as imperialist
devils. Mao Tse-tung and Chou En-lai also threatened to invade various offshore islands and reclaim their sovereignty as a part of World
War II agreements promising the return of all Chinese territories occupied by Japan.

Eisenhower would have preferred to follow Truman's policy toward
China and gradually disengage America from the civil war between
Formosa and the mainland. Truman had employed the Seventh Fleet
as a buffer to neutralize the Formosa Strait. To Eisenhower the presence of the navy was not meant to help Chiang "unleash" his forces
but to "shield" communist China from such an attack. Emphasizing
the defensive nature of America's commitment, Eisenhower rejected
arguments by his advisors to send troops to the Nationalist-held Tachen
Islands and instead ordered their evacuation. But when the communists began lobbing artillery shells on the off-shore islands of Ma-tsu
and Quemoy in early 1955, the administration concluded a defense
treaty with Formosa, and Dulles announced that the use of atomic
weapons might be necessary to resist aggression. Eisenhower deliberately left vague whether the treaty was meant to defend only Formosa
or Ma-tsu and Quemoy as well. The treaty may have had more to do
with placating the pro-Chiang and anticommunist elements within the
Republican party than with formulating a comprehensive Asian policy.
But Eisenhower and Dulles also feared that if the islands fell, the morale

of the Nationalists on Taiwan would collapse. Still, when he appeared before Congress to seek authorization to use force to defend Formosa in case of attack, he did not specifically include Ma-tsu and Quemoy, and thus he wisely kept the communists guessing about whether or not the United States would resist an invasion.

In Congress most Republicans regarded the shelling of the islands as evidence of Communist determination to launch military aggression at any time of their choosing. A small band of liberal Democrats in the Senate, led by Herbert H. Lehman, Hubert H. Humphrey, and John F. Kennedy, countered that the islands were politically insignificant and militarily indefensible. The Joint Chiefs of Staff also held that the islands were not essential to America's ability to defend Taiwan. But the Senate voted overwhelmingly with the president. In the meantime discussions had been underway in the summer months between American and Chinese diplomats at Geneva. Although the talks failed to resolve the matter of the islands and the future status of Formosa, they did allow China a pretext for ordering a cease-fire on Quemoy and Matsu and thereby bringing the crisis to an end.

In Eastern Europe the cold war intensified in the early fifties. Dulles's rhetoric about liberating the "captive peoples" of Eastern Europe, his determination to increase West Germany's rearmament program, and his reliance on Air Force General Curtis LeMay's Strategic Air Command (SAC) all combined to lend credibility to the new offensive character of American foreign policy. Before Eisenhower took office, Stalin had been predicting the economic collapse of the West and the inevitability of war. Invoking the spectre of "capitalist encirclement," he had embarked upon still another purge, the "Doctors Plot" involving the mass arrests of Russian medical specialists, many Jewish, for allegedly conspiring with British and American agents. These ominous events came to a halt with the unexpected announcement of Stalin's death in March 1953, possibly at the hands of Politburo members determined to prevent another reign of terror. Stalin's death eliminated the most grotesque features of a totalitarian system that derived in part from the pathological character of a cruel tyrant and his "cult of personality." Would it alter the nature of the cold war?

With Stalin gone and the Korean War wound down, Soviet officials could reassess both domestic and diplomatic developments. The first change involved accepting collective leadership as Georgi Malenkov, Secretary of the Communist Central Committee, had to share power with Molotov, Khrushchev, and others. Hoping to replace the dark night of Stalinism with the new dawn of "socialist legality," Malenkov emptied the forced labor camps and pardoned those arrested in the "Doctors Plot." He also announced to the world that international conflicts can be "settled peacefully by mutual agreement of the interested parties." This post-Stalinist effort at reducing tensions with the West, what came to be called detente, was brushed aside by Dulles, who regarded the American-Soviet rivalry as an "irreconcilable conflict." To Churchill's dismay, Eisenhower responded to the Soviet overture by asking for an immediate solution to every outstanding problem: reunification of Germany, democratic elections in Korea and Eastern Europe (not, however, Vietnam), UN control and inspection of disarmament, and an end to communist revolts in Southeast Asia. The last demand was characteristic of Eisenhower, who assumed that communism was monolithic and that the Soviet Union controlled communist activity everywhere and anywhere in the world. Whatever the validity of this "linkage" mentality, it scanted the more fundamental power realities of the era.

In the early years of the Eisenhower administration, while Soviet leaders were trying to redress the tense domestic and international problems left by Stalinism, the United States built an enormous strategic capability. In effective manpower the Soviet Union had the edge, with armed forces numbering some 5.7 million men to America's 3.5 million. When Eisenhower cut military spending by half from the $61 billion peak of the Korean War years, American expenditures matched Russia's at a similar level of $30 billion per annum. The decisive margin was nuclear vulnerability. With the expansion and modernization of General LeMay's SAC, the United States was amassing a bombing assault force, equipped with in-flight refueling techniques, that could penetrate the Russian heartland. SAC had four hundred nuclear armed B-47s capable of undertaking two-way attack missions against the Soviet Union and another 1,350 planes capable of dropping atomic bombs on any target from Moscow to Vladivostok. In contrast, the Soviet Union had only one-tenth the number of aircraft capable of such missions. In light of Russia's nuclear insecurity, not to mention economic problems that constrained increased military spending, Malenkov's offer of detente seemed a rational way to ease cold-war tensions. In the period from 1953 to 1955 the Eisenhower administration could have taken advantage of America's strategic nuclear superiority and negotiated with the Russians from a position of strength. For political reasons it did not do so. These reasons may be called the domestic determinants of the cold war.

THE DOMESTIC DETERMINANTS OF THE COLD WAR

Was Eisenhower's policy of liberation and massive retaliation meant to be used or was it simply a political flourish? It is worth noting that even after the United States stood helplessly by as Moscow ordered tanks into Berlin, Dresden, and Leipzig to put down anti-Soviet demonstrations in 1953, Dulles continued to mouth the language of liberation. Paradoxically, Dulles was more pessimistic about the Soviet Union than Eisenhower. The president at least believed that the United States and USSR had a common interest in reducing the armaments race and devoting their respective resources to economic development and the well-being of other countries. Dulles remained skeptical of all Soviet overtures. He was distrustful of diplomatic agreements, scornful of detente, and doubtful of any communist reform. On occasion Eisenhower even had to reprimand Dulles for his militancy, reminding him to add after using the expression "liberation" the important qualifier "by peaceful methods." Dulles fervently believed that communist systems could not deny indefinitely peoples' basic human aspirations. But his twin slogans "liberation" and "massive retaliation" seem almost incompatible: no Eastern Europeans wished to be free of communist domination at the risk of nuclear war. This disparity between theory and reality suggests that the new aggressive look in American foreign policy may have been only a useful myth, as indeed it would turn out to be in 1956.

The myth may have had more to do with internal domestic pressures than external diplomatic realities. Emmet John Hughes, an Eisenhower speech writer, has described the inhospitability of the political atmosphere in America at the time Malenkov made his peace offensive after Stalin's death. No Republican dared embrace Soviet offers of negotiation for fear of being seen as "soft on communism," a death warrant in American politics. Even Dulles could hardly forget how his predecessor, Dean Acheson, had been vilified by vindictive cold warriors. In the first years of the Eisenhower administration the Republican Right-wing, led by senators William F. Knowland of California and William Jenner of Indiana, and Congressman Walter Judd of Minnesota, had opposed the Korean settlement as a sell-out to the enemy. At banquets of the "China Lobby" they would shout with fists raised, "Back to the Mainland!" Moderate Republicans felt constrained and could not readily contemplate any agreements with the Soviets. Although Dulles himself had little faith in such agreements, pressures induced some other policy makers to refrain from exploring any possible basis for detente, at least as long as McCarthyism was still poisoning the air of politics.

Under Dulles's reign the State Department felt the hot breath of Joseph McCarthy. When the Russian expert Charles E. Bohlen was being considered for ambassador to the Soviet Union, McCarthy led an attack in the Senate, claiming Bohlen had deliberately misadvised Roosevelt during the Yalta Conference. Dulles did little to support the State Department's own officer against such accusations. Nor did he resist directives to the State Department to order the United States Information Agency (USIA) to remove from its overseas libraries all books "by Communists, fellow-travelers, etc." Included on the hit-list were such "radical" authors as Ernest Hemingway and Mark Twain. Dulles possessed a keen sense of power politics, but he also slipped easily into the McCarthyite mentality of assuming that communist activity everywhere was due to Russian conspiracy and that communist conquests anywhere to American responsibility. The columnist Richard Rovere once asked Dulles how he could blame the Democratic administration for standing by as the Soviets annexed the Baltic republics in 1939, a time when America was determined to stay out of World War II. Dulles replied: "They were in office when it happened, weren't they?" Herbert Hoover was in office when the Japanese invaded China in 1931, Rovere rejoined. "Should Hoover have been held to account for that?" Dulles had no answer, for the chain of argument had no logic, only the emotions of frustration that had entered the bloodstream of American politics.

Although the press had urged Eisenhower to go after McCarthy for his slanderous accusations, the president said little on the subject except for some vague comments against book-burning. He allowed his attorney general, Herbert Brownell, Jr., to harass Truman by reopening the case of Henry Dexter White, though he supported the former president when Truman refused (on constitutional grounds) to appear before a congressional committee. Eisenhower chose to remain aloof of the anticommunist controversy, believing it would demean the office of the presidency to engage McCarthy in the game of gutter politics, "to get into a pissing contest with a skunk," as he remarked privately in language that Truman would have used publicly. Such a stance displayed more wisdom than courage. Eisenhower said nothing when McCarthy told General Ralph Zwicker, the president's old friend who had been wounded and decorated in the D-Day landing, that he was not fit to wear a uniform. As did so many other politicians, Eisenhower feared

McCarthy, especially the prospect that the senator would turn on the Republican administration as he had on the Democratic. Eisenhower became particularly concerned when McCarthy charged that the H-bomb had been held up because of "Reds in government," a charge that came uncomfortably close to the findings of the administration's secret investigation of Oppenheimer. The physicist Oppenheimer had been judged a security risk. Whether Oppenheimer was guilty or innocent, Eisenhower feared that McCarthy's involvement in the case would create the impression that all scientists were disloyal and hence, ruin America's defense programs. "We've got to handle" the investigation ourselves, Eisenhower told his press secretary. "That goddamn McCarthy is just likely to try such a thing."

He would indeed. In McCarthy's feverish imagination every American institution had become a hotbed of radicalism. Government, schools, churches, even the CIA was "infiltrated" by communists, and the Atomic Energy Commission was about to be unless Eisenhower allowed McCarthy's subcommittee to investigate it. Serving on the subcommittee were Roy M. Cohn and G. David Schine, smart young lawyers who loved the power of subpoena and the glare of publicity while enjoying the illusion of invulnerability. Even Edward R. Murrow's exposure of McCarthy, watched by millions of Americans on CBS's "See It Now," resulted in the courageous broadcaster receiving bundles of hate mail. But when Schine was notified, in November 1953, that he had been drafted into the army, one of the most remarkable dramas in American political history began: the Army-McCarthy Hearings.

McCarthy had already been tangling with the army when stories began to spread in the press that Cohn had put pressure on officers at Fort Dix to make life easier for Private Schine. McCarthy reacted by claiming that the army was trying to force him to call off his exposure of communists in the military service. The Senate, embarrassed by the accusations of its fellow member, aware of McCarthy's drinking problem, and perhaps sensing that he was, at last, expendable, decided to hold public meetings carried live on national television. The army appointed as its special counsel Joseph Welch, a gentle, folksy sixty-three-year-old attorney with a devotion to fairness and civility. The hearings opened amid a barrage of television cameras and cables in the Senate Caucus Room on April 22, 1954. The television audience, estimated to be as high as twenty million, watched the proceedings for thirty-five days.

During the first several weeks McCarthy seemed invincible, holding forth faked documents and calling out, "Mr. Chairman, a point of order,"

Senator McCarthy dramatizing alleged communist strongholds in America, leaving army-appointed legal counsel Joseph Welch unconvinced and bored.

to interrupt any testimony that might turn against him. Then the hearings developed into a tense personal duel when Welch asked McCarthy questions he refused to answer, leaving the impression that the Senator was as duplicitous as communists who hid behind the Fifth Amendment. The audience began to warm to Welch's dignified manner and wit. Desperate, McCarthy played his last card. He informed the room that Welch's law firm had been employing a former member of the Communist party, a man named Fisher. The shaken Welch, trying to control his rage, calmly replied to McCarthy before the hushed audience. "Until this moment, Senator, I think I never really gauged your cruelty or your recklessness. Fred Fisher is a young man who went to the Harvard Law School and came into my firm and is starting what looks to be a brilliant career with us." He then told the television audience that he and others in the firm knew that Fisher had once belonged to the Lawyers Guild and had left it when he became aware of its procommunist politics. Welch knew that Cohn was aware of Fisher's background, so why was McCarthy bringing it up now? "Little did I dream," Welch continued staring McCarthy in the face,

> you could be so reckless and so cruel as to do an injury to that lad. It is true he is still with Hale and Dorr. It is true that he will continue to be

with Hale and Dorr. It is, I regret to say, equally true that I fear he shall always bear a scar needlessly inflicted by you. If it were in my power to forgive you for your reckless cruelty I would do so. I like to think that I am a gentle man, but your forgiveness will have to come from someone other than me.

Reeling from the moving rebuke, McCarthy grumbled that Welch had no right to mention cruelty since he had "been baiting Cohn here for hours." "Senator, may we not drop this?" Welch pleaded.

We know he belonged to the Lawyers Guild, and Mr. Cohn nods his head at me. I did you, I think, no personal injury, Mr. Cohn.

Cohn, biting his lips and trembling, whispered back, "No, sir."

I meant to do you no personal injury, and if I did, I beg your pardon.

Cohn again nodded, and McCarthy, now in panic, tried again to bring up the subject of Fisher.

Let us not assassinate this lad further, Senator. You have done enough. Have you no sense of decency, sir, at long last? Have you left no sense of decency?

The audience broke into applause and then hurried to leave the hearing room. "I was sick to my stomach," recalled one of the few remaining McCarthy supporters who stayed in his seat. Staggering back to his table, McCarthy turned his palms up and shrugged his shoulders, asking "What did I do?" The next day newspapers across the country provided the answer with headlines celebrating the defeat of "Cruelty" by "Decency."

Shortly after the hearings ended Eisenhower met privately with Welch and congratulated him for his handling of the army's case. Ought the president have done more than private gestures to put an end to McCarthy? Philosophers tell us that "ought implies can," and the political scientist Fred I. Greenstein tells us that Eisenhower could not have taken on McCarthy directly. In doing so he might have divided the Republican party, a possibility that worried Vice-President Nixon and press secretary James Hagerty. Further, an open confrontation with McCarthy would have divided and confused the public. Although the polls showed that McCarthy's popularity had dropped considerably in the spring of 1954, 79 percent of Americans still believed that there were communists in government, with half the number convinced that communists were "some danger" and the other half convinced that they were a "great danger." Probing further in his study *Communism, Conformity and Civil Liberties,* Harvard sociologist Samuel Stouffer asked Americans a telling question in a survey. How would they respond if the president told the country that the communist menace had been eliminated and the chairman of the congressional committee investigating communism said there was still a danger? Forty-nine percent replied they would believe the president, 40 percent would not, and the remaining 11 percent had no opinion. Americans would have had even less trust in the president if the committee chairman challenged his conclusion. In that case only 30 percent would have believed him.

Until Welch exposed McCarthy as a demagogue and fanatic, McCarthy had his cake and ate it too. Like a witch doctor, his power depended upon the claim that only he could eliminate evil and his future depended upon evil remaining a permanent danger. McCarthy needed the communists, however few they number; did America need McCarthy?

That question had been raised during the Senate debate on the proposal to censure McCarthy. Eisenhower, typically, remained aloof from the discussion. It was up to the Senate to put its own house in order, he advised. In early 1953 Democratic Senator Thomas Hennings of Missouri prepared a report for the Privilege and Election Committee recommending censure, which had the immediate support of Democratic Senator William Benton of Connecticut. Republicans William Knowland (California), Barry M. Goldwater (Arizona), and Everett Dirksen (Illinois) all opposed the move on the grounds that it would inhibit free debate. Hennings' report exposed McCarthy's dishonest campaign tactics and his financial irregularities. McCarthy predictably charged the committee members with parroting the communist line. With no sense of irony, he denied the constitutionality of a Senate investigating committee. When McCarthy later tangled with the army, Republican Senator Ralph Flanders of Vermont joined the move against him, as did the Democrat William Fulbright of Arkansas. In November 1954, McCarthy was finally censured, by a vote of 64 to 23. It took the Senate almost three years to condemn a fellow member who had made a mockery out of civil liberties and had turned anticommunism into a farce.

With McCarthy gone from the center of the political stage, America could better concentrate on the real problems of diplomacy. Foreign policy makers wanted to explore the possibility of detente with the Soviet

Union. In the summer of 1955 the first "summit conference" between the United States and USSR since Yalta and Potsdam took place at Geneva. The preparatory talks seemed encouraging as the Soviets agreed to on-site disarmament inspections. Eisenhower arrived at Geneva looking forward to meeting his old World War II ally Marshall Zhukov. But at the conference discussion broke down when America insisted upon the right of overflight surveillance as well as ground inspection. Germany was also a sensitive issue. Eisenhower wanted free elections as a means of reunifying East and West Germany. The Russians would not allow elections for much the same reason the United States would not allow them in Vietnam. But both sides assured one another of the absolute necessity of avoiding the horrors of nuclear war. Although no concrete agreements had been reached, East-West tensions had eased and Eisenhower and the world at large welcomed the "spirit of Geneva."

As Eisenhower entered the last year of his term he could take pride in having fulfilled his promise to end the war in Korea. If Eisenhower logged no great legislative achievements in his first term, that too was part of his strategy of strengthening and improving existing programs rather than embarking upon new social changes. Yet in the fifties American life flowed on, as we shall see in the following three chapters. If the president had the luxury of avoiding McCarthyism, other American were forced to face it directly. If Eisenhower evoked a quiescent mood of stability and consensus, society itself was creaking under the stresses of change, the confusion of new styles of popular culture, and in some instances even the anxiety of affluence and success. Finally, while Eisenhower symbolized the triumph of anti-intellectualism in politics, America witnessed the flowering of intellect in science, scholarship, and the fine arts.

PART TWO

PART TWO

5

Politics, Culture, and the Loyalty Controversy

HOLLYWOOD AND THE COLD WAR

When the European war broke out in September 1939, the United States was the only major power with neither an intelligence nor a propaganda agency. During the war secret intelligence operations were carried out by the OSS and its director, "Wild" Bill Donovan. If intelligence was essential for political and military objectives in Europe and Asia, propaganda was essential for psychological reasons in America. The Office of War Information assumed charge of arousing and sustaining citizen morale to promote the war effort. Staffed by advertising executives as well as intellectuals, OWI could never decide whether the war should simply be sold to the people with some propaganda gimmicks or be explained in deeper ideological terms. After awkwardly experimenting with posters and documentary films, OWI turned to more imaginative resources. "The easiest way to inject a propaganda idea into most people's minds," OWI Director Elmer Davis advised, "is to let it go in through the medium of an entertainment picture when they do not realize they are being propagandized." The poet Archibald MacLeish insisted that the OWI must neither control nor regulate the media but adhere to "a strategy of truth." But when the OWI sought the eager cooperation of Hollywood directors and actors, truth indeed became stranger than fiction and more responsive to politics than to art.

To a large extent American attitudes toward the rest of the world are shaped less by intimate knowledge than visual imagery. During the early forties when the United States was at war, much of what Americans learned about their enemies and friends derived from Hollywood movies. World War II was the first war to be treated in motion-picture feature films while the war was taking place, and many film scripts had to be cleared by the OWI. The war as seen on screen produced two national heroes—in John Wayne and Humphrey Bogart. It also produced some illusions that left Americans unprepared to grasp what would happen in the postwar world.

No one watching American movies about the war in the Pacific could have predicted that Japan and her people would become not only America's friends but our greatest economic competitors. Hollywood films led Americans to believe that Japan's military successes in the early part of the war were due to the sneaky and even cowardly conduct of its soldiers. The truth is that Japan enjoyed many technological advantages. American fighter planes were no match for the Japanese Zero, which was far superior in speed, altitude, and climbing rate. Even the famous Flying Tigers, the Curtiss P-40s that flew in China and whose pilots became folk heroes, had inadequate radios and gunsights. It took two years for the United States Navy to perfect the torpedo. What made Pearl Harbor possible was not only the element of surprise but the even more surprising fact that the Japanese carrier force was then the best in the world.

But in Hollywood Japanese technological superiority could be acknowledged, if at all, as something merely copied or stolen from America, and certainly not as important as the moral inferiority of its soldiers. The film *Destination Tokyo* was singularly exceptional in offering glimpses of the Japanese as wily and resourceful. More frequently they were portrayed as almost subhuman. Cruel and bellicose, angrily shouting orders, the Japanese military man was quick to kill with a smile and just as ready to take his own life. No wonder American movie-goers could similarly smile as they watched scenes of Japanese soldiers burning alive while being torched by flamethrowers. In *Purple Heart*, named after a medal given only to soldiers who have shed blood in battle, downed American fliers are captured, interrogated, tortured, and put on mock trial. When a Japanese officer quietly commits hara-kiri, the suicide is depicted as a cowardly deed and admission of defeat, with no allusion to the dignity of the Japanese military code of honor.

In contrast, actor John Wayne accepted defeat and death like a man.

They Were Expendable dealt with the futile efforts of American tor-
pedo-boat commanders to defend the Philippines. Wayne and his crew
face death heroically, and military defeat is turned into a glorious moral
victory of "American" values—loyalty, courage, pride, and sacrifice.
After the war Wayne became a staunch anticommunist and symbol of
the gung-ho marine. Against the Japanese Wayne dramatized the possibility of heroism without victory; during the cold war he accepted
General MacArthur's dictum that there is no substitute for victory.

Film treatment of Germany was more complex and even more
ambiguous. To be sure, there were out-and-out propaganda films such
as *Hitler's Children* and *Nazi Agent*, but these were generally espionage
or cheap sexual thrillers that shed little light on Nazi atrocities. Even
The Seventh Cross, which dealt with the concentration camps, obscured
the full horrors and depicted decent German people helping prisoners
escape. The Germans fared better than the Japanese probably because
of their common Anglo-Saxon heritage with America. The film *The
Moon Is Down*, based on the occupation of Norway, showed German
officers as civilized and reluctantly driven to executing hostages in order
to prevent sabotage. Alfred Hitchcock's *Lifeboat* provoked controversy
among film critics because it seemed to suggest that most of the Americans in the boat were helpless while the one German Nazi, although
ruthless and treacherous, possessed the knowledge and skills that would
enable them to survive. Certain films even hinted that Germans may
very well be superior and that against Nazi strong-armed methods and
cynicism, American innocence and idealism would prove no match.
What was needed was a "tough guy" who could symbolize the cynical
without being corruptible, a vital role superbly filled by Humphrey
Bogart.

The patriotic idealism of guts and glory symbolized by Wayne had
its opposite image in Bogart, who was familiar to Americans as a cagey
gangster. In *To Have And Have Not* Bogart's support of the antifascist
Free French is compromised by his willingness to make money from a
democratic political cause. In *Sahara* he played a tank captain whose
attitude toward prisoners of war verged on the callous. But it was in
Casablanca that American audiences sensed why the enemy could not
be defeated simply by invoking the honest platitudes of patriotism and
self-sacrifice. The film, which has since become a classic, is a great
Machiavellian drama warning Americans that those who merely want
to do good will be destroyed by the many who are not good. Portraying
a cafe proprietor in Vichy-occupied Casablanca, Bogart assures the
fascists that although he may have once fought for the Democratic

Humphrey Bogart and Ingrid Bergman in Casablanca, *a Hollywood World War II film that dramatized to Americans the heroism of the European resistance.*

Loyalists in Spain it was only because they paid him well. "I stick my neck out for nobody. The problems of this world are not in my department. I'm a saloonkeeper." The Vichy officer replies, "a wise foreign policy." Having deceived the enemy, Bogart is able to outwit him and survive, and by the end of the film he emerges as a hero who sides with the Free French. Yet his motives seem more romantic than patriotic. Instead of fleeing Casablanca to safety, he arranges for the husband of the woman he loves to take his place. In this melodramatic act of romantic sacrifice, the audience is assured that the devious means necessary to defeat fascism need not corrupt the human heart.

Films about Soviet Russia could also warm the heart, or so it seemed. *The North Star* dramatizes Russians courageously facing Nazi armies ravaging their villages. *Song of Russia* tells the story of an American musician falling in love with a Russian pianist of peasant background. Both become guerilla fighters until her village is overtaken and they return to the United States to promote the Russian cause. Such films did little more than to preach postwar peace and brotherhood with America's ally, even though scenes depicting peasants dancing happily under the banners of the Red star hardly conveyed the true feelings of the Russian people toward communism.

With the appearance of *Mission to Moscow* in 1943, however, a storm of controversy erupted in artistic and intellectual circles. Based on a book by that title written by Ambassador Joseph E. Davies, the film was produced by Warner Brothers at the request of Roosevelt, who believed that it was essential "to keep Stalin fighting." The millions of Americans who saw the film learned that Stalin had to purge all his rivals because they were agents of Germany; that the earlier non-aggression pact and Russia's invasion of Finland were essential to Stalin's war preparation strategy; that the American war effort was being obstructed by isolationists and congressmen who were more interested in "doing business with Hitler" than in defeating him; that Russia was a story-book land of smiling workers in love with their tractors; and that Stalin himself was a trusted leader adored by his people. A few conservative Hearst papers denounced the film as "Bolshevik propaganda," and some liberals joined with the Trotskyists in an effort to expose its lies. But other groups decried the attacks and defended the film as a "magnificent tribute . . . a truly epochal screen document" that was meant as "a gesture of international friendship made at the most crucial period in American history, with the highly laudable and important object of promoting trust instead of distrust in the Soviet Union."

Some of the pro-Soviet World War II films later became part of the communist controversy of the McCarthy era, a controversy that dragged on in Hollywood for several bitter years and turned former friends into life-long enemies. Many of the Hollywood actors and writers had been drawn to the CP and the promise of Soviet Russia because of the failure of England, France, and the United States to take a militant stand against fascism in the 1930s and to defend the Spanish Republic. With the Nazi-Soviet nonaggression pact in 1939, Hollywood liberals broke with the communists and declared the Popular Front over. During the war liberals and communists joined forces once again and united behind Roosevelt and the United States-USSR collaboration. All along, however, a budding actor named Ronald Reagan kept a watchful eye on the communists within the Screen Actors Guild. Then, after the war, with the ultra-patriotic élan ended, labor troubles erupted in the film studios while the Hollywood branch of the CP began to echo the Moscow line on the cold war. By the spring of 1947, when HUAC called for a purge of the film industry, the communist actor or writer had only two options: change politics or change professions.

The widely publicized HUAC hearings divided Hollywood into three groups. The anticommunists who cooperated with their interrogators were "friendly witnesses": Reagan, Budd Schulberg, Gary Cooper, and the Russian émigré novelist Ayn Rand. There were also noncommunists who organized to oppose the inquisition in the name of the First Amendment, liberals like John Huston, Humphrey Bogart, Lauren Bacall, Katharine Hepburn, and Judy Garland. Then there were the Stalinists who invoked the Fifth Amendment and refused to answer questions on the grounds of possible self-incrimination. This tactic on the part of the "unfriendly witnesses," who first numbered nineteen and then became the notorious "Hollywood Ten," proved a strategic mistake. Public opinion at first supported Hollywood and opposed HUAC's inquisition. But no matter how strongly Americans may venerate the idea of the Fifth Amendment, the majority of the American public could only conclude that anyone who refused to testify had something to hide. Some witnesses feared that they would be forced to name fellow CP members, other denounced HUAC as "fascist." As the hearings continued to grab headlines, Hollywood producers estab-

Russian émigré author Ayn Rand, testifying before the House Un-American Activities Committee on the pro-Soviet World War II movie, Song of Russia.

lished a blacklist prohibiting the employment of anyone who refused to testify or was cited for contempt. Among the great stars to fall victim to the blacklist were the actor Charles Chaplin, director Carl Foreman, and the black baritone Paul Robeson.

Although some of the Hollywood Reds would later become disillusioned with the Soviet Union, the majority of the Hollywood Ten remained ardent Stalinists, defending the Soviet Union every step of the way and demanding civil liberties in Malibu but not necessarily in Moscow. Other writers, such as Lillian Hellman, simply assumed that there was no inconsistency in defending a regime and at the same time not being responsible for what went on within the regime. Yet such a stance may only recall Samuel Johnson's adage that a "stubborn audacity is the last refuge of guilt." Even two scholars sympathetic to the Hollywood communists and severely critical of HUAC felt it necessary to offer the following judgment:

> Viewing the Hollywood Communists from the historian's perspective, it is necessary to conclude that on occasion these men and women undermined their credibility, misserved their cause, and misled their contemporaries with their behavior, their attitude, and their words. The American Communists in general, and the film Reds in particular, never displayed in this era any independence of mind or organization vis a vis the Comintern and the Soviet Union; hence, much as their activities and accomplishments in many realms—notably antifascism, domestic and international—redound to their credit, in the last analysis the CPUSA, and its Hollywood talent branches, could not escape some association with the actions, errors, and crimes of international communism. However perfunctorily and mechanically they may have defended the USSR, however "oblique" to their *major* preoccupying domestic and international goals the defense of Stalinism probably was for most of them, and however uninvolved in (and ignorant of) the actions of the Soviet regime they personally were, the screen artist Reds nevertheless defended that regime unflinchingly, uncritically, inflexibly—and therefore left themselves open to the justifiable suspicion that they not only approved of everything they were defending, but would themselves act in the same way if they were in the same position.

The purge of the film industry had a bizarre touch of poetic justice. One of the Hollywood Ten who went to jail for contempt found himself in the same prison as J. Parnell Thomas, the HUAC chairman who was later convicted of income-tax evasion after pleading the Fifth Amendment!

A group of Hollywood stars arriving at the Capitol in October 1947 to protest the House Un-American Committee's investigation into alleged Hollywood communism. Front row (left to right): Marsha Hunt, David Hopkins, Richard Conte, June Havoc, Humphrey Bogart, Lauren Bacall, Evelyn Keyes, Danny Kaye, Jane Wyatt, and Geraldine Brooks. Back row (from behind Bogart): John Huston, Sterling Hayden (partially obscured), Paul Henreid, Joe Sistrom, Sheppard Strudwick, John Shepherd, Ira Gershwin, and Larry Adler.

Writers responded differently to the purge. Some circumvented the blacklist by turning their scripts in under pseudonyms. The playwright Arthur Miller took the courageous position that he would cooperate with HUAC only in regards to his own past but would not answer questions involving the names and reputations of others. Miller went on to write *The Crucible*, a play suggesting parallels between McCarthyism and the Salem witch trials of the seventeenth century. The director Elia Kazan, a "friendly" witness who actually did name names, went on to produce the powerful film *On the Waterfront*. In addition to winning several Academy Awards, the film reversed an aesthetic and moral code that had been a convention in the art world for centuries. Its protagonist, the confused but sensitive Marlon Brando, struggles with his conscience as he realizes that the only way to fight the power and corruption of the union is by turning "stool pigeon." America now had a new hero—the informer.

THE PURGE OF THE PROFESSIONS

The ideological cleansing of Hollywood was more notorious only because its personalities were more famous. But anticommunism had deeper and more legitimate sources in America than the witch-hunt hysteria bred by HUAC and McCarthy. The first anticommunist purge in the trade unions, for example, began in 1946, in part an outcome of the bitter socialist-communist feuds of the 1930s. Those feuds subsided during the war when the United States and Soviet Union were allies and many radical unions agreed to a no-strike pledge. The feuds resumed with the onset of the cold war when members of the CP were once again told that only the Soviet Union could show the way to socialism. CP leader Earl Browder suddenly found himself replaced by William Z. Foster upon receipt of a cablegram from Moscow. One cynic who had observed this slavish behavior, common since the 1920s, was fond of asking American communists:

> What do you and the Brooklyn Bridge have in common?
> We are as hard as steel?
> No, you are both suspended by cables.

With the CP taking its orders from Moscow, leaders of the organized labor movement, spearheaded by the AFL and CIO, needed to declare their allegiance to America and disassociate themselves from the pro-peace activists who would become part of the Wallace movement. In several unions, especially maritime, transport, electrical, and automotive, leaders such as Walter Reuther and Joseph Curran struggled to wrest control from elements friendly to the CP and the Soviet Union. By 1949 all major American unions, with the exception of the San Francisco Longshoremen's, were directed by socialists or democrats. No doubt the struggle left many innocent victims, especially when HUAC began its red-baiting investigations and thousands of workers lost their jobs on grounds of insufficient loyalty. But in the trade-union movement, anticommunism came to be regarded by many—though by no means all—workers and officers as a legitimate component of American patriotism, an emotion deeply felt by first- and second-generation immigrant Americans.

But McCarthyism was another matter, based less on the presence of real communists than on suspicion in need of suspects, and pressures to succumb to it affected many other areas of American life. The

American Bar Association, the American Medical Association, and the National Education Association all proposed some form of a political test for its members. The teaching profession felt especially pressured by the public it served. Ninety-one percent of Americans believed communists should not be allowed to teach, and 21 percent advocated firing all teachers suspected of disloyalty. Many secondary school teachers felt fear and intimidation and seldom could look to their administrators for support. Often, over the protests of a faculty, a board of education would conduct an investigation of textbooks for subversive or un-American content. In some New York City schools administrators made use of anonymous informers to obtain information, or even rumor, about suspected radical instructors. In that city, where the Communist party was most concentrated, 321 school teachers and fifty-eight college teachers lost their jobs either because of past communist affiliations or refusal to comply with investigating committees.

Nationwide, the purge of higher education begun in the Truman era and continued into the Eisenhower fifties cost roughly six hundred teachers and professors their jobs. In the thirties communist student organizations thrived at such institutions as City College of New York, Harvard, Vassar, MIT, the University of Chicago, UCLA, and Berkeley. McCarthy had particularly singled out the Ivy League as a hotbed of bolshevism. Some faculty members subpoenaed to appear before HUAC cooperated under great guilt; the few who took the Fifth Amendment were often harassed by university administrators. At the University of Washington pressure from the Chamber of Commerce and the Central Labor Committee together with the American Legion led to the firing of several professors, even though students testified that their classrooms were free of political bias.

The most bitter controversy erupted at the University of California when its Board of Regents voted to impose a loyalty oath on the faculty. Professors were given two months to sign the oath or lose their jobs. The plight of California academics became a rallying cause as other campuses throughout the country sent contributions for legal defense and Albert Einstein and J. Robert Oppenheimer sent letters urging noncompliance. With the deadline approaching, the 20 percent of the faculty who refused to sign experienced depression, insomnia, incapacity to work, and anxiety about the decision they had to face. In the end many capitulated, while others took positions elsewhere, leaving approximately twenty-five non-signers, most of whom were not communists but highly principled scholars who regarded the oath as unconstitutional—as indeed the California Supreme Court declared in 1952.

The Hollywood blacklist and the university loyalty oath confronted liberals with a significant crisis regarding constitutional liberty and academic freedom. Is the communist entitled to benefit from such principles? On the whole, the Supreme Court ruled "no." In a few cases it found insufficient grounds for government or business to fire an employee simply on unsubstantiated rumor about disloyalty. But the Supreme Court generally upheld the state loyalty oaths (and thereby overruled the California court). States had a constitutional right, reasoned the Court, to obtain assurance that an employee was not knowingly belonging to a subversive organization dedicated to overthrowing the federal or state government by force or violence. If procedural safeguards were carried out, and if loyalty oaths were not used to punish teachers for past subversive affiliations, then refusal to testify about present political membership could be grounds for dismissal.

Curiously, while most writers and professors opposed the blacklist and loyalty oath because they were unconstitutional, the philosopher Sidney Hook opposed them because they were inconsequential. A former communist theoretician himself, Hook knew from experience that CP members would swear to any oath to conceal their political identity. Nevertheless, Hook also wanted to deny communists the right to teach on the grounds that Party members had surrendered their right to think and act independently of Moscow. He wanted the decision to be made, however, not by the courts or congressional committees but by university faculties on grounds of "professional ethics." As a genuine democracy, America must recognize all points of view as legitimate, even communism; but it is not necessary, Hook reasoned, to tolerate those who are intolerant of liberal and social democracy and remain apologists for totalitarianism. Hook took the position that America could cope with, and indeed thrive on, open intellectual heresy but must oppose what he regarded as covert political conspiracy. Hook's position drew criticism from the historian Henry Steele Commager and others who insisted that communists had a right to teach regardless of the nature of their political allegiances. The plea for absolute academic freedom Hook dismissed as "ritualistic liberalism."

The scrappy Hook had another cause to fight as well. "Most American intellectuals still do not understand the theory, practice, and tactics of the Communist movement," he complained during the height of the Red Scare in America. "Because McCarthy had made wild and

The philosopher Sidney Hook. Once America's leading Marxist theoretician, in the postwar era he became America's most vigilant anticommunist intellectual.

irresponsible charges, too many are inclined to dismiss the communist danger in its total global impact as relatively unimportant." How, then, could the anticommunist intellectual take anticommunism away from the anticommunist politician?

McCARTHYISM: THE INTELLECTUAL REPERCUSSIONS

The American intellectual of the forties and fifties has been doubly accused. During the McCarthy era the intellectual was regarded as either a closet communist who covertly supported the Soviet Union or as a liberal "dupe" whose innocence about the realities of Stalinism misled his readers and students into accepting a benign view of Russian behavior after World War II. Whichever the case, the intellectual, it was said, bore responsibility for the cold war because he failed to warn the public about the terrors of totalitarianism. The second accusation emerged a decade later with the Vietnam War. The sixties generation, the New Left, charged that the writers of the forties and fifties made the cold war inevitable by trying to "outdo the Right in its anticommunist zeal" and by even collaborating with the CIA in it counterrevolutionary activities. Ironically, while the Old Right labeled the American intellectual soft on communism, the New Left claimed he was too hard, so hostile as to lead the American people toward McCarthy and his witch hunts. Both of these accusations lacked the accuracy of historical sequence.

Rather than trying to "outdo the Right in its anticommunist zeal," the intellectuals who opposed communism had taken their stand long before the McCarthy era; indeed they tried to inform the public about the Soviet Union when the country was pro-, not anti-, Soviet. Many of these intellectuals had been radicalized in their teen-age or college years during the depression. They just as quickly became disenchanted with Russia when they read about the Moscow Trials and the Hitler-Stalin nonaggression pact. During World War II Americans heard much about the wonders of the Soviet Union in *Life* magazine. Even *Reader's Digest* was refusing, at the advice of the State Department, to print uncomplimentary articles on Russia. But all the while anti-Soviet writers tried in vain to alert the country to the dangers of Stalinism when it was decidedly unpopular to do so. The various writers who came to compose the noncommunist Left in American were passionately anti-Stalinist, long convinced that the Russian dictator had betrayed the democratic goals of Karl Marx. Their voices were faintly heard in small, obscure publications: the Marxist *Partisan Review*, the socialist *Call*, the Trotskyist *New International*, the quasi-anarchist *Politics*, and the Jewish *Commentary*, which first appeared at the war's end. Few of their readers were surprised, as was Truman and most Americans, by the Soviet Union's conduct after the war.

Ever since the eighteenth-century Enlightenment many Western intellectuals had regarded themselves as "citizens of the world," not narrow patriots. In the late nineteenth and early twentieth centuries Marxism reinforced the conviction that the intellectuals, "the engineers of the soul," would be internationalist in orientation and dedicated to the universal values of truth, freedom, and justice. This great hope, always more dream than reality, crashed into a confrontation during a notorious meeting in April 1949, at New York's Waldorf-Astoria Hotel, the Conference of Scientific and Cultural Workers for World Peace.

Some of the world's most illustrious intellectual figures attended the conference. The American participants were led by Hook, Dwight MacDonald, editor of *Politics*, and ex-radical Max Eastman, an older Greenwich Village activist who once joined John Reed in championing the Bolshevik Revolution. They demanded that the Conference address itself to issues of cultural freedom, specifically to the fate of the Russian novelist Boris Pasternak, whose writings had been suppressed by Stalin. To the dismay of the American composer Aaron Copland, the

New York anti-Stalinists protesting the communist-sponsored peace conference at the Waldorf-Astoria Hotel, March 25, 1949.

Russian composer Dimitri Shostakovitch responded by defending the Soviet attacks on Igor Stravinsky and other musicians experimenting with new symphonic compositions whose abstract notations were incomprehensible to "the broad masses." American scientists like geneticist H. J. Muller, Nobel-prize winner and once a friend of Russian geneticists, challenged the dominance in the Soviet Union of the teachings of Trofim Lysenko, an agronomist who insisted that evolution proceeds from inherent genetic mechanisms, a thesis at odds with the latest findings in molecular biology. Henry Wallace, to his credit, expressed some skepticism of Lysenkoism at the conference, and the philosopher Hook declared from the floor that the laws of science are universal and know no national boundaries or political requirements. But American intellectuals were not allowed to present their own papers at the conference. When it became clear that the values of intellectual freedom must be suppressed for the sake of world peace, most American participants charged that the conference was being dominated by the communists, and a small group withdrew and held their own counter-meeting. Several were old time Trotskyists or dissident communists who had opposed Stalinism in the thirties—writers like Hook, James Burnham, and Bertram D. Wolfe. Soon they would be organizing the American Committee on Cultural Freedom (ACCF), a counterpart to the Congress of Cultural Freedom that had been started in Berlin by writers like Arthur Koestler, author of *Darkness at Noon,* a penetrating psychological examination of the Moscow purge trials, and contributor to *The God That Failed,* a collection of essays by American and European ex-communists, among them the black novelist Richard Wright.

Another anti-Stalinist organization that emerged in the postwar years was the Americans for Democratic Action (ADA). It consisted of former New Deal liberals, labor leaders, civil libertarians, and academic intellectuals. ADA could agree with the Wallace Progressives about the need to expand the welfare state, develop a full-employment economy, preserve civil liberties against the assaults of McCarthyites, and extend civil rights to blacks and other minorities. But ADA had to sustain a delicate balance between its commitment to civil liberties and its commitment to anticommunism.

When eleven communists were sentenced under the Smith Act for conspiring to teach the violent overthrow of government, ADA members found themselves divided. Some feared losing touch with public opinion and appearing "soft" on communism if the organization defended the rights of the accused; but the majority issued statements publicly questioning the constitutionality of the Smith Act. ADA liberals had also to decide whether the CP was a legitimate party or a covert agency of a foreign power, and whether the government should prosecute communists as possible spies or simply because they advocated "un-American" ideas. ADA upheld the principle of academic freedom; it denied that professors should be dismissed for refusing to sign loyalty oaths; and it insisted that all ideas, even communist ideas, had the right to be advocated, if only better to be refuted.

Where ADA broke sharply with the Progressives was on the issue of the Soviet Union. The Progressives assumed that communist Russia was on the right course to progress, peace, and prosperity had it not been for America's "aggressive" containment policy. Underlying the assumption was the conviction that the United States and the USSR would become more and more alike, with America's economy tending more toward socialism and Russia's political structure more toward democracy.

This notion of "convergence" resulted in a curious irony in postwar intellectual history. In general liberals have been characterized as having forged a "consensus" view of political reality while radicals maintained a Marxist vision of "conflict" based on the ultimate irreconcilability of capitalism and socialism. Yet in international thought it was the Left-Progressives who believed in the possibility of Russian-American harmony while the Center-Liberals saw the continuation of conflict and rivalry. Many ADA and ACCF liberals saw ideological conflict—though not necessarily military confrontation—between the United States and USSR because both superpowers suffered from a proud arrogance that blinded each side to its own motives and intent. The view that power cannot reign innocently had been expounded by Reinhold Niebuhr, an ADA founder. Niebuhr's writings had profound impact on intellectuals as diverse as the poet W. H. Auden, the psychologist Robert Coles, the political theorist Hans Morgenthau, the theologian Will Herberg, the historian Arthur Schlesinger, Jr., the diplomat George Kennan, and the black minister and later, martyr, Martin Luther King, Jr.

According to Niebuhr, the error of both communism and capitalism was to replace the reality of sin and evil with an eighteenth-century belief in reason and progress. In doing so, communism and capitalism mistakenly assumed that power and conflict can be abolished: whether

Protestant theologian Reinhold Niebuhr, a founder of Americans for Democratic Action and an influential liberal intellectual in the forties and fifties.

by eliminating private property or preventing state intervention, both ideologies envisioned a future society essentially harmonious, providing people would be free to pursue their own ends unrestrained by political authority. But modern American liberalism, based on the interventionist welfare state, had been able to control the power and abuses of capitalism, whereas in the Soviet Union people had no means of opposing the power and abuses of the party and secret police. Nevertheless, both superpowers, fighting the cold war in the realm of propaganda, ideology, and even mythology, disclaimed power and identified their respective cause either with the will of God or the destiny of history. The sin of self-idolatry afflicts East and West alike. Niebuhr remained convinced, as did Abraham Lincoln, that God is inscrutable and the meaning of history incomprehensible. Cursed by original sin, "fallen" man is on his own, and he must accept power and the human corruptions from which it sprang. In some respects Niebuhr applied to the cold war the same lesson that the American framers had applied to the Constitution: since the sources of conflict cannot be eliminated they must be controlled.

Niebuhr's writings enabled liberals to develop a stance on containment that could be not only critical of communism but self-critical of America for its assumptions of innocence and pride and its equation of prosperity with virtue and God's blessings. Morgenthau's *In Defense of National Interest* (1951) drew on Niebuhr to question Senator Taft's claim that America's cold war policy was an exercise in pure, unselfish idealism. Schlesinger used Niebuhrian categories in *The Vital Center* (1948) to defend both the liberal and radical traditions grounded in the historical realities of social conflict and to expose the "doughface progressives" like Henry Wallace who remained sentimentally ignorant of such realities and regarded Russia as a farmer's utopia.

Years later writers like Schlesinger would be taken to task for belonging to the ACCF, an organization that had been partly financed by the European Congress of Cultural Freedom, whose own funds had come secretly from the CIA. But Schlesinger and most ACCF members remained unaware of the CIA connection and were hardly intellectual apologists for the State Department. Both ADA and ACCF liberals were anti-Stalinist and defended America in its confrontation with the Soviet Union; few, however, believed containment should be extended to Asia and many had reservations about the wisdom of America's intervention in Korea. What drove liberals apart was McCarthyism, an issue that became the focus of bitter debate within the ACCF.

Harvard historian Arthur Schlesinger, Jr., one of several Stevensonian liberals who switched to the younger Democratic candidate John F. Kennedy in the 1960 presidential election.

The McCarthy campaign forced ADA and ACCF members to address such controversies as the loyalty oath, the right of communists to teach, the propriety of the Fifth Amendment, and the security-clearance cases of fellow intellectuals like Owen Lattimore and J. Robert Oppenheimer. The question of taking a public stand on McCarthy proved divisive. The majority of the members believed it necessary to denounce McCarthy as a menace not only to civil liberties but to the cause of anticommunism itself. The trouble with McCarthyism, observed the *Partisan Review* editor Philip Rahv, was that it misled the people into thinking that communism posed a threat primarily *in* America rather than *to* America. Other members, for example the ex-Trotskyists James Burnham and Max Eastman, argued that while McCarthy himself might be repugnant, attacks upon him would only ease the pressure against communists in government and other American institutions. Still others like Irving Kristol denied that McCarthy was jeopardizing civil liberties, and Sidney Hook justified the Smith Act and the right of universities to fire communist teachers. Which represented a greater danger to American freedom, communism or McCarthyism? The literary scholar Diana Trilling concluded that both were repugnant, as did the sociologist David Riesman. By 1955 the ACCF suffered defections from both the Left and Right. The historian Schlesinger resigned after protesting that the ACCF had lost sight of cultural freedom in its

obsession with anticommunism long after the threat of internal conspiracy had passed. Burnham and Eastman resigned for the opposite
reasons, whereupon they joined the young Yale graduate William F.
Buckley, Jr., in launching the conservative weekly, *National Review.*

The phenomenon of McCarthyism continued to haunt as well as
divide the American intellectual community throughout the fifties.
Arthur Miller's play *The Crucible* (1953), focusing on the Salem witch
trials of the 1690s, made Americans aware of the villainy of false accusations and the thin dividing line between delusion and reality. The
deeper problem of interpreting McCarthyism was not simply the hysteria it bred but the popularity it commanded. Despite the stance of
ADA and ACCF, the majority of Americans saw communism as an
internal conspiracy as well as an external reality. They also believed
communists should be denied not only the right to teach but also the
right of citizenship, and they approved FBI's use of wiretapping and
felt it important for HUAC and other committees to continue their
investigations even if "innocent" people might be hurt. This widespread support of right-wing extremism chastened former left-wing
radicals who had once believed that "the masses" stood for reason,
progress, tolerance, and freedom.

President Truman and many liberal Democrats had also underesti-
mated McCarthy's appeal when he first went public with his wild accusations. Thus, in addition to fighting McCarthyism, many writers also
felt challenged to explain it. The sociologists Daniel Bell and Seymour
Martin Lipset began studying the "New American Right," which they
described as the intolerant behavior of the working class and the "status politics" of aspiring middle class small businessmen susceptible to
McCarthy's attacks on government and the eastern establishment.
McCarthyism was also interpreted as an anti-intellectual phenomenon
that drew on a "paranoid style" of politics that had roots in America's
traditional distrust of elites. McCarthy himself came to be viewed as a
"populist" who had inherited the Midwest's hostility toward Wall Street
and the Ivy League and as a classic "demagogue" who exploited fears
bred by the cold war. The conservative poet and historian Peter Viereck
regarded McCarthy as a vulgar rabble rouser who violated all the cul-
tivated human values that conservatism stands for: moderation, civility, decency, and tradition. But those who claimed to speak for the
"New American Conservatism"—Buckley, L. Brent Bozell, and
Willmoore Kendall—defended McCarthy against his many critics. To
the new conservatives the popularity of McCarthyism simply represented the desire of Americans to render their country inhospitable to

*The young William F. Buck-
ley, Jr., patriotically serving
his country in World War II.*

communism; the ways of McCarthy were a legitimate sanction against
subversion. Tolerance had its limits.

The years 1954–55 witnessed the founding of both William Buckley's *National Review* and Irving Howe's *Dissent*. In addition to dis-
agreeing over McCarthyism, both editors wanted America to move
toward different ideological poles. Buckley, a bright, witty polemicist
born into wealth and refinement, advocated a return to a pre-New Deal,
laissez-faire economy. Howe, an equally brilliant writer born into New
York City's working-class ghetto, argued for an economy that would
move beyond the welfare state and gradually adopt the principles of
democratic socialism. Both editors would be disappointed with the
Eisenhower administration, which seemed as reluctant to return to the
past as it was to advance toward the future.

6

The Pursuit of Happiness:
American Society and Popular Culture

ECONOMIC GROWTH AND THE SOCIAL LANDSCAPE

Although McCarthyism, the cold war, Korea and politics dominated front pages in the fifties, opinion polls profiled the American people as preoccupied with their own lives and largely nonpolitical. To most white, middle-class Americans the fifties meant television; bobby sox and the bunny hop; bermuda shorts and gray flannel suits; "I Love Lucy"; Marlon Brando astride a motorcycle and Elvis belting out "Hound Dog"; Lolita the nymphet; crew cut and duck's ass hairstyles; Marilyn Monroe; James Dean; cruising and panty raids; preppies and their cashmeres and two-toned saddle shoes; Willie Mays; Rocky Graziano; drive-in movies and restaurants; diners with chrome-leg tables and backless stools; suburbia; barbecued steaks; Billy Graham and the way to God without sacrifice; the Kinsey Report and the way to sex without sin. Few items in this list would strike one as serious, but many of them have proved durable. Indeed, such subjects fascinate even members of the post-fifties generation. In the seventies and eighties mass magazines like *Newsweek* and *Life* devoted special issues to the fifties as "The Good Old Days" and Hollywood produced *The Last Picture Show*, *American Graffiti*, and *The Way We Were*. Nostalgia even succeeded in trivializing the Korean War, as with the immensely popular "M*A*S*H."

Nostalgia is one way to ease the pain of the present. Those who survived the sixties, a decade that witnessed the turmoils of the Vietnam

War and the tragedies of political assassination, looked back wistfully on the fifties as a period of peace and prosperity. Many of those who survived the fifties, however, particularly writers and professors, passed a different verdict. "Good-by to the fifties—and good riddance," wrote the historian Eric Goldman, "the dullest and dreariest in all our history." "The Eisenhower years," judged columnist William Shannon, "have been years of flabbiness and self-satisfaction and gross materialism. . . . The loudest sound in the land has been the oink-and-grunt of private hoggishness. . . . It has been the age of the slob." The socialist Michael Harrington called the decade "a moral disaster, an amusing waste of time," and the novelist Norman Mailer derided it as "one of the worst decades in the history of man." The poet Robert Lowell summed up his impatience in two lines: "These are the tranquil Fifties, and I am forty. / Ought I to regret my seedtime?"

On the other side of the political spectrum, conservative writers tended to praise the fifties as "the happiest, most stable, most rational period the western world has ever known since 1914." They point to the seemingly pleasant fact that in the fifties, in contrast to the sixties, many nations like India and Burma achieved independence without resorting to armed force. The same era enjoyed a postwar prosperity and overcame a massive unemployment that had haunted the depression generation, and did it without raising inflation. Yet even conservatives conceded that the fifties were not a "creative time" in the realm of high culture. This was all right for many of them since "creative periods have too often a way of coinciding with periods of death and destruction."

Whatever the retrospective of writers and intellectuals, those who lived through the fifties looked upon them as a period of unbounded possibility. This was especially true of the beginning of the decade when the lure and novelty of material comforts seemed irresistible. Toward the end of the decade a barely noticeable undercurrent of dissatisfaction emerged and by the early sixties a minority of women and men would rebel against the conditions of the fifties and wonder what had gone wrong with their lives. A sweet decade for the many, it became a sour experience for the few who would go on to question not only the feminine mystique but the masculine as well. In dealing with the fifties one must deal with its contented and its discontents, two contrary states of mind that will be analyzed in the conclusion of the chapter.

The economic context is crucial. Between 1950 and 1958, the economy expanded enormously. A steady high growth rate of 4.7 percent heralded remarkable increases in living standards and other condi-

THE RATE OF INFLATION IN THE UNITED STATES, 1947–1960

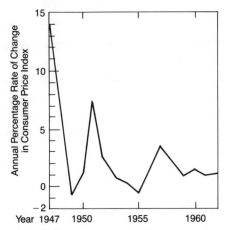

Source: U.S. Bureau of Labor Statistics. Reprinted from *History of the American Economy, Fifth Edition,* by Gary Walton and Ross M. Robertson. Copyright © 1983 by Harcourt Brace Jovanovich.

UNEMPLOYMENT IN THE UNITED STATES, 1944–1970

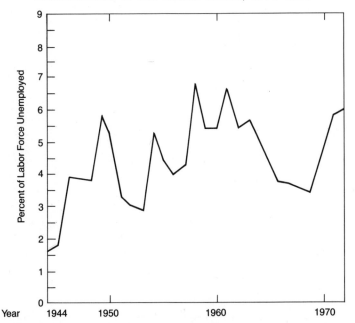

Source: U.S. Bureau of Labor Statistics. Reprinted from *History of the American Economy, Fifth Edition,* by Gary Walton and Ross M. Robertson. Copyright © 1983 by Harcourt Brace Jovanovich.

tions of life. This prosperity derived from a combination of factors: (a) the lingering postwar back-up demand for consumer goods together with increased purchasing power as a result of savings; (b) the expansion of plant and machine tool capacity, and other technological advances left by the war and revived by the cold war and Korean conflict; (c) the appearance of new and modernized industries ranging from electronics to plastics; (d) population growth and the expansion of large cities; (e) increases in the productivity, or output per man-hour, of the working force; and (f) the commitment to foreign aid, which made possible overseas credits and American exports.

Consumer Prices and Average Weekly Earnings of Production Workers in Manufacturing Industries, Selected Years, 1939–59

Year	Consumer price index (1947–49 = 100)	Net spendable weekly earnings,* worker with three dependents	
		Current (1960) dollars	1947–49 dollars
1939	59.4	$23.62	$39.76
1940	59.9	24.95	41.65
1942	69.7	36.28	52.05
1944	75.2	44.06	58.59
1945	76.9	42.74	55.58
1946	83.4	43.20	51.80
1947	95.5	48.24	50.51
1948	102.8	53.17	51.72
1949	101.8	53.83	52.88
1950	102.8	57.21	55.65
1951	111.0	61.28	55.21
1952	113.5	63.62	56.05
1953	114.4	66.58	58.20
1954	114.8	66.78	58.17
1955	114.5	70.45	61.53
1956	116.2	73.22	63.01
1957	120.2	74.97	62.37
1958	123.5	76.05	61.58
1959	124.6	80.36	64.49
Percent rise,			
1939–59	110	240	62
1950–59	21	41	16

SOURCE: U.S. Department of Labor, *Economic Forces in the U.S.A.*, 6th ed., pp. 73, 80; and *Statistical Abstract*, 1960, p. 336.

*Gross earnings minus social security and federal income taxes.

America experienced three mild recessions in the fifties, but through them all the rate of personal income grew and reached a record high of a 3.9 percent rise in 1960. If few became rich, the great majority lived more comfortably than ever before and enjoyed shorter hours on the job, as America moved to the five-day work week. Prior to the Second World War only 25 percent of the farming population had electricity. By the end of the fifties more than 80 percent had not only lighting but telephones, refrigerators, and televisions.

The generation that had borne the depression and the war was now eager to put politics behind and move into a bountiful new world. One strong indicator of confidence in the future was a sudden baby boom. Demographers had been predicting a postwar relative decline in fertility rates and no expansion of immigration quotas. Instead, population leaped from 130 million in 1940 to 165 million by the mid-fifties, the biggest increase in the history of the Republic. Population migrated as well as grew, spreading into the region that came to be called "the sun belt," states like Florida, Texas, Arizona, and California. Farms and small towns lost population. Many big cities, while still growing with lower-class and minority inhabitants, witnessed the flight of the middle class to the periphery. The massive phenomenon of suburbia would rip apart and remake the texture of social life in America.

Suburbia met a need and fulfilled a dream. During the depression and the war most Americans lived in apartments, flats, or small houses within an inner city. After the war, with GIs returning and the marriage rate doubling, as many as two million young couples had to share a dwelling with their relatives. Some settled for a cot in the living room, while married college students often had to live in off-campus quonset huts. Their immediate need for space in which to raise a family was answered by the almost overnight appearance of tracts, subdivisions, and other developments that sprawled across the landscape. Ironically, while suburban growth cut into the natural environment, felling trees and turning fields into asphalt streets, the emotional appeal of suburbia lay in a desire to recapture the greenness and calm of rural life. Thus eastern tracts featured such names as "Crystal Stream," "Robin Meadows," and "Stonybrook," while in the West the Spanish motif of "Villa Serena" and "Tierra Vista" conveyed the ambience of old, preindustrial California. In California the tracts were developed by Henry J. Kaiser and Henry Doelger, who drew on their war-time skills for mass production to provide ranch-style homes complete with backyards and front lawns. In the Northeast William Levitt offered New Yorkers and Pennsylvanians houses with shuttered windows and steep

The rush to suburbia in southern California in the early fifties.

pitched roofs to mimic the cozy Cape Cod look. Levitt had never liked cities. Having no patience with people who did, he saw his opportunity after the war when the government agreed to guarantee to banks the entire amount of a veteran's mortgage, making it possible for him to move in with no down payment, depending on the Veteran Administration's assessment of the value of the specific property. To keep building costs down, Levitt transformed the housing industry by using prefabricated walls and frames assembled on the site. In an effort to foster community spirit, he and other builders added schools, swimming pools, tennis courts, and athletic fields with Little League diamonds. For young members of the aspiring middle class, suburbia was a paradise of comfort and convenience.

Others were not so sure. "Is this the American dream, or is it a nightmare?" asked *House Beautiful.* Architectural and cultural critics complained of the monotony of house after house with the same facade, paint, and lawn inhabited by people willing to sign an agreement to keep them the same. One song writer would call them "little boxes made of ticky-tacky." Some children who grew up in them would agree, rebelling in the following decade against all that was sterile and standardized. The most angry critic was the cultural historian Lewis Mumford, author of *The City in History.* Mumford feared that Levitt was doing more to destroy the modern city than did the World War II aerial bombings. He also feared that suburbia was transforming the American character, rendering it dreary and conformist when it should be daring and courageous. "In the mass movement into suburban areas a new kind of community was produced, which caricatured both the historic city and the archetypal suburban refuge, a multitude of uniform, unidentifiable houses, lined up inflexibly at uniform distances, on uniform roads, in a treeless communal waste, inhabited by people in the same class, the same income, the same age group, witnessing the same television performances, eating the same tasteless pre-fabricated foods from the same freezers, conforming in every outward and inward respect to a common mold."

Admonishments aside, Americans were falling in love with suburbia—at least at first; some would have second thoughts and later wonder what they had bought, the theme of the cheerless film *No Down Payment* (1957). By the end of the fifties one-fourth of the population had moved to such areas. If not beautiful, suburbia was affordable, and thousands of homeless veterans were grateful to have their place in the sun for $65 per month on a full purchase price of $6,990 that included separate bedrooms for the children and a kitchen full of glittering gadgets. Such amenities also enabled housewives to be free of some domestic

HOUSING STARTS AND GROSS NATIONAL PRODUCT, JANUARY 1, 1946, TO MARCH 1, 1961

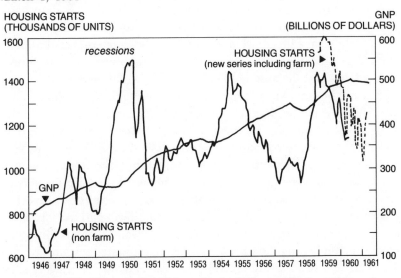

SOURCE: *Monthly Review*, Federal Reserve Bank of Minneapolis, June 1961, p. 3.

The Tupperware house party, a weekly gathering of housewives in search of companionship in new suburban communities.

chores as they became involved in community affairs while their husbands commuted to work in the cities. A frequent event was the Tupperware party, arranged by wives ostensibly to sell household conveniences but also to overcome isolation and boredom. The most serious drawback of suburbia was that its planners envisaged no need for public transportation. As a result, suburbanites became forever dependent upon the automobile. When their children reached driving age, some households became three- or even four-car families. But in the fifties, when gasoline was relatively cheap and the promising new freeways wide and uncongested, the car was seen as a solution, not a problem. Indeed, for proud teenagers it was the supreme status symbol, the one possession that with its "souped-up" carburetors and lowered chassis and various metallic colors, answered the need for freedom and diversity in a community of flatness and conformity.

In the fifties, car was king. Freeways, multilevel parking lots, shopping centers, motels, and drive-in restaurants and theaters all catered to the person behind the wheel. By 1956 an estimated seventy-five million cars and trucks were on American roads. One out of every seven workers held a job connected to the automobile industry. In suburbia the station wagon became a common sight. But really to fulfill the American dream one needed a Cadillac, or so advertisers informed the arriviste of new wealth with such effectiveness that one had to wait a year for delivery. Almost all American automobiles grew longer and wider. Their supersize and horsepower, together with more chrome and bigger tailfins, served no useful transportation purpose but were powerful enhancers of self-esteem. At the end of the decade, when many rich Texans, some country-western singers, salesmen, and even gangsters and pimps owned a Cadillac, it became what it always was, gauche, and its image declined from the sublime to the ridiculous.

In the fifties the spectacle of waste, once regarded by the older morality as a sign of sin, had become a sign of status. It was no coincidence that Americans junked almost as many cars as Detroit manufactured, thereby fulfilling Thorstein Veblen's earlier prediction that modern man would be more interested in displaying and destroying goods than in producing them. Veblen's insight into "conspicuous consumption" also took on real meaning in this era as Americans rushed out to buy the latest novelty, whether it was a convertible, TV set, deep-freeze, electric carving knife, or the "New Look" Christian Dior evening dress. The postwar splurge of consumption had been made possible by the $100 billion of savings Americans had banked during the war. Immediately after the war, household appliances were in demand, then luxuries like fashionable clothes and imported wines. For those who bought homes for $8,000 or more, luxuries were seen as necessities. The middle-class suburbanite looked out his window and "needed" what his neighbor had—a white Corvette or a swimming pool. Travel to Europe, once regarded as the "Grand Tour" only for the rich and famous, became accessible to millions of Americans in the fifties. For the masses who remained at home and took to the road, new tourist attractions sprang up, like Disneyland. Mass recreational mobility changed the nation's eating habits. In 1954 in San Bernardino, California, Ray Kroc, a high-school dropout, devised a precision stand for turning out french fries, beverages, and fifteen-cent hamburgers that grew rapidly into a fast-food empire: McDonald's.

Spending less time cooking and eating, Americans had more time for shopping. Discount houses such as Korvette's and Grant's opened up for the lower-middle class while the prestigious Neiman-Marcus catered to the needs of oil-rich Texans. Parents raised in the depression naturally felt that more was better, not only for themselves but particularly for their children. Teenagers splurged on phonograph records, bedroom decorations, cashmere sweaters, trips to Hawaii, motor-

DISTRIBUTION OF DURABLE CONSUMER GOODS IN AMERICAN FAMILIES

Year	Families owning automobiles* (percentage of all families)	Television	Refrigerators	Percentage of all wired homes with†				
				Freezers	Vacuum cleaners (floor)	Electric washers	Dryers (electric and gas)	Air conditioners
1946	n.a.	—	69.1	—	48.8	50.5	—	0.2
1947	n.a.	—	71.2	—	49.5	63.0	—	.2
1948	54	2.9	76.6	4.3	51.7	67.4	0.4	.3
1949	56	10.1	79.2	5.2	52.8	68.6	.7	.4
1950	60	26.4	86.4	7.2	56.5	71.9	1.4	.6
1951	65	38.5	86.7	9.3	57.7	73.5	2.4	.8
1952	65	50.2	89.2	11.5	59.4	76.2	3.7	1.4
1953	65	63.5	90.4	13.4	60.5	78.5	5.1	2.6
1954	70	74.1	92.5	15.1	62.2	81.3	6.6	4.0
1955	71	76.1	94.1	16.8	64.3	84.1	9.2	5.6
1956	73	81.0	96.0	18.0	66.7	86.8	11.9	7.6

SOURCE: Post-war Economic Trends in the United States, ed. Ralph Freeman. Copyright © Harper & Row, Publishers, Inc.
* Source: Board of Governors of the Federal Reserve System. Note: data relate to ownership of an automobile by some member of the family early in each year. Data are not available prior to 1948.
† Source: Electrical Merchandising, McGraw-Hill Publishing Company.

scooters, and hot rods. The seemingly infinite indulgence of the young worried many parents even as they contributed to it. In a survey 94 percent of the mothers interviewed reported that their children had asked them to buy various goods they had seen on television.

Television in America, unlike in England and much of Western Europe, was supported by the advertising industry, which did more than any other institution to fill the viewer's eyes with images of abundance. Advertisers spent $10 billion a year to persuade, not to say manipulate, the people into buying products that promised to improve their lives, whether frozen peas or French perfume. Professional football, the prime target for beer ads, invented the "two-minute warning" in the last quarter to accommodate commercials. Confronted by a medical report linking smoking to lung cancer, tobacco companies increased their ad campaigns with jingles like "Be Happy Go Lucky!" Television bloomed with romantic scenes of a dashing young man offering a cigarette to a seductively beautiful woman under a full moon. As violins rose, the match was lit, and her face turned into that of a goddess—young, eager, divine. Partial take-offs from the Bogart-Bacall films of the early forties, Madison Avenue could readily exploit such scenes, perhaps realizing that desire can always be tempted precisely because it can never be completely fulfilled.

What facilitated the illusion of fulfillment was a little rectangle of plastic dubbed the credit card. In 1950 Diner's Club distributed credit cards to select wealthy New Yorkers to give them the privilege of eating at swank restaurants without fumbling for money. By the end of the decade Sears Roebuck alone had more than ten million accounts for those who chose to live on credit or, more bluntly, to be in debt. Installment buying shot consumer indebtedness up to $196 billion, so high that certain department stores offered "debt counselors" for worried customers. One soothing nostrum was a good stiff martini, the favorite drink of suburbia and the commuters' circle. Drinking rose sharply in the fifties. So did prescription-drugs use. Sales of "tranquilizers" soared; by 1959, 1,159,000 pounds had been consumed. The following decade the Food and Drug Administration discovered that the once-popular pill "miltown" had no medicinal value. But for the fifties generation, coping with the boss's demands at work and the children's at home, popping tranquilizing drugs became a respectable adult addiction. That mental anxiety should accompany material abundance is no surprise. For centuries moralists had warned that people become unhappy when they get what they want—or think they want. Suburbia offered Americans the cleanliness and safety of a planned community, but nothing is more hopeless than planned happiness.

TELEVISION AND THE HEROES OF ENTERTAINMENT

Another form of escape from the stresses of the fifties was the amusement of the entertainment world. At the beginning of the forties, nine out of ten families had a radio. Americans spent more time listening to radio than on any other activity except work. By the end of the fifties many American households had TV sets. According to a Westinghouse Electric study, more person-hours per year were being spent watching TV than even working for pay. With a new viewing audience, TV producers had to predict Americans' taste: what they would laugh at and be moved by? What would hold their attention? For a while it was the documentaries of the Kefauver Crime Commission and the drama of the Army-McCarthy hearings. But producers soon recognized what social scientists had known for fifty years: every culture has a basic need to reassure its identity by experiencing the collective forms of popular symbolism. To fulfill that need there could be no better program than a situation comedy (soon known as "sit-com") that focused on the essential health of the American family.

The fifties watched a steady diet of that genre, which covered "The Adventures of Ozzie and Harriet," "The Danny Thomas Show," and "Father Knows Best." But by far the most successful was "I Love Lucy." The show featured Desi Arnaz, a Cuban bongo player with a thick Latin accent, and Lucille Ball, a former movie actress who played the role of a wacky housewife always threatening to leave hearth and home for a glamorous career in show biz. Her clownish antics expressed more confusion than conviction. By the end of the evening Desi was always ready to forgive, to the sigh of an audience reassured that domestic bliss can survive all marital tensions. So engrossed were Americans on Mondy nights that when Lucille Ball announced her pregnancy CBS issued weekly bulletins and then presented "Lucy Goes to the Hospital," a fictional show that took place at the same time the baby was actually delivered. It was seen by forty-four million people, twice the number of Americans who watched the inauguration of President Eisenhower the following day.

Almost as many Americans stayed home on Saturday evenings to turn on Jackie Gleason's television show. A comic genius, Gleason had a deep feeling for the dreams of the blue-collar worker who demanded

The long-running TV show, "I Love Lucy."

the best things in life. The contrast between Gleason's actual life (a mansion in the Catskills, a stretch Cadillac with bar and chauffeur) and his role as Ralph Kramden scraping by as a Brooklyn bus driver was not lost upon the audience. Teenage viewers knew what the lack of money had done to their parents' morale during the depression. The comforts of middle-class neighborhoods from which the audience viewed "The Honeymooners" contrasted with the Kramden home—a drab, two-room flat with nothing more than a bare table, chairs, sink, stove, and icebox. The audience responded not so much to Ralph's situation as his aspirations and frustrations. He was the lonely dreamer of get-rich schemes surrounded by contented neighbors and a fatalistic wife. He was also ambitious and proud and insensitive to the emotional needs of his wife Alice, whose main resources were a stoical fortitude and clever wit. "You know why I deserve that promotion, Alice?" Ralph complains upon returning from work. "Because I got it here," he shouts, pointing to his head. Without cracking a smile Alice responds "And here . . . and here . . . and especially here," pointing to each of her hips and then her stomach. "Pack your bags, Alice. You're going on a trip—right to the moon. Bang, zoom, smash, right to the moon, Alice."

Never once intimidated by Ralph's physical threats, Alice endures

Jackie Gleason in a scene from the TV show, "The Honeymooners."

his tirades and caters to his moods, eventually winning over his affections and even showing him to have been wrong, at which point he admits, in a concluding moment of both humility and endearment, "Baby, you're the greatest." Americans loved it. Perhaps the show made them feel good about themselves, especially those who had escaped both the inner city and the life of the working class.

In the fifties TV did much virtually to define, and perhaps determine, the subjects to which Americans attended: the tasteless amusement of Milton Berle and his pet monkey; the subtle and spontaneous wit of Groucho Marx and "You Bet Your Life"; the celebrity appearances, vaudeville acts, and glimpses of high culture on Ed Sullivan's "Toast of the Town"; the sophisticated repartee of Jack Paar's "Tonight" show; the detailed police work of "Dragnet" and the hardboiled Jack Webb; and the heightening drama of weekly quiz shows ("Twenty-One," "64 Thousand Dollar Question") that seemed to display the American intellect at its best. At first the winners of the quizzes were supposedly average Americans, like the Italian shoemaker who could answer the most obscure questions on opera. Then came the supreme master of knowledge, Charles Van Doren, an assistant professor of

English at Columbia University and son of the distinguished literary scholar Mark Van Doren. Week after week Van Doren stood in a glass booth seemingly wracking his brain to come up with last second answers and walk away with a bundle of cash. Instantly he became a campus hero. Once he walked into his classroom with a briefcase containing examination papers and asked his students what they thought he was carrying. "Money!" they all gleefully shouted. Then a losing contestant informed the district attorney that the program was rigged and Van Doren, after early denials, confessed before a congressional committee that he had indeed been "deeply involved in a deception."

Public reaction to the quiz scandals reflected the state of morality in the fifties. Van Doren had lied to his family, his lawyer, his colleagues, and the grand jury. But when he came clean some congressmen commended him, CBS received letters recommending that he not be fired, and Columbia students held a rally to protest his dismissal. Journalists reported that many Americans they interviewed saw nothing wrong with Van Doren's conduct. He only wanted what they wanted—money and fame, in that order. How can Van Doren be judged, Columbia students asked, when all morality is relative? Disgusted, Professor Hans Morgenthau informed them that "there is not a rebel among you," and he reminded them of German students who had risked all defying Hitler's lies. The novelist John Steinbeck wrote Adlai Stevenson a letter that the *New Republic* ran under the title "Have We Gone Soft?" "If I wanted to destroy a nation, I would give it too much and I would have it on its knees, miserable, greedy, and sick. . . . On all levels American society is rigged. . . . I am troubled by the cynical immorality of my country. It cannot survive on this basis."

In the early 1960s, Newton Minow, Chairman of the Federal Communications Commission, challenged broadcasters to spend an entire day watching television, which he judged "a vast wasteland." Teachers blamed TV for children's low reading scores and short attention span. Some communication experts claimed that because TV severs the connection between pictures and words, the viewer could only experience what he saw with no means of grasping it. Marshall McLuhan expected that TV could bring the whole world to focus on common concerns; yet he too feared that the visual image would replace the spoken word so thoroughly that written language would become obsolete. Such dire prophecies lacked historical perspective. Centuries earlier monastic scholars feared the coming of the printing press and literacy because such developments would render memory unnecessary and thereby destroy concentration and reflection. Ironically, the TV quiz shows taught

Americans to value such qualities as memory, however faked, because it would lead not to God but to Mammon.

While Van Doren faded into obscurity, other more genuine heroes of entertainment rose to preeminence in the fifties, especially in the field of athletics. Occasionally, scandals made the sports headlines too. Revelations emerged of a boxer taking a dive or of star players on leading basketball teams like University of Kentucky and City College of New York shaving points after being bribed by professional gamblers. While most people might condone a little cheating in order to win, as with the TV quizzes, losing is not part of the American way of life, as the philosopher William James noted when he lamented "the moral flabbiness born of the bitch-goddess of success." Yet James was not a jock. Vince Lombardi, a young assistant football coach at Fordham University in the fifties who would later become a national monument with the Green Bay Packers, knew what sports was all about when he uttered his now-famous epigram: "Winning isn't everything; it's the only thing."

The rising attendance at sports events in the forties, and the phenomenal number of TV viewers in the fifties, reflected the leisure time now being enjoyed in postwar society and the local pride of Americans cheering on their hometown teams. As in the twenties, the era of Babe Ruth and Jack Dempsey, interest in athletics in the fifties also signified decline of interest in politics and a need to find male idols in forms of competition whose outcome was, unlike the corporate life of the business world, suspenseful if not unpredictable. College stars were campus heroes, far more popular to coeds than a history major or a slide-rule-carrying engineering student. For many male youths, "Big League" professionals became more immediate role models of skill and finesse: Willie Mays throwing out a runner from New York's Polo Ground's deep center field; Y.A. Tittle breaking the National Football League's passing records with his well-timed long bombs; Bob Cousy dazzling Boston Celtics fans with the ball-handling moves of a magician and the footwork of a ballet dancer. Athletes in the early fifties were celebrities but not yet reborn capitalists. By the end of the decade, however, the huge revenues from TV advertisements made possible new franchises, spectacular players contracts, and other costs, some of which wealthy team owners could write off as tax deductions. The ABC network had a profitable association with the Gillette safety razor company sponsoring boxing matches and later Monday night football. The commercialization of sports added a corollary to Lombardi's doctrine: winning isn't everything; money is.

Even more important than money was the quality that makes athletic victory possible—talent. To appreciate that quality American society would have to face its own racial prejudices. The civil rights movement of the fifties was based on the constitutional principle of equality of opportunity. Ironically, the entry of black athletes into professional sports had less to do with equality than superiority. But recognition of the sheer natural ability of the black male was slow and grudging. In the immediate postwar years the most white Americans would concede in professional sports was the field of boxing. Here Joe Louis, the shy, slow shuffling black heavyweight who hit with lightening speed, would be succeeded by Sugar Ray Robinson, a multi-weight champion who thrilled white Americans with his blinding jabs and hooks even as they cheered Jake LaMotta and Rocky Graziano. But boxing had been racially mixed since the days of bare-knuckled fighting, even if the managers remained white and controlled the matches and the purse.

The important breakthrough in racial barriers came in spring 1947 when Jackie Robinson stepped onto Ebbets Field as the Brooklyn Dodgers' second baseman. "It just won't work," general manager Branch Rickey was told by a baseball buff convinced that a black would be unacceptable to players and fans alike. But Rickey defied the league and took a gamble. He also warned Robinson, a UCLA graduate who starred in several sports, that white players would try to hit or spike

Brooklyn Dodger second-baseman Jackie Robinson attempting to steal home against the Chicago Cubs.

him. "You can't fight back, boy. That's going to be the hardest part of all. No matter what happens, *you can't fight back.*" Some players did try to injure or insult him. But Robinson kept his cool, and by summer he was headed for the Rookie-of-the-Year award, quarreling with umpires, and enjoying the adulation of fans and the respect of fellow players. A few years later the first black players entered professional basketball. Soon NFL football scouts would prowl black colleges like Grambling to recruit halfbacks and linemen. Althea Gibson became the first black to play in the US Lawn Tennis Association championship matches. In amateur athletics blacks also became a familiar presence and, in other amateur events like the Olympics, a vital factor since the thirties. But all athletes, white as well as black, wanted to make the pros and earn the big money from commercial endorsements in addition to salaries. For the talented few, sports provided a ladder of social mobility; for the untalented many, a spectatorial drama of skill and stamina.

During the forties and fifties music became widely accessible to the masses of people. Elaborate hi-fi sets replaced the simple victrola and the jukebox lifted the spirits of the lonely, the tense, and the bored. Light operas like "Oklahoma," "South Pacific," and "My Fair Lady" played to packed theaters, and Americans listened to Mary Martin and Ethel Merman belt out popular songs.

One of the most curious shifts in popular musical tastes that separated the forties and the fifties involved the careers of Frank Sinatra and Elvis Presley. During World War II Sinatra suddenly became the idol of hordes of bobby soxers who were mysteriously mesmerized by his crooning serenades, some shrieking and swooning, others fainting or possibly pretending to. Wherever "The Voice" appeared he was mobbed by delirious teenagers. Watching the nation's craze, psychologists spoke of "mass hypnosis" and social scientists tried to make sense of crowd behavior and charismatic personalites. Yet the hysteria ended almost as suddenly as it began, and by the early fifties Sinatra could not land even a Hollywood film contract. Then another singer captured the youth's imagination and another mode of music determined the nation's sound and rhythm for years to come—Elvis and rock 'n' roll.

Contrary to popular impression, Presley did not enter the world a natural rebel. Born in Tupelo, Mississippi, in 1935, Elvis was a quiet, ordinary student who stayed close to his protective mother throughout his high-school years. Not until the mid-fifties did he become the legendary symbol of danger and dissonance. His revolutionary music, a fusion of white country and western and black rhythm and blues, would

Singer Frank Sinatra, at the height of his popularity among teenage "bobby-soxers" in 1943.

later influence such groups as the Beatles and Rolling Stones. (Curiously, most commentators in the fifties were certain that rock 'n' roll would quickly disappear as merely another fad, although at least one psychiatrist likened the "mass ecstasy" to a long repressed "prehistoric rhythmic trance.") Unlike Sinatra, who appeared so emaciated as to be starving, Presley exuded raw strength and sensuality. Parents brought up on the mawkish music of Bing Crosby tried in vain to shield their children from contamination by the new phenomenon sweeping the country. They were aghast watching "Elvis the Pelvis" with his tight pants, full, pouting lips, and shoulder-length black hair, grip the microphone and buck his hips in gestures so lewd that some TV producers would only film him from the waist up. Magnetic but aloof, self-possessed yet sad, Presley stood before screaming crowds as the icon of the fifties, charging teenagers with energy and emotion in scores like "I Want You, I Need You, I Love You," "Don't Be Cruel," and "Love Me Tender." A cult figure, Presley partook of the fifties consumerism. He purchased a fleet of Cadillacs (some merely to give away), a jet, a ranch, and mansions and estates. He flouted an assortment of rings, pistols, capes, and huge gold buckles. Although parents, teach-

Elvis Presley brings the new music of rock-and-roll back to his hometown, Tupelo, Mississippi, in 1956.

ers, and church leaders denounced him as vulgar and obscene, Presley was for the young the perfect symbol of all that was exciting and forbidden, a voice that seemed paradoxically both aggressive and tender, strong yet vulnerable.

Commentators in the fifties often compared Presley to Marlon Brando, James Dean, and Montgomery Clift, three new film stars who revolutionized acting methods and left audiences emotionally drained and confused. In the postwar years Hollywood had experienced a crisis of confidence, brought on in part by the Red Scare, the threat of television, and competition from European film makers. Desperately, American producers turned to panaceas like the "3-D" movie in which viewers wore dark, polarized glasses to create the illusion of depth. The traditional western featuring John Wayne continued to delight Americans, and in *High Noon*, starring Gary Cooper, the audience witnessed a simple morality tale in which the single individual is abandoned and left on his own to combat the forces of evil—a document that can be interpreted as a criticism of McCarthyism or of conformity itself. Yet it was Brando, Dean, and Clift who emerged as the new existential heroes of film. All were actors who conveyed complex emotions more felt than understood in an attempt to express what could not be voiced. In *On the Waterfront, East of Eden,* and *From Here to Eternity,* Brando, Dean, and Clift displayed a sensitivity and depth of pure feeling that rendered them almost defenseless against the world. Indeed the film *Rebel Without A Cause* is haunted by tragedy. All of its four stars—Dean, Natalie Wood, Sal Mineo, and Vic Morrow—would suffer tragic deaths.*

To the fifties generation, James Dean communicated the emotions of a crippled romantic, a moody idealist whose dreams about the world have already been destroyed by his resentment toward it. "My mother died on me when I was nine years old," he complained of his broken home. "What does she expect me to do? Do it all myself?" Raised in Indiana by a father and step-mother, Dean had little interest in school except for basketball, track, and dramatics. After dropping out of college in California, he held a string of odd jobs before heading for New York and acting school. There he was discovered and immediately compared to Brando in *The Wild One:* the same wandering, lonely eyes, the scornful lip, the inarticulate mumblings, and the controlled

---

*Dean died in an auto accident, Wood drowned, Mineo was stabbed to death, and Morrow was killed in a helicopter crash on a film set.

The moody, enigmatic actor James Dean, symbol of the confusions and unfocused defiance that seethed beneath the "quiet generation" of the fifties.

rage that made being "cool" the strategy of survival. Dean appealed especially to young Americans. They felt his need for love and knew why he was so misunderstood by an adult world incapable of rendering it. "And who in the audience, what creature that ever lived, felt he was loved enough?" wrote the film critic Pauline Kael of Dean's performance. But it was not only love. Dean also played the restless, searching youth, hungering for innocence, knowing too much about the compromises and complacencies of the world. Thus in films he appeared both wiser and sadder than the older characters. Yet he would make no reconciliation with reality. To do so was to adjust and settle down, precisely what society demanded of the fifties generation. "Whoso would be a man," wrote Emerson a century earlier, "must be a nonconformist." On September 30, 1955, Dean's speeding white Porsche-Spider collided with another car; the steering wheel went right through him. Lost and lovable, the symbol of troubled youth, James Dean was dead at the age of twenty-four. So many young Americans had modeled their dress and mannerisms after Dean that his sudden death wrenched a vital part of their own selves. Some denied the death, hoping he was in the hospital for facial surgery; others broke down in tears. One high school English teacher, feeling the grief of his students, suggested they read A. E. Housman's poem, "To an Athlete Dying Young":

··

Smart lad, to slip betimes away
From fields where glory does not stay
And early though the laurel grows
It withers quicker than the rose.

··

YOUTH CULTURE, STUDENT LIFE, SEX

"Live fast, die young, and have a good-looking corpse." The lines by the novelist Willard Motley haunted sensitive youths of the fifties generation, many of whom experienced the era with more unease than did their parents. As children they had come to know the horrors of the bomb from the media; in school they were taught "duck-and-cover" exercises in case of attack; at home some of the affluent heard their parents speak of building bomb shelters in the backyards. Teenagers often knew someone who had been killed in an auto accident or drag race. A best-selling novel, Irving Shulman's *The Amboy Dukes*, intended

Actor Marlon Brando in The Wild One *(1953).*

to expose the brutality of urban street gangs; for young males it had the opposite effect of glorifying courage in the face of violence. A similar response could be felt after watching such films as *Rebel Without A Cause, The Wild One,* and *Blackboard Jungle,* where the opening scene thunders with the theme song, "Rock-Around-the-Clock," a shrill of seething rebellion. Asked what he was rebelling against, Brando replied: "What've ya got?" Perhaps the quest for security on the part of the parents drove their children to desire risk and adventure all the more. Boys cruising in hot rods and quaffing six-packs of beer knew they were flirting with danger, as did those girls who risked pregnancy to discover the secret pleasures of the body. Why not? The fifties was the first generation in modern history to know that the world could end tomorrow.

If atomic war breaks out, "I'm going to sit right to hell on top of it. I'll volunteer for it, I swear I will." Thus spoke one of J. D. Salinger's characters in *The Catcher in Rye,* a novel read and treasured by millions of youths who also sensed that the best response to the idiocy of the nuclear age was a good dose of black humor. The character Holden Caulfield became a hero to students of the fifties generation, embodying their worries and their wonders, their revulsion against the phoniness of adult society and their quest for a sense of self in a vulgar and obscene world. The real world was as nauseating as the graffiti on the wall of a public school. "If you had a million years to do it in, you couldn't rub out even half the 'Fuck You' signs in the world. It's impossible." All the subjects of fifties—war, death, sex, personal relations, commitment, religion, happiness, suffering, love, marriage—render Caulfield both fearful and fascinated as he tries to preserve his innocence from life's inevitable involvements. A former English teacher quotes the German philosopher Wilhelm Steckel: "The mark of the immature man is that he wants to die nobly for a cause, while the mark of a mature man is that he wants to live humbly for one." Caulfield flees from such advice. By the end of the book, however, he recognizes that his own pose of virtuous innocence may be just as shallow as the compromises of everyday society. Some poems of Emily Dickinson are on his dead brother's baseball mitt. In them is embodied the connection between death and isolation, and the need to rejoin the world and accept the loss of innocence as part of the magic of youth that cannot be prolonged. But Salinger was hardly advocating the well-adjusted life of humble maturity. Although his clear-eyed criticisms of polite society were more focused than Dean's stuttering incoherence, he still sympathized with those teenagers whose cries for love and understand-

The means of transportation for adults, the car became a place to "make-out" for teenagers.

ing went unheard. The last thing the rebels without a cause wanted was more authority and discipline.

Indeed, authority seemed to have broken down in the postwar years as the youth culture showed signs of unruliness and disorder. In the inner cities juvenile delinquency and gang fights grew alarmingly. In suburbia newspapers reported stories of all-night drinking parties and secret "non-virgin clubs." "Teen-agers on the Rampage," announced *Time* after surveying a week of violence in high schools from Maine to California. According to the FBI, one half of all arrests for burglary, robbery, rape, aggravated assault, and even murder involved Americans eighteen or under. To many teenagers stealing a car meant not so much a criminal act as a "joy ride." Some social scientists blamed youth crime on lurid comic books and violence in the media. What puzzled criminologists and social scientists was that juvenile delinquency increased as America became more prosperous. How could respect for authority be taught in a culture of freedom and affluence?

According to the anthropologist Margaret Mead, it could not be taught. In *The School in American Culture* (1951), she noted that in previous eras education was responsible for transmitting the truths of the past. Now it needed to address the uncertainties of the future. Today's teachers, especially the experienced ones, Mead said, were disoriented precisely because their knowledge had become irrelevant due to the rapid pace of change. Small wonder they found students with little respect and even less curiosity for learning and willingness to work. Facing a "world which this adult generation is unable to grasp, to manage, to plan for," teachers needed all the more to convey "a readiness to use *unknown* ways to solve unknown problems."

One author who believed the problem was both knowable and soluble was Dr. Benjamin M. Spock. Spock's *Common Sense Book of Baby and Child Care* (1946) became the best-seller of the postwar era, with as many as twenty-two million readers poring over it as gospel. Before the child arrived at school he must be reared properly in an atmosphere of benevolent and systematic attention. It was natural for parents to want to raise their children traditionally, with punishments and spankings for rudeness, disobedience, thumb-sucking, crying for attention, and, later on in adolescence, masturbating in the bathroom. Do not be afraid of what others may think, Spock advised. "You know more than you think you do." With a nudging geniality, Spock explained why parents should not fear spoiling the child by meeting the basic needs not only for food but also for "comforting and loving."

The kindly Spock wanted to enlighten the task of parenting in order to save the child from the coercive and crippling repressions of past generations. Other writers, however, sensing that the loving mother, not the punitive father, would rear the child, saw a kind of soft tyranny where Spock saw only a healthy tenderness. The author Philip Wylie's *Generation of Vipers* (1942) opened up the prospect of "Momism." Wylie had in mind the American mother who had become both child cuddler and censor, a manipulative authoritarian presence whose constant sheltering led young boys to rebel against the female-dominated household. This same syndrome, Wylie thought, would lead girls to seek either a strong father figure in a future husband or to follow the mother and seek a weak object over whom she could exercise power. Other writers like Max Lerner speculated that a matriarchal upbringing could lead American boys to identify with the mother's moral values, too sissified for the real masculine world and so silent on carnal knowledge that sexual life becomes associated "with an impossible goal of purity." Yet most social scientists, including Lerner, recognized another truth—ultimately, peers, not parents, most influenced the attitudes and mores of young Americans in schools and colleges.

Spock spoke of home, but his message carried further, as an alleged "permissiveness" pervaded the nation's schools. Its presence led to considerable debate in the fifties over "progressive education," the "child-centered curriculum" and other experimental programs that derived from the pedagogic theories of John Dewey. From the turn of the century the benign and learned philosopher wanted to save America's children from dying of boredom in the classroom. He wrote scores of books advocating new teaching methods that emphasized the unstructured acquisition of knowledge. Students would learn "by doing," by undertaking practical, problem-solving activities that required working together with others. These activities would meet the needs and interests of the students themselves. Dewey's theory rested on his pragmatic assumption that all knowledge was interest-bound, but it failed to take into account that what students were immediately interested in might not help them in the long run. Dewey came to recognize dilemmas in his theory of learning, particularly its logical conclusion that led to the disappearance of authority in the classroom. But many of Dewey's disciples ignored his reservations and continued to experiment with experimental education. As a result America's elementary and secondary schools seemed to some critics a bedlam. The historian Arthur Bestor analyzed the problem in *Educational Wastelands:* too much time wasted on frivolous assemblies, excursions, and field trips.

President Eisenhower voiced a common complaint in *Life* magazine in 1959. "Educators, parents, and students must be continually stirred by the defects in our educational system. They must be induced to abandon that educational path that, rather blindly, they have been following as a result of John Dewey's teachings."

Most Americans who had read Rudolf Flesch's *Why Johnny Can't Read,* a best-seller published in 1955, would have agreed with the president. Flesch's book proved to be an alarmist tract, which assumed that teaching remedial reading indicated America was a nation of illiterates. Actually, by the end of the fifties the number of Americans over age twenty-five who were functionally illiterate (incapable of reading beyond the fifth-grade level) was 8.4 percent. In the early forties tests were conducted to measure the relative success of college students who had been educated by progressive methods against those from traditional schools. The progressive students came out on top, in grades and honors as well as in curiosity, ambition, and a sense of public responsibility. During World War II, however, the military services blamed progressive educators for lack of discipline and desertion among soldiers, and with the advent of the cold war Dewey and his followers were attacked for imposing a "collectivist philosophy" on America that allegedly derived from Karl Marx.

Dewey, a staunch critic of Marxism, was the wrong target. The real proposal for a collectivist form of education came from an opponent of Dewey and the pragmatists, the behaviorist B. F. Skinner. A Harvard psychology professor, Skinner claimed that by controlling the stimuli to which students are subjected, their responses can be controlled and directed, even by impersonal teaching machines. Skinner wanted to control thought in order to modify behavior; Dewey wished students to use their minds and think critically. Yet while Skinner's message was clear, Dewey's was ambiguous: students should think for themselves but work together with others and be cooperative rather than competitive. The aim of education was "life-adjustment."

The term that came to describe the college generation of the fifties was alienated, which Yale Professor Kenneth Keniston defined as "uncommitted." He and other observers of the campus scene were dismayed by students' indifference to participation in public affairs, their preoccupation with the present, their lack of conviction and curiosity, their sense that life had no deeper meaning than securing a career, their fear of involvement in anything other than the frivolities of a fraternity or sorority, their insouciance in the face of social problems, their unconcern about everything except their looks and popularity, their acceptance of the status quo—in two words, their complacency and conformity. This was the "silent generation" that the radical sixties would repudiate like a plague from the past, a generation more interested in staging panty raids on dormitories than in political assaults on the establishment. But if the generation was silent it was not inactive and it turned inward to seek adventures in private pleasures, particularly sex.

The amount of attention the media devoted to sex in the fifties may be misleading since there is reason to doubt significant changes in behavior actually occurred. Sex was then an emotion more felt than fulfilled. It was also a fantasy, and if fantasies reflect what people desire and not necessarily what they do, desires nonetheless are a large part of the human secrets of life.

During the decade, while teachers and professors were lamenting the decline in educational standards and ministers and priests the decline of morality, teenagers and college students were awakening to something stirring in their own bodies, something at once new, at least to them, and exciting and confusing, a subject more seen and felt than heard and understood. It could be seen in *Playboy*, which started publishing in 1955, exposing more naked angles to the female body than male students could ever imagine, fleshy images that aroused erotic fantasies and made one forget Somerset Maugham's witty warning about sex: the pleasure is momentary, the price damnable, and the position ridiculous. Sex could be read about in *Lolita*, Vladimir Nabokov's popular novel in which a professor who is sexually obsessed with a bobby-soxer, discovers it is she, wily nymphet, who ravishes him, all the while blowing bubble gum. Sex could be pondered in *The Apartment*, a film proving that the afternoon trysts of Shirley MacLaine and Jack Lemmon could do much to compensate for the dullness of office work. And it could be savored in the movies of Marilyn Monroe and Brigitte Bardot. Monroe dazzled the male audience with her luscious red lips, inviting open mouth, and mandolin-shaped buttocks; Bardot offered tousled blonde hair, a petite torso wrapped in a revealing blouse and skin-tight jeans tucked into risqué leather boots, and the cat eyes of a brazen coquette. Images seemed to mirror reality. Both actresses made it clear in their public lives that no one man could satisfy their sensual appetites. Morally, the fifties was a difficult time; visually, it was divine.

Educators vainly attempted to teach the young about sex, but usually in hygiene courses that dealt clinically with the mechanics of reproduction. Most students had to learn sex by themselves and often they learned it in automobiles, whether parked on some remote road or

Actress and sex symbol Marilyn Monroe, from a scene in the 1953 movie How to Marry a Millionaire.

under the looming screen of a drive-in movie. Lusting boys wondered how far they could go; "nice" girls wondered about how far to go before risking reputation and pregnancy. Not until 1960 did the United States Food and Drug Administration approve the safety of an oral contraceptive, soon to be called "the pill." It arrived too late to help the fifties generation overcome its fears and frustrations. Meanwhile, Americans young and old wanted to know more about sex.

Their curiosities were met by two postwar publications, *Sexual Behavior in the Human Male* (1948) and *Sexual Behavior in the Human Female* (1953), both by Alfred Kinsey and his colleagues of the Institute for Sexual Research at Indiana University. Trained as a zoologist, Kinsey was a collector with a passion for classifying and cataloguing the facts of natural history. His approach to carnal data was equally taxonomic, replete with graphs, charts, and tables. Kinsey has been criticized for confining his sample to midwestern states and for interviewing mainly white middle-class subjects, half of them college graduates. But the conclusions he drew from his 18,000 sex histories were nevertheless eye-opening, even to Mrs. Kinsey, who remarked of her husband, "I hardly see him at night since he took up sex."

Fifty percent of American husbands had committed adultery and 85 percent had sexual intercourse before marriage. Ninety-five percent of males had been sexually active before the age of fifteen and by the ages sixteen and seventeen the activity was at a peak. The average unmarried male had three or four orgasms a week. Nearly 90 percent of men had relations with prostitutes by their thirty-fifth birthday, and one out of six American farm boys had copulated with farm animals. As to females, two out of three had engaged in premarital petting. Fifty percent were non-virgins before marriage. One out of every six girls had experienced orgasm prior to adolescence, and one in four by the age of fifteen. More than one wife in every four had committed adultery before the age of forty (26 percent or over seven million), and three out of every four non-virgins did not regret their sexual adventures; the most promiscuous were the least regretful and the most regretful were the least promiscuous. When asked why they remained chaste, 22 percent of the virgins acknowledged the reason was "lack of opportunity." One out of every three males had some adolescent homosexual experience, as had one out of every seven females. Ten percent of men were "more or less exclusively homosexual" for at least three years of their lives, and 4 percent of the male population (2,600,000) were "exclusively homosexual throughout their lives, after the onset of adolescence."

No one knew how accurate Kinsey's figures were and no one knew what to make of them. Fearing the worst, a few politicians persuaded the Rockefeller Foundation to withdraw support of Kinsey's Institute for Sexual Research. A double standard prevailed. The male study aroused relatively little objection, but when the female document emerged a few years later some Americans regarded it as a threat to women's virtue. Such confusing and misleading subjects as the vaginal and clitoral orgasm could not be openly discussed in the fifties. Nor could homosexuality, despite public fascination with Christine Jorgensen, a transvestite who underwent a "sex change" in Denmark and commanded the headlines throughout the election year 1952; or the successful Broadway play *Tea and Sympathy*, which dealt sensitively with a shy male youth who could not consummate the act of love with the opposite sex because of his repressed secret. Very acceptable, however, were big breasts, and those who had them—Jayne Mansfield, Jane Russell, Mamie Van Doren, Marilyn Monroe, Elizabeth Taylor. These desirables covered magazines in poses that defied the laws of geometry.

But even these monuments to photography could mislead by confusing fantasy for reality. Was there a sexual revolution in the fifties? Hardly. Had there been, most likely the increasing sales of Hugh Hefner's

Playboy would have slackened as American males enjoyed real intimacy, not surrogate figures smiling mindlessly at the camera.

Among the lower classes uninvestigated by Kinsey and perhaps
untouched by *Playboy*, sex still had more to do with having a lot of
children than having multiple orgasms. Married middle-class adults
probably enjoyed more sexual intimacy with their marital partners than
their parents or grandparents ever contemplated. During the decade
there were rumors of commuting husbands having affairs with office
girls while their suburban wives slept with the milkman or the tennis
coach. Hollywood celebrities had their liaisons plastered all over the
headlines. The movie actress Ingrid Bergman shocked the world when
she left her husband, ran off with Roberto Rossellini, her Italian lover
and film director, had a child by him, and refused to repent. The
anthropologist Margaret Mead suggested that marital infidelity was
rooted in a modern democratic culture devoted to freedom of choice;
but her suggestion was as exceptional as Bergman's behavior was sensational.

The striking thing about the fifties was not the coming crisis of the
modern family but its enduring stability. True, the rising divorce rate
alarmed Americans in the immediate postwar years. But it soon leveled
off and then decreased so that at the end of the fifties the rate was near
that of the forties—1.4 percent versus 2.5 percent. Neither marriage
nor the family had been threatened by the Kinsey report. Monogamy
may have been strained by the freeing effect of carnal knowledge, but
most Americans remained inhibited and feared their sexual feelings as
soon as they felt them. "Sex is Fun—or Hell," was how J. D. Salinger
put it in one of his short stories. In the words of one memoirist, women
in particular vacillated between "titillation and terror." Ultimately most
married men and women accepted their situation, for better or for worse.
Society said they should, and in the fifties the pressures of society, not
the risqué pleasures of the body, dictated the conduct of life.

THE AUTHORITY OF SOCIETY AND THE FATE OF THE INDIVIDUAL

While sexual morality remained intact, in deed if not in thought, another
much quieter revolution was under way. Earlier in American history,
especially during the Progressive era of the pre-World War I years, it
was assumed that America could best be understood through study of
its political institutions. In the depression years of the thirties, radical-

ism dominated academic and intellectual circles, and the focus naturally shifted to economics and the "contradictions" of capitalism. The fifties found another focus—American society as a phenomenon governed by its own inherent nature.

Society now came to be seen as the key to social order and cohesion. Almost all behavior called for a sociological explanation based on the attitudes and values shared by Americans, forces that were often subtle if not invisible. Three books, very influential in their time, threw light on Americans in the fifties: William H. Whyte's *The Organization Man*, Will Herberg's *Protestant, Catholic, Jew*, and David Riesman's *The Lonely Crowd.* Whyte proposed to describe a transformation of values in the everyday world of work and career; Herberg sought to account for a reorientation of religion from a God-centered faith to a society-based utility; Riesman traced the forces that have changed the American character itself. All three authors were profoundly disturbed by their analyses, for what seemed at stake was the fate of the individual in modern mass society.

Ostensibly, Whyte's "organization men" dealt with middle-management workers in the all-inclusive modern corporation. But implicitly his analysis applied to almost all large-scale institutions in contemporary America. A former editor of *Fortune* magazine, Whyte was convinced that the ways of business would shape the larger culture as Americans became imprisoned in the new fetish of "togetherness," "team work," and "group think." Such tendencies derived from a variety of converging sources: new schools of industrial relations that conceived the labor force as a social system in which each worker found his identity; theories of progressive education that emphasized adaptation to norms and a practical curriculum designed to serve society rather than individual curiosity; empirical techniques of science in which investigators worked in smoothly functional units; and the interview methods and personality tests of corporations that screened out all potential employees who might be different, eccentric, or disruptive. As a result of these inexorable tendencies, Whyte saw a departure from the older Protestant ethic. Fading were hard work, frugality, entrepreneurial risk-taking, and individual self-reliance. Emerging to take their place was a "social ethic" based on cooperation, security, group well-being, and surrender to the "togetherness of the whole." Even ambition seemed at risk as more Americans chose to get along, rather than to get ahead. The important thing was to be well-liked. This meant adjusting one's behavior to the demands of the larger community, whether at the office or at home in suburbia. Whyte was so opposed to the individual's acquiescence to the all-absorbing systems of social organization that he even recommended cheating on personality tests. Thus, diversity and dissent could survive the quiet tyranny of total sociability. *The Organization Man* carried a curious message, at once radical and conservative: the task facing the true individual was not to challenge society but to infiltrate it, not to overthrow the system but to take it over by playing by its own rules. The message left a basic question unanswered: once "inside the whale," to use George Orwell's expression, where would the authentic person find means to resist the organization's enticements so that the autonomy of private conscience could be preserved?

For centuries conscience had been the province of religious conviction, the inner domain of faith and hope, doubt and guilt. For Will Herberg, however, even religion had become a social phenomenon. God was now less an acutely experienced presence than a shallowly accepted convenience. Paradoxically, Americans were both religious and irreligious at the same time, combining a "mounting religiosity" with a "pervasive secularism." In the fifties the upsurge of religion could be seen everywhere: the dramatic rise of church attendance; prayer at cabinet meetings and professions of faith by politicians and celebrities ("God is a living Doll," opined the buxom movie star Jane Russell); the enormous sums of money spent on religious literature; polls revealing that 96 percent of Americans believed in God; the popular Hollywood film *The Ten Commandments;* and in the top drawer of every desk in every hotel and motel room the ubiquitous Gideon's Bible. "Our government makes no sense," President Eisenhower advised Americans, "unless it is founded on a deeply felt religious belief—and I don't care what it is." Nor did Protestant ministers seem to care. "The storehouse of dynamic power on which you may draw is faith. Not religion, not God, but Faith," exhorted one minister. The popular evangelist Billy Graham informed Americans that "one fifth of all the teachings of Christ was given over to money and stewardship."

To Herberg, a former communist theoretician who converted to Judaism, all utterances of religious belief without a discriminating theological content were insidious and idolatrous. Surely Kierkegaard was correct in observing that Christians cannot bear the real burdens of Christianity. Modern religion had become a narcotic that eased the pains of existence, not a "fear and trembling" in the face of God's judgment. Herberg explained religious behavior much as Whyte had explained social behavior. But while Whyte traced the Americans' need for "belongingness" and "togetherness" to the logic of social organization, Herberg traced the same phenomenon to immigrant and ethnic tensions that compelled third-generation Americans to seek identity in one of the three dominant religions, Protestantism, Catholicism, and Judaism. In an ever-changing social environment, institutionalized religion functioned as "self-identification and social location." Saint Augustine believed in order to know; Americans believed in order to belong. To be seen in church or the synagogue was the best evidence that one was a solid member of the community.

Nothing in the findings of Whyte or Herberg would have surprised David Riesman. In *The Lonely Crowd* Riesman also saw America gripped by transformation from one social-character structure to another. Riesman posited the existence of three character types: the "tradition-directed" person who lived in stable, preindustrial communities and drew his values from his predecessors; the "inner-directed" man of the nineteenth century age of capitalism who relied upon the privacy of conscience to determine his ruggedly individualistic life-style; and the "other-directed" American of modern mass society who received his attitudes and values from his peer group or from the dictates of society itself.

According to Riesman, mid-twentieth century America was shifting profoundly from the older, inner-directed character—a man work-conscious and fearless even when alone against public opinion—to the contemporary, other-directed person who feared being different, even feared being too successful. This shift from character to personality implied a shift in values from achievement and industry to adjustment and conformity. Like Whyte and Herberg, Riesman believed Americans were suffering from oversocialization. Ultimately Riesman stood for autonomy and what the literary critic Lionel Trilling called "the poetry of individualism." Americans should know that it was right and healthy to lead a life outside the group and to hold unconventional values even though they may spell failure in the eyes of society.

While *The Lonely Crowd* became a minor classic in sociology, it has its share of critics. Some scholars pointed to the nineteenth century observations of Alexis de Tocqueville, who wrote that Americans have always been under the sway of group pressures, and have always succumbed to the vicissitudes of public opinion and the "tyranny" of the majority. Others insisted that certain ideals—equality, achievement—have shaped American character since the eighteenth century. How, also, could Riesman's conformists account for a youth culture that absorbed Salinger's *The Catcher in the Rye*, cheered James Dean and Marlon Brando as rebels with or without a cause, and listened to beatnik poets castigating American society as "an air-conditioned night-mare"? Possibly, the inner and other-directed man could exist within the same person. Consider, for example, the central character in Arthur Miller's play *Death of a Salesman,* which opened on Broadway just before *The Lonely Crowd* was published in 1950.

Willy Loman, the play's tragic protagonist, proudly declares that the most precious thing in life is to be well-liked. As a salesman he is decidedly other-directed, ready with a winning smile and handshake. For Willy, what one knew was less important than *who* one knew. Yet his deepest desire is to succeed and be on top. Thus Loman wants it both ways—to get along and to get ahead—two contrary attitudes according to the Whyte-Riesman analysis. Loman even advises his sons that it is all right to cheat and lie a little for reasons of self-advance-ment. But Loman cannot accept one fact—new forms of business orga-nization have rendered the friendly and garrulous traveling salesman obsolete. When Loman is fired, a neighbor offers him another job. Yet Loman is too ashamed to admit defeat and too proud to accept help. He goes to his suicide clinging to the rightfulness of the older values of work and achievement even though they can no longer be realized. In Willy Loman, the inner-directed conscience is still alive, and it is deadly.

Although Riesman's distinction between inner- and outer-directed-ness may have been overdrawn, his sociological insights, and those of Whyte, remain valid. For they were not alone in describing the demise of the individual amidst the subtle, coercive authority of society. Some women who would go on to become authors were feeling similar pres-sures to conform and submit. Reflecting on the fifties, Betty Friedan deplored the "death" of the self at the hands of "the feminine mys-tique." The other-directed woman had also succumbed to group pres-sures as she passively accepted her conventional role. Many women would come to feel that they had lost their identity without knowing it.

THE STATUS OF WOMEN AND THE DILEMMAS OF MEN

During World War II as many as 6.5 million women entered the labor force. The majority of them were married. In the immediate postwar years all federal funds for child-care centers were terminated on the assumption that mothers would naturally want to return to the home. Many did, and how many did not is a controversy among historians. A Women's Bureau survey indicated that 75 percent wished to continue at work outside the home, but Roper and Gallup polls disclosed considerably lower figures. Regardless of the discrepancy among the polls, the number of women workers first declined sharply after the war, then picked up in the late forties, and continued to increase throughout the fifties. By 1960 women workers grew at a rate of four times that of men; 40 percent of all women over sixteen had entered the labor force compared to 25 percent in 1940. But historians have also pointed to economic factors to explain the entry into the once masculine workplace. The breakthrough in female employment was more intimately tied to inflation than to feminine independence. Husbands needed help. How else to buy a new home and appliances and keep up with the cost of living? Even during the war women had to be cajoled into taking traditional male jobs. Afterward, women working as secretaries, bank tellers, waitresses, and in other jobs experienced discrimination in pay and promotion policies. This syndrome persisted. If there was a women's movement in the fifties, it led directly to the wedding chapel.

The institution of marriage, whether based on the hope of fulfillment or the fear of loneliness, was sacrosanct in the fifties. Everybody got married. "Whether you are a man or a woman," advised *The Woman's Guide to Better Living*, "the family is the unit to which you most genuinely belong. . . . The Family is the center of your living. If it isn't, you've gone far astray." "Marriage is the natural state of adults," exhorted the family counselor Paul Landis. Everywhere in film, television, and advertising one saw loving couples embracing under the trees of new suburban homes. Marriage was celebrated as a state of bliss. So, too, was having children. In diaper ads babies always smiled and never cried. Child-rearing was depicted as an exciting challenge rather than as an ordinary chore. Indeed, housewifely tasks were glorified as proof of the "complete" woman: chef, hostess, nurse, laundress, maid, story-teller, shopper, PTA member, flower-planter, interior decorator, not to mention chauffeur at the call of children at the playground or the husband at the railroad station. Young Americans avidly pursued the image. In 1950 men's average marriage age was 22.0 and women's 20.3, the lowest since the government started keeping that statistic in 1890. Many high school girls were more desirous of securing a husband than a college degree. It seemed so natural. Homemaking and birthing "are very rich and rewarding experiences," advised a pamphlet written for female teenagers. "You yourself feel more completely a woman, as, indeed, you are."

One thrill for college sorority girls was the prospect of being "pinned." Young men obliged by attaching their fraternity pin to the coed's cash-

The "American Dream" that many members of the fifties generation aspired to in search of the material happiness that the depression and war had deprived their parents.

mere sweater, a gesture that announced to the campus that the couple were exclusive and on the way to becoming engaged. By 1957 an incredible 97 percent of Americans "of marriageable age" had taken the vows. These ceremonies were often preceded by a bachelor party for the groom and for the bride a wedding shower of gifts that defined her duties: Osterizers, Sunbeams, Mixmasters. Then came the children, the move from apartment to a suburban house, patio barbecues, the Little League, Brownies, and Cub Scouts.

Soon, however, parts of the image faded and what had seemed a delight in prospect became a drag in reality. Raising children was a tough, relentless job. Answering the call for help, *The Ladies Home Journal* convened a roundtable discussion on "The Plight of the Young Mother." Something must be done for the woman who spent eighty-four hours a week doing all the household work and caring for the children as well. Many wives decided to have several children in rapid succession in order to get behind them the responsibilities of parenthood. "For our generation of housewives and mothers," recalls memoirist Benita Eisler, " 'getting it over with' was our promise to a future deferred. We would 'do something' with our college education (or finish it) when we 'got out from under' diapers, formulas, car pools."

Confining woman's "sphere" to the household rather than the workplace had been pronounced at least since the early nineteenth century, as the early feminists discovered. But in the fifties, intellectual currents reinforced the conviction that women's proper place was in the home. One was Freudianism, a theory of behavior that emphasized distinct gender differences, attributed woman's discontent to "penis envy," and advised women to find emotional stability in motherhood and domestic life. Another was functionalism, a theory of the organized structure of society resting on the assumption that each unit reflects the demands of its function, and in the case of women her function or role was destined by sex, which is biologically determined, and not by character or temperament, which may be culturally conditioned. No doubt writers exaggerated, and perhaps distorted, Freudianism and functionalism when they applied them to the women question in the postwar period. In *Modern Women: The Lost Sex*, Marynia Farnham and Ferdinand Lundberg traced almost every problem in modern society, be it alcoholism, juvenile delinquency, or war itself, to the "neurotic" career woman who refused her natural role, left her children to the indifferent care of others, and futilely competed with men, thereby increasing aggression in the world. Even Dr. Spock had assumed that woman should be hovering over the crib rather than pursuing a career. The psychiatrist Helene Deutsch advised woman to accept the path of "normal femininity," which meant sublimating her masculine strivings by identifying with her husband as a means of relating to the outside world. A sociologist discovered that young girls had been taught to select dolls to play with and later, as teenagers, to repress their intellectual curiosity for fear of scaring off prospective suitors and losing out on a marriage and family.

Every middle- and upper-class parent knew that the best place for young women to find a husband was in college, and on most coeducational campuses there was an abundance of available men. Yet to marry during these years often meant that the coed had to drop out of school to find a job in order to put her husband through college, frequently through to a graduate degree in science, law, or medicine. Then she functioned as the counterpart to Whyte's organization man, the organization's woman, who was forever polite and gracious, never strident or demanding, always courteous to the husband's boss, and concealing her boredom beneath a yawn that can be made to appear as a smile. Later she would be taking tranquilizers or visiting a psychiatrist.

What many women felt, few men noticed. An exception was the sociologist Max Lerner, whose *America as a Civilization: Life and Thought
in the United States* (1957) devoted a large section to the "ordeal" of
women in modern life. "The unhappy wife has become a characteristic
American culture type."

Truly, the dilemma of woman was "the problem that has no name"
until Betty Friedan gave it one with publication of *The Feminine Mystique.* Although Friedan's book appeared in 1963, its context lay in the
fifties—as did Marilyn French's *The Woman's Room* almost fifteen years
later—and numerous other feminist books that broke suddenly into
print with the desperation of a drowning diver coming up for air.
Women had been systematically smothered and deceived, Friedan
complained, by a media-driven culture that gulled them to believe they
could find fulfillment as wives and mothers. Accepting assigned roles,
the modern woman also accepted guilt—discontent was her own fault,
a failure to adjust, to be satisfied with the blessings of family and children. *The Feminine Mystique* is one of those remarkable documents in
intellectual history. Written out of a deep personal need, it struck into
the hearts of millions of readers. Women who responded to the book
no longer felt alone. Now that they shared the same emotions and

Betty Friedan, author of The
Feminine Mystique, *a book
that conveyed the frustration
of women in the fifties who
accepted their conventional
domestic role.*

aspirations, they no longer felt guilty. For those who needed her, Friedan did for American women in the twentieth century what Emerson did for American men in the nineteenth: delivered them from sin and anxiety and restored their sense of self-worth.

Yet Friedan's analysis could restore one sentiment only at the cost of losing another. "She found that love between unequals can never succeed," wrote Gloria Steinem of Friedan, "and she has undertaken the immense job of bringing up the status of women so love can succeed." Steinem's praise must be qualified. *The Feminine Mystique* contains no mention of love, romance, or the erotic. Rather, in Friedan's view, men and women join together as business partners working on some practical enterprise known as "the family," only to discover that the contract had been poorly drawn. Marriage breaks down because the rules are unfair, not because emotions that once drew the partners together have withered away.

Desiring to turn every woman into a worker, Friedan downplayed their potential as sensual lovers. She deplored what she saw as "the mounting sexual hunger" among female youths in the fifties. To her, love-making could only "fill the vacuum created by the denial of larger goals and purposes for American women." It is curious that *The Feminine Mystique* remained indifferent to sexual passion and the irresistible emotions of romantic love. Perhaps Friedan was warning women that they could not "fall" for a man and be in control at the same time. If so, her book did more to turn women into lawyers than into lovers.

Many young men of the fifties did not need Betty Friedan to tell them that suburban life could be suffocating. As Barbara Ehrenreich has observed, *Playboy* magazine, the beatnik movement, and humanistic psychology suggested that men had their own doubts about marriage and the family. Hugh Hefner's philosophy tried to convince men that getting laid need not entail deep emotional involvement. The writings of Jack Kerouac made it clear that being on the road is better than being at home. The self-realization theories of Abraham Maslow, Fritz Perls, and other psychologists taught men to believe that they were suffering from too much responsibility. For a small, dissident segment of the male population, hedonism, bohemianism, and radical individualism combined to question what might be called "the masculie mystique." That conformist archetype figured in Sloan Wilson's *The Man in the Gray Flannel Suit,* a 1955 best-selling novel in which the hero subordinates career to the comforts of a cozy wife and suburban home.

That some young American males were fleeing commitment and their role of breadwinner can be seen in the popular culture of the fifties. No longer prevalent were the romantic comedies like *The Philadelphia Story*, a 1940s film in which the heroine is won, lost, and rewon. The western movies of director John Ford and actor John Wayne, of course, still showed men fighting the chivalrous duel, honoring women, and defending a cherished, conventional way of life. But many other films and television series conveyed a different message. The popular TV program "Route 66" was patterned after Jack Kerouac's novel *On the Road*, with a shining Corvette the symbol of freedom and adventure. The movie idols Montgomery Clift, James Dean, and Marlon Brando projected a new male type, not the responsible husband and successful business executive but men in mumbling torment struggling to express confusing desires in a threatening world. Even Elvis Presley, despite the tenderness of his lyrics and his own devotion to his wife, could be cynical about commitment. Asked a few years before his wedding if he ever contemplated marriage, Presley replied: "Why buy a cow when you can get milk through a fence?" The movie *Young at Heart*, featuring Frank Sinatra and Doris Day, depicted women the way Mark Twain had once depicted Huck Finn's Aunt Polly, the custodian of middle-class manners forever nagging young men to dress neatly and behave properly. Most of the male film heroes of the fifties dramatized the power of raw sex or the pains of unfulfilled love, not the virtues of marriage. The one successful film that treated love and marriage sentimentally, *Marty*, starred Ernest Borgnine, who seemed less a rugged hero than a soft teddy bear. Indeed, when Frank Sinatra crooned a popular song about marriage, many young men knew what he meant by the title, "The Tender Trap." No doubt the great majority of men went willingly to the altar. In 1950, for example, 65 percent of people in the work force were men with a wife at home taking care of children in a traditional nuclear family. Still, at least for some Americans, marriage remained in the fifties the same game that H. L. Mencken found it to be in the twenties: woman's pursuit and man's surrender.

The "feminine mystique" was not all that was going on during "the silent generation." The dilemmas of men were also acutely felt, even by Adlai Stevenson, whose own marriage was on the rocks. "Why is the American man so unsure today about his masculine identity?" asked the historian Arthur Schlesinger, Jr., in 1958. "The basic answer to this is plainly because he is so unsure about his identity in general. Nothing is harder in the whole human condition than to achieve a full sense of identity—than to know who you are, where you are going, and what you are meant to live and die for." Did young American males feel they had to marry to prove their manhood? "You go steady and the first thing she wants you to spend all your time with her," complained a teenager. "She starts talking about that marriage stuff. None of that going steady for me." "What can you do when you have to be a man?" James Dean asked his father in *Rebel Without A Cause*. Dean projected the image of a sagacious adolescent who would stay clear of marriage because it turned his father into a wimp. A similar warning to young members of the opposite sex had been earlier conveyed in the film *Mildred Pierce*. Here actress Joan Crawford played the sacrificing mother who loved too much her spoiled, greedy daughter and, until the very end of the movie, denied her own need for emotional fulfillment and romance.

All in all, in the late forties and fifties young women and young men received mixed messages from American culture. Nowhere was this clearer than in advertisements. Some ads showed women happily doing the laundry with soap that worked magic. Others depicted women sporting high fashion, jewelry, and cosmetics. In the home, women's image was plain and robust; in the bigger world, slender and elongated. One implied middle-aged responsibility and the absence of glamour; the other elegance, suaveness, curvaceousness, the swish of silk and the lush of mink. Aging, work, or children were nowhere to

A leisure-class style at odds with women's role as suburban housewife.

be seen. One type of ad informed women how to raise a family, the other how to win a man. Both stimulated consumption, but whether either enabled young women to identify their role seemed doubtful since each image was almost mutually exclusive.

The mixed messages were only part of the many paradoxes of the fifties. It was an age of stable nuclear families and marital tension, of student conformity on the campus and youth rebellion on the screen and phonograph, of erotic arousal before the visual and sexual hesitancy before the actual, of suburban contentment with lawns and station wagons and middle-class worry about money and status, of high expectations of upward mobility and later some doubts about the meaning and value of the age's own achievements. Members of the fifties generation were unique. They had more education and aspirations. They married younger and produced more babies. They possessed more buying power and enjoyed more material pleasure than any generation of men and women in American history. And it is a measure of the complexity of the fifties that its members could reach no consensus about the meaning of their accomplishments and disappointments. Looking back from the eighties, one male member, a building contractor and multimillionaire, put it this way:

> If you had a college diploma, a dark suit, and anything between the ears, it was like an escalator; you just stood there and you moved up.

Another member, a dental surgeon and medical-school dean, replied impatiently to the escalator comparison:

> Come on! We worked harder than anybody else; we took advantage of every opportunity, every scholarship, every loan. We knew, being where we came from, we just couldn't walk into the bank or the law firm. We had the wrong accent, we went to the wrong schools, we knew we had to make our own way.

The fifties remains a generation in search of itself.

7

High Culture: The Life
of the Mind in a "Placid" Age

Historians who call the 1950s a "placid decade" no doubt have in mind the unadventurous politics of the Eisenhower era and the mood of contentment and complacency that supposedly characterized an America dead from the neck up. This judgment may be valid as regards politics and society, but it breaks down when the world of high culture is considered. In all of the arts and letters the postwar era exploded in excitement and controversy. It also plunged into angst and worry, and not without reason, for postwar high culture perforce probed the nature of existence in a world shadowed by the Holocaust and Hiroshima. While politics reflected a stable consensus and the people a hopeful conformity, the postwar intellectual saw life as problematic, at times even fearful. In part this uneasiness was due to the bomb and the unexpected cold war. But society and the vulgarities of popular culture also induced a sense of displacement, especially among men and women of ideas driven to think independently, even originally.

All doubt that America was predominantly a middle-class society vanished in the fifties. All about them writers saw mass society and bourgeois prosperity. Few intellectuals and artists could make a separate peace with such a society. Instead, they questioned its certitudes, revealed its predicaments, and searched for its ideals. And when not thinking about politics and society, artists and writers did their best to mold a high culture to overcome the torper of the Eisenhower era. When all else failed, the intellectual could still grasp his last possession—the life of the mind.

The Refugee Intellectuals and
the Issue of Modernism

One catalyst for the cultural ferment of the era was the European refugee intellectual. In the 1930s such organizations as the Emergency Committee in Aid of Displaced Foreign Scholars, the Rockefeller and Carnegie foundations, and New York's New School for Social Research did everything possible to facilitate the arrival of European intellectuals fleeing totalitarianism. During World War II many European refugees worked with American scholars in the Office of Strategic Service or the Office of War Information. America lost only two great cultural figures to fascism and communism, the poet Ezra Pound, a disciple of Mussolini, and the black baritone Paul Robeson, a victim of McCarthy. What Mussolini, Hitler, and Stalin lost to America remains the greatest cultural migration in modern history.

Many refugees came to America in search of the new, and their innovating impulse created a further source of tension between modernity and tradition that had been developing for decades. Modernism— the desire to make a self-conscious break with the past and establish new forms of expression—would influence arts and science and stir up controversy for years to come. A sense of historical discontinuity and openness to experience implied that nothing could be defined or settled, especially once-honored ideas like truth, justice, and beauty. Not surprisingly, refugees who contributed to the fine arts embraced modernism, whereas their fellow exiles who were political philosophers rejected it.

The refugees made their first contribution to American culture in such fine arts as symphony orchestras and ballet. The incomparable Italian conductor Arturo Toscanini organized the NBC Symphony Orchestra, and with his infallible ear and clarity of texture gave Americans a feast of the traditional classics. More experimental were Serge Koussevitsky of the Boston Symphony, Otto Klemperer of the Los Angeles Philhamonic, George Szell of the Cleveland Orchestra, and Bruno Walter of the New York Philharmonic-Symphony, all of whom felt freer in America to introduce the avant-garde works of Igor Stravinsky, Béla Bártok, and Gustav Mahler. Mahler's brooding, wistful, elegiac Ninth Symphony, which juxtaposed the warm whispers of nature to the cold hand of death, seemed to Leonard Bernstein the exact musical reflection of the postwar "age of anxiety" even though it had been composed in the pre-World War I age of Victorian optimism.

Maestro Arturo Toscanini, a virtuoso conductor and one of a number of European refugees who enriched the fine arts in America.

Several European musicians taught at American universities. At the University of Southern California Gregor Piatigorsky demonstrated the sublime purities of the cello and at Mills College Darius Milhaud synthesized classical forms with jazz rhythms. But the composer who pushed the range of music beyond all conceivable limitations was Arnold Schoenberg, another exile who taught at both USC and UCLA and made American students aware that a new culture required a complete break from tonal structures. Traditional chromatic, tonal music conveyed the sense of logical coherence to the extent that the opening phrase of a composition provided a familiar key and cadence to which all other movements gravitated and returned. Schoenberg's atonal, serial music defied convention. It introduced a new sense of permutation where notes and scales appear mathematically organized only to disappear as all familiar elements such as melody, theme, and harmonic progression are lost to the ear. One of Schoenberg's students was John Cage, who would later devise his own method of "minimalism" to heighten the tension of silence and stillness as percussionists intermittently played on bowls, metal bars, and oriental gongs to evoke the meditative trances of Zen Buddhism.

In ballet American audiences also felt the influence of European innovators. Especially noteworthy was the Russian choreographer George Balanchine, who arrived in America in the thirties. By the post-war era Balanchine had turned the New York Ballet into one of the great cultural triumphs of the twentieth century. Balanchine combined his classical old-world training with the fresh materials of the new: the spontaneity of long-limbed American ballerinas, the earthy jazz beat, leading with the hip, and the concentration on action and tempo and less on plot and music. This combination of technical complexity and primitive simplicity influenced American choreographers and later, the Dance Theater of Harlem. An art form belonging almost solely to czarist Russia took on new meaning in America as modern ballet supplanted the discipline of position with the dynamics of movement.

Another profession transformed by the influence of European émigrés was architecture. After the war American architectural schools were teaching the designs of the émigrés Walter Gropius, Charles Le Corbusier, and Ludwig Mies van der Rohe. To the soaring verticality of the American skyscraper these Europeans brought the Bauhaus School of the 1920s, a style that emphasized rectangular forms, the use of

Famous Russian émigré choreographer George Balanchine and ballerina Suzanne Farrell rehearsing "Clarinade."

An example of the steel-and-glass motif of post-World War II "high-rise" architecture is exemplified in the Seagram Building, designed by Ludwig Mies van der Rohe and Philip Johnson.

glass and steel, functional efficiency, and classically perfect proportions to dramatize unity and harmony. American architects like Philip C. Johnson and I. M. Pei swiftly adopted some newer European motifs. They designed hotels, office buildings, museums, and apartment houses in ways that allowed modern structures to fit graciously into older surroundings. But not all Americans were pleased by what appeared to be the boring monotony of "glass boxes" going up on New York's Park Avenue and elsewhere. The urban writer Jane Jacobs argued that huge new city buildings discouraged the vitality of street life and made alienation and crime a greater problem. Postmodernist critics called for a return to richer ornamentation and traditional detail. The writer Tom Wolfe later pointed out an embarrassing irony: the simple, austere Bauhaus structures, originally designed in Germany as public housing projects for the working class, became in America luxury highrises affordable only to the wealthy few.

American science also flowered from European seeds. The "illustrious immigrants," as Laura Fermi called them, included her own husband, Enrico Fermi, who worked with Oppenheimer on the atomic bomb, and the Hungarian physicist Edward Teller, later called "father of the H-bomb." In the years just before Hitler came to power, Germany was bubbling with excitement over new developments in quantum mechanics, a system that attempts to relate the problematics of

*Hungarian émigré physicist
Edward Teller, "father" of
the hydrogen bomb.*

measurement to the indeterminate behavior of atomic particles. Hitler
dismissed modern physics as a "Jewish science." When the Nazis con-
solidated their dictatorship after 1933, more than sixteen hundred
scholars, many of them Jewish scientists, were dismissed from their
academic posts. In some instances the purges were abetted by the support of university students who identified with the promises of the Third
Reich.

Most refugee scholars found positions in American universities and
research centers. Several of the physicists and mathematicians had been
or would become Nobel Laureates. European scientists soon came to
appreciate America's technological sophistication and abundance of
resources for laboratory experiments. From the fruitful collaboration
of European and American scientists, the United States would soon
lead the world in research on everything from mathematical game theory to electronic computers to the break from the formalism of classical
genetics that later led to the discovery of DNA, the body's gene code
and the "secret of life."

No less influenced by the arrival of the European scholar was the
subject of psychology. American experimental psychology in thinking,
memory, perception, and learning came to be shaped by "Gestalt" theorists who tried to explain behavior not by looking for single factors
but instead by appreciating the simultaneous configurations of experiences that mutually interact to produce it. Sigmund Freud's ideas,
long known in America, revolved around the subconscious, repressed

Albert Einstein and J. Robert Oppenheimer, physicists who helped develop the atomic bomb, at Princeton's Institute for Advanced Study, 1947.

sexual desires, the death instinct, and the hopelessly divided state of the mind, in which reason struggles against aggressive emotional drives for its very survival. These thoughts seemed too pessimistic and tragic in an America dedicated to freedom, rationality, and moral progress. Yet several medical scientists had recognized the value of Freudian theory in treating neurosis, psychosis, and other mental disorders. During the war Dr. William C. Menninger, Surgeon General of the United States Army and Air Force, selected Jewish refugee analysts to teach young American MDs the latest developments in theoretical research and therapy. After the war New York and Los Angeles would become the world's leading centers of ego psychology, a school of thought that would dispense with much of Freud's focus on the subconscious in order to strengthen the patient's ability to cope with social demands.

The arrival of European psychoanalytic theorists would also profoundly alter the academic and intellectual world. Most popular was the German-born Erik H. Erikson, whose *Childhood and Society* and *Young Man Luther* made Americans aware that personality goes through stages of human development and is not fixed by unconscious determinants. Erikson also showed how the self can experience an "identity crisis" when subjected to conflicting loyalties or aspirations. The Austrian Bruno Bettelheim wrote *Love Is Not Enough* to explain his therapeutic efforts with disturbed children and *Symbolic Wounds* to revise Freud's idea of penis envy. Bettelheim posited that men envy women's capacity for giving birth and nurturing. Karen Horney, born of Nor-

wegian and Dutch parents and raised in Germany, went further. She denied Freud's thesis that women's condition is biologically determined ("anatomy is destiny") and formulated the first, major feminist anti-Freudian position by tracing neurotic behavior to the modern competitive culture of success which renders every person, regardless of gender, anxious and insecure. The German émigré Erich Fromm, a best-selling author in college bookstores and airports alike, synthesized Freudianism and Marxism in order to locate aggressive, selfish behavior not in the psychic stresses of the libido but in a society's class structure and economic conditions. Fromm's *Escape from Freedom* convinced many Americans that the rise of Nazism stemmed from an authoritarian culture. This culture had led German people to submit to a powerful father figure rather than decide their own fate by exercising the existential agony of choice and responsibility. It was a chilling message to discover that modern man would flee from freedom. But other books by Fromm, like *The Sane Society* and *The Art of Loving*, also had wide appeal in the fifties. They conveyed an optimistic reformism based on the familiar American idea that pleasure and happiness can be achieved in an economy of abundance.

For the most part it was a happy union, this marriage of European musicians, scientists, and psychologists and an open friendly America; but in political and social thought European writers who identified with America's liberal traditions were the exception. To be sure, the Germans Franz Neumann and Hans Morgenthau respected America's political founders. They admired statesmen like Lincoln and regretted that Germany lacked a progressive reform movement that might have eased the evils of industrial capitalism and prevented Hitler's rise to power. The Italian legal scholar Max Ascoli also championed democratic liberalism and the welfare state in his influential magazine *The Reporter*. But other émigré scholars, especially Austrian and German, brought with them an arsenal of political and economic ideas that did more to question America's institutions than to reinforce them. Some even believed America would follow Europe's path to totalitarianism unless its liberal principles were drastically altered; and to the extent that liberalism had identified with the experimental ethos of modernism, European classical economic and political thought sought to save America from both.

The notion that the welfare state, not the power of big business, threatened the future of liberty startled old New Deal liberals. That thesis had been propounded by Friedrich von Hayek in *The Road to Serfdom*, which the University of Chicago Press quietly published in

1944. The slender volume exploded like a bombshell after the war and became the gospel of American conservatives. Although von Hayek remained at the London School of Economics, his fellow countryman Ludwig von Mises came to America in 1940 and would later teach the "Austrian School" of economics at New York University, where a stream of admiring graduate students came to listen and spread the word. Von Hayek and von Mises argued that even "liberal" societies were unwittingly welding their own chains of slavery. Why? Well-meaning reformers who sought to relieve hardship had turned to government to regulate business activity without realizing that a planned society would prove incompatible with personal freedom. As European refugees, the Austrians remained convinced that all collectivized systems, whether the platform of England's socialist Labour Party or the proposals to expand America's New Deal, would lead to the same state-controlled economy that had brought Stalin and Hitler to power. American conservatives now had a shibboleth and a specter: "creeping socialism." The idea that there could be some "halfway" experiment with economic planning is, said the von Hayek disciple Max Eastman, "a little like hoping a boa constrictor will eat only half your cow." The democratic socialist Sidney Hook replied forcefully to Eastman and the Austrians, pointing out that in Russia and Germany the Bolsheviks and Nazis first captured state power and then collectivized the economy. The "road to serfdom" had been paved not by economic planners but

The émigré economist Friedrich von Hayek, who taught Austrian free-market theories at the University of Chicago.

by dictators like Lenin, Stalin, and Hitler who had contempt for democracy.

What really angered the Austrians about modern American liberalism was its departure from the nineteenth-century "true" liberal tradition based on free-market economics, small government, and no state intervention. All of these principles were defied by New Deal Keynesianism. This critique from the conservative Right rested on the assumption that capitalism was being crippled by the modern liberal state. Yet at the same time another critique was rising quietly from refugees of the radical Left. And they assumed, ironically, that capitalism reigned supreme in America.

These were the German scholars who had studied at Frankfurt's Institute of Social Research in the 1920s and had come to America in the following decade to escape Nazism. Among the chief theoreticians of the Frankfurt School were Theodor Adorno, Max Horkeimer, and Herbert Marcuse. All were uncompromising Marxist radicals who first played down their politics to become affiliated with Columbia University and to work for the government during the war years. Relatively unknown in the forties and early fifties, Adorno, Horkeimer, and especially Marcuse would later enjoy considerable influence in America. They laid the foundations for a school of thought called "critical theory." In briefest terms, the critial theorist accepts the philosopher Hegel's conviction that history is the process of "reason" arising to self-consciousness. Ultimately, "reason" will reconcile man to his spirit and essence. The duty of the critic is to point out all those forces impeding the process of liberation and self-emancipation. The dominant impeding force was capitalism, not so much as an economic system of production but as a cultural phenomenon that had hindered the development of revolutionary class consciousness. In America Adorno and Marcuse studied various aspects of mass culture such as radio and television, astrology columns, popular music, and fashion trends. They concluded that the masses of people recognize themselves in their commodities and possessions and thereby unconsciously submit to the structures of power. Deeply pessimistic, the German philosophers were certain that all of American life would be absorbed and homogenized by the culture of capitalism. They soon learned what Thorstein Veblen concluded a half-century earlier: the American consumer in pursuit of social status and material happiness is too alienated, too full of pride about his possessions, to experience his own alienation.

The Austrian economists believed liberty to be threatened by the

The German émigré political philosopher Hannah Arendt, whose writings were widely discussed in the postwar era.

state. The Frankfurt scholars assumed freedom as a self-actualization had already been lost to bourgeois society and its cage of illusions and creature comforts. One group of refugees insisted that only capitalism could save America. The other claimed that capitalism had already destroyed America and reduced its people to a state of happy slavery.

Two European intellectuals in particular did much to revitalize the study of political philosophy. In doing so, they sought to preserve the values of the past from the corrosions of modernism. Hannah Arendt arrived in New York in 1940 and later taught at the New School. In her widely discussed book, *The Origins of Totalitarianism,* she wrote that the totalitarian regimes of Germany and Russia had filled the vacuum of rootlessness and meaninglessness that had accompanied the breakdown of bourgeois values in the twentieth century. In *The Human Condition* she attempted to find the basis for an alternative set of political values. Drawing upon Aristotle, Arendt located freedom exclusively in the political realm. Her stance contrasted strikingly with the Austrian economists, who identified freedom with private enterprise, and the Marxists, who regarded labor as the source of value as well as freedom. Arendt later became an admirer of the Founding Fathers and wondered how the American Revolution could be made relevant to the modern world.

To Leo Strauss, another refugee who first taught at the New School, the modern world was also the problem. Strauss went on to teach political philosophy at the University of Chicago and had a remarkable influence on generations of brilliant disciples. Deeply absorbed in Plato, Strauss taught that philosophy should liberate society from the perishable and contingent, and to do so the contemporary thinker must have access to the eternal wisdom of the past. One perennial idea was natural right, the knowledge of which presumably enables citizens to act according to reason and virtue. With the American Revolution, however, the ancient idea of natural right receded and was replaced by the modern idea of natural liberty. Liberalism gave man the grounds for resisting government and postulated a human nature driven by "passions and interests" and a citizenry more concerned about opportunity than duty. Thus, for Strauss the dilemmas facing modern man could only be overcome by a return not to America's past but to his beloved ideals rooted in classical antiquity.

If the merit of a teacher is measured by influence, some European intellectuals must be judged outstanding. Although the political ideas of the German refugees seem to lay dormant in the fifties, they would soon come almost to possess the minds of many students. By the mid-sixties the scholarly meditations of the Frankfurt scholars were discovered by the New Left, and Marcuse's students embraced Hegel and Marx as keys to liberating bourgeois America from its hegemonic "false consciousness." Then, the following decade, the disciples of Strauss began to articulate the case for neo-conservatism. When President Ronald Reagan triumphantly entered the White House in 1981, the Straussians, together with the Austrian-struck free-market advocates, descended upon the capital to take up residence in "think tanks" and proffer policy advice on every subject under the sun. Thus the political legacy of the refugee intellectuals served to inspire American radicalism and conservatism alike. Both the Left and the Right émigrés were at war with the open, tolerant world of liberalism and modernism. Radicals wanted to transform, conservatives to preserve. Both opposed experimentation, whether in politics or in art.

THE FINE ARTS AND THE LITERARY IMAGINATION

Music in America found a responsive audience after World War II. In a prosperous postwar era symphony halls and opera houses sprang up across the land and classical musical festivals boomed at various summer reports. On Sundays millions of Americans watched and listened to "The Joy of Music" as Leonard Bernstein explained the technical complexities of composition and the relative merits of one melody versus another. The articulate composer-conductor added to his fame with the popular Broadway musical, *West Side Story*, which transformed the family feuds of Romeo and Juliet into a contemporary tale of teenage street-gang warfare accompanied by a brilliantly vibrant musical score.

It was in this era that the subtle and often intentionally unclear compositions of Charles Ives were discovered and acclaimed. Aaron Copland, who had studied in Paris under the conductor and teacher Nadia Boulanger, composed ballets based on Cuban and Mexican dance rhythms and gave American music international distinction with his Third Symphony and Piano Sonata. Elliot Carter, who also studied with Boulanger in Paris, experimented with new pitches and harmonic mixtures to integrate disparate materials, and in Los Angeles the Improvisational Chamber Ensemble was founded to see how far the premeditated writing of music could relate to and perhaps be shaped by the act of performance itself.

Nowhere was the magic of improvisation more developed than in jazz. After the war the nuances of modern jazz were recognized as a serious art form. Some classical musicians defended jazz and envied its instrumental virtuosity and seemingly complete structural freedom (which the German Frankfurt scholars dismissed as "bourgeois decadence"). The young composer and horn player Gunther Schuller advocated a synthesis of classical and jazz forms in what he called "Third

The often aching love ballads of Billie Holiday indicate the forties and fifties had romantic longings.

John Coltrane, a saxophonist whose elaborate harmonic progressions and polyrhythmic patterns elevated modern jazz to a serious art form.

Stream" music, which included the sounds of the soft, disciplined Modern Jazz Quartet and the unpredictable saxophonist Ornette Coleman, who often had the audience on its feet by starting his solo where most music ends—with a climactic crescendo. More popular with music lovers were the well-crafted compositions of Duke Ellington, who combined ragtime rhythms with sweet melodies reminiscent of George Gershwin. The pleasant piano numbers of Erroll Garner and Dave Brubeck were also a hit among college students, as were the sad love songs of Billie Holliday. But among jazz musicians themselves, white as well as black, the great legendary figure of the postwar era was John Coltrane. Coltrane was the heir of an even greater legendary figure, Charlie Parker, affectionately called "Bird" and worshipped and studied like "a fertility god," as the black novelist Ralph Ellison aptly put it. The tenor saxophonist Coltrane's chordal progressions, which could range from low moans to wailing shrieks, were always sustained by a delicate rhythmic sense and the steady syncopated beat of the drummer. A shy, deeply spiritual person, Coltrane reached for sounds that seemed to carry music into the spheres. But jazz is a complex, demanding medium, for listener as well as player. Toward the end of the fifties the "progressive" music of Coltrane, Miles Davis, and others was drowned out by the rise of rock 'n' roll and its electronic cacophony. Some black musicians, seeking an audience more responsive to the introspective delicacy of jazz, fled to Europe to find work.

Modern painters were also rejecting the notion of any hierarchy in visual forms. No doubt many Americans in the postwar era continued to respond to the familiar realism of urban and natural land-scapes in paintings: the portraits of human longing by Andrew Wyeth, the boundless desert landscapes by Georgia O'Keeffe, the stark city scenes of Edward Hopper. Especially admired in liberal circles was Ben Shahn, who continued to depict victims of social injustice as he had during the depression era, and who was commissioned by *Time* magazine to do a cover etching of Adlai Stevenson. But in intellectual circles the most exciting artistic event was the rise of "abstract expressionism."

This mode of painting, also referred to as "The New York School," emerged in the late forties. By the mid-fifties it was the talk of the town. It had been influenced in part by refugee artists who brought with them the traces of cubism and surrealism. But abstract expressionism proved to be a unique American contribution to the world of art. The New York painters seemed charged by a restless energy that could be both savage and subtle, wildly pagan and quietly religious. Willem de Kooning shocked the sensibility of viewers with a series of paintings of women, particularly one of Marilyn Monroe in which the distortions of the body become a satirical metaphor for the anxiety and rootlessness of the age. In contrast, Mark Rothko lured viewers into

Robert Motherwell, Elegy to the Spanish Republic, *1955.*

Jackson Pollack at work in his Long Island studio (1950) perfecting the new art of painting as dripping and pouring.

the serene mysteries of the inner world in a series of soft-edged, blended color rectangles that had the effect of whispering voices of contemplation as though one were inside a church. The more bohemian Franz Kline depicted the vastness and hectic pace of city life with white canvasses on which black brushstrokes frantically sped in seemingly opposite directions. Robert Motherwell, influenced by Freudian psychoanalysis, painted a series of *Elegies*, first in blackness massed against white and later in color, to dramatize the brave republic that died in the Spanish Civil War. Cryptic, haunting, the figures in the paintings appear as ovoids in pregnant female bodies threatened by dark, sinister forces in an everlasting struggle of life against death.

The most notable abstract expressionist was Jackson Pollock. Born and raised in Wyoming, Pollock started out as an artist under the tutelage of Thomas Hart Benton and western landscape realism. In the forties all recognizable forms began to disappear from his work, and by the fifties Pollock astounded the art world with his new technique of floor painting. With violent bursts of energy, he worked with an unstretched canvas laid flat on the floor, circling around it like a frenzied tribal dancer as he dripped paint, seemingly at random. The result was brilliant skeins of color, textured in transparent layer over layer, with browns, greys, and blacks bouncing off one another to suggest autumn leaves rustling in the wind. Pollock likened his method to that of "the Indian sand painters of the West" whose ritual images derived from dribbling coloured grains and pebbles on the ground to the dancelike movements of the body. Critics have also likened Pollock's painting to the poetry of Walt Whitman, who similarly believed that the vastness and complexity of America could be captured in a single blade of grass recollected in spontaneous ecstasy. With Pollock American painting achieved a sense of awe and grandeur.

With its concentration of abstract expressionists, New York replaced Paris as the world's art capital. Such daring innovation generated controversy and bitter accusation. Aware that the New York painters had been exhibited in the prestigious Venice Biennale, the US State Department purchased seventy-nine oil paintings and thirty-eight watercolors to circulate abroad in an exhibition titled "Advancing American Art." But traditional painters objected so strongly that the show was withdrawn and the works tastelessly sold off by the government. In the McCarthy era abstract expressionism was also accused of being "communist art." Congressional hearings were held to get at the bottom of the subversive conspiracy allegedly taking place in art studios and galleries. Ironically, communists and radical art critics themselves denounced the "decadence" of abstract expressionism. They claimed its painters had lost sight of social reality and indulged in a shameless preoccupation with the self that ignored Marx's dictum: the task of mind is not to interpret reality but to change it. McCarthyites and communists could at least agree that American art had gone to the dogs. The former wanted to see portraits of George Washington crossing the Delaware; the latter wanted paintings of tractors and farm youths with bulging biceps. What the abstract expressionists themselves wanted was the freedom to be free of all dogmas and strictures.

Abstract expressionism also intensified the debate over modernism, which continues to this day. In the world of culture, modernism implies a sensibility toward discontinuity, fragmentation, and introversion. The result is that such thoughts and expressions cannot easily be subjected to rational analysis. In art this signified a decisive break with the traditional principle of "mimesis," the notion that art must imitate or at least approximate reality and objective experience. In this respect modern abstract expressionism seems formless and nonrepresentational— no identifiable object is the subject in these works. The art critic Clement Greenberg defended the New York painters' use of paint itself, and not the object painted, as a new method of bringing order to disorder and imposing unity on the resistant chaos of diverse materials. Another critic, Harold Rosenberg, coined the term "action painting" to explain the state of mind of the New York painters. "At a certain moment the canvas began to appear to one American painter after another as an arena in which to act—rather than as a space in which to reproduce, redesign, analyze, or 'express' an object, actual or imagined. What was to go on the canvas was not a picture but an event." One artist referred to "psychic automatism" to suggest a kind of free association that allows the brush to wander undirected by the conscious mind; another whimsically mentioned the "laws of chance" to convey the unpredictable excitement of subjective expression in the creative process. Several abstract expressionists were also influenced by philosophy of existentialism and its conviction about risks and danger. Life was a situation in which one cannot avoid the responsibility to choose and to act. Thus modern art became an act rather than a representation, a deed rather than a thing. Such a formulation placed more emphasis upon what one does than what one understands and left viewers wondering how to explain something that does not represent anything.

Because abstract expressionism seemed so inexplicable, its critics were tempted to charge that the spontaneous creations were no more than doodlings or "drip paintings." Cartoonists delighted in showing a human being and an ape scratching their heads and peering quizzically at a Pollock canvas. Years later the writer Tom Wolfe would dismiss the whole enterprise as a sham in *The Painted Word.* According to Wolfe, abstract expressionism had less to do with genuine art than with the social life of Peggy Guggenheim, the wealthy heiress who promoted it, and the chic ambitions of New York's Museum of Modern Art. Wolfe and others ridiculed and dismissed abstract expressionism because of its apparent incomprehensibility. Yet it could very well be, as Edmund Burke first pointed out in the eighteenth century, that the properties of great art lie in obscurity rather than clarity. The viewer's imagination is aroused by what is suggested and hinted at, not by what is clearly represented and stated. Whatever the case, Pollock, Motherwell, and other New York painters had every right to say with Emerson: "To be great is to be misunderstood."

The crisis of understanding could also be seen in one of the most widely discussed plays of the era, the Irishman Samuel Beckett's *Waiting for Godot.* Here viewers felt the same tension of silence, emptiness, and the tedium of eventlessness found in much of modern art and music. If the challenge of the art critic was to describe what had been painted when nothing had been represented, the challenge of the theater critic was to interpret what was being performed when seemingly little was going on. Yet there were American playwrights who did sat-

Eugene O'Neill, Nobel Prize winner, and America's first playwright of international fame.

isfy the need for dramatic action. Indeed, in the immediate postwar years American drama enjoyed a "golden age." When these writers held the mirror up to American realities, however, they saw not a "placid" age of contentment but the human pathos of confusion and desperation.

That theme was driven home in the debut of Eugene O'Neill's *The Iceman Cometh* in 1946. A decade earlier O'Neill had received a Nobel Prize for his repertoire of plays experimenting with masks, choruses, scenic effects, interior monologues, symbolic figures, and characters with split personalities. O'Neill shouldered the burden of being a "black Irish Catholic," one who ceased believing in God in his youth yet could not fully accept an existence without spiritual meaning. O'Neill, America's greatest playwright, could find little religious nourishment in America. In contrasting the passions and joys of his young characters with the hardness and lovelessness of a Calvinist life of work and striving, he rejected America's Protestant heritage as acquisitive and materialistic. Like the historian Henry Adams, O'Neill saw how people could transfer their worship of God to the worship of science, and its intoxicating promise of power. In the forties he intended to work on a cycle of plays tracing the tragic story of an American family from colonial times to the present. "I am going on the theory," he said in an interview right after America emerged victorious in the war, "that the

United States, instead of being the most successful country in the world, is the greatest failure." The American ethos seemed to be "that everlasting game of trying to possess your own soul by the possession of something outside it." It was this theme of the soul's self-estrangement that gave *The Iceman Cometh* and *Long Day's Journey Into Night* such compelling power. The death of illusions, the collapse of the "pipe dreams" that enabled the characters to cope with reality, could be the end of life itself. O'Neill's plays were driven by his own obsessions, and none was more telling than his lifelong quarrel with God and the "curse of the misbegotten" world He created. But O'Neill also wanted to make the audience feel his characters' inner humanity, which lay hidden by the outward pose of conformity. In an age that demanded adjustment, O'Neill's characters could not forgive themselves for being who they were.

Some of the same themes of seeking and suffering can be seen in the works of Tennessee Williams. Born Thomas Lanier Williams, he broke into American theater as a relatively unknown playwright with the production of *The Glass Menagerie* in 1945, one of the saddest plays of the postwar era. Partly autobiographical, it depicts the emotional plight of a young and delicate girl, Laura (created from Williams' sister, whose own withdrawals led to her being institutionalized), and her mother's efforts to match her with a "gentleman caller" in order to secure her a husband in the throes of the depression years. But the semi-invalid Laura is rejected, and as the audience watches her turn to her fragile glass animals for companionship, we hear from Williams a desperate cry of compassion and a plea for illusions to ward off the cruelties of reality. Like O'Neill, Williams felt deeply the loss of religious faith. "What has become of compassion and understanding?" he protested in an earlier play. "Where's God? Where's Christ?" He also made the family the institution in which memory, guilt, and hope meet in combat. He, too, allowed his characters their desperate illusions. In *A Streetcar Named Desire* the audience watches as Blanche DuBois, a neurotic woman whose refined manners barely conceal her sexual hunger, hangs a colored paper lampshade over a light bulb to hide her encroaching age and to seek salvation through fantasy. Her rape by Stanley Kowalski meant to Williams the brutal ravishment of all that was tender and delicate. Blanche's final remark before being taken away to a mental institution asks for forgiveness, pity, and mercy: "I've always depended on the kindness of strangers." Williams could endow women with redeeming humanity and still imbue female characters with sufficient complexity to embody the traits of both genders.

The film version of Tennessee Williams' Streetcar Named Desire, *staring Marlon Brando, Kim Hunter, and Vivien Leigh.*

In other hits like *Cat on a Hot Tin Roof,* the women are aggressive and possessive and want their men strong, handsome, and masculine. Whichever sex he was writing about, Williams always showed deep sensitivity toward the unfortunate, the eccentric, the fearful, and the fragile, and he condemned cruelty and mendacity. He, as well as his characters, was haunted by impermanence, and thus he offered aging athletes and fading beauties—not to scorn their vanity but to dramatize their mortality. In the pleasure-seeking fifties, he wrote of people of pain.

A different kind of pain afflicted the characters in Arthur Miller's plays. His subject was the fate of the individual who allows society to shape his identity and define his existence. Miller's first broadway hit, *All My Sons,* dealt with a responsible, hard-working businessman, Joe Keller, who accepted society's achievement standards. During the war, in a moment of panic, Keller gave the order to ship defective machine parts to the air force, which resulted in the crashing of twenty-one planes in the Pacific. At the trial his partner was blamed and Keller released. While his friends and neighbors knew he was far from innocent, they respected him for being "smart" enough to get off. Keller continued to suffer guilt. When he discovered that his son knew he was responsible and died in combat as a kind of family expiation, he claimed the twenty-one airmen "all my sons" and, in his own act of contrition, killed himself. More sympathetic was Willy Loman of *Death of a Salesman*, (discussed on p. 211), which swept the theater awards when it appeared in 1949. Willy swallowed the Horatio Alger myth about honesty, thrift, enterprise, and popularity at any price. Like the protagonist in *The Iceman Cometh*, he was a peddler whose illusions make him both victim and victimizer, one whose inability to accept failure and acknowledge his own lies "comes with the territory." In two other plays society was also judge and executioner. In *A View from the Bridge* the protagonist refuses to admit his sexual desire for his niece and is destroyed by his need to preserve his reputation in the neighborhood. In *The Crucible*, a parable on McCarthyism, the victim must either side with his accusers and make a confession, thereby joining a community that turns man into a liar, or lose his life. In having the Puritan John Proctor choose death over life in a society with its deceitful demands, Miller showed nobility being reborn from the materials of tragedy.

Although the theater provided a curious commentary on American life in the post-war years, it would be facile to regard its productions as simply "social criticism." With the exception of Proctor, most of the characters created by Miller, Williams, and O'Neill were lacking in authentic awareness and human greatness; hence they were too fated, and often too willing, to do anything but participate in their own destruction. Once the curtain went up, the die was cast from the open-

A scene from Arthur Miller's Death of a Salesman, *with Lee J. Cobb playing the title role of Willy Loman.*

ing of the play and there was no possibility of either rebellion against society or reconciliation with it. Blanche DuBois and Willy Loman accepted their roles and played them well, and they were caught in the act.

In poetry, America's "golden age" occurred three decades earlier, during what Gertrude Stein called the "lost generation." By the post-World War II era the eminent poets of the 1920s had died, moved abroad, become recluses, committed suicide, or gone mad. The latter fate befell Ezra Pound, one of the giants of twentieth-century literature. Pound's earlier diatribes against banks, usury, and Jews led him to identify with the dictator Benito Mussolini and to make propaganda broadcasts for Fascist Italy during the war. After American forces liberated Italy, Pound was arrested on thirteen counts of treason. He was first placed in a make-shift cage in Pisa, where he continued writing brilliant poetry, then returned to the United States and committed to a psychiatric hospital. When he was awarded the prestigious Bollingen Prize for his *Pisan Cantos,* a bedlam of controversy broke out in the literary world. Those who defended Pound, including some of America's leading poets and critics, claimed that the form and technique of a work of literature can be considered apart from its content and meaning.

The idea that art could be considered independently of politics was a necessary principle to the modernist intellectual who wanted to uphold the latest innovations in literary technique. Older writers and critics knew that some of their European literary heroes were conservative politically no matter how radical their aesthetic sensibility.* Thus when Wallace Stevens finally won the recognition and honors he had long deserved with the publication of his *Collected Poems,* many young writers were surprised to discover upon his death in 1955, that he had worked as the vice-president of an insurance company in Hartford, Connecticut, and voted Republican! A number of these budding authors of the fifties sought to develop their creative powers by studying at the University of Iowa's Writers Workshop, San Francisco State's Poetry Center, Kenyon College, or at North Carolina's Black Mountain College. A visit by the wild Welshman Dylan Thomas, who occasionally showed up drunk, had students holding their breath as they listened to his impassioned poems.

The fifties may be called the "placid decade" but out of it came a

---

*Conservative in the sense that they did not feel there were easy political solutions to deeper moral problems. Among them were D. H. Lawrence, Franz Kafka, Marcel Proust, William Butler Yeats, Thomas Mann, and James Joyce.

galaxy of implacable poets.† Two in particular registered the peculiar sensibilities of the era, especially its understanding of the need for authority and the desire for freedom.

The poetry of Robert Lowell viewed the modern world as a conflict of opposites. On the one side there was custom and convention, on the other liberation and openness to experience. Memories of youth and the threatening encroachments of age concerned him, as did the possibilities of life that remain after the conditions of life have been almost exhausted. Partaking of the New England tradition, Lowell saw America as founded on a covenant with God and the Republic, and his poetry resonated the conflict between a majestic past and a miserable present. The covenant had been abrogated with the passage of time, and the poet must find the possibilities of its renewal. The vows of marriage suffered the same fate, and it was a measure of the genius of Lowell's poetic imagination that he could tell the story from the wife's point of view:

> "The hot night makes us keep our bedroom windows open.
> Our magnolia blossoms. Life begins to happen.
> My hopped up husband drops his home disputes,
> and hits the streets to cruise for prostitutes,
> free-lancing out along the razor's edge.
> This screwball might kill his wife, then take the pledge.
> Oh the monotonous meanness of his lust. . . .
> It's the injustice . . . he is so unjust—
> whiskey-blink, swaggering home at five.
> My only thought is how to keep alive.
> What makes him tick? Each night now I tie
> ten dollars and his car key to my thigh. . . .
> Gored by the climacteric of his want,
> he stalls above me like an elephant."

Another writer whose life as well as work seemed to symbolize both the aspirations and the repressions of the fifties was the poet Sylvia Plath. Born in Boston in 1932, Plath had her first verse published at the age of nine and went on to become a brilliant student at Smith. As a teenager Plath succeeded in placing her poems and short stories in

---

†Aside from the more publicized beatniks (discussed later), talented poets of the postwar era include John Ashbery, John Berryman, Elizabeth Bishop, Robert Bly, John Ciardi, James Dickey, Richard Eberhart, Jean Garrigue, John Hollander, Randall Jarrell, James Merrill, Josephine Miles, Theodore Roethke, Adrienne Rich, Delmore Schwartz, Robert Penn Warren, Karl Shapiro, Peter Viereck, Richard Wilbur, and William Carlos Williams, who, though starting earlier, wrote his first poem in the forties.

Sylvia Plath, a novelist and poet who spent the fifties in a painful, creative female identity search.

Mademoiselle and *Harper's* and in winning collegiate literary honors. On a fellowship at Cambridge University, England, she met a number of prominent writers including a rising star, the poet Ted Hughes, whom she married. The marriage brought two children and a productive life for husband and wife. All along, however, Plath had bristled at the conventional role women were supposed to assume:

> A living doll everywhere you look.
> It can sew, it can cook.
> It can talk, talk, talk.
> It works, there is nothing wrong with it.
> Will you marry it, marry it, marry it.

When her marriage broke up after six years, Plath first grew depressed then determined to put her life together as an independent woman. She continued working on her autobiographical novel, *The Bell Jar,* and on a series of poems that would later be published as *Ariel.* These and other works reveal what was troubling her almost to the point of mental torture: the loss of her father at the age of eight, the end of her "purely happy" years; miscarriages and nervous breakdowns; Hiroshima and the Holocaust, the Rosenbergs' execution, and the destructive power of modern science; nature, especially water, as both mysterious and menacing; the joy and pain of love; and a narcissistic search for identity by a poet who oould accept paradox in literature but not in life. On the evening of February 11, 1963, Sylvia Plath left a plate of milk and bread for her children, sealed her kitchen's doors and windows with towels, then turned on the gas oven and laid her head in it.

> Dying
> Is an art, like everything else.
> I do it exceptionally well.

The tensions that were building up in Ernest Hemingway's life in the fifties were different but just as murderous. The publication of his disappointing *Across the River and into the Trees* in 1950 led many of his followers to believe that the great novelist of the lost generation was washed up. Two years later "Papa" surprised everyone with *The Old Man and the Sea,* a moving allegory in which Hemingway once again proved his mastery at using man and nature to portray ambiguous emotions. In many respects the novella summarizes the moral code that ran through almost all of Hemingway's works. The old man loses to the ravenous sharks the giant marlin he has caught. But life itself is a losing proposition; what counts is the courage and endurance with which one conducts oneself even while going down to defeat. Hemingway never published another novel after *The Old Man and the Sea,* and apparently he could not abide by his own code. In 1961 he took his favorite shotgun and blew half his head off. In his last years he had succumbed to paranoiac madness, but throughout his life he was as preoccupied with death as Sylvia Plath had been. Hemingway's father had also died by suicide and the thought remained with him like a thorn in the brain. "Why did he kill himself, Daddy?" asks the son in one of Hemingway's earlier short stories. "I don't know, Nick. He couldn't stand things, I guess."

Prose fiction and the novel lost their splendor in the postwar era. For decades Hemingway had been America's most famous writer. Several of his great contemporaries, like F. Scott Fitzgerald and Thomas Wolfe, had died just before the war; others such as John Dos Passos, John Steinbeck, and William Faulkner continued publishing novels in the forties and fifties, but without the acclaim that had greeted their earlier works. The war itself produced four outstanding novels: John Horne Burns's *The Gallery,* James Jones's *From Here to Eternity,* Norman Mailer's *The Naked and the Dead,* and Irwin Shaw's *The Young Lions.* After the war Burns's life was cut short by an untimely death in Italy,

Jones and Shaw would eventually move to Europe, and Mailer would find, after attempts with unsuccessful novels like *Barbary Shore* and *Deer Park*, that his forte lay in nonfiction.

Unlike Hemingway and several writers of the "lost generation," most of the younger novelists who emerged after the war took America as their subject. But their literature scarcely "mirrored" society. While many Americans climbed the slippery pole of ambition and success, characters in prose fiction seemed to be scurrying for survival. John Updike's *Rabbit, Run* offers domesticity and middle-class, small-town life in all its dreary social detail only to illustrate why one must run away from wife and community. Philip Roth's *Goodbye, Columbus* comes close to suggesting why a Jewish-reared young man must run away from himself. John Barth's *The End of the Road* has readers wondering whether there is an "I" from which to run. The protagonists in Saul Bellow's *The Adventures of Augie March* and *Henderson the Rain King* are "displaced persons" who move through life without a sense of purpose except endless desire ("I want, I want"); a brilliant depiction not only of Jewish rootlessness but of the existential angst of modern man. The following decade Bellow would win the Nobel Prize for literature and have admirers everywhere from Africa to Asia. Perhaps the only writers with a firm sense of place were New Englanders like John Cheever, who offered small-town ceremony as a defense against modern chaos; and southerners such as Flannery O'Connor, who made hillbilly country her subject in order to extract the largest possible moral truths hidden in the most local tales.

The only important institution postwar novelists delighted in exposing was higher education. The hypocrisies of college life, especially petty faculty politics, received satirical scorn in Bernard Malamud's *A New Life*, Randall Jarrell's *Pictures from an Institution*, Mary McCarthy's *The Groves of Academe*, and Ralph Ellison's *Invisible Man*. But politics and social protest would be hard to find in the literary agenda. Readers in the postwar era learned that the south must handle its own racial relations (William Faulkner, *Intruder in the Dust*); that authority, however incompetent, must never be challenged (Herman Wouk, *The Caine Mutiny*); that liberal activists are devious (Allen Drury, *Advise and Consent*); that voting and civic participation change nothing (Morton Thompson, *Not as a Stranger*); that laws are made to be broken (John O'Hara, *Ten North Frederick*); and that political ideals are corrupted by the means used to realize them (Robert Penn Warren, *All the King's Men*).

In the politically quiet years of the Eisenhower era, American fiction turned inward as writers made the act of writing its own justification. What many novelists offered was a literature of revelation that concerned itself with the problem of identity and the fate of freedom in a mass society. Sensing the loss of self to society and its compromises, writers like Bellow, Roth, and Updike wanted to live in touch with their own values and desires, however vaguely articulated. Such a stance could be sufficient for the literary artist who was free to fabricate a personal world of mock heroes on the run. Other American intellectuals, however, felt the need to take society seriously and to grasp politics and the nature of power.

"THE END OF IDEOLOGY" AND THE CONTROVERSY OVER "CONSENSUS"

One such intellectual was Daniel Bell. A former radical who had come to recognize the limitations of Marxism in foretelling the future, Bell spent the postwar years trying to analyze the nature and direction of modern society. With a series of essays in the fifties that culminated in *The End of Ideology* in 1960, and also Seymour M. Lipset's *Political Man* a few years later, controversies erupted in the social sciences that have still to subside. Bell and Lipset explored the social cohesion of democracy, the alientating character of work and yet, paradoxically, the conservative nature of the working class, the emergence of status rather than class to explain social behavior, and the phenomenon of mass society in which individual differences become obliterated. In defending contemporary social trends, Bell in particular denied that mass society imposes a relentless conformity and stifles intellectual leadership. The most controversial aspect of the Bell-Lipset stance was the "end of ideology," by which they meant the "end of chiliastic hopes, to millenarianism, to apocalyptic thinking." The cataclysmic assumptions that characterized prewar Marxist thought were now "exhausted," and hence the impassioned doctrines of the Old Left could not be expected to reemerge. Although the two scholars still saw themselves as taking a "critical" stance toward society, they recommended an "empirical" analysis that would specify what goals are to be proposed, how they are to be realized, and who will pay the cost and provide the justification. Anything less, Bell was convinced, would sacrifice present generations to the hopeless visions of the ideologue who mistakes politics for religion and commits the sin of pride. Bell was fond of quoting Max Weber: "He who seeks the salvation of souls . . . should not seek it along the avenue of politics."

Within a few years Bell and other sociologists of the fifties would be accused of divorcing morality from social thought and settling for an empirical, descriptive approach devoid of ethical questions. It may have been true, critics pointed out, that Weber was worried about the excesses of passion and righteousness in his seminal essay, "Politics as a Vocation." But did not Weber still believe that utopian ideals were necessary to keep alive a sense of what ought to exist? "Certainly all historical experiences confirms the truth," wrote Weber, "that man would not have attained the possible unless time and again he had reached out for the impossible." How to interpret Weber became a central concern in postwar American sociology. Since the turn of the century Weber's methodological approach to the study of society had been regarded as an alternative to Marxism. Some Americans who had been influenced by Weber advocated a sociology that began with social facts alone and confined itself to the immediate data of experience. Others used, as did Weber, theoretical constructs to discover how social systems worked. This school of thought came to be known as "structural functionalism," and its most influential exponent in the forties and fifties was Talcott Parsons of Harvard University.

Parsons' writings and teachings, which did much to shape postwar American sociology, purported to explain how all human societies are held together by basic organizing principles that seem to be as necessary to social "systems" as cells are to biological organisms. In part, structural functionalism drew on the earlier works of John Dewey and other American scholars who emphasized the symbolic and social nature of thought and conduct in the context of human interaction. But Parsons' primary influence came from Weber and the European tradition of seeing social order as deriving from the structure and patterns of human activity in which action is guided by values that have been internalized in the individual's personality and institutionalized in society and culture. Although a dense writer, Parsons was a compelling teacher. To classes packed with admiring students, Parsons would explain how society functioned as a "system" that united men and women into a bond of infinite relationships. It is important to note that Parsons came from a long line of congregational ministers, and thus saw himself as something of a preacher with the Christian duty of justifying society's ways to man while looking to society for answers that had once been the domain of religion. Many students influenced by Parsons became convinced that modern social pressures served the same function as older religious imperatives, rewarding good behavior through its increasing achievement norms and punishing bad or "deviant" conduct as the rules of meritocracy replaced older dictums of morality. In a word, society became religion.

Few of the playwrights, poets, or novelists of the postwar era would have been converted to the Parsonian perspective on modern society. To them, society itself was the problem, and the challenge of the writer was to "wake the spirit's sleep" (Bellow) by arousing the self to search for its own personal identity. But if Parsons drew on Weber to overcome Marx, he shared with Marx and Dewey—indeed, with all modern social theorists—a deep conviction that humanist thinkers found threatening: there is no self apart from society.

It was not only literary humanists who would be unable to stomach structural functionalism as a system where everyone relates and has his place in the total scheme of things. A few sociologists began to question this dominant school of thought that seemed to ignore such problems as class stratification, power and influence, and legitimization, that is, the reasoning used to justify a given social system by reference to something other than its functional performance, to an end or value like equality or justice. It took the maverick scholar C. Wright Mills to put forward such a critique in his *The Power Elite* and *The Sociological Imagination.* A colorful, burly Texan who drove to his classes at Columbia University on a motorcycle, Mills questioned the cherished faiths of American democracy by proposing that the Republic had come to be ruled by an interconnected network of "establishments" consisting of big business, the military, and the government bureaucracy. Mills shared with the Marxists the assumption that the exercise of power by one cluster of groups would be antithetical to the interests of other groups. But he dismissed the notion of a revolutionary working class as part of Marx's nineteenth-century "labor metaphysic"; hence, he offered a theory of power based on elite domination rather than class exploitation. Mills's theory resembled his rugged temperament, "a fiercely grinding sort of power that came down like a fist," Irving Howe recalls in his memoirs. No distinguished sociologist could ignore his challenge and in the late fifties students and professors were debating, "Is there a ruling class in America?" Bell, Parsons, David Riesman, and other sociologists sought to refute Mills by pointing out that elites often quarrel among themselves; that certain decisions are made by those who have had authority conferred upon them and thus they rule on the basis of consent, not coercion; and that modern bureaucracy, rather than concentrating power, actually disperses it by creating numerous administrative units which veto each other's actions and achieve a workable equilibrium. Few scholars gave credence to Mills' thesis. But in January 1961, when President Eisenhower warned of the dangers of "the military-industrial complex" in his farewell address, some eyebrows were raised; within a short time the New Left of the sixties would see illegitimate power everywhere and, acting on their suspicions, would find what they suspected and embrace C. Wright Mills as a prophet.

The sociologists' conviction that power in America fragmented into a healthy equilibrium had its economic counterpart in the writings of John Kenneth Galbraith. His *American Capitalism: The Concept of Countervailing Power* acknowledges that power has been concentrating in various constellations of influence. But such institutions and interest groups as big business, labor, farmers, government, and the broad mass of consumers could only contend with one another and never command power and impose their will on society. Self-checking mechanisms, "countervailing powers," arise to balance the demands of each segment of society. Thus, labor organizations join with government to resist the power of business, which in turn joins with the scientific community to increase its productive capacity while the people

Sociologist C. Wright Mills, one of the few dissident critics of the fifties.

Harvard professor John Kenneth Galbraith, an economist who tried unsuccessfully to change America's wasteful consumption habits in the fifties.

benefit from economic efficiency in the form of lower prices. Such a view led Galbraith to more firmly believe that large corporations should be accepted as a technological inevitability. But by 1958, when he published *The Affluent Society*, Galbraith doubted that people enjoyed "consumer sovereignty" sufficiently to exercise any meaningful choice in the marketplace. In part this powerlessness was due to inflation, which decreases purchasing power and forces buyers to accept the seller's going prices. But Galbraith also came to see what the German exiles had discovered in the forties: Americans are too eager to accept whatever Madison Avenue advertises as they indulge themselves in an orgy of wasteful spending on this gadget and that garment. A day in the life of the consumer leaves Galbraith in sardonic dismay:

> The family which takes its mauve and cerise, air-conditioned, power-steered, and power-braked automobile out for a tour passes through cities that are badly paved, made hideous by litter, blighted buildings, billboards, and posts for wires that should long since have been put underground. They pass into a countryside that has been rendered invisible by commercial art. (The goods which the latter advertise have an absolute priority in our value system. Such aesthetic considerations as a view of the countryside accordingly come second. On such matters we are consistent.) They picnic on exquisitely packaged food from a portable icebox by a polluted stream and go on to spend the night at a park which is a menace to public health

and morals. Just before dozing off on an air mattress, beneath a nylon tent, amid the stench of decaying refuse, they may reflect vaguely on the curious unevenness of their blessings. Is this, indeed, the American genius?

Galbraith wanted to see less private consumption and more public spending on schools, hospitals, highways, cultural activities and other social services and aesthetic priorities. But the mentality behind America's economy functioned to create artificial wants and instill in people such insatiable demands that they become as dependent on their desires as an addict on drugs. Yet while Galbraith believed that affluence was ruining the American character, another scholar wanted to show how economic abundance had shaped it.

David Potter expounded that thesis in *People of Plenty*. A historian by training, Potter drew on various disciplines to demonstrate how the very "personality formation" of the American people evolved from conditions of abundance and opportunity. Attitudes toward status, mobility, wealth, equality, success, and democracy itself were historically shaped by the presence of surplus. In America democracy evolved in the absence of class conflict since wealth, rather than being distributed by taking from the few and giving to the many, simply expanded.‡ Potter was too sensitive a scholar not to notice that economic abundance had some unhealthy consequences for the American character. He cited the writings of the European refugee psychoanalysts Fromm and Horney to show how the prospect of abundance drives Americans to be overly competitive, anxious about failure, and to crave acceptance and recognition. But all in all, Potter regarded economic abundance as the key to America's historical success. In the Eisenhower era *People of Plenty* provided further evidence of why Americans could count their blessings.

Other social scientists were also trying to explain the key to America's success and stability. One was Robert Dahl, a Yale University political theorist who became an influential academic intellectual in the fifites. In his *A Preface to Democratic Theory*, Dahl described Amer-

‡The development of economic abundance was something that neither Karl Marx nor the American Founders had anticipated. Their thinking rested on the assumption of scarcity and struggle. Classes or "factions" would always be in conflict because the property of the few would be threatened by the power of the many. The framers believed that the Constitution had to be devised to protect property and control democracy because they feared that "overbearing" popular majorities would, if left unchecked, use political means to achieve economic ends. That Americans would turn out to be "people of plenty" pursuing their own ends as workers and entrepreneurs is another reason why the class conflict the Founders had expected failed to materialize.

ican society as "polyarchy," a mass of self-interested minorities each lobbying intensely to pursue a few issues of special concern rather than dedicating themselves to a public philosophy. This reduction of politics to interest-group activity, commonly referred to as "pluralism," rested on two assumptions a future generation of political scientists would challenge: that groups compete on roughly equal terms and that there is no ruling class in America. But in the fifites pluralism remained the dominant school of political thought in the academic community. It reinforced the "end of ideology" mood in so far as politics was conceived to be about means and haggling details rather than ends and ultimate doctrines. And in the wake of European totalitarianism, a theory of democracy that did not require the mobilization of mass participation seemed a godsend.

In no discipline was the impact of totalitarianism more clearly felt than in the study of American history. In the teens and twenties the eminent historians Carl L. Becker and Charles A. Beard wrote books on the Declaration of Independence and the Constitution. Readers were told that the ringing statements in the Declaration may have been mere rationalizations rather than true convictions and that the Constitution had more to do with protecting property than promoting liberty and equality. Becker and Beard also became leading exponents of relativism, the view that beliefs and values have no universal or timeless validity but are simply produced by differing historical conditions. Relativism had been rampant in almost all the social sciences in America. But the rise of totalitarianism forced intellectuals and scholars to consider that certain behavior must be judged by standards that are universal rather than conditional, and for many it would be the eighteenth-century Enlightenment and its ideals of liberty and equality. Thus, during the war, Becker and Beard took another look at the Declaration and the Constitution; now they praised such documents for preserving liberty and hailed the ideas that inspired them as the "generalities that still glitter."

Totalitarianism and the war also had an enormous impact on those who had first come to American history from a Marxist perspective. Historians like Louis Hacker started out in the late thirties writing articles on the "crisis of capitalism." After the experience of war showed America's economy performing with unexpected efficiency, Hacker went on to write books in praise of the productive achievements of American business. Another historian who had to come to grips with Marxism was Arthur Schlesinger, Jr., not because he ever became a convert to the doctrine but simply because it pervaded the intellectual community in the thirties and forties. At Harvard and elsewhere Schlesinger had listened to leftist friends claim that Roosevelt's New Deal was a fraud and that, given the structural "contradictions" of capitalism, the American political system could not survive the depression and the war. Schlesinger's *The Age of Jackson* was written during the war years. It sought to show how the political state had been used in early American history to control the power of an emergent capitalist sector and why no one, socialist or conservative, should expect history and society to be without conflict. "One may wonder whether a society which eliminated struggle would possess much liberty," wrote Schlesinger, who had in mind what he regarded as the real struggles between capital and labor in the Jacksonian era. Indeed, Schlesinger was the only American historian in the postwar era to identify liberty with conflict and struggle, even class struggle.

By the fifties all sense of struggle tended to disappear from American historiography as a new generation of scholars began to emphasize cohesion rather than conflict. One historian was Daniel J. Boorstin, then at the University of Chicago and later the Librarian of Congress (and now Librarian Emeritus). As a student at Harvard in the thirties Boorstin had belonged to a communist "cell" and studied Marxist doctrine. When he broke with his radical past in the forties he remained distraught by the way ideas can seduce people into holding utopian beliefs that have no bearing on reality. "Ideology" was one such disease of the brain, and Boorstin wrote *The Genius of American Politics* to explain why Americans had no need of it. Whereas European society remains ridden with ideological conflict, American history succeeded because abstract ideas were never important, even to the Founders, who drew their political thought from nature and experience rather than theory and ideology. The "genius" of the American people was their instinct for deriving knowledge and value from nature and man's interaction with the environment rather than from ideological doctrine. Boorstin's thesis would be challenged the following decade, but in the fifties it resonated the anti-intellectual mood of America.

Another fifties thesis that would become the subject of intense controversy was the idea of "consensus." The idea had been formulated by historians, several of whom had been influenced by Marxism in their student years. The consensus argument emerged as an alternative to the conflict interpretation of American history that had been pronounced in the radical thirties. Having been misled to believe that America was so conflict-ridden that it would collapse from the stresses of depression and war, former radical students, now professors in the postwar era, felt the need to figure out why they allowed themselves to be misled and, in addition, why American institutions survived the depression and the war relatively intact. Since the catastrophe predicted by Marxists had failed to occur, the challenge now was to explain continuity.

Richard Hofstadter tackled that challenge in *The American Political Tradition*. He found "a kind of mute organic consistency" in the platforms of all major statesmen from Jefferson to Herbert Hoover, a philosophy of economic individualism that bound Americans to the values of competitive capitalism and made America a "democracy of cupidity rather than a democracy of fraternity." Episodes of populism and progressivism that once had seemed like radical insurgencies emerge in Hofstadter's works as essentially conservative movements that aimed at restoring old principles rather than realizing new ones. This temperament was not what Marx had in mind when he urged the critical thinker to draw his "poetry" from the future, not the past.

Why, then, did class conflict fail to develop in America? Louis Hartz offered a brilliant analysis of this problem in *The Liberal Tradition in America*. Drawing on Tocqueville, Hartz provided a two-fold explanation: the absence of feudalism and the presence of Lockeanism. Because America skipped the feudal stage of history it did not experience a real social revolution in 1776 and hence its people were "born free" (Tocqueville's phrase). Lacking an ancient regime resisting the forces of change, America also did not need a mass socialist movement struggling for radical change. Both the working class and the middle class subscribed to the same Lockean values of property, opportunity, and individual liberty. And since America lacked an aristocracy (except for a pseudo-aristocracy in the plantation South), both workers and merchants lacked an identifiable enemy against which a hostile class consciousness might have developed. Without a landed aristocracy to destroy or a landless mob to denounce, America's political culture became homogenized, flat, and uneventful in the more dramatic European sense of genuine class conflict. In a word, liberalism absorbed America.

Unlike Boorstin, Hofstadter and Hartz deplored rather than celebrated their own consensus interpretation of American history. Indeed, there was nothing in their interpretation that would have been incompatible with the equally saddened thoughts of the German exile Herbert Marcuse, who would soon describe America as similarly "one dimensional," a country of uniform people consuming standardized products. How could America be possessed of "genius" and yet be so monotonous?

Because the consensus interpretation would become so controversial in subsequent decades, it is important to clarify what was being said, particularly by Louis Hartz. Unfortunately, many recent historians have criticized Hartz for praising the "uniqueness" of American liberalism and the "autonomy of American history." It is true that Hartz did partake of what the Old Left of the thirties called "American exceptionalism," the view that America is different and must be interpreted in terms that avoid the European-grounded categories of Marxism. But Hartz despaired at the spectacle of an "irrational" and "absolutist" liberal ideology that had so consensualized America's political consciousness that the American mind could not critically reflect upon itself. Hartz also achieved what has always been the great dream of Marxist scholarship: to combine an analysis of ideology with an analysis of social structure, in this instance the omnipresence of Lockeanism and the missing presence of feudalism. Yet the irony is that the more Hartz came to feel he understood America the more he became convinced that America would fail to understand the world. To the extent that America was truly "unique" and "exceptional," America would have little to offer the rest of the world. The liberal nature of the Declaration and the individualist nature of American society deprived America of a genuine revolutionary heritage that would enable its people to sympathize with others who must struggle to overcome backwardness and the remnants of feudalism. The ideals of 1776 could not be easily transported to the underdeveloped world, for the simple reason that political liberalism based on property and individual rights could not easily be translated into class struggle. "Can a people 'born free' ever understand peoples elsewhere that have to become so? Can it even understand itself?" asked Hartz.

An important dimension of American history that the consensus historians seldom emphasized was religion, the subject of Perry Miller's masterful scholarship. Unlike Hartz, Hofstadter, and Boorstin, Miller never went through a Marxist phase in his college years and it seemed to matter little to him whether consensus or conflict explained American history. What mattered to Miller was "the life of the mind," which he found flowering in seventeenth-century New England Puritanism. Influenced in part by Reinhold Niebuhr, Miller came to appreciate the Calvinist theologian Jonathan Edwards as a modernist thinker whose insights into the "human condition" presaged those of the Danish philosopher Søren Kierkegaard. But Miller had to wage an uphill struggle against conventional historical scholarship. For years the prevailing view had been that of Vernon L. Parrington in his three-volume text,

Main Currents of American Thought, which depicted Puritanism as a gloomy, morbid body of European ideas that had to give way to the more "enlightened" ideas of Jeffersonianism before liberty could prevail in America. Similarly, Miller's contemporary Daniel Boorstin had dismissed Puritanism as another false "ideology" that America quickly overcame as the stale strictures of "dogma" yielded to the fresh breeze of "experience." Miller, on the contrary, saw liberty originating in the Puritan covenant, and he admired Calvinism for its intellectual richness and philosophical depth. Among Miller's outstanding graduate students were Bernard Bailyn and Edmund S. Morgan, who in turn would go on to become eminent historians at Harvard and Yale and produce a galaxy of bright young historians. One of the great intellectual harvests of the forties and fifties was the rediscovery of the colonial past. For years to come it would remain the most fertile field in American historical scholarship.

"THE NEW FAILURE OF NERVE": PHILOSOPHY, THEOLOGY, AND GOD AND MAN AT YALE

During World War II and for several years afterwards there took place in America a war within a war. Since it was fought by intellectuals no one got hurt, but the arguments filled the air with acrimony and venom. At issue was the question seemingly on every writer's lips: who is to blame for modern totalitariansim? In England controversy erupted at the end of the war with the publication of Karl Popper's *The Open Society and Its Enemies,* which did wonders with intellectual history by tracing Hitler not only to Hegel but all the way back to Plato. A few years later Eric Hoffer, a once-blind, self-taught longshoreman who loaded cargo on San Francisco's docks, wrote *The True Believer,* a bestseller that would become one of President Eisenhower's favorite books. Hoffer argued that the horrors of modern mass political movements sprang from the minds of rootless intellectuals who arrogantly identify their own wishes with the course of history as they try to bend history to their will. As if this indictment were not enough, totalitarianism also came to be explained not by the intellectuals' drive toward power but by their denial of knowledge. This accusation roared through the halls of a conference, held in the early war years, on "Science, Philosophy, and Religion in Their Relation to the Democratic Way of Life." Here the scholastic philosopher Mortimer J. Adler went so far as to claim that "the most serious threat to democracy" was not Hitler but "the positivism of the professors," the "nihilistic" liberal educators who failed to teach their students the aboslute, eternal truths that keep the flames of freedom burning. At a similar conference the following year eight Protestant professors from Princeton University issued a manifesto titled "The Spiritual Basis of Democracy." By the war's end there developed a conviction among Christians of various persuasions that totalitarianism, whether fascist or communist, was the political disease of all forms of modern thought that had lost sight of God. Father William J. Kenealy, a Jesuit professor at Loyola University, convinced himself and many of his listeners that even the death camps could be attributed to the perils of modernism:

> The fire of human liberty is extinguished, because there are no inalienable natural rights; there are no inalienable natural rights, because there is no natural law; there is no natural law, because there is no eternal law; there is no eternal law, because there is no God—no God, that is, but Caesar. Would you judge this philosophy by its fruits? Then behold the rotting corpses, the mangled bodies, the crippled minds, the broken hearts, the crushed liberties—the stench of physical and spiritual death—in the lands across the sea.

What was "this philosophy" that allegedly wreaked so much havoc? It was modernism, which consisted of the following: positivism, the view that the only valid knowledge is that which can be scientifically verified; behaviorism, a positivist school of psychology that studies only the physically observable and measurable; naturalism, the rejection of anything supernatural or transcendent; and, above all, relativism, the denial of eternal standards of right and wrong. All that twentieth-century philosophy had contributed to knowledge, and much of which had been central to American pragmatism, was now hauled before the court of Christian judgment and declared guilty. Was it a fair trial?

Jewish intellectuals, not only pragmatists like Sidney Hook but art critics like Meyer Shapiro, had every reason to be outraged by this indiscriminate indictment. With the Holocaust burning in memory, they could not help but recall that the Catholic and Protestant establishments scarcely lifted a finger to help stop it. Nor did the Vatican and the Protestant hierarchy openly criticize Mussolini and Hitler when they were marching to power. Even before the war John Dewey tried to point out that it was not empirical skepticism but ideological dogmatism that animated European totalitarian movements. Aside from politics, what was at issue intellectually was the question whether religion provided the only grounds of morality. To rebuke that assumption Hook organized a symposium on "The New Failure of Nerve" in the *Partisan Review*. The atheist Hook charged that instead of resolutely facing the complexity of the modern world, theologians were running away from it and seeking spiritual shelter under the roof of religious dogma. The more gentle John Dewey, who had been raised a Congregationalist and always retained a sense of piety, made a spirited defense of scientific naturalism and called upon Americans to renew their faith in reason and intelligence.

But the philosophy of pragmatism, which for almost a half-century had dominated American thought in fields like education, law, sociology, and political theory, was also losing its following among intellectuals who were secular and equally skeptical of formal religion. One reason for the disillusionment with pragmatism was that Dewey and some of his disciples had no answer to Hitler's aggressions and refused to support America's entry into the war. Dewey had looked to education, especially the development of scientific intelligence, as the answer to all problems. But the despair modern man felt after witnessing totalitarianism was not despair over human ignorance but human wickedness. Could education arrest man's passion for self-destruction? Many younger American philosophers ceased to believe so and as a result they turned to a new philosophy that arrived like a deliverance after the war.

That philosophy was existentialism, another contribution to American intellectual life by European refugees like Hannah Arendt and Walter Kaufmann, who explicated its meaning and significance. Almost overnight it became a fad and the topic of highbrow conversation. At cocktail parties society ladies would run a hand across the brow and in a slow, jaded accent utter, "La vie est absurd." College students who had read J. D. Salinger could understand such a complaint. But when their philosophy professor took another puff from his pipe and told the class, "You have no essence, only existence," students stared at one another in puzzlement. In the evening, over their beer, students continued to wonder why the professor was talking about "being and nothingness" and "anxiety and nausea." At least their curiosities were provoked, proving again that philosophy begins in wonder.

Existentialism might be defined as the philosophy of the last resort, for it emerged as a desperate answer to a desperate question: where does one turn when all other modes of thought have failed? It appealed particularly to the World War II generation of European writers who felt that all traditional sources of knowledge, including religion and science, had proven impotent in the face of fascism. Religion seeks transcendent truths and science requires a patient accumulation of data. But existentialism is a crisis philosophy in which each individual must decide although there is no assurance of being right. It holds that the critical situations man finds himself in cannot be described or understood in either scientific or idealistic terms. The former purports to predict what man will do, the latter prescribes what he ought to do. For the existentialist, deciding what he is to do can only come from himself, from the resources of his own conscience and will. Profoundly introspective, existentialism provides a way for human beings to analyze critical borderline situations that induce such emotions as guilt and anxiety. Its aim is to show why making decisive choices is an expression of freedom in a world that is uncertain, contingent, and maybe even purposeless. Its motto could well be:

I choose, therefore, I am.

In America existentialism became popular on campuses through the writings of William Barrett, who clarified its various dimensions in his widely read *Irrational Man*. College introductory courses in the humanities often required students to read Albert Camus's *The Stranger* to appreciate the absurdity of putting a man to death for the wrong reasons. More advanced students tackled Jean-Paul Sartre's difficult treatise *Being and Nothingness* and his more lucid plays and novels. There they learned that man has no nature or fixed essence; that freedom is felt in the dread of existence and the agony of decision; that man cannot escape creating value in the free act of choosing; and that therefore he is "condemned to be free." Arthur Schlesinger, Jr., adopted that Sartrean theme from Erich Fromm, and in *The Vital Center* he argued that totalitarian man wants to eliminate anxiety whereas freedom compels liberal man to live with it. Yet while existentialism in Europe culminated in a fierce political debate between Camus and Sartre over Stalinism and Russia's labor camps, in America its ultimate significance would be felt in religion rather than politics.

The central figure here was Paul Tillich, a German refugee who was brought to America in the thirties through the help of Reinhold Niebuhr. Eventually, after learning English, Tillich became one of the most important religious philosophers of the postwar era, especially with the publication of his influenctial *The Courage To Be*. Tillich's American readers were made aware that belief is not necessarily based on the church's dogma or institutions but instead on humankind's own ultimate concerns and commitments. In addition to showing his followers how to overcome anxiety about meaninglessness, guilt, and death, Tillich insisted that there is no need to worry about God because a supernatural symbol can have no philosophical proof of existence.

By making religion dependent on emotion and need rather than reason and evidence, existentialism did much to revive it and liberate it from modern skepticism. But a number of American thinkers doubted that Protestant existentialism could resolve the moral problems of the contemporary world. In 1952 the *Partisan Review*, the most prestigious high-brow journal of the era, ran a symposium on "Religion and the Intellectuals." Aware that the bomb and the collapse of political faiths had turned some writers toward religion, the editors asked contributors to address such questions as whether culture required religion and whether religious values needed to be grounded in a belief in the supernatural. Only a few of the contributors insisted that religion provided an answer to modern doubt and despair; the great majority felt it only provided a desperate assurance that there was an answer.

While intellectuals debated the merits of a European-derived existential religion, a young American Trappist monk living in rural Kentucky, Thomas Merton, published *The Seven Storey Mountain.* The book appealed to hundreds of thousands of college students who followed the course of this Columbia graduate struggling with the problems of existence. They read of Merton watching the world succumb to the dark nightmare of war and totalitarianism, flirting with Marxism and Freud, discovering booze and sex, and finally entering the Catholic priesthood and accepting the strict discipline of the Cistercian order. Later Merton would turn to Eastern philosophies in an attempt to incorporate mysticism and seek higher truths found in the silence of the contemplative life. He would also become an ardent supporter of the civil rights and antiwar movements and a guru to the beatniks.

The various expressions of religion in the fifties disturbed the more orthodox Christians and Jews who had been trained on the Bible and the Torah. This was particularly the case of Catholics brought up on the teachings of Saint Thomas Aquinas. A philosopher who drew on Aristotle and Saint Thomas Aquinas, Mortimer Adler saw existentialism as fetishizing choice without giving any guidance as to what one's choices should be. Jewish existentialist theologians like the German Martin Buber and his American disciple Will Herberg failed to convince even non-Catholic Thomists that religion was possible without the authority of revealed truth. Many Thomists even felt the need to disagree with so devout a Catholic thinker as the French philosopher

Gabriel-Honoré Marcel, who believed that we cannot prove God's existence through reason but only "encounter" Him in the act of love. They also saw no need to turn toward mysticism since reason was adequate to the demands of faith. Such scholastic thinkers, who as Thomists and Aristotelians would become prominent at the University of Chicago and St. John's College (Annapolis), wanted to see America adopt a "great books" approach to education so that students would absorb the timeless classics. Liberals who were skeptical of the idea that timeless truths exist, criticized the proposal as impractical and elitist. The fundamental assumption underlying the proposal was the ancient argument that some initial agreement regarding the ends of life provide the indispensable prerequisite to a rationally ordered society. Many of the thinkers who advocated such ends as a goal of education saw American society in the fifties in a state of chaos rather than consensus. But there was one exception, a young author who felt he saw agreement and consensus everywhere and dissent nowhere.

William F. Buckley's *God and Man at Yale* became the subject of bitter controversy when it appeared in 1951. It attempted to document the pervasive antireligious bias of the intellectual community in general, including the media, and of the Yale faculty in particular. In addition to implying that secular humanism was corrupting the soul of the student body, Buckley also accused professors of hypocritically upholding the liberal ideal of tolerance while in reality refusing to allow devoted Christians to become members of the faculty. The current fads in religion such as existentialism, personalism, and mysticism seemed a babble of nonsense to Buckley, who wanted his Christianity based on the rigors of authority and obedience. Buckley's dismissal of academic freedom as a "superstition," his call to the alumni to establish at Yale the orthodoxy they wished to pay for, and his advocation of outright religlious "indoctrination" in the classroom created a furor across the country. But ultimately the most curious feature of Buckley's thesis was that it paralleled much of the argument that some of the more radical German refugee scholars observed in the fifties, though they felt constrained not to voice it until the sixties. The argument was that America had been dominated by a liberal consensus which allowed no dissent. Both Buckley and Herbert Marcuse, whether for the sake of God or of Marx, declared their intolerance of liberal tolerance as a fraud and their intention to go after the minds of the young, whether it be through "indoctrination" or what later come to be slyly called "consciousness raising."

Yet it would be misleading to describe the "new conservatism" that

Buckley helped inaugurate as deriving solely from an impassioned religious impulse. For *God and Man at Yale* contained another indictment that could delight atheists as well. Not only did Yale refuse to teach religion, Buckley charged, it also refused to have Austrian free-market economics become part of the curriculum. The demand that Yale teach both profits and piety contained some theoretical difficulties. The Austrian scholars were secularists and agnostics who based their economics on science and the self-regulating laws of the market, whereas Buckley was a devout Catholic convinced that values must be grounded in a sense of the supernatural. To arrive at a consensus of both required synthesizing capitalism, which had its origins in Protestant individualism and its revolt against authority, and Roman Catholicism, which made acceptance of papal authority the supreme duty. In Buckley's *National Review* conservative individualism and religious conservatism would remain in tension. Editors did their best to fuse the values of liberty and freedom on the one hand and tradition and divine order on the other. Nevertheless, the magazine witnessed the defection of agnostics like Max Eastman and libertarians like Ayn Rand. But *National Review*'s writers and readers could still sustain a consensus based on a common enemy—the ubiquitous liberal intellectuals.

The New York Intellectuals and the San Francisco Beatniks

Although liberalism fared poorly in the political arena during the Eisenhower era, in high culture and intellectual life it enjoyed a large following. The academic world was also dominated by liberal professors teaching the virtues of consensus, pluralism, and Keynesian economics. Few liberals advocated "collectivism," as Buckley had charged, but the majority did believe in the welfare state and the necessity of a controlled economy. But liberalism so pervaded intellectual matters that even liberals felt the need to expose its easy assumptions about consensual harmony, organizational efficiency, human reason, and the inevitability of moral progress. Since the forties Niebuhr and Schlesinger had been familiar liberal critics of liberalism. Then in 1950 Lionel Trilling published *The Liberal Imagination*, a widely discussed series of essays in which literary criticism addressed politics and society. Trilling called upon liberals to explore the more difficult realm of subtlety, ambiguity, and irony in order to overcome their complacent assumptions. The role of the liberal intellectual was not to continue providing

Columbia professor Lionel Trilling, hero of both the beatniks and later, the neoconservatives.

simplistic portraits of reality but to turn easy answers into harder questions by developing a consciousness of the rich variety and complexity of experience.

Although Trilling was not quite asking for a separation of literature and politics, he was bringing to fruition several theoretical concerns that had been troubling American writers for decades. Literary critics brought up on liberal and radical traditions felt obligated to champion literature that dealt with politics and society in the cause of justice. Yet their aesthetic sensibility led them to praise novels and plays that illuminated solitude, estrangement, and tragedy. Moreover, while the standards of modernism encouraged the liberal to hail whatever was new and experimental, the most radically innovative writers were often conservative and had no use for the values of democratic liberalism. Liberals knew that William Faulkner was a segregationist, T. S. Eliot a royalist, and Ezra Pound a fascist. Can the greatness of literature be established solely on literary grounds by disengaging form from content?

That question was one of many debated day and night by a group of writers who thrived on controversy as though agreement meant the last breath of life. Most of the leading intellectuals in America, many of whom had subscribed to Marxist ideas in the thirties, had plenty of thinking and clarifying to do in the postwar era, and whenever they gathered at someone's apartment "disputes seemed to go off like small firecrackers all over the place." These were the "New York intellectuals," writers who emerged from the depression and war bitterly anti-commuist, skeptical of Marxism, ambivalent about America and the cold war, and intensely dedicated to cultural modernism and the life of the mind. One author called them "a herd of independent minds" to suggest their endless internecine quarrels; another called them "truants" to convey the sense of waste and futility on the part of those who came to view their earlier radicalism as an escape from responsibility. "I pissed away my life in talks," moaned one veteran. Daniel Bell regarded himself and his contemporaries as part of a "twice-born" generation, too old and wise to reenact the optimistic hopes of the thirties and too young and restless to give up completely the adventure of a political cause. The "movement" had died; the mood remained.

The inner circle of New York intellectuals consisted of those who had gone to City College of New York, engaged in fierce debates about Trotsky, wrote for *Partisan Review*, and who in the postwar years hung out in Greenwich Village bars and engaged in equally fierce debates about abstract expressionism. The more numerous Jewish members, many from East European immigrant backgrounds, strove to be cosmopolitan and steeped themselves in European writers and philosophers. Hence Philip Rahv, an editor of *Partisan Review*, had to come to terms with Dostoevski, a literary genius but a political reactionary. The outstanding exception of the old-world Jewish orientation was Alfred Kazin, whose magisterial *On Native Grounds* stimulated a revival of interest in American literature and history. The author and critic Leslie Fiedler astounded the academic world with a Freudian interpretation of *Huckleberry Finn* that viewed male-bonding as homosexual. He also upset many on the Left with his *An End to Innocence*, which charged that intellectuals had repressed their guilt rather than face the truth about Soviet Russia. Two pieces of writing in particular foreshadowed the radical uprisings of the sixties. Paul Goodman's *Growing Up Absurd* convinced numerous readers that America did not provide meaningful work, allow sex without shame or guilt, or give the young a sense of community. More shocking was Norman Mailer's much discussed essay "The White Negro," which hailed the black "hipster" as an existential hero of blood and instinct whose dangerous street life and use of marijuana helped him dare the unknown and thus set an example of rebellion in an age of conformity.

Whatever subject they took up, the New York intellectuals went at ideas, theories, and concepts with such "analytic exuberance" it seemed as though writing itself could compensate for the frustrations of politics. When they participated in the symposium "Our Country and Our Culture," which ran for several issues in *Partisan Review* in 1952, their frustrations and guarded hopes poured forth like a long-withheld confession. As intellectuals they were asked how they felt about their country and their role in it. Had the symposium been held in the twenties, American writers would have disparaged their country and praised the superiority of European culture. Had it been held in the thirties many would have foretold of America's capitalist economy succumbing to Marx's prophecies. In the postwar aftermath of European totalitarianism, the American writer felt—for the first time in decades—it was no disgrace, no shallow provincialism, to accept America and admire it. The single exception was Mailer, who disagreed with the whole idea of the symposium. Many contributors became vehement when they discussed the cheapening of artistic and intellectual life by the forces of mass culture. Most agreed with the editors about the need to sustain a "critical non-conformism." No one dared predict the future. Knowing history had failed them in the past, all seemed to be waiting in darkness for the future to reveal itself.

Meanwhile, literary criticism excelled in the postwar era. Edmund Wilson had made his reputation in the late twenties and its brilliance remained undiminished with his learned essays in the *New Yorker* in the fifites. Cleanth Brooks extracted hidden religious themes from prose fiction and Irving Howe analyzed the novel for its political import. Kenneth Burke, who anticipated the various schools of post-structuralism and deconstruction that would flourish in the eighties, explained why all thinking was linguistic in nature and why all writing turned on rhetorical strategies. Among the New York intellectuals the most impressive literary critic was Lionel Trilling. Gracious, urbane, subtle; Trilling may not have convinced everyone that the refined truths of literature were more noble than the crude realities of politics. But like some of the European refuge scholars, he had an enormous influence on students at Columbia University. One was Norman Podhoretz, who became editor of *Commentary* in the fifites and in the eighties would loom as perhaps the leading neo-conservative intellectual and ardent supporter of President Reagan. It was a measure of the rich delicacy of Trilling's mind that he would also leave a lasting impression in the decidedly non-liberal imagination of some students who would become

New Left activists or bohemian dropouts. Ironically, Trilling wanted students to expand the range of human awareness; when they did so in the sixties he called their rebellious behavior "modernism in the streets."

One of Trilling's most promising pupils was Allen Ginsberg, a history major who would take up poetry after being thrown out of Columbia University for writing obscenities on a dormitory wall. No two temperaments could have been more different. Trilling looked to Matthew Arnold to appreciate literature as a criticism of life; Ginsberg turned to Whitman and embraced literature as a celebration of life. The professor felt at home in the high culture of the academic world; the poet found a home in the underground culture of the bohemian world. Trilling valued discipline, Ginsberg debauchery.

Ginsberg left New York to pursue in California a homosexual affair with Neal Cassady, a legendary figure of the fifties whose life symbolized a frenzied search for the soul's salvation through the pleasures of the body. When Cassady's wife objected to Ginsberg staying at their house in San Jose, he headed for San Francisco carrying with him a letter from William Carlos Williams introducing him to another poet, Kenneth Rexroth. In the early fifties San Francisco had become a mecca for a marginal generation of dropouts and wanderers who scorned the Ivy League and its button-down collars and Wall Street and its Brooks Brothers suits. Rexroth had come from Chicago to try to find traces of the romantic radicalism of the early Wobblies and Jack London. During the war he remained a pacifist and identified with Dwight Mac-Donald's lively but short-lived anarchist journal, *Politics.* But most San Francisco writers were antipolitical. Following the composer John Cage, they rejected all the conventional aesthetic forms and all the stale political formulas. They saw themselves as prophetic bards announcing the coming apocalypse of a dehumanized, exploitive, bomb-shadowed, consumer-driven technocratic civilization. Like their hero, the novelist Henry Miller, they preferred to rejoice to the end rather than try to find the basis for a new beginning:

> It may be that we are doomed, that there is no hope for us, *any of us;* but if that is so then let us set up a last agonizing, blood-curdling howl, a screech of defiance, a war whoop! Away with lamentations! Away with elegies and dirges! Away with biographies and histories, and libraries and museums! Let the dead bury the dead. Let us living ones dance about the rim of the crater, a last expiring dance. But a dance!

San Francisco writers frequented City Lights bookstore, owned by the poet Lawrence Ferlinghetti and reportedly the first store in America to deal in paperbacks. In the evening they gathered at the Hungry I or Miss Smith's Tea Room to hear poetry recited to the accompaniment of a saxophone. The atmosphere was as sensual as it was solemn, with the aroma of pot working its uninhibiting magic. Then one evening in 1955 at the Gallery Six the San Francisco "renaissance" was suddenly born. A poem Ginsberg had been working on for two weeks, day and night under the influence of peyote, amphetamine, and dexedrine, was read to an electrified audience shouting "Go! Go! Go!" First titled "Wail," the poem was published as "Howl." Ginsberg read it as a desperate, hysterical chant, as though he were on top of Miller's volcano railing against the gods. Like a Puritan conversion experience, it begins with a confession of helplessness and despair:

> I saw the best of my generation destroyed by
>   madness, starving hysterial naked,
> dragging themselves through the negro streets at dawn
>   looking for an angry fix,
> angelheaded hipsters burning for the ancient heavenly
>   connection to the starry dynamo in the machinery
>   of night. . . .

Then the entry of evil in the form of Moloch, the god of wars:

> Moloch! Solitude! Filth! Ugliness! Ashcans and unob-
>   tainable dollars! Children screaming under the
>   stairways! Boys sobbing in the armies! Old men weeping in the parks!
> Moloch whose mind is pure machinery! Moloch whose
>   blood is running money! Moloch whose fingers
>   are ten armies! Moloch whose breast is canni-
>   bal dynamo! Moloch whose ear is a smoking
>   tomb!

Ginsberg's resolution offers neither a political solution nor a turn to religion but an identification with the apoetically mad seers and lost visionaries in New York's state mental hospital at Rockland:

> I'm with you in Rockland
>   where you scream in a straightjacket that you're
>   losing the game of the actual pingpong of the
>   abyss. . . .

I'm with you in Rockland
    where fifty more shocks will never return your
    soul to its body again from its pilgrimage to a
    cross in the void.

Sitting on the floor of Gallery Six that evening was Jack Kerouac, drunk on red wine and exhilarated by Ginsberg's screaming visions of a cold, loveless world of outcasts hungering for deliverance. Kerouac had also gone to Columbia University and like Ginsberg he, too, looked to Neal Cassady as a vital force of raw energy and physical fearlessness born of the western frontier. Earlier Kerouac and Cassady took a long car trip across the country, savoring the wide-open spaces, speeding here and there, and seemingly searching to find in motion what had been lost in time. Kerouac then composed his impressions on a continuous roll of paper in a three-week high of creative tension. Like Pollack, Kerouac and the beatniks were concerned with creativity not as art but as process. After several rejections, the novel was published as *On the Road* in 1957. It enjoyed enthusiastic reviews and impressive sales. The *New York Times* literary editor claimed that *On the Road* would do for Kerouac's "Beat Generation" what Hemingway's *The Sun Also Rises* had done for the Lost Generation.

Since *On the Road* came out the same year as Sputnik, the Beat

Poet Allen Ginsberg reading to a gathering of beats and academics.

Generation of San Francisco writers came to be called "beatniks." What precisely did the term mean? The public was puzzled, but then, as now, no one could give a precise definition. The person who first used the expression, the novelist John Clellon Holmes, had in mind a "generation of furtives" who were weary of all conventions. Others thought the term "beat" referred to jazz rhythm, and Kerouac himself confounded everyone when he maintained the term was meant to imply religion as in beatitude, a state of exalted blessedness. Whatever the term meant—down and out, disillusionment and alienation, inner moral resistance, vagrancy as virtue, spiritual bliss and supreme happiness—it represented a mystical search for salvation based upon poetry, jazz, sex, and meditation.

Was there a direct ideological descendency between the beatniks of the fifties and the Hippies and New Left of the sixties? Certainly for Ginsberg, who would go on to become an antiwar activist and apostle of psychedelic drugs and tantric yoga. But Kerouac grew more conservative in the sixties, took to alcohol, retained his bad Catholic conscience, and continued to be haunted by the death of his saint-like tragically ill brother, which he witnessed at the age of four, a model of purity he could never be. In the late sixties he moved with his third wife into his mother's house in Florida. His closest friend, Neal Cassady, died in Mexico in 1968 from an excess of drugs and liquor. The following year Kerouac suffered a massive hemorrhage while watching TV and drinking whiskey; he died eighteen hours later in a hospital. In his last known interview Kerouac was asked whether he identified with the hippies. After scolding their use of acid drugs like LSD, Kerouac sought to separate himself by putting first things first. "I wasn't trying to create any kind of new consciousness or anything like that. We didn't have a whole lot of heavy abstract thoughts. We were just a bunch of guys who were out trying to get laid."

And what did the New York intellectuals think of their literary offspring? Not much. With the single exception of Norman Mailer, who praised their outrageous life-style in *The Village Voice*, most other New York writers treated them as naughty children. Norman Podhoretz dismissed the beatniks as the "know-nothing bohemians." Diana Trilling thought them a throwback to the thirties, and Paul Goodman admired their sexual adventurism but criticized their affectless manner of not caring about society and its problems. Irving Howe doubted that they "could dream themselves out of that shapeless nightmare of California, and for that, perhaps, we should not blame them, since it is not certain anyone can." The poetry and prose of the San Francisco writers seemed to the New York intellectuals shrill, crude, confessional, striving for innocence rather than irony, purity instead of paradox, novelty at the expense of subtlety. Their elders wanted them to give up their abandon, to grow up and accept the responsibilities of adulthood. The beatniks preferred to dance on the rim of the volcano and to prove T. S. Eliot wrong: the world will end not with a whimper but a wail.

Yet the New York intellectuals and San Francisco beatniks did share a common distaste for American politics and society in the Eisenhower era. The former writers found little inspiration in suburbia, mass consumer culture, indiscriminate cold-war rhetoric, and politics as the spectacle of lobbies and the scramble of interest groups. The beatniks expressed their repudiation of the fifites in life as well as literature. Women beatniks shunned high fashion and wore black leotards and no lipstick, but they used so much eyeshadow that people joked about their "raccoon eyes." While society was upholding the stability of marriage and family, the beatniks stood for the wild delight of wandering and sexual freedom, city night-life in dark cellars of iniquity, slovenly clothes, sandals, and beards, and work as the last resort—the curse of the creative class.

To survey intellectual life in the postwar era is to become aware that the America of those years cannot be encapsulated in simple epithets like "consensus" and "conformity." The possibility that intellectuals are notoriously inaccurate guides to their times cannot, of course, be denied. But however society may have been guiding itself "the bland leading the bland," as it was then put—the intellectual assumed a critical position toward it. The "affluent society" that made life better for the masses of people left many artists and writers troubled, if not alienated. Even those who benefited from the prosperity of the era doubted that all its problems could be solved by the endless acquisition of money. Perhaps feeling it themselves, the intellectuals wanted to give society a guilty conscience by trying to shake it out of its complacency. Yet their demands that life be elevated and dedicated to higher pursuits than material satisfactions fell on deaf ears. When Truman ridiculed abstract expressionism as the painting of "scrambled eggs," nothing further needed to be said about the relation of art to politics. The intellectuals of the proud decades had their own pride, and thus they were often dismissed as being so wrapped up in musty books and meaningless thoughts that they had lost touch with life. But the aim of modernism was to rise above the smiling certitudes of the Truman and Eisenhower eras and, instead of talking down to the American people, challenge their capacity for accepting "the shock of the new" and for examining life as well as living it.

> The goal of intellectual man
> Striving to do what he can
> To bring down out of uncreated light
> Illumination to our night.

PART THREE

8

Black America, the Constitution, and Civil Rights

Black Consciousness and the Roots of the Civil Rights Movement

The exciting innovations in high culture in the postwar years influenced black intellectuals as well as white. Many black writers grew up in the staid, provincial South before moving to New York City, where they became caught up in the exotic jazz world and Harlem night life. Despite their disparate roots, black writers had several things in common with New York intellectuals.

Novelists Richard Wright and Ralph Ellison, for example, had also flirted with American communism in the thirties and they would later break with the party and expose its deceptions and allegiance to Moscow. Wright and Ellison were similarly influenced by literary modernism and the daring prose techniques of the Lost Generation, and like their predecessors they too were fleeing small-town life. Their cosmopolitan sensibility toward the bold and new also affected their political outlook. As black writers they had difficulty identifying with either Africa or Russia. Although sympathetic with the struggle against colonial imperialism, their modernist temperaments alienated them from both the ancient cultures and religions of the underdeveloped world, and from Marxist determinism and its denial of freedom. Their stance contrasted stikingly to that of the great black Marxist historian, W. E. B. Du Bois, who had been raised in cosmopolitan Boston and educated at

Harvard University. After being tried and acquitted as an unregistered agent of a foreign government, Du Bois left America during the McCarthy era and traveled through Russia and China before settling in Ghana, where he identified with tribal culture and his long-sought dream of Pan-Africanism. Wright and Ellison, however, were closer to the New York intellectuals in rejecting both communism and ancestor worship and identifying freedom as the intellectual's capacity to question and to choose.

When Wright and Ellison began to publish, they were welcomed by the intellectual world, as was the younger James Baldwin, whose *Go Tell It on the Mountain* registered the religious tensions felt by a southern Baptist adolescent smoldering with fear and guilt. Wright broke into the literary scene with his first novel *Native Son*, and his autobiographical *Black Boy* became a best-seller and Book-of-the-Month Club selection. Ellison regarded *Native Son* as "the first philosophical novel by an American Negro," and he compared *Black Boy* with works by Dostoevski and James Joyce. Both authors had been influenced by the American philosopher William James and his celebration of "the unguaranteed existence" and by French existential philosophy, which appealed to the rootless condition of black intellectuals and challenged them to approach life not as victims but as creators. Ellison's *Invisible Man*, which won the prestigious National Book Award, was a complex, ironic novel whose protagonist accepts the challenge of finding out the truth about himself in a white society that refuses to recognize his worth as a black.

The issue of blackness was uppermost even if the artistic self wanted to deny it. In battling for their humanity, black writers looked to the novel as the vehicle of protest and the birth of consciousness. "He knew he was black but he did not know he was beautiful," Baldwin wrote of his father, who had died several years earlier in 1955. Other writers, like the poets Claude McKay and Langston Hughes, used verse to articulate the emotions of the inarticulate. The challenge was to fight false shame with racial pride. In "Children's Rhymes" in *Montage of a Dream Deferred*, Hughes drew upon be-bop jazz rhythms to capture the thoughts of Harlem youths:

> By what sends
> the white kids
> I ain't sent:
> I know I can't
> be President.

The World War II years gave black writers and artists an opportunity to challenge government and society on several fronts. They worked with the Office of War Information in efforts to persuade Hollywood producers to improve the image of blacks in films. But while Nazism and its denial of racial equality led OWI writers to propagandize the virtues of democracy, Hollywood continued to depict black as Sambo-type entertainers who existed solely to humor white audiences. The singer Lena Horne refused to perform at segregated military bases— at one camp black soldiers had to sit behind German prisoners of war. Some blacks protested the draft. The novelist Ellison joined the merchant marine because he "wanted to contribute to the war, but didn't want to be in a Jim Crow army." A few months after Pearl Harbor a black gardener in Long Island came home from work, opened his mail, and sat down and calmly wrote:

> Gentlemen: I am in receipt of my draft-reclassification notice. Please be informed that I am ready to serve in any unit of the armed forces of my country which is not segregated by race. Unless I am assured that I can serve in a mixed regiment and that I will not be compelled to serve in a unit undemocratically selected as a Negro group, I will refuse to report for induction.
>
> Yours respectfully,
> Winfred W. Lynn.

Blacks like Lynn were willing to risk going to jail; many others simply failed to show up when summoned for induction, and the government was reluctant to prosecute for fear of publicizing the problem. But later during the war an event took place that left the government no choice.

On the evening of July 17, 1944, at the Port Chicago Naval base in California, two munitions cargo vessels suddenly blew up in a terrifying blast. The explosion shook the surrounding community like an earthquake and its glare shone twenty-five miles away in San Francisco. Annihilating the ships and the pier, it was the most powerful man-made explosion prior to the bomb that would fall upon Hiroshima. Some 320 sailors were killed instantly and numerous others maimed or blinded. Of the dead, all ammunition loaders, two hundred were black. Three weeks following the blast, after investigators failed to detect its cause, the 328 surviving black sailors were ordered to return to work loading ammunition. But 258 of them, some still virtually in a state of shock, refused until they could be assured of safety. They were incarcerated and cajoled and threatened by naval officers. Then fifty men were singled out and charged with mutiny. The ensuing naval court-martial became the first mutiny trial of World War II and the greatest mass mutiny trial in American military history.

The court took only eighty minutes of deliberation to find all fifty guilty for conspiring to stop work on the docks. The trial received wide publicity in the black press and Thurgood Marshall, special council for the NAACP, gave legal assistance to the accused to the extent allowed in a military court. He sent Secretary of the Navy James Forrestal a letter pointing out that the sailors' grievances had not been presented at the trial. Why were they not given proper training in handling munitions, as longshore officials had advised, and why were only blacks loading ships at Port Chicago? Sensitive to the racial issue, Forrestal replied that at other bases whites loaded munitions and that the order to return to work at Port Chicago was meant to prevent the men from building "an emotional barrier" of fear the longer they stayed off the job. Forrestal said nothing about the severity of the punishment: ten men were sentenced to fifteen years in prison, twenty-four to twelve years, eleven to ten years, and five sentenced to eight years. All would be dishonorably discharged from the navy.

The black community and many liberal white groups reacted angrily to the Port Chicago trial. Campaigns were organized to build popular pressure for the release of the men, and the NAACP's Legal Defense Fund had its officers file an appeal. Eleanor Roosevelt worked with the National Urban League in sponsoring protest meeetings and collecting petitions. The public had now been made more aware than ever of segregation in the military services, and newspapers reported other protest work stoppages on the island of Guam and within the Seabees. In June 1945 the navy announced that segregation in training camps and other programs would be discontinued; six months afterwards Forrestal's office ordered the release of the Port Chicago fifty, who were given clemency now that the war was over.

The Port Chicago trial provoked one of the largest mass campaigns in behalf of racial justice. It brought together black, liberal, and labor organizations in a common cause. The outcome also proved a victory for the NAACP and its budding legal scholar, Thurgood Marshall, appropriately christened Thoroughgood. His next victory, involving school desegregation, would be a turning point in American history.

THE WARREN COURT AND THE *BROWN* DECISION

One morning in September 1950, Oliver Brown walked his eight-year-old daughter Linda four blocks to their neighborhood school in Topeka, Kansas, expecting to enroll her after finding a registration notice on his doorstep. The principal refused Linda permission, and, citing a law in force in Kansas and in sixteen other states requiring black children to attend segregated educational facilities, he suggested that she ride a bus a half-hour across town to an all-black primary school. Oliver Brown and other black parents protested and joined the NAACP in filing a suit against the Board of Education of Topeka, Kansas. The suit claimed that refusal to admit Linda Brown violated the equal protection clause of the Fourteenth Amendment. The case quietly worked its way up the appeal system and reached the Supreme Court in 1954.

The previous year President Eisenhower had appointed as Chief Justice of the United States California's Governor Earl Warren. Neither Eisenhower nor anyone else expected significant changes in the Court's decisions under Warren, who at the time was assumed to have a "middle-of-the-road" philosophy. His earlier approval of the Japanese-American relocation during World War II as California's attorney general and his silence during the Port Chicago mutiny trials also boded ill for civil rights. Although he had criticized McCarthyism and California's loyalty oath, he had uttered no comments on racial segregation in public facilities. Then on May 17, 1954, Warren handed down the Court's unanimous ruling in the now-famous *Brown v. the Board of Education* declaring school segregation unconstitutional. Eisenhower was upset by the boldness of the decision, the liberal press and the NAACP were jubilant, the South first mute then infuriated, and the rest of the nation confused and apprehensive.

Although the *Brown* decision came down like a bombshell, the struggle for racial equality had been fought for years through legal channels. Thurgood Marshall, barred from staying at downtown hotels when he went to Washington to argue a case in the Supreme Court, had been using the resources of the NAACP to orchestrate litigation campaigns. The Court had already struck down southern state laws prohibiting blacks from attending law school, and in South Carolina, Virginia, and Delaware cases had been filed challenging separate schools for races maintained through constitutional or statutory provisions. The black sociologist Kenneth Clark had also been gathering evidence to prove that racial segregation harmed black children's self image and stamped them with "the badge of inferiority." In the last months of the Truman administration, Chief Justice Fred M. Vinson declared that segregation fell within the jurisdiction of the Constitution and that the *Plessy v. Ferguson* (1896) ruling could be challenged. That ruling held that if blacks were furnished public accommodations equal to those of whites (in that legal case, railway coaches), there was no violation of the Fourteenth Amendment's provision, "nor to deny to any person . . . equal protection of the laws." The principle of "separate but equal" came to imply that segregation did not entail discrimination.

By the time of *Brown*, the real question facing the Warren Court was not whether the Fourteenth Amendment was designed to give equal protection to black Americans—a point acknowledged by every legal theorist—but whether segregation under conditions of equal facilities amounted to a denial of equal protection. Chief Justice Warren, together with the NAACP's resourceful legal scholar Marshall and activist Roy Wilkins, convinced the court to depart from precedent and employ a new mode of thinking. They and others recognized the difficulty of judging the validity of the Fourteenth Amendment's provisions by trying to establish the original intent of the authors who wrote them. Instead, the Warren Court held that it was not possible to determine whether those who drafted the Fourteenth Amendment in 1866 meant to ban

NAACP attorney Thurgood Marshall preparing a civil rights brief.

school segregation as well as to assure equal political rights for black Americans as an outcome of the Civil War. The Court then reasoned that all racially segregated school systems, even those with similar facilities, were "inherently unequal" because they breed "a feeling of inferiority" in the "hearts and minds" of young black children, an argument that rested on problematic evidence provided by sociologists. At issue was not the equality of facilities but the emotional effects of being identified with separate facilities. Along with the psychological damage done by segregation, separate schools also deprived black pupils of equal educational opportunities and thus denied them the equal protection of the laws guaranteed by the Fourteenth Amendment.

The unanimity of the Court's decision made it appear that the Constitution had declared its authority in a single voice. In truth, the Court was deeply divided. While all members agreed that *Plessy* had to be overturned and that segregation in trains and law schools was unconstitutional, they were reluctant to pass judgment on public schools. Justice Hugo L. Black, a Roosevelt appointee from Alabama, feared that the KKK would take to the streets in violent demonstrations. When Philip Elman, a civil rights expert in the Solicitor General's office, became aware of such apprehensions, he submitted a revised brief proposing that the district courts be given a reasonable period to work out the details and timing for implementing the decree. Justice Felix Frankfurter, another Roosevelt appointee who had, with some impropriety, been keeping Elman informed, could now bring other members of the Court to see the imperative of issuing a unanimous decision. Thus the most important Supreme Court decision of the twentieth century, one that had the potential for affecting twelve million school children, deliberately avoided an implementation decree and left it up to local school authorities to assume responsibility for carrying out the law.

The executive also had the responsibility to enforce the law. But President Eisenhower, piqued by a ruling that made his political life more difficult than he thought it should be, and later angered by the Court's civil liberties decisions, would call his appointment of Warren "the biggest damn-fool mistake I ever made." Nevertheless, he moved swiftly to integrate the District of Columbia's schools after the Court ruled that segregation violated the Fifth Amendment's due process clause. Blacks were also hired to White House positions for the first time on a significant scale. Beyond that, Eisenhower showed little interest in the drive toward equality and civil rights. Meanwhile, various southern state governors convened meetings with political and school officials to decide how they would respond to the Court's decision. When it became clear that many states were delaying or making excuses to ignore the ruling, the Court issued another judgment, the so-called "Brown II," stating that all segregated school systems must make "a prompt and reasonable start toward full compliance" and to do so "with all deliberate speed."

The second *Brown* decision proved to be even more controversial than the first, dividing the country, the Eisenhower Administration, and the Supreme Court itself. Two justices began to worry that the Court would be put in the awkward position of issuing judgments it had no means of enforcing. Warren himself never made it clear whether school segregation "solely on the basis of race" was unconstitutional or whether separate educational facilities were unconstitutional because they were "inherently unequal." Such ambiguities could be exploited by the claim that custom and tradition, and not race, was the issue. Thus southerners and some conservative scholars insisted that segregation was part of the South's way of life and could not be altered by judicial fiat. That view was challenged by Professor C. Vann Woodward in *The Strange Career of Jim Crow* (1955). By showing that the legally defined exclusion of blacks from public accommodations occurred in the South only after the Civil War and as late at the 1880s, Woodward tried to demonstrate that there was no direct continuity between slavery and segregation and that southern race relations, rather than being permanently rooted in historic conventions, were amenable to change and adaptation.

Since several school desegregation cases were being decided concurrently, the practice of segregation throughout the nation as a whole came under scrutiny. Yet constituency was almost as important as geography in determining results. Where black populations were relatively small, below one-fourth of the student body, some educators would comply with the Court's order; where blacks exceeded one-fourth, various strategies of resistance developed. Thus in Topeka, Kansas, where the *Brown* decision originated, desegregation proceeded smoothly in a city with a black population of only 8.3 percent. In the District of Columbia, where blacks were in the majority, white students and parents boycotted local court orders. In Delaware, the integration of rural school districts went well but not in the highly black populated city of Wilmington. White South Carolinians succeeded for a decade in resisting court orders involving various "black-belt" regions, and in Prince Edward County, Virginia, which had been cited in the *Brown* case, a white school board chose to close its public schools rather than to desegregate them.

The historic *Brown* decision raised arguments and stirred controversies for years. Constitutional critics charged that it marked the beginning of government by an unelected judiciary. In many parts of the South it met massive resistance as state governors prepared to "interpose" themselves before the authority of the federal government. In the North, several years after the decision, many large cities witnessed a "white flight" of middle-class Americans to the suburbs. And when the policy of busing children into different neighborhoods was adopted, an irony became embarrassingly evident: a judicial decision that had earlier been made to prohibit racial discrimination would now have to recognize it as a means of bringing about "racial balance" in various school districts. Liberals and blacks, however, would defend the Warren Court's decision as part of a broader civil rights movement which was beginning to move against racism in public facilities, restaurants, the workplace, and voting booths. Warren himself came to believe that the *Brown* decision may have been a little too precipitous. But he never had second thoughts about the Court's ruling, which meant that the rights of black Americans could no longer be violated under the United States Constitution.

Showdown at Little Rock

But the Supreme Court can only pronounce the law; it is up to the president to enforce it. Eisenhower refused to endorse the *Brown* decision; he claimed it was his responsibility to execute the law, not to comment upon it. In truth, he was reluctant to put the federal government squarely behind the civil rights movement and school desegregation. Indeed, he showed even less interest in taking risks in domestic race relations than in the field of foreign affairs. His idea of the presidency, which reflected the nation's mood of moderation, was to maintain an equilibrium rather than lead the country into new social experiments. "I personally believe," he stated in addressing racial integration at a press conference in 1957, "if you try to go too far too fast in laws in this delicate field that has involved the emotions of so many Americans, you are making a mistake." Ultimately he believed that race relations remained a private and not a public responsibility. In respect to changing peoples' values, he informed Booker T. Washington's daughter, Portia, "we cannot do it by cold lawmaking, but must make these changes by appealing to reason, by prayer, and by constantly working at it through our own efforts."

Not all Americans agreed. In the Senate civil rights had the strong support of liberals like Hubert Humphrey of Minnesota and Lyndon Johnson of Texas. Within the administration the attorney general's office, headed first by Herbert Brownell, Jr., and then William P. Rogers, articulated the case for a strong civil rights bill to Congress. But Eisenhower would support only the mildest of its provisions and he accepted a revised Senate amendment that eliminated the attorney general's authority to bring civil action against violation of not only voting rights but civil rights in general. The Civil Rights Act of 1957 did little to address such problems as job discrimination, access to public accommodations, and school desegregation, which several states were either quietly evading with the consent of the white community or engaging in defiant massive resistance. Despite the appeals of such black leaders as Ralph Bunche, Jackie Robinson, and A. Philip Randolph, Eisenhower refused to lend the prestige of his office to the cause of racial equality.

The most that can be said of the president is that he was consistent. For he remained similarly indisposed toward sexual inequality. At the time the civil rights bill was being debated, the journalist May Craig, after praising the president for doing something about racial discrimination, asked: "Why have you not been active in trying to wipe out discrimination based on sex, namely the equal rights amendment?" Surprised by the question, Eisenhower replied: "Well, it is hard for a mere man to believe that woman doesn't have equal rights." The nearly all-male press corps roared at the innocence of the response. Eisenhower promised he would "take a look" at the problem, one that would take another decade to agitate the nation's political consciousness.

But the question of equal rights in respect to race would not wait. The Supreme Court had declared what the law of the land was and should be in *Brown*. Liberals began to look upon the courts as instruments of social change, and the NAACP expanded its Legal Defense and Education Fund to work with government agencies to expedite racial integration. Yet in 1957, three years after *Brown*, only four southern states were complying with the ruling. Several had also passed laws against barratry, the "stirring up of quarrels and lawsuits," in an effort to drive the NAACP out of legal practice in the South, a move that the Supreme Court would strike down as a violation of equal protection in racial litigation. Senators like Harry F. Byrd of Virginia and

The John Birch Society, a right-wing extremist organization founded in the late fifties, saw communism everywhere, including the Supreme Court.

Herman Talmadge of Georgia invoked the South's antebellum argument of states' rights to oppose the power of the federal government. In the deep South, "Citizens' Councils" organized to take a last stand on segregation and racial supremacy. Even outside Old Dixie, right-wing organizations like the John Birch Society saw the government as the enemy. The Birchers convinced their followers that racial integration was a communist plot. In California and the Southwest billboards alongside freeways told drivers what they must do as their patriotic duty: "IMPEACH EARL WARREN."

Meanwhile in the South, federal district judges did their best to uphold the Supreme Court's decision on desegregation, often in the face of angry threats from white citizens. Yet court orders to comply could be circumvented by a variety of strategies. One was to admit a few blacks to all-white schools, a tactic which observed the Constitution's ban against desegregation but fell short of integration by achieving a racial mix of students proportionate to the community's population. Another was to organize classrooms according to "ability groups" with each race attending different times of the day, or to require so many application forms, lengthy personal interviews, and even longer lines that black parents would be dissuaded from trying to enroll their children.

Some school districts, such as the Little Rock Board of Education in Arkansas, sincerely wanted to carry out the *Brown* decision but to do it slowly, starting the integration process at the upper levels of high school and year-by-year working down to the lower grades, a schedule that was to be started in 1959 and completed by 1963. But the Arkansas NAACP wanted immediate integration at all levels, and when the school board refused, it filed suit in the federal court. The court found in favor of the school board, holding that Little Rock was in compliance with the "all deliberate speed" principle in respect to local conditions.

But the court decision did little to cool tempers in Little Rock as the fall semester approached in 1957. Racists and demagogues organized citizen's councils to run candidates for the school board on a white supremacy platform. Despite defeat at the polls, the bigots continued their campaign and threatened massive resistance—even violence if necessary—when the schools opened. Little Rock city officials called upon Governor Orval Faubus to take responsibility to enforce the law. Although no staunch segregationist, Faubus first hesitated, knowing it would be politically damaging to intervene on behalf of desegregation. Yet he had taken no stand when Arkansas had amended its state constitution to oppose *Brown* and he failed to consult with President Eisenhower when he eventually directed the Arkansas National Guard to oppose the federal court-ordered enrollment of nine black students at Little Rock's Central High School.

For three weeks the armed troops stood shoulder to shoulder to prevent blacks from entering the building, in defiance of the city's school board, which wanted to carry out the court order. As tension mounted the NAACP judged it unsafe to send black children from their homes until the students' safety could be guaranteed. But the parents of one girl, fifteen-year-old Elizabeth Eckford, had not heard of the NAACP's decision. When Elizabeth arrived at Central High School, white mobs shouted, "A nigger! . . . Here they come!" She continued against the taunting crowd, holding back her tears, trying not to show any fear. Then a national guardsman barred her from entering the school door and she turned around, confused, alone, afraid. The white crowd continued to harass her when she reached a bus-stop bench and began to sob with her head in her arms. A white woman who sat down to comfort the trembling Elizabeth and escort her home on the bus was jeered as "You nigger lover." "Don't you see she's scared?" the woman pleaded. "She's just a little girl." The next day photographs of Elizabeth Eckford walking past a gauntlet of hate-mongers appeared on the front pages of the nation's newspapers. The country was outraged at such meanness and cruelty. Turning with disgust from Little Rock, Americans now looked to the White House for leadership in the school desegregation crisis.

All along Eisenhower had been reluctant to intervene. Not only did he doubt that racial attitudes could be changed by legal means, but he also had great sympathy for the white South and he had to consider the possibility that southern states would simply abolish the public school system. But Faubus's defiance of federal court orders and his decision to withdraw the state National Guard, instead of asking the president to put the state troops under federal authority, made Little Rock vulnerable to mob violence and left Eisenhower no choice but to resort to force to uphold the law. He dispatched one thousand paratroopers of the 101st Airborne Division to Little Rock to surround Central High School. Protected by the fully armed paratroopers, black students entered the school and went quietly to their desks. The president tried to conciliate southern politicians by reminding them that he was not trying to enforce integration but simply carrying out his oath of office. For once his charm and gentle persuasion failed him. Senator Richard Russell of Georgia likened the federal intervention to Hitler's storm troops and a Louisiana politician called for secession from the Union.

Except for some northern liberals, the Democrats approached the

Elizabeth Eckford, attempting to enter Central High School, Little Rock, Arkansas, in 1957.

desegregation controversy with caution and tact. On the television program "Face the Nation," Adlai Stevenson told reporters he would not advocate resorting to force in Little Rock. After Eisenhower had done so, Stevenson agreed with the president that there was no alternative. But Eisenhower's action would do little to solve the "national disaster" unless he would "now mobilize the nation's conscience as he had mobilized its arms," advised Stevenson. Easier said than done, especially for a Democratic party that could not afford to lose its southern wing. Even Stevenson, the symbol of the statesman who would not stoop to politics, had to court the segregationist Senator Russell if he were to remain the leading contender for the party's nomination in the 1960 election. With Eisenhower, however, politics mattered less since the Constitution prohibited his running for a third term. His failure to take a strong stand on desegregation was more a matter of conviction about the limits of government intervention in racial affairs. Perhaps his most enlightened act was appointing to the Civil Rights Commission Father Theodore M. Hesburgh, the president of Notre Dame University, who proved to be a strong supporter of equal opportunity for blacks. But at the highest level of leadership, the president failed to address the greatest social problem facing America.

"I HAVE A DREAM": MARTIN LUTHER KING, JR., AND THE CIVIL RIGHTS MOVEMENT

Most revolutions begin in mass protest and passion; the civil rights movement of the fifties began with a single gesture of exhaustion. On the evening of December 1, 1955, Mrs. Rosa Parks, a neatly dressed, middle-aged black woman, was riding home on a Montgomery, Alabama bus, seated behind the section for "Whites Only." She held a shopping-bag full of groceries on her lap. When two white passengers got on and saw all the seats in the white section occupied, the driver announced, "Niggers move back," ordering the blacks to give up their seats as prescribed by law. Three black passengers got up and stood at the back of the crowded bus. Rosa Parks stayed in her seat. The driver, grumbling under his breath, pulled over to the curb, set the brakes, rose from his seat, and with a few steps stood above her. "I said to move back, you hear?" Everyone on the packed bus fell into complete silence; no one moved, especially Mrs. Parks, who continued to look out the window, refusing to even acknowledge the driver's presence. He waited; the passengers listened and watched for even a gesture of

Rosa Parks being booked for disobeying public transportation segregation laws, Montgomery, Alabama.

a reply. He repeated his order; she continued to stare into the darkness of the night. No one in the bus that evening realized they were witnessing a historic moment that would change the course of modern American history. Not even Mrs. Parks, who later stated that she was simply too tired and "bone weary" to move to the back.

But Mrs. Parks had been working with E. D. Nixon, president of the Alabama NAACP and who had earlier worked with A. Philip Randolph planning the March-on-Washington during the war. When she called him from jail that evening, he phoned Clifford Durr about bail and legal advice. Clifford and Virginia Durr were members of a small group of southern white liberals who worked with black leaders on the Alabama Council on Human Relations to find ways to improve the South's racial situation. Durr was a distinguished lawyer who had once worked in New Deal agencies and left government in protest of Truman's loyalty program. He suggested challenging the constitutionality of Alabama's segregated public transportation services. Nixon realized such an effort would require the full backing of Montgomery's black community. He then approached the Reverend Ralph Abernathy, a young, militant Baptist minister, and together they planned a bus boycott on the day that Mrs. Parks had to appear in court. It was a risky tactic, for almost all black workers in the city had to use public transportation to get to their jobs. To reach as many neighborhoods as possible and assure the full cooperation of all blacks, Abernathy called Rev. Martin Luther King, Jr., the young new pastor of the Dexter Avenue Baptist Church. On the day of the boycott King and his wife Coretta were up before dawn to check bus stops to see how many blacks were aboard. They felt they could expect no more than 60 percent to honor the boycott, but that would be a sufficient threat to Montgomery's transportation revenue. On a regular day the early buses would be jammed with black domestic workers on their way to wealthy white residential districts. The day of the boycott, the first bus arrived empty; so, too, the second; the third had two passengers, both white. As the morning wore on, those on the boycott planning commission saw a sight that surpassed all expectations: young black students thumbing rides, cars overloaded with hitchhikers, older black workers cheerfully walking, a few using horse-drawn buggies, and at least one seen riding a mule. Even those who had to trek six miles to work sang as they walked along. "A miracle had taken place," King later wrote in *Stride Toward Freedom*. "The once dormant and quiescent Negro community was now fully awake."

That evening a mass meeting took place at the Holt Street Baptist Church. It was here that King, then only twenty-seven and unknown to the community and America at large, entered the pages of history. Montgomery's black leaders had sensed King's genius for pulpit oratory and late in the day they asked him to deliver the evening's sermon. Although unprepared, King rose to the occasion. He aroused the audience by shouting: "We are tired! Tired of being segregated and humiliated!" Then he led them back to reflection by calmly reminding them: "Once again we must hear the words of Jesus: 'Love your enemies. Bless them that curse you. Pray for them that despitefully use you.' If we fail to do this, our protest will end up as a meaningless drama on the stage of history." The conclusion was a perforation of duty and destiny:

If you protest courageously, and yet with dignity and Christian love, future historians will say, 'There lived a great people—a black people—who injected new meaning and dignity into the veins of civilization.' This is our challenge and our overwhelming responsibility.

The audience rose, applauding, cheering, with hosannas of "Amen, Brother, Amen." Everyone understood why the boycott must be continued; no one present could forget the impact King had made upon their lives. One elderly woman later recalled that she "saw angels standing all around him when he finished, and they were lifting him up on their wings."

The young man who would go on to become the spiritual catalyst of the civil rights movement, a Nobel Prize winner, a symbol of courage to the sixties generation, and ultimately, the victim of an assassin's bullet, was born in Atlanta, Georgia, in 1929. His father, Martin Luther King, Sr., was the respected pastor of the prestigious and well-endowed Ebenezer Baptist Church. Although raised in a comfortable middle-class neighborhood, young Martin knew the meaning of racism. A friend on the block was told not to play with him because he was black and once a woman in the department store suddenly slapped his face. "The little nigger stepped on my foot," she complained. He was a precocious, gifted student, always reading and distracting his parents with a battery of questions. The sight of black unemployed workers standing in line in tattered clothes during the depression saddened him. Assured of his own meals, he wondered if there were children who would have enough to eat. The sight of racial cruelty was worse. When he saw police brutalizing black children or witnessed night-riding Klansmen clubbing his people in the streets, he struggled to control his rage and obey the commandments. "How can I love a race of people who hate me?" he asked. Even as a youth King took it upon himself to bear the crushing weight of guilt for both the white man's deeds and the black man's thoughts.

When he was fifteen, King attended Morehouse College, a segregated liberal arts school affiliated with Atlanta University. Upon graduation he chose not to follow his father's advice and go directly into the ministry. Instead he went to Crozer Theological Seminary in Pennsylvania and received a Bachelor of Divinity degree, graduating first in his class. In 1955 he earned a Ph.D. at Boston University, where he also met his future wife Coretta Scott, a beautiful, talented singer who had been training at the New England Conservatory of Music. Coretta originally wanted to remain in Boston, but she did not hesitate to support her husband's sense of moral duty at the expense of her own career so he could return to the racially tense South.

School for King was not simply an accumulation of degrees and credentials but a voyage of discovery into two fields that became his daily passion: religion and philosophy. He undertook an omnivorous, systematic inquiry into Plato, Rousseau, Hobbes, Locke, Nietzsche, and Kierkegaard. He attended seminars on personalism and existential philosophy and took survey courses on Hinduism and Islam. He wrote his doctoral dissertation on the contrasting theisms of Paul Tillich and Henry Nelson Wieman. Tillich was a monist who claimed God remained transcendent and beyond the things of the world; Wieman, a pluralist who believed in God's immanence and direct involvement in all worldly things. King thoughtfully sought to synthesize both. He wanted to preserve the need for unity from the relativistic threat of pluralism and the value of individuality from the all-absorbing oneness of monism. His professors were impressed with his probing, restless mind and looked forward to his career as a prominent scholar.

As much as King valued the life of the mind, the Christian gospel of social justice was a higher imperative. In developing his own intellectual vision of politics, he drew on three distinct sources and managed to assimilate them into a coherent theory of action. The first was a book that had also influenced Progressive intellectuals after the turn of the century, *Christianity and the Social Crisis* by Walter Rauschenbusch. It called upon Christians to build a new social order by replacing capitalism and the laws of Darwin with the example of Christ and the laws of love, cooperation, and solidarity. But King's anticapitalism never drove him to be tempted by the ideas of Marx, although the FBI suspected he was a communist and kept close surveillance of his personal life. His reading of Tillich's existential theology led him to conclude that communism was a "grand illusion," a false doctrine that denied man's spiritual nature, substituted for God the self-propelled movement of matter, and endowed history with its own redemptive power. King was equally skeptical of pacifism. Rauschenbusch had rejected the notion that man was the source of evil, and Christian pacifists like A. J. Muste carried the conviction of human innocence to the point of renouncing all uses of power to resolve problems. More and more King doubted that Christian love itself could effect social change or prevent human suffering. Slavery and the Holocaust were tragic reminders of the impotence of brotherly love. To overcome the dilemmas of Protestant liberalism King turned to a second source, Reinhold Niebuhr's *Moral Man and Immoral Society, The Irony of American History,* and *The Nature and Destiny of Man.* Niebuhr reminded King that Christian pacifists themselves were responsible for Nazism for refusing to take up arms against it. King also came to understand how man's sinful nature caused him to rationalize his own sinful deeds, the most conspicuous example being the American Founders' validation of slavery.

Reverend Martin Luther King, Jr., before a photo of the Indian pacifist and leader, Mahatma Gandhi.

Above all, King obtained from Niebuhr a vision of "the glaring reality of collective evil," the tendency of otherwise decent individuals to join groups and remain unaware of how their own egoistic and aggressive nature becomes magnified in group behavior. Through Niebuhr's writings King transformed himself from a Protestant moralist to a Christian "realist."

While making King aware of the reality of evil and the duty of using force to oppose it, Niebuhr's writings nevertheless were insufficient to meet the needs of black America. King knew from reading about Nat Turner's insurrection in 1831 that force and violence would be suicidal for blacks. He was far more impressed with Henry David Thoreau's dictum that small minorities, even "one honest man," could regenerate an entire society. But Thoreau's tactic of trying to change society by denouncing it and "washing" his hands of it did not make a difference, at least not politically. What was needed was not the pose of the alienated poet but an effective theory of civil disobedience. For this third source of inspiration King went outside America to learn from the life and writings of Mahatma Gandhi.

In the postwar years the dramatic Indian independence movement was led by a saintly person who challenged the moral imagination in an age of power politics. Trained as a lawyer, Gandhi chose to wear native loincloth, shawl, and sandals, fitting symbols of his belief in gentleness, persuasion, and the utmost simplicity of needs. Gandhi had learned from Thoreau the tactic of individual passive resistance to change the wrongs of society, but he transformed the lesson into an epic mass movement to purge British colonial power from India. When King first heard a lecturer explain Gandhi's idea of *satyagraha*—the "truth force" that reconciles love and power—he was spellbound. Through nonviolent strikes, boycotts, and protest marches Gandhi and his followers succeeded in winning their freedom from their oppressors. What moved King was not so much that Gandhi had won but how he had won. For Gandhi represented the first example in modern history of realizing political ends through spiritual means. King absorbed Gandhi's conviction that nonviolence implies the willingness to endure suffering without retaliation. He also shared Gandhi's conviction that the aim of nonviolence should not simply be to win victory or humiliate the opponent; instead, every effort must be made to reach the opponent's conscience and ultimately to try to achieve a reconciliation based on a new level of moral understanding. Thus Gandhi's Hindu idea of satyagraha reinforced King's interpretation of the Christian idea of agape—the love of all humanity as a single chain of brothers and sisters, the only chain that could withstand the ever-recurring forces of hatred.

During the bus boycott King preached his Gandhian inspired theory of civil disobedience to the Montgomery Improvement Association, which then set up workshops throughout the city on non-violence and direct action. Out of such efforts evolved the Southern Christian Leadership Conference (SCLC), organized in 1957 to work for black voting rights and school desegregation. Three other organizations promoted the civil rights movement in the fifties. The National Urban League, started decades earlier during the Progressive era, concentrated mainly on northern industrial cities and was of little help to southern blacks. The Congress of Racial Equality (CORE), which grew out of the prewar Fellowship of Reconciliation, combined Christian pacifism with Gandhian tactics but it, too, failed to penetrate into the deep South after the war. Meanwhile the NAACP had been fighting the cause through the courts, but when it won a legal victory, as in the *Brown* case, black America could not count on the president to implement it. Moral confrontation would have to supplant litigation. King and SCLC officials realized this when they finally obtained a meeting with President Eisenhower in June 1958. He was "surprised" to hear that respected black leaders had become impatient with the federal government. As the meeting broke up, Eisenhower passed by King and with the shrug of his shoulders sighed, "Reverend, there are so many problems . . . Lebanon, Algeria . . ."

Although King would become disgusted with the Eisenhower administration, his own movement had been picking up support since the Montgomery bus boycott, when he was indicted the following year for having hindered business without "just cause or legal excuse." King's arrest and trial had made the boycott front-page news and brought journalists from Europe and as far away as Taiwan, Japan, and the Philippines. Reporters were delighted when King responded to the charge that he was a communist by giving an erudite lecture on Marx, Engels, Hegel, and Feuerbach and then explained why he preferred theological existentialism to dialectical materialism. Busily taking notes, reporters were impressed listening to an activist who could be as profound as he was persuasive. An intellectual's intellectual, he knew more about communism than most members of the Communist party.

The Montgomery boycott succeeded in integrating the bus service, but all other public institutions, including schools, remained segregated. The same resistance prevailed throughout the deep South. Autherine Lucy, a black coed, tried to enter the University of Alabama and was almost murdered by white students. In Birmingham, Alabama, Nat King Cole, the famous black singer, was attacked and beaten while singing from the stage of the city auditorium. Afterwards, the same gang of whites jumped a black youth on the street and mutilated his genitals. The mob lynching of fourteen-year-old Emmet Till in Mississippi in 1955, shocked the nation. King himself received threatening phone calls, hate mail from the KKK, was stabbed in the chest by a deranged woman, and had his house bombed. Yet like Gandhi King never lost faith in nonviolence, and like Abraham Lincoln he sensed that his political mission might result in his own fatality. "Lord, I hope no one will have to die as a result of our struggle for freedom here in Montgomery," he said. "But if anyone has to die, let it be me." After his house was bombed, he assured his followers on the street outside that his wife and children were safe. He then stated: "If I had to die tomorrow morning, I would die happy—because I've been to the mountaintop, and I've seen the Promised Land."

The civil rights movement that Martin Luther King, Jr., inspired in the fifties would realize many of its goals the following decade and after his assassination, on April 4, 1968, America would celebrate his birthday along with Washington's and Lincoln's. King always felt uncomfortable when some of his followers referred to him as a savior or the Messiah. Yet he was a spiritual force who changed the hearts and minds of black and white Americans alike, if only by making the latter feel guilty and the former proud. "We got our heads up now," said a black janitor in Montgomery, "and we won't ever bow down again—no, sir—except before God."

9

Neither War nor Peace

Eisenhower had learned from observing the Truman administration the difficult political lesson of allowing America to become bogged down in a land war in Asia. But after he had successfully extricated the United States from the Korean War and refused to commit troops to the French cause in Indochina, Eisenhower still had to confront the reality of China, numerically the largest communist power in the world. Although Britain and other Western states had extended diplomatic recognition to China, the United States refused to do so, in part because of China's bitter ideological offensive against capitalist America, and in part because Eisenhower's advisors assumed that China was an integral part of a united world communist "bloc" that included North Korea, Eastern Europe, and the USSR. The assumption was more apparent than real. Not only was the communist world on the verge of dissolution in the mid-fifties, but the refusal to explore the possibility of normalizing relations with Mao meant that America would be forced to continue defending the Nationalist regime on the island of Formosa as the legitimate government for all of China. One recalls Tom Paine's warning to the British in 1775: an island cannot rule a continent.

The tense Formosa Strait crisis of 1954–55 (discussed in Chapter 4), had wound down with no improvement in United States-China relations. During the crisis the Eisenhower administration had hinted strongly that nuclear weapons would be used if China undertook invasion operations against the offshore islands. The chief of naval operations even reported to the press that the president was considering a preemptive strike to end China's "expansionist tendencies." It is not at all clear that the administration's threat to resort to nuclear weapons proved successful in deterring the Red Chinese, for they would resume shelling of the islands several years later. But the tactic convinced many Republicans that the best way to avoid conventional warfare was to prepare for nuclear war. "The ability to get to the verge without getting into war is the necessary art," Secretary of State Dulles stated in an interview in *Life* magazine. "On the question of enlarging the Korean War, on the question of getting into the Indo-China War, on the question of Formosa, we walked to the brink of war and looked it in the face." Dulles's use of the threat of war as a deterrent came to be known as "brinksmanship," a calculated gamble that seemed to have succeeded in Asia. But the policy did little to win the support of noncommunist Asia or to consider how America could improve relations with Mao's China without sacrificing Formosa's security. If nothing had been lost by Dulles' saber rattling, neither had anything been gained. Relying on the doctrine of massive retaliation did fulfill the administration's promise to reduce defense expenditures, but as a diplomatic strategy it was as dubious as it was dangerous. Eisenhower himself recognized the difficulty of keeping a nuclear war limited even as he threatened its use in Asia.

The doctrine of nuclear retaliation actually had more meaning in Europe than in Asia. Russia had no irredentist claims, had met its security requirements, and as a satisfied power had everything to lose by challenging containment and embarking upon revolutionary adventurism. China, in contrast, was by no means satisfied with Formosa and its nationalist leaders threatening to return to the mainland. Moreover, in areas like Korea and Indochina, where insurgent movements were not controlled by outside superpowers, the threat of massive retaliation could hardly deter guerrillas from continuing civil war in the countryside. Should the United States annihilate the city of Peking for what was happening in the jungles of Laos? Nuclear warfare, in short, would not be clearly applicable to the internal revolutions which came to characterize the cold war in the Third World. Nor could its threat be continually invoked over a long period without America losing its credibility. In the end "walking to the brink" amounted to a diplomacy not so much of success as of stalemate and recognition of the status quo.

Yet it was precisely the status quo in the communist world that the Republican party had set out to repudiate. Dulles had long opposed the Democratic policy of "containment" as too accommodating. Instead he advocated "liberation" of people living under communist domination. The idea that there could be a "rollback" of communism was the great hope of right-wing Republicans, and many saw Indochina as merely a ploy on the part of the Soviets to draw American forces into minor wars all over the world with her alleged satellites. Thus, the Eisenhower administration looked on with approval as Radio Free Europe called upon peoples of Eastern Europe to rise up against their captors. Nineteen-fifty-six was an election year, a tempting time for the Republican party to claim to have the means with which to turn the tide of totalitarianism.

Meanwhile, in the summer of that year, events in the Mideast caught the Eisenhower administration so by surprise that the United States found itself aligned not against but with the Soviet Union. Little attention had been given to the Mideast at the outset of the cold war, and when America quickly recognized the state of Israel in 1948, few politicians or journalists foresaw any trouble with the Arab world. But in 1955 Israeli troops, in retaliation of border skirmishes by the Egyptians, staged a raid on the Gaza Strip, whereupon Egypt's new nationalist leader, Gamal Abdel Nasser, negotiated an arms deal with Russia and Czechoslovakia. In an attempt to persuade Egypt to remain out of the Soviet bloc, Eisenhower committed America to help finance the construction of the Aswan Dam, a vast irrigation project on the Nile

Egypt's President Gamal Nasser, a hero to his people for defying the imperial influences of England and France.

River that was to be the showpiece of Nasser's modernization program. Then in May 1956, Nasser recognized Red China, an act that infuriated Dulles, who always had contempt for "neutrals" who would exploit both sides in the cold war. Eisenhower agreed with Dulles that the offer of economic assistance, opposed by many congressmen, must be withdrawn. When Israel, furious about Arab guerrilla harassment, began to mobilize for a full-scale war against Egypt in July, Nasser denounced the French for selling arms to the Israelis and aroused the hostility of the British government by nationalizing the Suez Canal. He also informed the world that he would build the Aswan Dam without American or Russian money, but instead from the canal profits. The French, who had considerable stock in the Suez Canal, held another grievance against Nasser for his support of the Algerian rebels. Israel was even more angry when Nasser singled it out as the only nation that would be denied the right to use the Canal.

The Suez Crisis tested the limits of an American diplomacy that sought both to be noninterventionist and influential at the same time. Eisenhower and Dulles wanted to use Arab nationalism as a foil to Soviet communism, and they refused to deny, as did some British leaders who wanted Nasser dead, that Egypt was within legal rights in seizing the

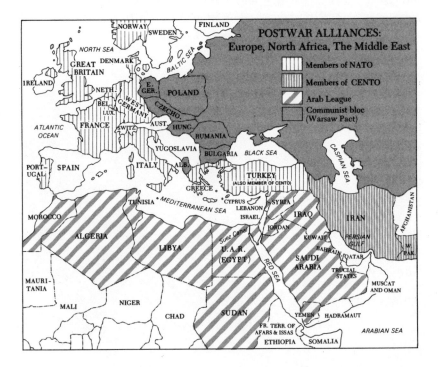

Canal. They also wanted to see the waterway kept open to all nations. But how could this objective be guaranteed? Having withdrawn economic aid, and having insisted that arms sales to Egypt must be paid for in cash, while the Czechs had been accepting cotton, the Eisenhower administration had no bargaining leverage and hence no means of controlling an explosive situation.

While America looked to the UN for a solution, France was secretly plotting with Israel to send its own troops into the Canal area, an anti-Nasser collusion that the British soon joined. Israeli soldiers made short shrift of the Egyptian army in a brilliant four-day Sinai campaign in October. Sir Anthony Eden, England's foreign minister, kept Dulles in the dark as Britain, France, and Israel collaborated in joint military operations. The uninformed Eisenhower administration was outraged, and the United States joined Russia in condemning the British and French intervention and supporting the arrival of the UN Emergency Force.

Eventually the UN presence stabilized the Mideast, but the Suez Crisis left all participants feeling betrayed. The British and French felt that the United States let them down by refusing to support their attempt to regain influence in the Suez. The Israelis were frustrated at losing the chance to finish off the Egyptian army and discredit Nasser. The Egyptians were insulted by Dulles's insistence that they lacked the technical knowledge to operate the Canal. And Americans, while praising Eisenhower for upholding international law, grew angry at the French when President Charles de Gaulle later denied the United States the use of French airfields and proceeded to develop their own atomic bombs and to threaten to withdraw from NATO. Above all, the Suez Crisis seemed to dramatize the dangerous misunderstanding among the three major Allied countries. For the British and French apparently acted on the assumption that the presidential election would compel Eisenhower to keep America neutral in the Mideast imbroglio in order not to risk losing the Jewish and isolationist vote. Some journalists speculated apprehensively about a forthcoming break-up of the Western alliance.

Ironically, it was the Soviets who assured the survival of the Western alliance by their actions in Eastern Europe at the time of the Suez Crisis. What did much to create unrest behind the Iron Curtain was Khrushchev's address to the Twentieth Communist Party Congress in February 1956, the earthshaking "Crimes of Stalin" speech that provided a vivid account of the dictator's paranoiac and tyrannical behavior. When word of the secret speech, unpublished in Russia, leaked out, the faith of hard-core Stalinists in Poland and elsewhere crumbled in confusion. A new Polish leader, Władysław Gomułka, now spoke of "democratization" and finding new roads to socialism independent of the Soviet Union. The brave stance of the Poles sparked demonstrations in Hungary and a demand that Imre Nagy and other reform-minded communists be returned to power and that the police state be ended. Defying the Stalinist, pro-Soviet Hungarian Communist party, students and workers fought the secret police in the streets of Budapest, and they were soon joined by Hungarian army soldiers and officers. At first Russia hesitated to intervene, perhaps convinced that Nagy's popular movement was an inevitable result of the mistakes and terror of the previous Hungarian Communist leadership. But when Nagy announced his plans to transform the one-party dictatorship into a genuine coalition government by means of free election, and, in addition, proclaimed Hungary's desire to leave the Warsaw Pact, the Soviets resorted to brute force rather than risk destruction of the satellite system. Clearly, to allow Hungary to become independent like Austria or Finland would have ignited a chain reaction as other anti-Stalinist communists within the Soviet orbit, perhaps even within the Soviet Union itself, took courage and made similar demands for political freedom. The entry of Soviet tanks into Budapest in November 1956 resulted in a bloodbath as students and workers tried to fight back with rocks, rifles, and home-made bombs. The world watched in dismay the sheer heroism of the helpless.

Before the Soviets intervened, Eisenhower announced that the United States was prepared to give economic assistance to new and independent states in Eastern Europe. When the invasion came, he refused the CIA permission to parachute arms and supplies to the Hungarians and made it clear that he would not consider dispatching American troops. He realized that the United States had no available military power for Eastern Europe other than nuclear weapons, which would do more to annihilate than to rescue Hungary. The president assuaged his conscience as well as that of the American people by revising immigration laws to allow many of the hundreds of thousands of Hungarian refugees to enter the United States. But nothing was said about the tragic irrelevance of America's policy of liberation. The doctrine of liberation rested on the assumption that communist regimes were inherently unstable and could be overturned by either internal revolt, external force, or the threat of force. It proved to be a deadly sham.

Most historians agree that Eisenhower acted responsibly in not intervening in Hungary. Any attempt to help freedom fighters would

Budapest freedom fighters, having toppled the statue of the hated Soviet dictator Joseph Stalin in the Hungarian uprising of 1956, delight in desecrating it.

have risked a nuclear confrontation with the Soviets and the likelihood of a third world war that would have been a war in which, as Khrushchev once remarked, the living would envy the dead. True enough. But fear of a nuclear holocaust should not lead one to conclude that America was powerless to help the Hungarians. Indeed, Eisenhower had at least a potential option whereas Khrushchev was the victim of his own policy. Had the Hungarian uprising successfully defied the Soviet Union, it would have discredited the leadership of Khrushchev, who was the agent and symbol of "the new course" of liberalization and reform in the post-Stalinist communist world. Eisenhower, however, was in a position to at least explore the possibility of seeing whether Hungary's new course could be followed with the cooperation of Russia. Hungary's desire to break out of the Soviet orbit may have been made tolerable to the USSR by a mutual agreement with America to withdraw from Western Europe on the condition that the Red Army pull out of Eastern Europe. All conditions, of course, would have had to be acceptable to the NATO allies, and no doubt some American cold warriors would have screamed that the Soviets could not be trusted with agreements of any kind. But the Soviets had long wanted to see a gradual and simultaneous dissolution of the NATO alliance and Warsaw Pact, and thus a staged withdrawal of American troops could possibly have been made dependent upon the freedom and independence of Eastern Europe. Although Eisenhower had been too preoccupied with the Suez Crisis to concentrate on such a proposal to the Soviets, a few days after the election he conferred with his cabinet about withdrawing forces east of the Rhine. But for the Soviets to accept such a proposal for a mutual withdrawal, another condition had to be met: America must cease claiming the right to send high reconnaissance flights over Soviet territory, an intelligence operation that Eisenhower refused to negotiate. The previous year at the Geneva Conference Eisenhower had offered his "open skies" proposal, whereby both superpowers were to allow overflights deep inside their respective borders. Khrushchev squelched the proposal as an espionage plot and the CIA continued covert aerial reconnaissance. We shall never know whether a dual agreement to disengage American troops and end spy overflights would have induced the USSR to withdraw from Hungary and allow democracy and independence peacefully to evolve in the satellite regimes. Whatever the case, genuinely responsible statesmanship may have more to do with responding to a possible opportunity than issuing excuses for inaction.

THE ELECTION OF 1956

In the presidential campaign of 1956 the Democratic party offered Americans a foreign policy position that amounted to little more than a distinction without a difference. Candidate Adlai Stevenson stated eloquently that critical areas in international affairs must be above politics. Nevertheless, in his campaign he expressed fear that Indochina was "falling to the Communists" and he charged Eisenhower with losing Egypt to the Soviet bloc. A week before the election he described Republican foreign policy as an "abysmal . . . complete and catastrophic failure." It was one thing to tell voters that the "United States lost control of events in areas vital to its security." It was altogether another thing to explain how the United States could regain control of events through clear diplomatic initiatives applicable to specific crisis areas like the Suez and Hungary. On the eve of the election Stevenson sent Eisenhower a telegram urging him to appeal to the United Nations to take up the Hungarian situation. But what could the UN do? In the Korean War the United States turned to the UN for an explicit legitimization to intervene *after* America had intervened; in the Hungarian crisis both the Democrats and Republicans wanted an implicit legitimization from the UN for United States nonintervention. But neither the Democrats nor the Republicans suggested that the UN could possibly supervise a mutual disengagement of American and Soviet forces in the hope that the Hungarians could have their freedom and the Russians their security. In all probability such a proposal, made in the midst of a tense international crisis, may have alarmed Americans and exposed either candidate to the charge of recommending retreat when the Soviets appeared to be expanding.

That domestic politics would hinder diplomatic imagination can be seen in the issue of a nuclear test-ban policy. In the early fifties the Eisenhower administration had been charged by McCarthy with holding up development of the H-bomb. Eisenhower himself recognized that bigger megaton bombs, whether hydrogen or proposed cobalt, had little military value, and thus he wanted a moratorium, especially given the growing public fear of radioactive fallout. But in 1956, when the Soviets undertook another round of tests, Eisenhower accepted the advice of the Atomic Energy Commission that further tests were necessary to find ways to attach nuclear warheads to missile systems. Late in the campaign Stevenson came out against the "H-bomb race," emphasizing that since the United States was ahead of Russia a freeze would be to its advantage. He also quoted the physicist Einstein: "I don't know what terrible weapons will be used in World War III. But I do know the weapons that would be used in World War IV—they will be sticks and stones." Eisenhower regarded Stevenson's position as campaign theatrics at best and demagoguery at worst, and he pointed out to the press that "it is a little bit of a paradox" for the Democratic candidate to advise continuing with missile development while halting the H-bomb since research data on both were interrelated. Eisenhower was just as committed to disarmament as was Stevenson, but when it became a partisan campaign issue, the public was more confused than informed.

Republicans had reason to be concerned about the 1956 election. Although polls showed Eisenhower as far more popular than Stevenson, the president had suffered a coronary thrombosis in September. With the press abuzz about the president's condition, the electorate had to consider the possibility that Eisenhower could die or become incapacitated during his second term and that the country would then be stuck with Vice-President Richard Nixon. Many journalists, especially the liberals who recalled the McCarthy era, regarded the difference between Eisenhower and Nixon as the difference between respectability and ruthlessness. In the 1954 congressional elections the Democrats had regained a narrow margin of power in both the House and the Senate. To many Americans the Republican party continued to be identified as the party of big business and the Democratic the party of the masses of ordinary workers. How could the Republicans appeal to the masses? One way was to take a lesson from the old Whig party of the 1840s and deny there was any difference between the two parties. This was the theme of the "New Republicanism" spelled out in Arthur Larson's *A Republican Looks at His Party*. Eisenhower's undersecretary of labor, Larson tried to depict the Republican party as the worker's best friend by pointing to the president's support of minimum wage increases and other social welfare measures. Whether or not Republicanism was simply the art of appearance, 1956 was an election in which both parties moved toward the middle in search of the independent voters who desired a politics of moderation.

On the issue of civil rights, for example, Stevenson was as reluctant as Eisenhower to endorse the Supreme Court's *Brown* decision. To the disappointment of northern Democratic liberals like Senator Paul H. Douglas of Illinois and Senator Herbert Lehman of New York, Stevenson did little to promote the cause of racial equality, in part because he remained aloof from the plight of poor blacks, but also because he realized the necessity of holding the loyalty of southern Democrats who were threatening massive resistance to school desegregation. His selection of Tennessee's Senator Estes Kefauver as vice-presidential candidate was one attempt to hold the "solid South." On other domestic issues like social security and budget deficits, Stevenson and Eisenhower were in agreement that the first was sacred and the second scandalous.

With little disagreement over platforms and programs, the 1956 campaign turned more on images than on issues. This was the first presidential race that received such wide and sustained television coverage. Both candidates went before the cameras after being treated with pancake make-up to disguise the bags under their eyes, and being told how to throw their shoulders back and how to project. In this contest Stevenson's wit and urbanity was no match for Eisenhower's charm and simplicity. Eisenhower, moreover, was the candidate of peace who had ended the Korean War, and he enjoyed the fortune of running when the economy was healthy and the people were caught up in the pleasures of abundance. On election night Americans did not have to wait long to hear the results.

Eisenhower won the popular vote by close to ten million—35,581,000 to Stevenson's 25,738,765—more than 50 percent larger than the margin by which he had won in 1952. And the electoral vote increased from 442 to 89 in 1952 to 457 to 73, with Stevenson carrying no state outside the South, and even the "solid" South continued to collapse, with Virginia, Florida, Louisiana, and Texas going Republican. Eisenhower could look forward to his second inaugural triumphantly. Yet his overwhelming victory was somewhat misleading for the future of the Republican party. In 1956 Eisenhower ran far ahead of Republican congressional candidates. In the House, Democrats increased their margin to 33. In 1958 the Democrats would improve their hold in the House to 282 to 154 and in the Senate 64 to 34. The Republicans had yet to build a national majority that could be counted on to vote the party ticket. This dilemma would have pleased the authors of the Constitution, who feared popular majorities controlling the executive as well as the legislative branches of government. But it was no consolation to the GOP, whose respected and winning president could not, due to the Constitution's Twenty-second Amendment, run for a third term.

THE EISENHOWER DOCTRINE AND THE DEBATE OVER DISENGAGEMENT

Although Eisenhower had earned his early reputation as a military hero, he knew war could no longer be fought in the nuclear age. Rather than relishing conflict, he always desired to reduce tensions. In his second inaugural address he looked forward to the day when the peoples of East and West could live in peace and friendship. But he also foresaw that in the immediate future the challenge would be to accommodate North and South, the blessings of industrial society with the burdens of the underdeveloped countries, what has since become known as the "Third World." The "winds of change" were blowing across this section. "From the deserts of North Africa to the islands of the South Pacific," he told Americans, "one-third of all mankind has entered upon an historic struggle for a new freedom: freedom from a grinding poverty." In part Eisenhower was trying to arouse America to its economic and moral responsibility to the Third World, but he also feared that America would be cut off from raw materials if the Third World went communist. Yet he could never convince either his treasury secretary, George Humphrey, or the American people and their congressional representatives of the urgency of extending loans to developing countries. Foreign aid, Republican Senator Henry Styles Bridges complained, was nothing but "a do-gooder giveaway." Trying to convince Congress of the need for such programs was the most frustrating experience of Eisenhower's second term.

But Eisenhower did succeed in obtaining from Congress a resolution expressing America's willingness to use its armed forces in behalf of any Middle Eastern nation threatened by "international communism." There was some criticism in Congress against what came to be known as the "Eisenhower Doctrine," for the president could not take action on his own without the Congress's right to approve of war. Formulated in response to the weakening of Anglo-French influence in the Middle East, the new executive prerogative derived from heightening tensions when Nasser set out to unite the Arab world by fanning the flames of nationalism. In April 1957, young King Hussein of Jordan, under attack from pro-Nasser elements in his own country, asked America for help on the grounds his opponents were communists. Whether or not they were communists, or most likely Nasserites, Eisenhower quickly responded by sending $10 million to Hussein and ordering the Sixth Fleet to the coast of Lebanon. The following year the pro-Western Baghdad Pact seemed to be crumbling. The pact originated as a mutual security treaty between Turkey and Iraq in 1955, and shortly after became part of the western defense system when Britain, Iran, and Pakistan joined. With a military coup in Iraq in 1957, the Lebanese Maronite Christian president, Camille Chamoun, fearing his overthrow by Nasser's followers, asked for emergency support from the United States. Eisenhower dispatched 14,000 marines who, under cover of the Sixth Fleet, landed unopposed on the beaches of Lebanon to the astonishment of bikini-clad sunbathers. Within a few months American forces were withdrawn, and for the time being Jordan and Lebanon had been saved.

Saved from what? Although Eisenhower defended his actions by citing the threat of "international communism," much of the unrest in the Mideast stemmed from an emergent Arab nationalism raging against Western colonialism. Indeed, many Arab communists who recently had emerged from years of illegality and persecution, stood against any union with the United Arab Republic, the recent merger of Syria and Egypt that had been advocated by military officers from both countries as a means of resisting Soviet influence. During the Senate hearings Dulles admitted that there was no evidence of Soviet "volunteers" in any mideastern country and that no Arab state appeared to be going communist either by a coup or by free choice. But the great oil resources of the Mideast, together with the UAR's control over the northern and eastern approaches to the African continent, was of great concern not only to the United States but to England and France as well. Thus when Iraq began to fall under Soviet influence in 1958, America shored up its relations with the northern remnants of the Baghdad Pact, Iran and Turkey, with economic aid in exchange for access to oil and the use of missile bases. In other parts of the Mideast, America's policies angered the Israelis, especially the granting of military aid to Saudi Arabia and the administration's demand that Israeli troops be withdrawn from Gaza. The "Eisenhower Doctrine" declared the right of America to save the Arab world from communism without necessarily acknowledging the right of Israel to save itself from Islam.

Eisenhower's concern about the threat of "international communism" to the Third World, though understandable in some respects, rendered him less sensitive to the deeper forces of nationalism and anticolonialism, forces so indigenous to particular countries that international alignments would be more shibboleth than substance. Neither Eisenhower nor Dulles took seriously the growing rift between the USSR and Red China. In 1958 China embarked upon its "Great Leap Forward" program of forced collectivization on the farms and ideological indoctrinization of the minds. Mao was attempting to avoid the seemingly less radical Soviet path, with its heavy party bureaucracy, indifference to doctrinal purity, and its alleged emphasis on consumer goods rather than on military supplies essential to sustained revolutionary struggle. Not only did the Soviet idea of coexistence differ from China's more impatient idea of peasant insurrection, but Mao denied that communist parties could be run from a single center such as Moscow and he insisted that Khrushchev was unworthy of world leadership. Thus, unlike the Russians in Eastern Europe, the Chinese did not attempt to intervene directly in the affairs of other Asian communist movements in order to establish a satellite system. Yet the Eisenhower administration continued to look upon Asia and the Third World as though world communism remained what Lenin wanted it to be: an intact monolith subservient to Moscow.

The Geneva Convention of 1954, which included Red China and an Indochina about to win its freedom from French colonialism, represented an attempt on the part of the West to preserve Southeast Asia from communist domination. Although Eisenhower wisely refused to commit American ground forces to such an effort, his policies did much to globalize the cold war and extend it into Southeast Asia. When South Vietnam's President Diem called off scheduled national elections in

1956, he had the complete support of the Eisenhower administration, whose diplomatic advisors knew full well that the communist Ho Chi Minh would have won decisively. In the face of Diem's violation of the Geneva accords, and America's extension of military and technical assistance to South Vietnam, Ho's followers organized a guerrilla movement known as the Viet Cong, which grew in strength as Diem became increasingly unpopular and repressive. The United States also moved covertly through the CIA to depose a neutralist government in the newly formed country of Laos in the northwest province of Indochina. The installed pro-Western regime angered both the neutralists, who had significant influence among the Laotian military, and the Pathet Lao communists, who could now pose as anti-imperialist liberators. By 1959 Burma, Indonesia, and South Vietnam were receiving as much as $547 million in foreign aid under the Mutual Security Program.

In Vietnam and Laos the communist struggles were more in the nature of internal civil wars than internationally coordinated movements. China or Russia might exploit such insurgencies, but there is no evidence that they had created them. Nevertheless, in August 1958 China resumed shelling of the islands of Quemoy and Ma-tsu, and to Eisenhower and Dulles it appeared that the Red Giant was on the move. The bombardment occurred while the United States was bogged down in another Mideastern crisis, and perhaps Mao was expecting the island garrisons would surrender without China having to stage an invasion. Instead the American Seventh Fleet escorted Nationalist forces and supplies to the islands and American marines installed artillery capable of firing atomic shells. The Nationalist leader Chiang wanted to escalate the confrontation, as did Dulles and the Joint Chiefs of Staff. But General Nathan F. Twining advised the president that the islands were indefensible and "probably not" required for the protection of Formosa. In October, China announced it would engage in shelling only a few specified days a week, reducing it to such a bizarre level that Eisenhower "wondered if we were in a Gilbert and Sullivan war."

It is worth noting that when the United States sent troops into Lebanon and intervened in the Formosa Strait, the Soviet Union made no countermove other than to issue predictable verbal denunciations. The Hungarian tragedy illustrated that America would shrink from risking an armed confrontation with the Soviets, and events in the Mideast and Asia indicated that the Soviets may have felt the same with America and her nuclear superiority. Thus the cold war seemed more and more to be characterized by the "dual hegemony" of the two superpowers. Yet the fate of Hungary continued to haunt the conscience of the West, the status of Poland remained precarious, and the question of German reunification unresolved. At the same time the arms race between the two superpowers continued to escalate. In an effort to begin to find a way to help Eastern Europeans move out of the orbit of Soviet domination and to ease tensions between the East and West, several statesmen and writers explored the possibility of removing armed forces from the center of Europe. This new policy of "disengagement" had been proposed by the Polish foreign minister Adam Rapacki in the fall of 1957. Meanwhile, George F. Kennan, the original theoretician of "containment" who had left the foreign service in 1953, delivered a series of lectures calling for the mutual withdrawal of military forces as the only way to reduce the risk of war and expand the area of human freedom. No doubt there were serious obstacles to such a proposal. The maximum aim of the West was to remove all Soviet forces from Eastern Europe, reunify and possibly neutralize the two Germanies, and establish the basis for Eastern countries to transform their Communist regimes and free themselves from Soviet domination. While the Soviet Union wished to see all the American forces out of Europe, obviously it had no wish to see the disintegration of the satellite system.

Still, there remained certain minimum aims that might have been explored, such as the establishment of demilitarized neutral zones of politically free countries, guaranteed by both superpowers, with Germany remaining divided and troop withdrawals on both sides, perhaps under the supervision of the UN. But in America such proposals went unexplored, in part because Kennan used disengagement to question whether the cold war could not be reconceived as a rivalry that might depend upon some defensive strategy other than thermonuclear weapons and the threat of annihilation. Specifically, he recommended a halt to shipping nuclear arms to West Germany as a bargaining chip to see whether Russia would agree to neutralization of Central and Eastern Europe. To Kennan, the lesson of Hungary proved the nuclear weapons of mass destruction were too "suicidal" to be usable as instruments of either war or diplomacy, and thus NATO countries must be prepared to defend themselves by other means, not only traditional ground forces but the "spiritual will" to resist to the end any invasion and occupation of their territories. Kennan's proposal provoked considerable debate. Former Secretary of State Acheson, Dulles, and several English writers claimed Kennan had no grasp of power relationships. If American troops were withdrawn from Europe, they insisted, and the Soviets violated a disengagement pact by renewed military intervention, the nations of the West would be left to their own fate. No doubt. But Kennan was trying to show why Russia as well as the West had a stake in disengagement, for NATO had no available military response to the Soviet Union other than nuclear weapons. His proposal, alas, was never translated into American policy and forwarded to the Soviet Union. As the arms race continued and the threat of nuclear war grew like a technological nightmare, the possibility of disengagement loomed as one of the missed opportunities of the cold war.

SPUTNIK, THE SPACE RACE, AND ARMS CONTROL

When Americans awoke on the Friday morning of October 4, 1957, to learn that a Russian satellite was circling the earth every ninety-two minutes, traveling 18,000 miles per hour, and emitting a "beep, beep, beep," they were stunned. They could hardly complain that they had not been forewarned. American citizens as well as government officials had simply refused to believe the Russians when they boasted of their missile development and plans to launch space vehicles. "Sputnik," no more than the size of a beach ball, filled Americans with apprehension and recrimination. One senator proclaimed "a week of shame and danger," another called for a special session of Congress. Democrats attacked Eisenhower's lack of leadership in science and technology, and even Republicans who once praised the president's fiscal responsibility now criticized his alleged lack of interest in defense and cutbacks in military spending. Chastened at home, Americans also felt humiliated abroad as they read of reports of foreign journalists claiming the USSR had overtaken the United States and was now the number one superpower. Sputnik appeared shortly after the publication of John Kenneth Galbraith's *The Affluent Society*, a critique of America's overindulgence in conspicuous consumption. What better proof could there be that Americans valued their Cadillacs and Chevrolets more than their country?

If it pays to be a winner there is also a cost to pay, and the truth is that America was unwilling to match Soviet expenditures on research and development in space technology. Neither Eisenhower nor any other American had foreseen the urgency of such expenditures, nor did the president like the idea that the federal government would have to be heavily involved in the entire spectrum of scientific research, development, and technology. Perhaps the only people in America who wanted to push as rapidly as possible on ballistic-missile research were the German scientists. Toward the end of the war OSS agents searched for them in Germany. Operation "Paperclip" remained covert, for several German scientists either had Nazi pasts or had worked in laboratories in which brutal forced-labor resulted in the deaths of thousands of Jews. Once found the scientists were secretly brought to Huntsville, Alabama. Such pioneers of modern rocketry as Wernher Von Braun had been inspired since childhood by the dream of space flight. And they well knew they had their counterparts intensely working on the same projects in Russia, where science had depended upon the support of the state since its introduction from the West by Peter the Great.

In the United States rocket-missile research had developed sporadically since the end of World War II. Both the Truman and Eisenhower administrations imposed budget cut-backs and cancellations. As America concentrated on the atomic and hydrogen bombs, the idea of a "moon rocket" seem to remain the fantasy of only Von Braun and his colleagues and Walt Disney and his wide-eyed fans. The famous mathematician John von Neumann and the "think tank" Rand Corporation urged the acceleration of missile programs in the early fifties, only to encounter bureaucratic resistance in government. The United States Air Force was authorized to go ahead with further development on the guided ballistic missile Titan, but the space program stumbled along in fits and starts. Nevertheless, by the time Sputnik was launched the United States was abreast and perhaps even ahead of Russia in electronic guidance systems and solid-fuel technology.

Until Sputnik the United States had spent only a half-billion dollars per year on space research and development. Six months after the shock, tho figure increased to $10.5 billion, still not as much as was being spent in the Soviet Union. The impression that Russia would remain ahead in the space race so terrified Admiral Hyman G. Rickover, architect of the nuclear submarine, that he urged America to imitate Russia's educational system. What was really needed was institutionalized coordination. With the air force developing the Atlas missile system, and the army and navy rivaling each other with their own systems, competition among the armed services for government contracts seemed almost greater than rivalry with the Soviet Union. In 1958, Eisenhower steered through Congress a bill establishing the National Aeronautics and Space Agency (NASA). To the distress of the military and the Pentagon, NASA was a civilian agency that would work with the Department of Defense and the scientific community. It was Eisenhower's way of meeting the demands of the space and missile era without turning the cold war completely over to the military services and their worship of weaponry.

"Whew! At First I Thought It Was Sent Up by One of the Other Services"

Yet no one could fail to see that the space race was intricately involved in the cold war. Even before Sputnik the United States had been unsuccessful in working out with the USSR an "atoms for peace" policy whereby each superpower would jointly stockpile uranium and fissionable materials for nonmilitary purposes—though such efforts did lead to creation of the International Atomic Energy Commission (IAEC) and helped control the proliferation of nuclear weapons in other countries. Nor had Eisenhower been successful in proposing an "open skies" policy whereby planes would be allowed to photograph each nation's ground installations to insure against a surprise attack, which Khrushchev rejected as an infringement on the USSR's territorial sovereignty. The failure of such proposals augured ill for the post-Sputnik era. For one of the by-products of rocket research, in Russia as well as the United States, was the development of the intercontinental ballistic missile system (ICBM); and with the dreaded ICBM the whole course of the cold war had changed, in theory as well as practice.

The presence of the ICBM turned the cold war into a theoretician's nightmare. Specialists knew that the shadow of the atomic bomb created a completely new form of warfare, and the thousands of Americans who built bomb shelters in their cellars or under their backyards were expecting the unthinkable. Warfare by means of conventional aircraft bombers still required long-range flights in which missions could be called back in case of some disastrous miscalculation such as a mistaken report of a surprise attack. With the ICBM the time element shrank from several hours to a few minutes and both superpowers were more vulnerable to a preemptive strike or error judgment or even a fatal flaw in the operational machinery—even if some authorities promised the world that the system was "fail-safe."

In an attempt to assure the West that America could offer something less than a world holocaust, Henry Kissinger wrote *Nuclear Weapons and Foreign Policy* (1957). Kissinger argued that there could be such a thing as "limited nuclear war" based on new, small tactical weapons which could be both "destructive" and "discriminating." But neither Kissinger nor any other theorist advocated reducing the then-limited ICBM stockpile, and thus America was left with the doctrine of deterrence. The most thoughtful analyst of that doctrine was Bernard Brodie of the Rand Corporation, author of *Strategy in the Missile Age* (1959). Brodie pointed out that whereas in the past the building of a military establishment was meant to win wars, now its chief purpose was to avert them. Previous wars may have been rational in that they served a political purpose. But what could America achieve by waging a nuclear

USAF Atlas intercontinental ballistic missile being launched January 10, 1958, from Cape Canaveral, Florida.

war against a nuclear power? In raising such questions, Brodie tried to demonstrate that in the cold war both sides could lose and neither could win.

Perhaps nothing better illustrates Thorstein Veblen's dictum on "the penalty for taking the lead" than the plight of the Soviet missile program after Sputnik. Not only was NASA surmounting formidable technical problems with great efficiency and speed but the space race led America to begin to develop an ICBM retaliatory force, whereas the relative inefficiency of Soviet rocketry slowed the pace and perfection of their SS-6. This Soviet counterpart to the ICBM was not even truly intercontinental since only France, England, and West Germany were within striking distance. Actually, the Soviets were using the space program as a deception to cover up their inability to deploy effective, long-range ICBMs. By the end of the fifties the United States, after suffering the initial shock of falling behind, had overtaken the USSR in both space and weapons research.

Yet America's lead, while militarily essentially, undermined all prospects of arms control. Ever since Eisenhower took office he had been distraught by the awesome destructive power of nuclear bombs, and at the first summit, the Geneva Conference of 1955, he pressed upon the Soviets the necessity of detente and disarmament combined with mutual inspection and UN supervision. But he was unable to convince Khrushchev and Nikolai A. Bulganin, Chair of the Council of Ministers, that they had nothing to fear from a more open world. After Hungary and Sputnik, the USSR was more vulnerable ideologically and militarily. In 1958, Eisenhower offered to cease testing nuclear weapons if the Soviets simultaneously accepted a ban on further weapon production. Instead Bulganin proposed a two- to three-year moratorium on all nuclear tests, which was unacceptable to England and France since they were about to develop their own missile systems. But ultimately the impasse between the two superpowers derived from a curiously ironic predicament. Eisenhower wanted nuclear testing halted and disarmament begun, but he also wanted America to remain ahead of the Russians. Khrushchev wanted a moratorium for as long as three years, but he also wanted no inspections since America would find out that it was indeed ahead. "I believed at the time that the U.S. might be willing to cooperate with us," Khrushchev later wrote in his memoirs, "but we weren't willing to cooperate with them. Why? Because while we might have been ahead of the Americans in space exploration, we were still behind them in nuclear weaponry. . . . Our missiles were still imperfect in performance and insignificant in number." Thus, while

America insisted on inspections so that the Soviets would not violate any disarmament agreements, the Soviets insisted on no inspections so that America would not violate the delicate *modus vivendi* between the two superpowers. Again, Khrushchev:

> I must say that the Americans proposed certain arms control measures to which we could not agree. I'm thinking about their insistence that a treaty include a provision for on-site inspection anywhere in our country. In general, the idea of arms control was acceptable to us. Zhukov, who was our defense minister at the time, and I agreed in principle to on-site inspection of the border regions and to airborne reconnaissance of our territory up to a certain distance inside our borders, but we couldn't allow the U.S. and its allies to send their inspectors crisscrossing around the Soviet Union. They would have discovered that we were in a relatively weak position, and that realization might have encouraged them to attack us.

Did Khrushchev really believe that the United States might turn aggressive as soon as the USSR's relative weakness had been discovered? Or was he merely using the call for a moratorium without testing as a means of catching up with the United States? Whatever the answer, Eisenhower himself was feeling pressure from two sides. On the one hand, growing world opinion against further tests was convincing him that the United States should announce a moratorium and beat the Russians at their own propaganda game. On the other, many of his advisors reminded him that research and testing were necessary to develop an antiballistic missile, make progress on small, tactical nuclear weapons, and perhaps even build a "clean" bomb that could leave civilian populations unharmed. Yet Eisenhower was encouraged to proceed with disarmament talks with the Soviet Union by an unexpected turn of mind by Secretary Dulles late in the spring of 1958. To the surprise of everyone, Dulles, who was nearing death from cancer, called for a reduction of military expenditures, a study of the possibility of disengaging American forces from Europe, and a resumption of serious disarmament talks even if the no-inspection stance on the part of Soviets carried certain risks. Discussions took place in Paris, but no agreements could be reached. By 1960, Eisenhower realized that the arms race was out of control and that America, after having built a nuclear arsenal of six thousand weapons, was more insecure than ever.

One reason for the dangerous impasse was the ambiguity inherent in new forms of weaponry. Any possible understanding between the United States and USSR turned on the precise nature and purpose of nuclear missiles. Were they offensive or defensive? Both sides claimed that their nuclear arsenals were for retaliatory purposes only, and each side insisted on a first-strike capability to preempt the other from attacking. In the late fifties both countries anxiously monitored the technological progress of the other out of fear that some immanent breakthrough would give the other a decisive advantage. In this respect, discoveries in science, instead of leading to greater control of power, only increased political instability and distrust. Thus the cold war, having its deeper origins in ideology, would continue to be propelled by technology. And the doctrine of deterrence, based on the perfectibility of technology, would tragically fail the moment its weapons were used.

10

The End of the Ike Age

THE STATE OF THE NATION AND CONGRESSIONAL ELECTIONS

With the approach of the mid-term congressional elections of 1958, Americans had the opportunity to send the Eisenhower administration a message. Both the restraint Eisenhower showed in the Hungarian uprising and the calculated display of force he called upon in Lebanon created the impression that world events could stabilize themselves without the loss of American lives; and the Suez Crisis seemed to have had more to do with European duplicity than American diplomacy. But four issues hung unaddressed: desegregation, civil liberties, public education, and the state of the economy; a fifth issue remained to be discovered: corruption in high office.

Black people and the NAACP were not the only Americans frustrated by Eisenhower's evasive stance on Little Rock and school integration. So too were liberal Democrats and the ACLU. Some progress had been made outside the deep South. In Little Rock in 1959, prosegregationist extremists were convicted for planting bombs, and in Florida black students were admitted to the state's university system for the first time. But in Mississippi and elsewhere in the lower South racial barriers stood fast. In 1960, "freedom riders" traveled through the South attempting to integrate public facilities and secure black voting rights. They had no indication from the White House that their efforts would be supported even if their lives were in danger. It was not until January 20, 1961, the day Eisenhower officially left office, that the black student and air force veteran James Meredith sent for an application to enroll at the all-white University of Mississippi.

In the fifties it was the Supreme Court, acting independently of Congress and the executive, that pushed hardest in school desegregation and race relations. The Court denied appeals from southern states to gain a stay of integration orders and it upheld the right of a local federal judge to declare void Louisiana's segregation statutes. Three members of the historic Warren Court—Hugo Black, William O. Douglas, and Felix Frankfurter—had been appointed by Roosevelt; three others, William J. Brennan, John Harlan, and Potter Stewart, by Eisenhower, who had also named Earl Warren to be chief justice. Thus the predominantly Republican Warren Court did its best to protect and promote the rights and needs of black Americans who voted Democratic. Ironically, the Supreme Court, once the bane of FDR and Truman, became the bastion of the old New-Deal coalition.

In the late fifties the Supreme Court also promoted the cause of civil liberties, so crippled during the McCarthy era. Justices Black, Brennan, Douglas, Harlan, and Warren constituted a libertarian bloc devoted to restoring the fabric of civil freedom. In *Yates v. United States* (1957), the Court denied that communists could be prosecuted under the Smith Act for advocating "a mere abstract doctrine of forcible overthrow" of government as opposed to inciting persons to undertake such an action. In two other cases, *Sweezy* and *Watkins,* the Court upheld the right of defendants to cite the Fifth Amendment, warned congressional committees to restrict their investigations to legislative objectives instead of sensational exposure, and declared that resolutions creating such committees suffered from the "vice of vagueness" and hence violated due process of the law. In *Kent v. Dulles* (1958), the Court ruled that the State Department's denial of passports to communists was an unconstitutional violation of the "right to travel" guaranteed by the Fifth Amendment. With the passing of the Red Scare the Warren Court was more inclined to insist upon a principle that would have caused McCarthy to groan from his grave—all political opinions deserve equal protection of the law.

Higher education received an unexpected boost in the late fifties. Eisenhower had promised to make public education a top priority of his 1956 campaign. But the program of federal loans he later offered to state educational systems entailed such high interest rates that one school official felt it was "written with the tone of a mortgage banker lending money to a pauper." Yet even the cost-minded Eisenhower went along when Congress overwhelmingly passed the National Defense Education Act of 1958. NDEA made available substantial loans for college students, established a program for graduate fellowships, gave assistance to high school counselors responsible for vocational instruction, and reserved highest funding for the teaching of science, mathematics, and foreign languages. NDEA was as successful as the older GI Bill. It sponsored many thousands of budding physicists, anthropologists, economists, and historians through to a Ph.D. degree. But in some respects it represented less a commitment to knowledge and learning than to "national defense." For the bill was passed in a mood of near-panic after Russia had put into orbit the first space satellite, a dramatic conquest for science but a blow to America's pride.

In the late fifties the nation's economy, once the pride of the Eisenhower administration, no longer seemed robust. Two recessions, in 1957–58 and 1960, were allowed to run their course by a president who was reluctant to resort to government spending because of its presumed inflationary consequences. Working Americans enjoyed annual increases in disposable income, as did those receiving social security benefits. Unemployment lingered at about 5 percent; but even when it increased to 7 percent the president's economic advisors remained convinced that a full-employment economy would be incompatible with price stability and fiscal responsibility. Yet Eisenhower, for all his faith in balanced budgets, which he did succeed in attaining in three of his eight years in office, presided over the largest peacetime deficit in American history.

Unable to look to a Republican administration, organized workers looked to their unions. Under the leadership of George Meany of the AFL and Walter Reuther of the CIO, the union movement had remained strong in the early fifties, particularly in the industrial Northeast and upper Midwest. Labor also became sophisticated politically and hired "professionals" to work in research, education, publications, public relations, and legal affairs. Even so, layoffs and unemployment were always a possibility in some industries, and wages managed to stay only slightly ahead of the rising costs of living. Union membership had also peaked and begun its decline as the economic expansion of the fifties took place in the South and Southwest where union activity had always been weak. Equally serious, the cause of labor no longer had the support of public opinion as it had in the depression years. Although there was no move to turn back legislation giving unions the power of collective bargaining, several states passed right-to-work laws which made employment no longer dependent on union membership. Moreover, large unions began to resemble corporations not only in their similar bureaucratic structures but also in racism and exploitation. The

International Ladies Garment Workers Union (ILGWU), once the bastion of Jewish and Italian radicalism in the twenties, turned to black and Puerto Rican workers in the fifties without allowing any of those members to rise to higher paid leadership positions.

Years earlier American writers on the Left had looked to the labor movement as the last great hope of idealism. In the fifties writers felt it was their duty to expose the connection of some labor leaders to the underground criminal world of prostitution and gambling. In *The End of Ideology* Daniel Bell analyzed "the racket-ridden longshoremen"; in *Midcentury* John Dos Passos brought to light the strong-arm tactics of David Beck, Jimmy Hoffa, and other teamster officials; and in the film *On the Waterfront*, which won eight Academy Awards, viewers recoiled at the sight of goons terrorizing dock workers. The press also reported stories of labor-union racketeering involving the misuse of pension funds, and a congressional committee turned up tales of murder, arson, blackmail, kidnapping, and beatings and torture. The Landrum-Griffin Act of 1959, which Eisenhower strongly supported, attempted to control labor racketeering by banning ex-convicts from union office, requiring frequent elections of officers, and establishing regulations for financial disclosure of union investments. The legislation also tightened restrictions on secondary boycotts and picketing, thus making it appear that Eisenhower was against unions as well as crime.

The Democratic party maintained an uneasy relationship with labor in the fifties. Its standard bearer, two-time presidential candidate Adlai Stevenson, was more comfortable with Wall Street bankers than Detroit auto workers. "The Democratic Party is the best friend American business has," he informed *Fortune* magazine. Yet more activist Democrats, liberals like Senator Humphrey and Joseph Rauh of ADA, continued to champion the cause of labor and civil rights. In 1957 the Democratic Advisory Council was established, which included such reform-minded figures as Truman, Humphrey, and Eleanor Roosevelt as well as the more aloof Stevenson. Intellectual advisors like the historian Arthur Schlesinger, Jr., and the economist Leon Keyserling may have been impressed by the extent of abundance in the Eisenhower years. Even so, they took pains to remind Americans of the pockets of poverty in Appalachia and elsewhere. The Democrats supported the passage of Senator Paul Douglas's Area Redevelopment Bill, which called for public works, job retraining, and increased welfare benefits. Eisenhower vetoed the bill as costly and inflationary.

American agriculture was the one major sector of the economy that remained excluded from the prosperity of the fifties. By the end of the decade only 8 percent of the population lived on farms, a demographic shift that reflected the acute decline in agricultural income. The farm family stood in the lowest one-fifth of the national income scale, and in the late fifties income per person on farms had dropped to about 45 percent of incomes per person of the nonfarming population. During the Eisenhower administration farmers experimented with restricted acreage, flexible price supports, sliding parity payments, marketing quotas, and selling excess commodities abroad with the government accepting foreign currency in order to pay growers in stronger dollars. Nothing seemed to work. In the postwar era American agriculture benefited from a hungry Europe in need of grain and other exports. But in the fifties farm surpluses, produced by increasing technological efficiency as well as the loss of foreign markets, began to drive prices down. Farmers became disgruntled with Agricultural Secretary Benson. His policy of aiming only to stabilize prices through government purchase of surpluses left many farmers wondering whether Washington was the solution or part of the problem.

One particularly notorious entrepreneur knew how to use the government's policy in ways that had more to do with chicanery than husbandry. The Texan Billy Sol Estes demonstrated why an American born poor could become a millionaire. Estes built an empire based on government cotton allotments and low-interest loans intended for constructing grain storage bins. He used the money instead to build shabby prefabricated homes and exploit the housing crisis. For his business savvy the US Chamber of Commerce selected him as one of the nation's then outstanding young men on the rise. But the US government saw things differently and sentenced him to serve in the federal penitentiary for swindling.

But the crimes of private enterprise are seldom as shocking as those involving public trust. At a time when the country was reeling in disbelief from the TV quiz scandals, journalists had been uncovering stories of corruption within the administration involving Sherman Adams, assistant to the president and a close, trusted friend. When Eisenhower ran in 1952, the corruptions of the Truman administration proved an easy campaign target as Republicans promised to sweep the "mess" from Washington and give the people a government as pure as falling snow. Six years later Americans discovered that to campaign against vice is no guarantee of virtue, at least not in American politics, which, as the Founders feared, would have more to do with money and opportunity than morality and duty.

In the summer of 1958 a House subcommittee brought forth evidence charging that Adams had intervened on several occasions with the Federal Trade Commission and the Securities and Exchange Commission. He allegedly tried to obtain information and prevent the investigation of a friend, the wealthy New England manufacturer Bernard Goldfine, who was suspected of mislabeling textiles. In return Goldfine had given Adams several "gifts," including a $2,400 oriental rug and a new-fashioned vicuna fur coat. When the sordid details began to emerge, Democrats were jubilant as were a few conservative Taft Republicans who resented the more liberal Adams. Many Americans were also perplexed as to why Adams, a former governor of New Hampshire with a reputation for integrity, had allowed himself to become involved with a sleazy millionaire like Goldfine. When Goldfine testified before the House subcommittee, he passed around a gold watch with an engraving of initials indicating that it had been given to him by Adams on inauguration day 1953. People in the audience winced with disgust. But if the immorality was appalling, the stupidity was amusing. Here was a man charged with buying influence thinking he would acquit himself by proving how much influence he enjoyed!

Meanwhile, Eisenhower had been defending his assistant and claiming that Adams's misdeeds were a matter of "imprudence" and "carelessness," hardly the grounds to demand his resignation. Then at a press conference Eisenhower stated: "I admire his abilities. I respect him because of his personal and official integrity. I need him." Although the statement had been gone over by his press secretary and advisors, it backfired. The "I need him" allowed critics to depict Eisenhower as old and tired, and dependent upon assistants whatever their ethical lapses. Whether out of weakness or loyalty, Eisenhower had no stomach for confronting his friend Adams with a request that he resign. He left the task to Vice-President Nixon.

The congressional elections of 1958 reflected not only the uneasy sentiments of farmers and industrial workers but also the effects of a recession that in 1957 had begun to take its toll in rising unemployment and declining gross national product and income. The electorate had grown impatient with a president it had overwhelmingly elected for a second term. "Things are in an uproar. But what is Eisenhower doing?" asked the *Chicago Daily News*. "All you read about is that he's playing golf. Who's running the country?" In the Southwest bumper stickers began to appear reading: "Ben Hogan for President (If We've Got to Have a Golfer in the White House, Let's Have a Good One)." Republican party officials knew they were in trouble throughout the summer and their worries were confirmed in the November elections.

The Democrats captured the House 282 to 154 and the Senate 64 to 34. Thus Eisenhower became the first president in American history who had to deal with three successive congresses with majority opposition in both houses. In 1950 the Republican party carried 49 percent of the electorate; in 1958 its total polling draw had dropped to 43 percent. Republicans also controlled only fourteen of the forty-eight governorships of the country. No matter how popular Eisenhower remained, the Republican party was in the worst shape it had been since the peak of the New Deal in 1936. Looking forward to 1960, Democrats could for the first time since FDR begin to feel "Happy days are here again."

The Environment, the Hidden Perils of Nuclear Energy, and the Peace Movement

Although the term "ecology" was not widely used in the fifties, Americans were becoming aware of the dangers to the environment brought by science, technology, and population growth. It was in this period that Rachel Carson gathered data to write her best-selling book, *The Silent Spring*, which warned of the poisonous effects of pesticides on food crops and water resources. In *The Conduct of Life*, Lewis Mumford carried on his Thoreauvian effort to convince Americans to return to the organic rhythms of the environment in order to restrain man's assault upon nature. At the end of the decade Vance Packard wrote *The Waste Makers* to show Americans that unless they restrained their consumer habits they would forever be exploited by the planned obsolescence and "throwaway" psychology of Madison Avenue. No doubt most Americans remained deaf to Thoreau's advice: "simplify, simplify, simplify." In an era when consumer credit soared 800 percent, Americans were clearly more interested in purchasing tail-finned cars than in pursuing the simple life. Yet Americans were not entirely oblivious to the deeper emotions that put them in touch with the more enduring truths of nature. Even amidst the clutter of chrome and plastic they could appreciate the purer sights of the natural world. Thoreau once claimed that those who do not read newspapers are "blessed" for only they will see nature. In the fifties not only those who read the news but even those who watched TV had the wild delights of nature brought right into their living rooms.

The man who made this possible was Jacques Cousteau, the French marine biologist who became a popular fixture on American TV after the classic "Omnibus" show hosted by Alistair Cooke ran his films on underwater archeology. Cousteau and his crew adapted TV filming techniques by building the first submersible cameras. In 1956 he won an Academy Award for his feature documentary, *The Silent World.* It was through the daring camera work of Cousteau and his team that millons of Americans had their first glimpse of the strange and exciting universe beneath the coral formations and crashing waves. But Cousteau was more educator than entertainer, and he always concluded his show with a reverential praise for the natural environment and a sober warning about its ecological fragility.

Americans were mindful of the dangers to their own wilderness and open spaces. In the early twentieth century, when the conservation of national resources became the goal of Theodore Roosevelt and other reformers, the problem was industry's demand to explore for oil, to cut down forests, and in general exploit the earth as though it were a natural right. In response the federal government brought some of America's great natural wonders like Yellowstone, Yosemite, and the Grand Canyon under the jurisdiction of the National Park Service. In the postwar years part of the problem was people themselves, especially tourists whose cars and trailers threatened to turn nature's treasures into "national parking lots." To prevent the trampling and paving of remaining wild spaces areas such as the Florida Everglades were declared national parks in the postwar era. Yet even with the establishment of national parks, preserves, and wildlife refuges, some Americans worried about the impact of masses of people on nature's delicate balance and wondered how long the last frontiers would last. In politics the leading advocate of outdoors preservation was Oregon's Senator Richard L. Neuberger, who observed that the president's interest in nature went little further than a devotion to well-mowed golf greens.

At the turn of the century the automobile was hailed as the invention that would replace the horse and buggy and eliminate forever the stench of horse shit on the streets. What the postwar automobile did to the air, however, stung eyes and irritated nostrils. In major cities across the continent skies were being polluted by exhaust emissions and sulphur dioxide pouring from oil refineries and chemical plants. The most affected city was sprawling Los Angeles, which in 1950 established an Air Pollution Control Office to find a solution to "smog," odious formations of brown and yellow layers of air that were damaging vegetation and rendering crops like lettuce unfit for consumption. Radios carried "smog alerts," doctors reported increases in respiratory illnesses, and some scientists speculated that air pollution may cause an increase in lung cancer. Yet Americans were not fully alarmed over what they were doing to the environment. The automobile had made the growing ecological crisis a race between convenience and catastrophe. Not until the late sixties would America awake to the crisis.

Meanwhile, Americans worried about what seemed to be a more immediate threat—radioactivity. The problems of fallout, the disposal of toxic materials, and the building of nuclear reactors created considerable controversy. In 1958, the scientists Linus C. Pauling and Willard F. Libby debated the issue of fallout on Edward R. Murrow's "See It Now" TV program. Pauling argued that a diplomacy based on nuclear arsenals condemned the world to the likelihood of a war on annihilation; Libby contended that testing had to proceed for reasons of national security. Many Americans scarcely knew who to trust. Some cold warriors wanted to believe that modern weapons technology was so sophisticated as to be accident proof (what in the early sixties led to a debate over the "fail-safe" fallacy). But in 1958, an atomic bomb slipped from a B-47 flying over South Carolina. Fortunately the triggering device had not been set, though the impact of the bomb shattered a nearby house. The previous year an accident occurred that would be suppressed until uncovered decades later through the Freedom of Information Act (FOIA). In New Mexico, a B-36 had been making a landing approach in turbulent air currents when an officer mistakenly grabbed a release mechanism and dropped a hydrogen bomb. The impact of the bomb set off conventional explosives attached to it. Had the nuclear component detonated, an explosive power of ten megatons—one thousand times greater than that of the bomb that fell on Hiroshima—would have been released. Americans who could imagine such accidents shuddered as they tried to deny their own visions of sudden holocaust or, perhaps worse, a human species wracked with genetic deformities. On March 1, 1954, the United States dropped a hydrogen bomb on Bikini Attoll in the South Pacific. Scientists had failed to predict that prevailing wind currents would carry fallout to nearby inhabited islands. For years afterwards some children would be born with unnaturally large heads, rolling eyes, and bodies without muscular control.

In 1957 the British author Nevil Shute wrote *On the Beach*. Later made into a film, it depicted the final days of human existence in the aftermath of a thermonuclear war started in 1963 by India and Pakistan. In Cambridge, Massachusetts, a young Harvard mathematician and songwriter, Tom Lehrer, wrote in mordant graveyard humor a hideously funny song that conveyed the resignation of many students:

And we will all go together when we go,
Every Hottentot and every Eskimo;
When the air becomes uranious,
We will all go simultaneous,
Yes we all will go together when we go.

Some Americans preferred shelter to humor. After the election of
Nelson Rockefeller as governor of New York in 1958, a campaign was
started to provide every home in the state with a fallout bunker. Elsewhere kits were sold so that families could build their own, equipped
with toilets, hand-operated generators, canned food, and protective suits.
It has been estimated that about 5 percent of the population either had
bomb shelters or had made structural changes or additions to their
homes to prepare for survival, and another 20 percent had stocked up
food and emergency supplies.

"Freedom from fear" was one of President Roosevelt's four freedoms declared at the outset of World War II. The cold war made fear
and dread a daily reality, and for the first time in history knowledge
and science seemed helpless to render the human race unafraid. In
1957 Congress held hearings on the effects of radioactive fallout, only
to discover the existence of strontium 90, a radiation-producing sub-

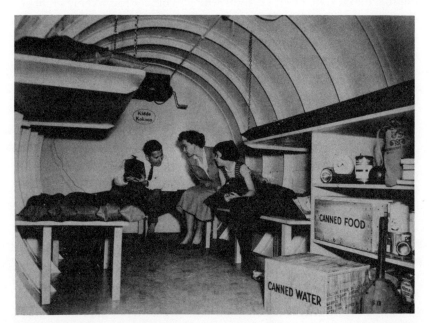

"H-bomb hideaway" in Garden City, New York, 1955.

stance that supplants calcium in the body and destroys bone marrow. This unexpected spin-off of the H-bomb intensified the controversy over nuclear weapons. Chairman Lewis Strauss of the Atomic Energy Commission maintained that strontium 90 was more dangerous to cattle chewing grass affected by fallout dust than to people safe in their houses or shelters. The Federal Civil Defense Administration distributed one million copies of the pamphlet, *What You Should Know About Radioactive Fallout,* which maintained that nuclear testing in the upper atmosphere would produce harmless radioactive particles given the weeks or months it would take them to reach the earth. In case of an attack, only people living in proximity of the bomb site were in danger; those several hundred miles away, so the map indicated, would be safe. Nothing was mentioned about contaminating wind currents or ground water. Some scientists suggested that people may be able to receive small dosages of radiation without danger to life or genetic malformation. Linus Pauling challenged the notion that there could be a threshold level, claiming that continued testing endangered the lives of thousands of children. In 1959 *The Nation* magazine alleged that the AEC was withholding a report showing that strontium 90 deposits had been discovered in the bones of babies and had been increasing in proportion to nuclear testing.

The building of nuclear power plants also resulted in bitter controversy. While nuclear bombs and missile warheads could be justified on grounds of national defense, reactors were sold to Americans on the basis of reducing energy costs. Utility companies waged a public campaign to convince Americans that nuclear power could be put to peaceful uses and that it was cheaper and less polluting than electricity produced by fossil fuel. Lest some children were budding skeptics with a distrust of the adult world, they, too, had to be convinced. Thus in the *Walt Disney Story of Our Friend the Atom,* kids were assured that "we hold the Atomic Genie under control. He comes forth at the beckoning of modern science—a smiling, magic servant to all mankind." Some Americans living in the vicinity of planned reactors protested their potential danger. The AEC dubbed them "nervous neighbors." The government agency also suppressed a scientific study opposing the building of a plant in Detroit. In Bodega Bay, California, a utility company planned to build a reactor only one thousand feet away from the earthquake-prone San Andreas Fault. It took environmentalists years of litigation in court to halt the construction. Unknown to the public, the AEC ordered a report on the possible consequences of accidents at another plant site, but the conclusions of the Brookha-

ven Report proved too frightening to be publicized. In case of an accident there would be no violent explosion; instead the reactor's core
would melt down and its container break apart and shoot radioactive
material into the surrounding area, killing approximately 3,400 people, severely injuring 43,000 more, and producing $7 million in
destruction and clean-up costs. Twenty years later, the Union of Concerned Scientists successfully concluded their efforts to release the report
through the Freedom of Information Act. (In the mid-seventies several
engineers would resign from General Electric and the Nuclear Regulatory Commission to protest the inadequate safety systems in various
power plants, some of which had been constructed in the fifties.)

Government was no more candid on the problem of disposing radioactive wastes. Not until articles appeared in *The Nation* and *The Saturday Evening Post* in the late fifties did the people of Massachusetts
learn that the AEC had been dumping "hot" toxic products near Boston Harbor since 1946. Environmentalists succeeded in moving that
dumping ground further out to sea, and in Houston a toxic dump was
banned altogether. Still, the government was secretly transporting by
airplane, and by truck through crowded Manhattan, shipments of plutonium, a potentially lethal chemical that, in the event of an accident
or a leak, could instantly fill the air with deadly, lung-cancer producing
fumes. By opting for cheaper energy, the fifties generation committed
America to a technology of both promise and peril.

But what became known at the beginning of the sixties was as frightening as what had been suppressed. With the publication of Herman
Kahn's *On Thermonuclear War*, Americans were told that they must
stop denying what they desperately hoped was impossible and begin
thinking the unthinkable. A thermonuclear war would be tragic, but it
could be winnable if Americans took the steps necessary to assure that
some would survive—build plenty of deep shelters, stock up on first-
aid kits and food supplies, and distribute radiation counters to the pop-
ulace. A scientist at the Rand Corporation, Kahn had an almost morbid
interest in calculating expected death counts in the event the United
States and USSR chose their own version of the "final solution." The
answer to total war was total preparation for civil defense. Not all
Americans accepted this bunker mentality. When a mock thermonuclear attack was staged on American cities in 1955, thirty people in
New York refused to go inside shelters and instead held a prayer vigil
outside the city hall. They were arrested and called "murderers' by the
judge who sentenced them. But peace activists began to organize in the
fifties and gathered support from small groups of environmentalists,

Quakers, and pacifists. One figure who had been known since the thirties for his Christian antiviolence philosophy was A. J. Muste. In the early fifties he wrote *Of Holy Disobedience* to urge the young to resist the draft and follow in the footsteps of Thoreau and Gandhi. The chemist Linus Pauling challenged the wisdom of Edward Teller's H-bomb and questioned the safety of nuclear testing in *No More War!* In 1957, in response from appeals from Bertrand Russell and Albert Einstein, the first Pugwash Conference was held. Financed by the Cleveland industrialist Cyrus Eaton, and held at his summer home at Pugwash, Nova Scotia, the conferences called upon scientists of the world to devote themselves to peace and disarmament.

The most significant peace organization to come out of the fifties was SANE, founded in New York as the Committee for a Sane Nuclear Policy. Within a year after its founding in 1957 it had 25,000 members and 130 chapters. Among its officers were John Hersey, Norman Cousins, Erich Fromm, and Walter Reuther. In the early sixties Dr. Benjamin Spock became a prominent SANE activist and the historian H. Stuart Hughes ran for political office under its banner. Connecticut Senator Thomas Dodd accused SANE of being an instrument of the Kremlin. As usual, Dodd provided not a scrap of evidence to back up his charge. Most SANE members, an amalgam of writers, academic intellectuals, and pacifists, believed that some form of *modus vivendi* with the Soviet Union was the only prospect for reducing tensions and averting armed conflict. In *An Essay for Our Times*, H. Stuart Hughes expressed a glimmer of hope that the communist world would live up to its "humanist" promise and cease betraying the ideals of Marx. He also hoped that the Western world would adhere to the values of the Enlightenment. Only with the possibility of peace could modern man move "beyond despair."

CASTRO'S CUBAN REVOLUTION AND THE U-2 INCIDENT

Yet throughout the fifties Professor Hughes and many other writers and intellectuals had been assuming that communism as a monolithic system had disintegrated forever. Many hopeful signs had pointed in this direction, especially Yugoslavia's break with the Soviet Union in 1947 and the subsequent bitter rift between Peking and Moscow. Such schisms had generated discussion of "polycentrism," a term coined by the Italian Communist leader Palmiro Togliatti. In the mid-fifties, when destalinization led to a spirit of independence within Communist parties in various countries, writers and political leaders grew confident that each nation could develop its own path to the goal of Marxism. The conclusion seemed to be that no communist leader, especially one who had come to power without help from the Kremlin, would be so mindless of history as to allow his country to succumb to Soviet domination. That conclusion would be put to a test with Fidel Castro's Cuban Revolution in January 1959.

Much of America greeted the revolution with open arms. Castro's 26th of July Movement and his heroic guerrilla battles in the Sierra Maestra had been acclaimed by Herbert Matthews of the *New York Times*. When Castro marched triumphantly into Havana, the Eisenhower administration immediately recognized the new regime. Earlier Eisenhower had refused to come to the aid of dictator Fulgencio Batista y Zaldivar, who had been charging that Castro's movement was communist dominated. Allen Dulles of the CIA had also issued similar warnings. But Undersecretary of State Christian A. Herter, who would succeed Dulles in 1959, advised Eisenhower that there was insufficient evidence of the extent of communism, that Batista had lost the support of 80 percent of the Cuban people, and that the only solution was for him to relinquish power and leave the country.

At first Castro seemed an exciting example of the new possibilities of polycentrism. Whereas the Cuban Communist party had been collaborating with Batista's dictatorship, probably on orders from Moscow, Castro promised a third way between communism and capitalism— "neither bread without liberty nor liberty without bread." A romantic caudillo with a rugged beard and battlefield fatigues, he emerged as the authentic answer to Latin America's desires and frustrations. Upon coming to power he instituted a sweeping social transformation, purging the Cuban bureaucracy, disarming the military, building hospitals and turning barracks into school rooms, confiscating foreign property, increasing the wages of workers and peasants, and ordering an end to racial segregation. His initial reforms in land distribution, housing, rent control, and public recreation aimed to improve and equalize living conditions. In contrast to orthodox communist regimes in Eastern Europe, where stress was placed on heavy industry and capital accumulation, Castro seemed to be meeting the immediate needs of his people. In America some sympathizers on the Left hailed his revolution as the dawning of a "new humanist socialism." Many other Americans also approved of the long-needed changes Castro was undertaking, as did Cuban businessmen and landowners who financed his guerrilla movement.

Cuban Prime Minister Fidel Castro addressing the National Press Club in Washington, D.C., April 20, 1960. Castro assured American journalists, "We are against communism and all dictatorships of all kinds."

Within a year, however, Castro undertook an unexpected political course that began to alienate both the American government and the Cuban middle class. He allowed members of the Communist party to assume important roles in his government, turned to the Soviet Union for economic assistance, and started making public speeches attacking America, incredibly long harangues that often lasted five hours. Then, on a good-will visit to the United States, he assured Americans that he and his men were not communists but "Roman Catholics, mostly." Although Eisenhower refused to see him, he charmed politicians and reporters with his grimy field jacket, fifty-cent cigars, and the cases of rum he gave away as gifts to his neighbors to the north. Vice-President Nixon was almost alone in suspecting Castro of either being a communist or being naïve about the dangers of communists in his government. For once he was right. Back in Cuba, Castro suspended habeas corpus, established military tribunals and show trials, held public executions, jailed writers (and later, homosexuals), called off promised elections, described the United States as a "vulture . . . feeding on humanity," and dared the Yanquis to invade Cuba.

The unexpected transformation of Cuban society forced many middle-class professionals into exile. When they arrived at the docks in

Tampa some were met by CIA agents, interrogated, given code names and passwords, and then sent to camps in Louisiana and Guatemala to train secretly for the invasion that Castro dared America to stage. Eisenhower was looking for "some kind of nondictatorial 'third force' neither Castroite nor Batistiano." While plans were being concocted by the CIA to assassinate Castro, probably without the president's knowledge, Eisenhower suspended the American purchase of Cuban sugar, a devastating blow to the island's economy. Castro responded by arranging with the USSR an agreement to accept sugar exports. He would also announce to the world that he had been a "Marxist-Leninist" all along; and Khrushchev, who originally had misgivings about Castro's theories of revolution and his treatment of old Cuban communists, embraced the *Fidelistas* as true comrades. Thus the dream of polycentrism collapsed and the cold war entered Latin America.

With the enemy now "only ninety miles away," as car bumpers warned, right-wing cold warriors charged that once again America had been taken in by revolutionary movements that spout democratic slogans and turn into communist dictatorships. The temptation to fan Americans' fear by describing Cuba as the beachhead for launching revolution throughout the Western hemisphere was also difficult to resist, particularly by those unaware that Latin American radicalism had an indigenous, nationalistic, anarcho-syndicalist tradition hostile to international communism. The American left similarly believed the Eisenhower administration had blundered in its Cuban policy, albeit for entirely different reasons. The Left charged that Castro was forced into alignment with the Soviet Union as the only means of protecting his revolution from subversion by the forces of American imperialism. In 1960 C. Wright Mills spelled out this thesis in *Listen, Yankee*. It would become gospel to the New Left of the mid-sixties and endorsed and elaborated upon by influential radical historians like William Appleman Williams. Before long a veritable mythology emerged that depicted the Cuban Revolution as a genuine "proletarian" phenomenon that represented a direct challenge to corporate capitalism and American liberalism. The major difficulty with this interpretation is that Castroites themselves rejected it.

Writing in *World Marxist Review* six months before the revolution, Blas Roca, a Communist party official, stated that in Cuba, "the armed struggle was initiated by the petty bourgeoisie. Working-class action could not be the decisive factor of the revolution owing to a number of circumstances," among which he specified "the weight of 'economism' in the labour movement," that is, the tendency of workers to value better wages and working condítions more than communism. Castro himself realized this when he later imposed state-ownership of farms instead of allowing the self-regulating cooperative farms, one of the revolution's goals, to flourish. "We wanted small-scale agriculture so that we would not be substituting for the old boss a new administrator, for the old owner a new state owner," recalled Carlos Franqui, who had been at Fidel's side in the struggle to power. "But Fidel had an innate distrust of the people; he preferred militarization to organization." According to Franqui, Castro deliberately provoked a confrontation with Washington in order to induce Moscow, which had been reluctant and apprehensive, to take up Cuba's cause. Moreover, those who fought with Castro in the mountains were mainly middle-class professionals. Castro himself was a lawyer, Ernesto "Ché" Guevara a physician, and among their followers were so many teachers, professors, merchants, and technicians that the overthrow of Batista could almost be called a white-collar revolution. The manifestos of the 26th of July Movement made no mention of Yanqui imperialism, confiscation, or collectivization; instead, they stipulated free elections, representative government, and constitutional safeguards along with a vast program of social reforms. Theodore Draper, the American historian who unearthed such embarrassing facts in his research, would be called the "conscience" of the Cuban Revolution for showing that Castro had betrayed it. In the sixties and for years afterwards, the New Left and its followers would fear Draper for the same reason that the old Stalinists feared Trotsky—he knew too much.

To the extent that Castro was determined to transform the revolution from a liberal-socialist reform movement into a communist dictatorship, there was probably little the United States could have done to prevent Cuba from falling into the Soviet camp. Throughout 1959 the Eisenhower administration kept a friendly ambassador in Havana who conveyed America's sympathies and willingness to negotiate economic assistance. But Castro instructed his subordinates to turn a cold shoulder to such proposals. Perhaps for ideological reasons he needed America as an enemy even more than America needed Cuba as a friend.

Throughout the fifties the Eisenhower administration had worried about the spread of communism in South America. In 1958 Vice-President Nixon was confronted by a spitting, rock-throwing mob when his limousine made its way through the streets of Caracas, Venezeula. But only after Castro came to power did Eisenhower persuade Congress to appropriate a half-billion dollars in aid for South America. The State Department also reaffirmed in stronger terms its support for progressive reforms to be carried out through the Organization of American States, and the CIA gave assistance and encouragement to the opponents of the despised General Rafael Trujillo Molina, the right-wing dictator of the Dominican Republic.

But in his last years in office Eisenhower's attention was fixed on Europe. Many issues, like the proposed test-ban treaty, remained unresolved and the complex question of Germany's reunification still simmered. In November 1958 Khrushchev renewed the Berlin crisis by declaring the Soviets intention to sign a separate peace treaty with East Germany. The move may have been calculated to countervail America's and Britain's NATO treaty rights to use European sites for missile installations. An independent East Germany would also eliminate Russia's nightmare of a nuclear-armed and united Germany aligned with the West, and by cutting off West Berlin as a free city the Soviets could reduce the flow of refugees from East Germany. Whatever his motives, Khrushchev had set May 27, 1959, as the deadline for settling the Berlin question once and for all, and the possibility that he might take some action like closing the Autobahn made his ultimatum seem threatening. As the six month deadline approached fears of war began to sweep through Western Europe and America. To everyone's relief, Khrushchev implicitly withdrew his ultimatum and agreed to a foreign ministers' conference, which had been urged upon Eisenhower by British Foreign Secretary Harold Macmillan, who made clear his fear that in the event of war Britain would be the first country to be wiped out by Soviet missiles. When the conference failed to lead to significant agreement, Khrushchev accepted an invitation to visit the United States and meet personally with Eisenhower, who in turn agreed to visit the USSR in 1960.

Khrushchev's tour of America proved to be a journalist's delight. At times he behaved boorishly, particularly toward Eleanor Roosevelt. But Americans followed his talks with Iowa farmers and his inspection of Hollywood studios, and shared his disappointment at not being able to visit Disneyland for security reasons. He spent two days at Camp David with Eisenhower and was a hit with the president's grandchildren. But Eisenhower was unhappy when Khrushchev avoided serious diplomatic discussion and seemed so unimpressed with America's middle class comforts. The pride of America, the flashy automobile, struck Khrushchev as wasteful; it was evidence that Americans always wanted to be on the move and that they had no roots. Nevertheless, reporters praised the "spirit of Camp David" as the beginning of the end of mutual distrust and everyone looked forward to the Geneva Summit

Conference on May 14, 1960. Then came the U-2 incident.

The U-2 espionage aircraft almost seemed a technical dream out of science fiction. Long and black, a thin shell with no guns, and designed to be flown by a single pilot at altitudes of 80,000 feet (approximately fifteen miles), the U-2 was more of an aerial camera than a war plane. Its elaborate, infrared photographic equipment could take pictures of land below with ranges as wide as 125 miles and as long as 3,000 miles. Unbelievably, interpreters who analyzed the enlargements could read a newspaper headline ten miles below the aircraft. It was the U-2 that provided the photos to the Department of Defense showing that France and Britain were preparing to attack Egypt during the Suez Crisis. The same high-powered cameras informed the Eisenhower administration that Russia was not embarking upon a crash ICBM build-up after Sputnik, and in 1963 they would detect the installation of Soviet missiles in Cuba.

The U-2, it was assumed, could not only fly out of reach of Soviet antiaircraft missiles but if hit would disintegrate along with the pilot and the photographic equipment—a grim fact that seemed to have been confirmed when nearly a dozen U-2s crashed in training missions with no survivors. U-2 pilots were supplied with cyanide capsules in case they had to bail out over enemy territory because of mechanical failure. For neutral territory they were given sophisticated survival kits and a silk banner stating in fourteen languages: "I bear no malice toward your people. If you help me you will be rewarded." On May Day 1960 a U-2 was shot down over Sverdlovsk, probably at the height of 70,000 feet, on an intelligence flight from Peshawar, Pakistan, to Bodø, Norway. The pilot, Francis Gary Powers, parachuted and survived after failing—perhaps because the gravitational forces were so strong in the spinning plane—to throw the destruction switch.

When the U-2 failed to land in Norway, NASA released a cover story on May 3 that a weather plane was missing. The CIA and Joint Chiefs of Staff assured Eisenhower that it would be impossible for the Soviets to capture an American pilot alive. The following day the State Department told reporters that the United States had never deliberately violated Soviet air space. This is exactly what Khrushchev was waiting to hear, for he needed an excuse to torpedo the summit after being informed that under no circumstance would China go along with a test-ban treaty. Now he went before the world and on TV showed the pilot, the aircraft remains, and the camera equipment. Eisenhower responded by assuming full responsibility for ordering the flight and implied that such activity would continue. Thus, America had been caught at espionage, lied about it, and then compounded the error by justifying it.

The summit conference took place in an atmosphere of gloom and rancor. When Eisenhower's turn came to speak, he made no apology for the U-2 flight but did concede such flights would not be resumed. Khrushchev angrily announced he would not attend another summit until after a change in American presidents. Eisenhower later lamented to President de Gaulle: "What a splendid exit it would be for me to end up . . . with an agreement between East and West." Instead he exited the White House leaving United States-Soviet relations in the worst shape they had been since the height of Stalinism. Yet the American people did not blame Eisenhower for the summit fiasco. Instead they praised his "dignity" in the face of Khrushchev's boorish tirades. Thus he left office with his popularity assured even though his diplomacy was in disarray.

THE ELECTION OF 1960

In June 1960 a Gallup poll asked Americans who they would prefer to represent the United States as president in the event of another summit meeting the following year. Americans overwhelmingly preferred Vice-

Soviet leader Nikita Khrushchev speaking before the United Nations, 1960.

President Nixon to several Democratic candidates. Having exposed Alger Hiss and sided with Joseph McCarthy, Nixon had earned his reputation as a combative anticommunist. The image had been reinforced when he engaged Khrushchev in the famous "kitchen debate" which took place in a model ranch house on display at an American exhibition at the Sokolniki Park in Moscow. Before journalists and photographers Nixon stood toe-to-toe with the Russian dictator. Khrushchev pushed his thumb against Nixon's chest and boasted how strong the Russians were. Undaunted, Nixon wagged his finger at Khrushchev and replied: "In some ways you are stronger than we are. In others, we are stronger. . . ." They then picked up a bottle of California wine and drank a toast. The debate, such as it was, did little to lesson cold-war tensions, but Nixon returned as the macho hero who proved he could stand up to the Russians. What had the Democrats to offer?

There was the eloquent, meditative Adlai Stevenson, twice defeated by Eisenhower yet still a sentimental favorite of the liberal wing of the party and of Eleanor Roosevelt. Senator Hubert Humphrey, who had his roots in the radical tradition of Minnesota's Farmer-Labor Party, was also liked by liberals but he was not well known outside the Midwest. Senator Stuart Symington of Missouri had a similar handicap, while the nationally recognized Lyndon Johnson of Texas was too southern for northern Democrats. Massachusetts Senator John F. Kennedy had the burden of being Catholic and the reputation of being a playboy who had shown little respect to some of the senior members of the party. Kennedy was also suspect to liberals for his failure to vote with the Senate in censuring McCarthy, his unwillingness to fight for a stronger civil rights bill, and his multimillionaire father who, as America's ambassador to England, had in the thirties supported appeasement.

But Kennedy could also turn handicaps into advantages. His senior thesis at Harvard, *Why England Slept* (in part ghostwritten for the book version by Arthur Krock of the *New York Times)* questioned the assumptions of appeasement held by an older generation. His Pulitzer prize-winning best-seller, *Profiles in Courage,* which extolled principle over expediency in politics, created the impression he stood for lofty standards. That he may not have lived up to such standards and, like Stevenson, had to go slow on civil rights to win the support of the South, was obscured by the high moral tone of his writing. Kennedy's religion could also help the Democrats regain many Catholic voters who had gone over to the Republicans—although he had to do everything possible to distance himself from the Vatican on moral issues like birth control. His marriage to the attractive Jacqueline Bouvier seemed to put to rest his reputation as a swinger as well as offer the possibility of glamour and taste in the White House. And his father's wealth freed him of many concerns and enabled him to elevate politics to a conception of national purpose rather than private interest, of challenge and sacrifice rather than comfort and satisfaction. He could also use his family's wealth to put together a formidable political organization that no other Democrat could afford.

The latter advantage proved itself in the primaries. In Wisconsin Kennedy had fully staffed headquarters in eight of the state's ten congressional districts. Humphrey had only three and failed to win a decisive victory in his neighboring state. By the time of the West Virginia primary Humphrey was in debt and had to travel through the state in an old bus. Kennedy campaigned on a plane with a huge staff of highly motivated pollsters, typists, and advance scouts. When Humphrey lost in West Virginia he had to withdraw from the race. In addition to giving Kennedy the lead, and burying the religious issue in a Protestant state, the West Virginia primary exposed him and the rest of the nation to Appalachia, the vast coal-mining region of jobless miners, poverty, and disease. It was an awakening to a rich, young politician who knew nothing of deprivation and despair. "He climbed back into the car after a visit to a jobless miner's shack visibly moved," Theodore C. Sorensen recalled. "He shook his head in dismay and said nothing."

Although Kennedy made references to the plight of the poor and hungry in his campaign, he was not prepared to launch a crusade against such conditions. As a candidate he well knew that Eisenhower's popularity derived from avoiding the issue of the economic needs of the lower classes. Kennedy's challenge was to appear prudent and moderate and at the same time not alienate the older elements of the Roosevelt coalition. He was a liberal Democrat facing a conservative electorate.

At the Democratic Convention in Los Angeles Kennedy arrived with enough delegate votes committed to him to win the nomination. Stevenson's supporters staged a thunderous demonstration in the balcony of the sports arena, a last hurrah to the precious voice of liberal reason. After Kennedy was nominated on the first ballot, he surprised everyone by offering the vice-presidential candidacy to Lyndon Johnson. Some Kennedy advisors were assuming that Johnson would abide by his previous statements and turn down the offer in order to remain Senate majority leader. Had not John Nance Garner, another Texan who had been FDR's running mate, advised Johnson that "the vice-presidency isn't worth a pitcher of warm spit"? Kennedy men wanted Johnson's support to carry Texas, not necessarily his acceptance. They got both, to the disappointment of the Stevensonian liberals, and younger brother Robert F. Kennedy, who had a running feud with Johnson.

Nixon's nomination had been a foregone conclusion. Only some liberal elements within the Republican party had reservations, and thus when Nixon offered the vice-presidential position to Nelson Rockefeller, the New York governor turned it down and the Republicans found themselves with the rather lackluster Henry Cabot Lodge, Jr., of Massachusetts. During the campaign Eisenhower remained aloof, possibly at the request of Nixon, who had heeded Mamie Eisenhower's warning about her husband's heart condition. But in August Eisenhower dealt Nixon a low blow that seemed out of character for a decent man. Asked at a press conference, "What major decision of your administration has the vice-president participated in?", the president replied: "If you give me a week, I might think of one." In *Six Crises* Nixon later wrote that Eisenhower telephoned him to apologize and said he had only meant to be "facetious."

Perhaps the most significant event of the close campaign was Nixon's decision, against the warning of his advisors, to accept Kennedy's challenge to a series of TV debates. Nixon felt confident after his kitchen encounter with Khrushchev. He had also studied closely Kennedy's acceptance speech, a stiff, colorless performance delivered by a tired candidate. It never occurred to Nixon that the four debates would give his opponent the national exposure he needed. On Monday evening, September 26, 1960, seventy million Americans were glued to their TVs. After the first debate, the remaining three were inconsequential. Both candidates had been cramming for weeks; neither made a false slip, and in verbal exchange the opening debate was close to a draw. In visual performance, however, there was no question who had won. One reporter even heard the debate on his car radio and judged Nixon the victor; then he watched a replay on TV and reversed the decision. Kennedy looked handsome, confident, youthful, with eyes that twinkled just before he cracked a joke. Nixon, recovering from a leg infection and underweight, seemed haggard, grim, nervous, and aggressive, his brow perspiring and a five o'clock shadow covering his cheeks. The journalist Ralph McGill grasped the significance of TV for the future of American politics when he observed that the "audience looked more than listened."

Aside from images, both candidates appealed to the broad center on

The Nixon-Kennedy debates of 1960 did much to change American politics as more and more people would vote with their eyes.

substantive issues and differed mainly on details rather than doctrines. Nixon campaigned on the administration's record, accepted the premises of the welfare state, and reminded Americans of how good they had it for eight solid years. Kennedy promised increases in social security, called for "vigor," and claimed he could "get the country moving again." On foreign policy, Kennedy exploited cold-war fears by charging that the United States had a "missile gap" with the Soviet Union. He also held that Quemoy and Ma-tsu were indefensible while chastising the administration for allowing communism to establish a beachhead in Cuba. Nixon countered by implying that Kennedy was immature, naïve, and under the influence of the "radical" Americans for Democratic Action. Six years after the demise of McCarthy, innuendos of being "soft" on communism could still be the kiss of death in American politics.

The public followed intensely the exhausting, grueling campaign. At the end of October, George Gallup concluded that the race was too close to call. On election eve CBS, using IBM computers, predicted an overwhelming Nixon victory. At 10:30 P.M., when a Kennedy landslide seemed inevitable, Jacqueline whispered joyously, "Oh, Bunny, you're president now!" Kennedy quietly replied, "No . . . no . . . it's too early yet." And so it went throughout the night and into the morning. Not until midday was Kennedy declared the winner, and for weeks afterwards some Republicans urged Nixon to challenge the outcome since there seemed to be ample evidence of ballot-stuffing in the two crucial states Kennedy won, Texas and Illinois. In Chicago, Mayor Richard J. Daley waited out the downstate Republican districts to report before he brought in his decisive bloc of Democratic votes. Later in December an official count gave Kennedy 34,227,000 to Nixon's 34,109,000, a razor-edge margin of only 118,000, less than two-thirds of 1 percent of the popular vote. The Republicans also gained seats in the House and Senate. It was a tense, dramatic presidential election and the closest since 1888. Two-thirds of eligible voters went to the polls, one of the highest turnouts in the history of the Republic.

Perhaps the most telling aspect of the election was the black vote, which overwhelmingly went to Kennedy, for good reason. Across the country the vigorous movement that Kennedy had promised had been stirring in the streets during the exciting election year. In February four black college students sat down at a whites-only Woolworth's lunch counter in Greensboro, North Carolina; soon similar sit-ins were car-

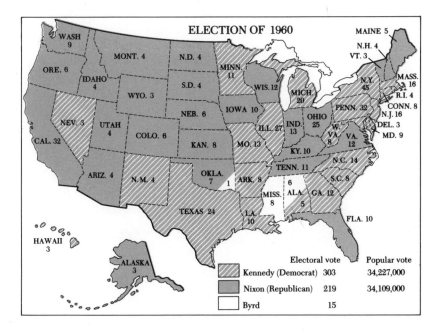

ELECTION OF 1960

	Electoral vote	Popular vote
Kennedy (Democrat)	303	34,227,000
Nixon (Republican)	219	34,109,000
Byrd	15	

ried out in other parts of the South. In May students sat down in the corridors of San Francisco's city hall to protest hearings of the House Un-American Activities Committee, and shortly afterwards the same students picketed businesses that refused to hire blacks. In October, just weeks before the election, Martin Luther King, Jr., was arrested for staging a sit-in at an Atlanta department store. When he was sentenced to four months hard labor, reporters asked Nixon for his view, and he replied that he had none. Privately he wanted the Justice Department to look into the matter but Eisenhower squelched the request. Kennedy made a personal call to Coretta King extending his desire to help, and his brother Robert phoned a Georgia judge and obtained King's release on bail. Quickly the news spread through the black neighborhoods across the country. King's father, a Baptist minister, had never thought he could bring himself to vote for a Catholic. In 1960 he did.

Conclusion

The closeness of the 1960 election reflected a society not yet prepared to accept any challenge to its way of life. Although the economy was in a mild recession, people only had to look around and to recall their plight, or that of their parents, during the depression to realize that they were better off than any previous generation of Americans. Before the recession the national productive output had reached an unprecedented 7 percent, and in 1960 real disposable income—the amount remaining after taxes and adjustments for inflation—was 44 percent higher than in 1929. Economists spoke of discretionary income and leisure spending and wondered what Americans would do with their wealth in future years. Many children born after the Second World War had come to know so much material satisfaction that it would be easy for them, as college students in the 1960s, to conclude that material satisfaction was not enough. What once made many parents proud would make some children guilty.

The year 1960 did witness one area of American life where the challenge of change was unmistakable—civil rights. Freedom riders were mobilizing blacks in southern cities with such growing numbers that segregationists could no longer blame the protest marches and sit-ins on "outsiders." School desegregation had also been making strides. In southern states the number of black students attending schools with whites increased from less than 350 to more than 2,600. The rate of desegregation was painfully slow compared to the two million or so black school children in the South. But southern resistance had begun to crack. In 1958, a Gallup poll asked southerners whether they thought they would ever see the day when whites and blacks would attend the same schools, eat at the same restaurants, and share the same public accommodations. Only 57 percent answered yes. When the same question was put to southerners in January 1961, 76 percent believed they would see such changes taking place.

In foreign affairs American attitudes remained steadfast, particularly toward the cold war. The Kennedy administration would seek to revise Dulles's doctrine of massive retaliation by devising newer tactics of flexible response that entailed conventional and even paraguerrilla forces. But the principles of containment and deterrence remained axiomatic premises of superpower rivalry. After Sputnik the American people were susceptible to Kennedy's claim of a "missile gap" between the United States and the USSR, and Eisenhower had difficulty refuting the erroneous impression since he had, to the frustration of the intelligent agencies, halted all U-2 flights in 1960. In his farewell address Eisenhower uttered his now-famous indictment of "the military-industrial complex" for profiteering from the arms race, but he himself had in eight years quadrupled military spending. The logic of the cold war would continue, and deterrence would depend upon the threat of retaliation that others feared possible, what came to be called "mutually assured destruction," a scenario that included civilian populations. The world had come a long way since Pearl Harbor.

The nuclear legacy is perhaps the one permanent aspect of the forties and fifties that cannot be pointed to with pride. It almost seemed that world events conspired to bring about the frightful predicament. Fear that Hitler's Germany was working on the atom bomb motivated refugee and American scientists to develop it. The desire to save American lives led to its use against Japan. After the Berlin blockade Truman approved of atomic bombs on SAC aircraft. The Korean War hastened the decision to proceed with the H-bomb. Sputnik reinforced the Eisenhower administration's decision to amass an arsenal of nuclear missiles. Even though strategic superiority gave America little political leverage, the build-up continued, and it would only be a matter of time before both superpowers would have almost parallel nuclear capabilities. The British military scholar Lawrence Freeman, himself a defender of deterrence, realized its inevitable dangers. "An international order that rests upon a stability created by nuclear weapons will be the most terrible legacy with which each succeeding generation will endow the next. To believe that this can go on indefinitely without major disaster requires an optimism unjustified by any historical or political perspective."

Eisenhower inherited Truman's cold-war legacy and passed it on to Kennedy without having secured his long-sought test-ban treaty. To the extent that detente eluded him, it is therefore curious that Eisenhower's presidency has come to be praised by a younger generation of American historians. In the fifties Eisenhower's middle-of-the-road politics pleased neither conservatives nor liberals—though some liberals were thankful that he prevented the Republican party from returning to isolationism and a laissez-faire economy. Even so, many journalists and scholars who evaluated his presidency as it unfolded, or from the perspective of the sixties when liberalism again animated the nation's political temper, were critical of his inaction and absence of vision. Problems like civil rights, poverty and unemployment, education, health, and the environment were not so much faced as postponed. Yet after the sixties the post-Vietnam generation would come to esteem Eisenhower's inaction in the diplomatic arena. He ended the Korean War and undertook no other course of action that would lead to another bloody quagmire. Thus it is understandable that historians of the post-Vietnam generation would admire him for avoiding a nuclear confrontation with the Soviets and his restraint in regards to military intervention in Indochina.

This "revisionist" reappraisal was perhaps inevitable, but carried too far it obscures Eisenhower's more troubling legacy, specifically his covert use of the CIA in Iran and Guatemala and his brandishing of nuclear weapons against China. Not only did the president and his secretary of state prolong the cold war instead of confronting it in all its complexity, they also planted the seeds of some of the diplomatic disasters of the sixties—namely, the planned Cuban invasion and the "falling domino" mentality regarding Southeast Asia. Eisenhower proved to be one of the very few presidents who left office more popular than when he entered. For many Americans who wanted nothing more than to bask in the pleasantries of suburbia, perhaps that was sufficient. But the world was no safer and humankind continued in the coils of the nuclear peril.

Yet Eisenhower's extraordinary popularity, the envy of every politician then and now, cannot be dismissed lightly. It derived from the sense of dignity and trust he brought to the White House and to his well-earned reputation as a military hero. He was a curious kind of hero, not an event-making leader but a respected administrator who got things done. Kenneth S. Davis, who had been close to Eisenhower during the war years, later discovered some notes he had taken while preparing a book on the general. Davis doubted he could write a biography of any depth since his subject was devoid of it. Eisenhower's entire mental life "is involved in external strategy. If he cares about *meanings*, even historical ones, I am not aware of it. . . . Yet he is caught up in historical circumstances." Davis's personal notes reveal a string of perplexities. "Meaning, significance, is not rooted in him," he observed of Eisenhower, "it only *adheres* to him. His significance is all external, imposed. He drifts with a destiny he probably does not understand, and he does nothing (practically) to determine it." Eisenhower preferred to live life without examining it, and if destiny called upon him to lead, he did not care to know where. "He is in a heroic position without being himself a hero. None of that moody grandeur, depth, et cetera, which inspires men to be better than themselves. One can't imagine him leading a great historic movement. No *creative* will. There is no *beyondness* in him."

Davis would go on to perceive the more positive qualities of Ike, particularly his awareness of his symbolic role as the architect of Allied unity, his genuine dedication to peace, and his belief in American cooperation and unity. But it is worth noting how differently Harry S. Truman saw himself. History was nothing to Truman if not pregnant with meaning and significance. Truman's memoirs are full of boasts that he took his bearings from the lessons of the past. Whether he looked to history simply to sanction his actions or whether he truly believed that present events had antecedent causal relations, Truman was fond of invoking history, especially at times of crisis, like his decision to overcome the Berlin blockade or to resist the communist invasion of South Korea. Even the most controversial episode of his administration, the decision to relieve General MacArthur of his command, reminded Truman of the situation that Abraham Lincoln had faced in dealing with General George B. McClellan during the Civil War. But for all Truman's devotion to the study of history, it was Eisenhower who convinced Americans that he was in control of events even if he had little comprehension of their significance.

The Truman and Eisenhower years gave Americans a sense of pride in themselves and confidence in the future. It is questionable whether either sentiment survived the fifties intact. The America that emerged victorious from World War II was not the same America fifteen years later. The decline of confidence resulted in part from the changing nature of warfare brought by modern technology. After the Second World War Americans could take pride in the performance of their soldiers. With the increasing complexity of the cold war, which offered the possibility of either covert CIA operations or nuclear attack and retaliation, warfare seemed more and more a choice between the dishonorable and the suicidal; and if new inventions in sophisticated missile weaponry would make some Americans feel proud of their technological achievements, it was a pride born of fear.

The cold war itself, however, is not the only explanation for the decline of self-assurance that came to be felt at the end of the Eisenhower years. Equally troubling was the sense of unease and discontent. No one had predicted it. In 1950, for example, *Fortune* published a book with the curious title, *U.S.A., the Permanent Revolution*. The title, taken from Leon Trotsky, was meant to depict a new way of life founded on unlimited prosperity, active citizen participation, winning friends aboard with generous foreign aid and free-trade policies, and proudly accepting the burdens of history as a great world power. America must be understood not as a nation of definite goals but of indefinite growth. "Americans wish that other people could see their country as it really is: not as an achievement but as a *process*—a process of becoming." But can there be growth without conscious direction and meaning? "Why should we assume that America has *any* meaning?" the editors asked. "Rightly understood, the principles that embody the meaning of America are the very forces that have done most to change America."

By 1960, all confidence that America could simply be accepted as a process of continual growth and change came to be questioned and in many instances rejected. "What is wrong with America?" queried the *U.S. News and World Report*. "What shall we do with our greatness?" asked the editors of *Life*. President Eisenhower set up a "Commission on National Goals" and Walter Lippmann analyzed the "Anatomy of Discontent," which he specified as a willingness of Americans to extend their political commitments and an unwillingness to fulfill them. The Reverend Billy Graham thought Americans overextended themselves in more concrete ways. "We overeat, overdrink, oversex, and overplay. . . . We have tried to fill ourselves with science and education, with better living and pleasure . . . but we are still empty and bored." Adlai Stevenson doubted that America's "permanent revolution" would have any impact on the rest of the world. "With the supermarket as our temple and the singing commercial as our litany, are we likely to fire the world with an irresistible vision of America's exalted purpose and inspiring way of life?" "Something has gone wrong in America," complained the novelist John Steinbeck of his fellow people. "Having too many things, they spend their hours and money on the couch searching for a soul." Everywhere Americans were engaged in the "great debate" about "the national purpose." Americans have become worried, journalists concluded, because they feel they lack inspiring ideals and because they have been led to believe that they do not need them.

"The case of the missing purpose," wrote a philosopher in *The Nation,* "is a case of human beings missing the purpose of life." The proud decades were over.

Or were they? Several months before Eisenhower's farewell and Kennedy's inauguration, things were changing. Within a few years America would be addressing problems it never knew existed and some people would be singing "We Shall Overcome!" Yet even before the sixties ended America would be more divided than ever, the two Kennedys and King dead, and the Republicans back in office. Now it was Nixon who promised to bring Americans "back together again." Henceforth, the period of the fifties, once regarded as a dreadful aberration standing between the more compassionate thirties and activist sixties, would seem more and more the steady norm of America's political temper. The generation of the sixties experienced the previous decade as a burden that had to be radically transformed, and some of its worst aspects were confronted and eradicated. But as the radical sixties petered out, it became all the more clear that the two decades beginning with the Second World War shaped the nation's environment and consciousness in more enduring ways than had once been expected. The forties and perhaps especially the fifties are still living in the present, and the assumptions and values of the two decades have become ingrained in our habits and institutions. "What is the national purpose?" asked Dean Acheson in response to the great debate of the late fifties. "To survive and, perchance, to prosper." In doing both well, America still had good reason to be proud of itself.

A Note on Sources

CHAPTER ONE

American reactions to Pearl Harbor are in Studs Terkel, *"The Good War": An Oral History of World War II* (New York, 1984); the student is quoted on p. 36. The revisionist and antirevisionist historigraphy on Pearl Harbor is vast. A sampling of different perspectives may be found in the anthology, *Pearl Harbor, Roosevelt and the Coming of the War*, ed. George M. Waller (Boston, 1953). The first major revisionist assault was Charles A. Beard's *President Roosevelt and the Coming of the War, 1941: A Study of Appearances and Reality* (New Haven, 1948). More balanced interpretations are Roberta Wohlstetter, *Pearl Harbor: Warning and Decision* (Stanford, 1962), and Gordon W. Prange, *At Dawn We Slept: The Untold Story of Pearl Harbor* (New York, 1981). See also Richard W. Steele, "Franklin D. Roosevelt and His Foreign Policy Critics," and the "Comment" by Arthur Schlesinger, Jr., *Political Science Quarterly* 94 (1979): 15–35.

For American attitudes toward fascism in Europe, see John P. Diggins, *Mussolini and Fascism: The View from America* (Princeton, 1972); *Public Opinion, 1935–1946*, ed. Hadley Cantril (Princeton, 1951); William W. Kaufmann, "Two American Ambassadors: Bullitt and Kennedy," in *The Diplomats: 1919–1939*, eds. Gordon Craig and Felix Gilbert (Princeton, 1953), 2, 649–81. On the varieties of isolationism and nonintervention ism, see Selig Adler, *The Isolationist Impulse: Its Twentieth Century Reaction* (New York, 1957); Manfred Jonas, *Isolationism in America, 1935–1941* (New York, 1966); and Burton K. Wheeler, *Yankee from the West* (New York 1962). The intellectuals voiced their opposing positions in John Dewey, "No Matter What Happens, Stay Out," *Social Frontier* 7 (March 1939): 11; Bruce Bliven, "This Is Where I Came In," *New Republic* 93, Jan. 5, 1938, 245–46; Waldo Frank, "Our Guilt in Fascism," *New Republic* 102, May 6, 1940, 603–8; Archibald MacLeish, "The Irresponsibles," *Nation* 150, May 18, 1940, 618–23.

Statistics on domestic life during the war years are drawn from *Public Opinion, 1935–1946*. See also *Homefront: America During World War II*, eds. Mark Jonathan Harris, Franklin D. Mitchell, and Stephen Schecter, (New York, 1984); Terkel, *"The Good War"*; John Morton Blum, *V Was for Victory: Politics and American Culture During World War II* (New York, 1976); Richard Polenberg, *War and Society: The United States, 1941–1945* (Philadelphia 1972). More specific studies are D'Ann Mae Campbell, *Women at War with America: Private Lives in a Patriotic America* (Cambridge, 1984); Louis Ruchames, *Race, Jobs, and Politics: The Story of FEPC* (New York, 1953); R. M. Dalfiume, *Desegregation in the United States Armed Forces: Fighting on Two Fronts: 1939–1953* (Columbia, Mo., 1969); Roger Daniels, *Concentration Camps USA: Japanese America and World War II* (New York, 1971); Harvey Sitkoff, "The Detroit Race Riot of 1943," *Michigan History* 53 (Fall 1969): 1 83–206; Alice Kessler Harris, "Rosie the Riveter: Who Was She?" *Labor History* 24 (Spring 1983): 249–53. For the domestic side of the war years, the author has drawn a good deal from Geoffrey Perrett, *Days of Sadness, Years of Triumph: The American People, 1939–1945* (New York, 1973); and from the following contemporary accounts: "Shifts of Civilian Populations During the War Period," *Monthly Labor Review* 58 (June 1944): 1186–89; Susan B. Anthony, II, "Working at the Navy Yard," *New Republic* 110, May 1, 1944, 59–99; Gene Dickson, "Housewife War Worker," *ibid.* 109, Oct. 18 1943, 518–19; Edith Stein, "Brains in the Kitchen," *The Nation* 158 Jan. 22, 1944, 95–96; Carey McWilliams, "The Zoot-Suit Riots," *New Republic* 108, June 21, 1943, 818–20; "Los Angeles Pachuco Gangs," *ibid.* 108, Jan. 18, 1943, 76–77; "The Negro: His Future in America: A Special Section," *New Republic* 109, Oct. 18, 1943, 535–50; Walter White, "Behind the Harlem Riot," *ibid.* 109, Aug. 16, 1943, 220–22; Charles Williams, "Harlem at War," *The Nation* 156, Jan. 16, 1943, 86–88; Horace R. Cayton, "The Negro's Challenge," *ibid.* 157, July 3, 1943, 10–12; Carey McWilliams, "California and the Japanese," *New Republic* 106, Mar. 2, 1942, 295–97; Isamu Noguchi, "Trouble Among Japanese Americans," *ibid.*, 108 Feb. 1, 1943, 142–43; Wallace Stegner, "The Nisei Come Home," *ibid.*, July 9, 1945, 45–46; Eleanor Roosevelt, "Race, Religion, and Prejudice," *ibid.*, 106 May 11, 1942, 630.

On President Franklin D. Roosevelt's enduring hold on the America political imagination, see William E. Leuchtenburg, *In the Shadow of FDR: From Harry Truman to Ronald Reagan* (Ithaca, N.Y., 1983). The closing phases of the New Deal are described in John Chamberlain, *The American Stakes* (New York, 1940); and the last chapters in Broadus Mitchell, *Depression Decade: From New Era through New Deal 1929–1941* (New York, 1947), and William E. Leuchtenburg, *FDR and the New Deal* (New York, 1963). For the Roosevelt administration during the war years, see James MacGregor Burns, *Roosevelt: The Soldier of Freedom, 1940–1945* (New York, 1970); Robert Dallek, *Franklin D. Roosevelt and American Foreign Policy, 1932–1945* (New York, 1979).

World War II as military history is covered in A. Russell Buchanan, *The United States in World War II*, 2 vols. (New York, 1964); Ronald H. Spector, *Eagle against the Sun: The American War with Japan* (New York, 1985); B. H. Liddell Hart, *History of the Second World War* (New York, 1971; Dwight D. Eisenhower, *Crusade in Europe* (Garden City, N.Y., 1948); David Eisenhower, *Eisenhower: At War 1943–1945* (New York, 1986); Ronald Schaffer, *Wings of Judgment: American Bombing in World War II* (New York, 1986); David Wyman, *The Abandment of the Jews: America and the Holocoust, 1941–1945* (New York, 1984).

On America and the Holocaust and Hiroshima, see Hannah Arendt, "The Concentration Camps," in *The 1940's: Profile of a Nation in Crisis*, ed. Chester E. Eisinger (Garden City, N.Y., 1969), 129–140; Robert Abzug, *Inside the Vicious Heart: Americans and the Liberation of Nazi Concentration Camps* (New York, 1985). Deborah E. Lipset, *The American Press and the Coming of the Holocaust* (New York, 1985); Paul Boyer, *By the Bomb's Early Light: American Thought and Culture at the Dawn of the Atomic Age* (New York, 1985), examines the cultural and psychological impact; for opposing views on the decision to use the bomb, see Herbert Feis, *The Atomic Bomb and the End of World War II* (Princeton, 1966); and Barton Bernstein, "Roosevelt, Truman, and the Atomic Bomb: A Reinterpretation," *Political Science Quarterly* 90 (1975): 23–70.

The opinion of the communists is examined in Paul F. Boller, "Hiroshima and the

American Left," *International Social Science Review* 57 (1982): 13–27; for American attitudes in general see Rita James Simon, *Public Opinion in America, 1936–1970* (New York, 1974), 157–59.

CHAPTER TWO

The revisionist case is argued in Gar Alperovitz, *Atomic Diplomacy: Hiroshima and Potsdam* (New York, 1965); Gabriel Kolko, *The Politics of War: The World and the United States Foreign Policy* (New York, 1968); Lloyd Gardner, *Architects of Illusion: Men and Ideas in American Foreign Policy, 1941–1949* (Chicago, 1970); William Appleman Williams, *The Tragedy of American Diplomacy* (New York, 1962). A penetrating, systematic critique of the revisionists is offered in chapters 7 and 8 of Arthur Schlesinger, Jr.'s *The Cycles of American History* (Boston, 1986); see also Hugh Thomas, *Armed Truce: The Beginnings of the Cold War, 1945–46* (New York, 1987); a useful anthology and bibliography is *The Evolution of the Cold War*, ed. Richard H. Miller (New York, 1972).

For critical but balanced treatments see the valuable studies by Walter LaFeber, *America, Russia, and the Cold War* (New York, 1980) and Adam Ulam, *The Rivals: America and Russia since World War II* (New York, 1972); Daniel Yergin, *Shattered Peace: The Origins of the Cold War and the National Security State* (Boston, 1977).

Other works to consult are John Lewis Gaddis, *The United States and the Origins of the Cold War, 1941–1947* (New York, 1972), and his *Strategies of Containment: A Critical Appraisal of Postwar American National Security Policy* (New York, 1982); Vojtech Mastny, *Russia's Road to the Cold War* (New York, 1982); William Taubman, *Stalin's American Policy: From Entente to Detente to Cold War* (New York, 1982); and George C. Herring, *Aid to Russia, 1941–1946: Strategy, Diplomacy, the Origins of the Cold War* (New York, 1973).

The briefing paper for the Yalta Conference is quoted in Alan J. Levine, "Some Revisionist Theses on the Cold War, 1943–1946: A Study of a Modern Mythology," *Continuity* I (Fall 1980): 82; the Duclos letter in Joseph R. Sarobin, *American Communism in Crisis, 1943–1957* (Cambridge, 1972), 78–81; descriptions of Stalin in Nikita Khrushchev, "The Crimes of Stalin," *New Leader*, July 16, 1956, section two, 2–67. See also Milovan Djilas, *Conversations with Stalin* (New York, 1962), 132–33; and Franz Borkenau, *World Communism: A History of the Communist International* (Ann Arbor, 1962), 429. On Keynes and the Bretton Woods Conference, see Alfred E. Eckes, Jr., *A Search for Solvency: Bretton Woods and the International Monetary System, 1941–1971* (Austin, 1975); Luce is quoted in Robert Dalleck, "The Postwar World," in *Estrangement: America and the World*, ed. Sanford J. Unger (New York, 1985), p. 32.

Truman's speech on the Greece-Turkey crisis is in *Containment and the Cold War: American Foreign Policy Since 1945*, ed. Thomas G. Paterson (Reading, Mass., 1973); Henry A. Wallace spelled out his opposition in "My Alternative for the Marshall Plan," *New Republic* 118, Jan. 12, 1948, 13–14.

Congressman Judd's perception of the double standard is discussed in Robert H. Ferrell, *American Diplomacy: A History* (New York, 1959), 447–48; Truman's description of Chiang Kai-shek is in his *Memoirs*, 2, 90; John K. Fairbank's comment is from his "America and the Chinese Revolution," *New Republic* 121, Aug. 22, 1949, 11–12; Lippmann's hopeful expectations about Poland are from *Public Philosopher: Selected Letters of Walter Lippmann*, ed. John Morton Blum (New York, 1985), 452, 460; for Mao's suspicion of Stalin, see André Malraux, *Anti-Memoirs* (New York, 1968), 442–69.

On the Kennan-Lippmann debate, see George F. Kennan, "The Sources of Soviet Conduct," *Foreign Affairs* 25 (July 1947): 566–82; and Walter Lippmann, *The Cold War: A Study in US Foreign Policy* (New York, 1947). The diplomatic dimensions of the atomic bomb and the control of atomic energy are dealt with in Martin J. Sherwin, *A World Destroyed: The Atom Bomb and the Grand Alliance* (New York, 1975), and Gregg Herken, *The Winning Weapon: The Atomic Bomb in the Cold War, 1945–1950* (New York, 1982). On China and the Korean War, see Akira Iriye, *The Cold War in Asia: A Historical Introduction* (Englewood Cliffs, N.J., 1974); Michael Schaller, *The United States and China in the Twentieth Century* (New York, 1979); and Harold R. Isaacs, *Images of Asia: American Views of China and India* (New York, 1962). Max Hastings, *The Korean War* (New York, 1987) appeared too late for use here.

On General MacArthur and the Korean War, see William Manchester, *American Caesar: Douglas MacArthur, 1880–1964* (Boston, 1978), and Richard Rovere and Arthur Schlesinger, Jr., *The MacArthur Controversy and American Foreign Policy* (New York, 1965). For the Berlin blockade, see the close analysis of Soviet intentions and American reactions in Alexander L. George and Richard Smoke, *Deterrence in American Foreign Policy: Theory and Practice* (New York, 1974); the public reaction was expressed in "The Great Air Lift Sustains Berlin," *Life* 25, Aug. 9, 1948, 15–19; Arnold Toynbee's observation is in his essay, "Symbols Men Live and Die For," *New York Times Magazine*, Nov. 20, 1960, 12–13, 126.

For earlier views on the Soviet Union, see Christopher Lasch, *American Liberals and the Russian Revolution* (New York, 1962); and Peter Filene, *America and the Soviet Experiment, 1917–1933* (Cambridge, 1967). Samples of the hopeful pro-Soviet views during the war are Freda Kirchway, "End of the Comintern," *The Nation* 156, May 29, 1943, 762–63, and Max Lerner, "After the Comintern," *New Republic* 108, June 7, 1943, 753–55.

CHAPTER THREE

The best sources for Truman are his own lively, argumentative *Memoirs*, 2 vols. (New York, 1955–56); Merle Miller, *Plain Speaking: An Oral Biography of Harry S. Truman* (New York, 1974); and *Off the Record: The Private Papers of Harry S. Truman*, ed Robert H. Ferrell (New York, 1980). For vivid narrative history, see Robert J. Donovan's two volumes, *Conflict and Crisis: The Presidency of Harry S. Truman*, (New York, 1977), and *Tumultuous Years: The Presidency of Harry S. Truman, 1949–1953* (New York, 1982). Two valuable reappraisals are William E. Leuchtenburg, "Give 'Em Harry," *New Republic* 190, May 21, 1984, 19–23; and Geoffrey S. Smith, "Harry, We Hardly Knew You: Revisionism, Politics, Diplomacy, 1945–1954," *American Political Science Review* 70 (June 1976): 560–82.

For the economics and politics of the era, see Alvin H. Hansen, *The Postwar American Economy: Performances and Problems*, (New York, 1964); Allen J. Matusow, *Farm Politics and Policies in the Truman Years* (Cambridge, 1967); Samuel Lubell, *The Future of American Politics* (New York, 1952); and Alonzo L. Hamby, *Beyond the New Deal: Harry S. Truman and American Liberalism* (New York, 1973) and *The Imperial Years: The US since 1939* (New York, 1976).

Quotes by Vaughn, veteran student, Stone, Roper, Thurmond, FBI agent, Reuther, *Washington Post*, and jokes about Truman are in Joseph C. Coulden, *The Best Years, 1945–1950* (New York, 1947), 214, 230, 316, 350, 399, 403, 421; and John Bartlow

Martin, "Middletown at Peace: Muncie Revisited," in *American Thought: 1947*, ed. Philip Wylie (New York, 1947), 390; the suburbanite is quoted in Eric Goldman, *The Crucial Decade and After: America, 1945–1960* (New York, 1960), 89; Kempton is quoted in Miller, *Plain Speaking*, 132–33; Truman's remark on the tomb epitaph is quoted in William Manchester, *The Glory and the Dream: A Narrative History of America, 1932–1972* (Boston, 1974), 608; the liberal criticisms are in the scathing evaluation, "Truman as Leader," *New Republic* 118, May 17, 1948, 13–27.

On the extent to which the loyalty oath and congressional committees investigating subversion went beyond the intent of the framers, see Alan Barth, *The Loyalty of Free Men* (New York, 1951), and Alan D. Harper, *The Politics of Loyalty: The White House and the Communist Issue, 1946–1952* (Westport, Conn., 1969). Elizabeth Bentley's career is discussed with insight in Murray Kempton, *Part of Our Time: Some Monuments and Ruins of the Thirties* (New York, 1955), 217–30; on McCarthy and the Red Scare, see Thomas C. Reeves, *The Life and Times of Joe McCarthy* (New York, 1982); Allen Weinstein, *Perjury: The Hiss-Chambers Case* (New York, 1978), and Victor Navasky, "Allen Weinstein's 'Perjury': The Case Not Proved Against Alger Hiss," *The Nation* April 8, 1978, 2–11; for the revisionist argument that traces McCarthyism to liberalism, see Athan Theoharis, *Seeds of Repression: Harry S. Truman and the Origins of McCarthyism* (Chicago, 1971), and Robert Griffith and Athan Theoharis, eds., *The Specter: Original Essays on the Cold War and the Origins of McCarthyism* (New York, 1974); the argument that McCarthyism represented an elite rather than a popular phenomenon is presented in Michael Rogin, *The Intellectuals and McCarthy: The Radical Specter* (Cambridge, 1967); for the older liberal position, see Owen Lattimore, *Ordeal by Slander* (Boston, 1950) and "McCarthy's Great Red Scare," *New Republic* 122, Mar. 20, 1950, 5–7.

CHAPTER FOUR

On Dwight D. Eisenhower, see Stephen Ambrose's scholarly, two-volume study, *Eisenhower: Soldier General of the Army and President Elect, 1890–1952* (New York, 1983) and *Eisenhower: The President* (New York, 1984); also Emmet John Hughes, *The Ordeal of Power: A Political Memoir of the Eisenhower Years* (New York, 1962); Robert Griffith, "Dwight D. Eisenhower and the Corporate Commonwealth," *American Historical Review* 87 (1982): 87–122; and *Eisenhower as President*, ed. Dean Albertson (New York, 1963). On the Democrats, see John Barlow Martin, *Adlai Stevenson and the World* (New York, 1977).

Other important works are Samuel Lubell, *The Revolt of the Moderates* (New York, 1956); Arthur Larson, *A Republican Looks at His Party* (New York, 1956); Manchester, *The Glory*; Geoffrey Perrett, *A Dream of Greatness: The American People, 1945–1963* (New York, 1979); Fred Siegel, *The Troubled Journey* (New York, 1984); Charles Alexander, *Holding the Line: The Eisenhower Era, 1952–1961* (New York, 1957). Eisenhower has also been the subject of revisionist interpretations by recent scholars who praise him for keeping America out of foreign interventions and for his presumably then unseen talents as a politician. See Blanche Cook, *The Declassified Eisenhower: A Divided Legacy* (New York, 1981) and Fred I. Greenstein, *The Hidden-Hand Presidency: Eisenhower as Leader* (New York, 1982); see also Vincent P. De Santis, "Eisenhower Revisionism," *Review of Politics* 38 (1976): 190–207; and Arthur Schlesinger, Jr., "The Ike Age Revisited," *Reviews in American History* 11 (1983): 1–11.

For the Korean War, see Joseph C. Goulden, *Korea: The Untold Story of the War* (New

York, 1982), and Adam Ulam, *The Rivals;* Max Hastings, *The Korean War.* The historian Robert A. Divine's defense of Eisenhower's threat to wage atomic warfare in Korea is in his *Eisenhower and the Cold War* (New York, 1981), 31; pilot Jabara is quoted in "Korea: Trial and Achievement," *New Republic* 124, June 25, 1951, 9; Richard Strout and Charles Wilson in Manchester, *The Glory,* 649, 652–53; Lippmann in *Letters,* 514; Nixon, Dulles, and Reston in Samuel F. Wells, "The Origins of Massive Retaliation," *Political Science Quarterly* 96 (1981): 31–52. On the CIA, see Gregory F. Treverton, *Covert Action: The Limits of Intervention in the Postwar World* (New York, 1987); on diplomacy, see Townsend Hoopes, *The Devil and John Foster Dulles* (Boston, 1973). Taft's attack on Truman in R. Alton Lee, *Truman and Taft-Hartley: A Question of Mandate* (Lexington, 1966), 38, and his skepticism about business leadership in Richard P. Rovere, *Final Reports: Personal Reflections on Politics and History in Our Time* (Garden City, N.Y., 1984), 121; Stevenson on Peale in Stephen Whitfield, "The 1950s: The Era of No Hard Feelings," *South Atlantic Quarterly* 76 (Autumn 1977): 550–68; Eisenhower on McCarthy in Ambrose, *Eisenhower,* 2, 166; Molotov in LaFeber, *America, Russia, and the Cold War,* 147; Stevenson's campaign speeches in "Stevenson Speaks," *New Republic* 127, Oct. 20, 1952, 9–23, and "Toward the Big Great Tomorrow," Aug. 4, 1952, 5; description of Congressman Kennedy's campaign in *Time* 60, Nov. 10, 1952, 27; Rovere's exchange with Dulles in Rovere, *Final Reports,* 146. On McCarthy's censure, see Donald J. Kemper, *Decade of Fear: Senator Hennings and Civil Liberties* (Columbia, Mo., 1965); data on relative nuclear capability drawn from Zbigniew Brzezinski, "How the Cold War Was Played," *Foreign Affairs* 51 (Oct. 1972): 181–209.

CHAPTER FIVE

On Hollywood and World War II, see Clayton R. Koppes and Gregory D. Black, *Hollywood Goes to War: How Politics, Profits, and Propaganda Shaped World War II Movies* (New York, 1987), Davis and MacLeish quoted on pp. 64, 66; Roger Manvell, *Films and the Second World War* (New York, 1974); Colin Schindler, *Hollywood Goes to War* (London, 1979); Alistair Cooke, "Humphrey Bogart: Epitaph for a Tough Guy," *Atlantic* 199, May 1959, 31–35. The critical judgment about the Hollywood communists comes from Larry Ceplair and Steven Englund, *The Inquisition in Hollywood: Politics in the Film Community, 1930–1960* (Berkeley, 1983), 241. On communism and the trade unions, see Bert Cochran, *Labor and Communism: The Conflict that Shaped American Unions* (Princeton, 1977); for the purge of the professions, see David Caute, *The Great Fear: The Anti-Communist Purge Under Truman and Eisenhower* (New York, 1978); Ellen W. Schrecker, *No Ivory Tower: McCarthyism and the Universities* (New York, 1986); and Sidney Hook, *Heresy, Yes—Conspiracy, No* (New York, 1953).

On intellectuals and communism and anticommunism, see Sidney Hook, "From Alienation to Critical Inquiry: The Vocation of the American Intellectual," *Partisan Review* 19, Sept.–Oct. 1952, 569–74; the charge that the liberal intellectual was trying to "outdo the Right" was made by Christopher Lasch in the symposium, "Liberal Anti-Communism Revisited," *Commentary* 44, Sept. 1967, 64; for a more supportive view, see John P. Diggins, *Up From Communism: Conservative Odysseys in American Intellectual History* (New York, 1975). On the infamous Waldorf-Astoria conference, see Joseph P. Lash, "Weekend at the Waldorf," *New Republic* 120, April 18, 1949, 10–14. Liberals and the ADA are treated critically in Mary McAuliffe, *Crisis of the Left: Cold-War Politics and American Liberals, 1947–1954* (Amherst, 1978); and Irving Howe, "Liberalism—A Moral

Crisis, the ADA: Vision and Myopia," *Dissent* 2 (Spring 1955): 107–13; and are defended in Arthur Schlesinger, Jr., *The Vital Center: The Politics of Freedom* (New York, 1949); see also Schlesinger's recent further thoughts in his "The Vital Center," *Partisan Review* 51 (Winter 1984–85): 868–70. On Niebuhr's influence, see *Reinhold Niebuhr: His Religious, Social and Political Thought*, eds. Charles W. Kegley and Robert W. Bretall (New York, 1956); *The Legacy of Reinhold Niebuhr*, ed. Nathan Scott, Jr. (Chicago, 1975); and Richard Fox, *Reinhold Niebuhr: An Intellectual Biography* (New York, 1985).

On McCarthyism and the intellectuals, see *The Radical Right: The New American Right Expanded and Updated*, ed. Daniel Bell (Garden City, N.Y., 1963); *The Meaning of McCarthyism*, ed. Earl Latham (Lexington, Mass., 1973); Dennis Wrong, "Theories of McCarthyism," *Dissent* I (Autumn 1954): 385–92; Peter Viereck, *Shame and Glory of the Intellectuals* (Boston, 1953); and Nelson Polsby, "Towards An Explanation of McCarthyism," *Political Studies* 8 (1960): 250–71.

CHAPTER SIX

The quotes about the fifties by Goldman, Mailer, Harrington, and Lowell are in *Eisenhower*, ed. Albertson, x; Douglas T. Miller and Marion Nowak, *The Fifties: The Way We Really Were* (Garden City, N.Y., 1977), 6; *The Fifties: Photographs of America*, introd. by John Chancellor (New York, 1985), no pagination; the conservative view is John Mander, "In Defense of the Fifties," *Commentary* 48 (1969): 63–67.

On the economy, see Hansen, *Postwar American Economy*; Edmund S. Phelps, "Perspectives on Economic Growth," in *The Changing American Economy*, ed. John R. Coleman (New York, 1967), 161–69; and Herbert Stein, *Presidential Economics: The Making of Economic Policy from Roosevelt to Reagan and Beyond* (New York, 1984), 65–87.

On social changes, see Kenneth T. Jackson, *Crabgrass Frontier: The Suburbanization of the United States* (New York, 1985); Mumford and *House Beautiful* are quoted in Ron Rosenbaum, "The House that Levitt Built," *Esquire* 100, Dec. 1983, 378–91; on automobiles, see John Brooks, *The Great Leap: The Past Twenty-five Years in America* (New York, 1966); and Eugene D. Balsley, "The Hot Rod Culture," in *American Culture: Approaches to the Study of the US*, ed. Henig Cohen (Boston, 1968), 266–71; on consumption and the martini set, see John O'Hara, "The New Expense-Account Society," *Flair* I, May 1950, 23, 110–11; the growth of fast foods and McDonald's is examined in Tom Robbins, "Ray Croc Did It All For You," *Esquire* 100, Dec. 1983, 340–44; the mothers interviewed about television and children are in Manchester, *The Glory*, 723; for a valuable analysis of the Gleason show, see David Mark, *Democratic Vistas: Television in American Culture* (Philadelphia, 1984), 99–128; the TV scandals are discussed in Goldman, *The Crucial Decade*, 316–24; Van Doren's students are described in Jeffrey Hart, *When the Going was Good: American Life in the Fifties* (New York, 1982), 54, and they are criticized in Hans Morganthau, "Epistle to the Columbians," *New Republic* 141, Dec. 21, 1959, 8–10; John Steinbeck, "Have We Gone Soft?" *New Republic* 142, February 15, 1960, 11–15; John Steinbeck and Adlai Stevenson, "Our Rigged Morality," *Coronet* 47, March 1960, 144–47; the optimistic assessment of TV is in Marshall McLuhan, *Understanding Media: The Extensions of Man* (New York, 1964). On sports and the media, see Benjamin Rader, *In Its Own Image: How Television Has Transformed Sports* (New York, 1985); Rickey is quoted in James Gilbert, *Another Chance: Postwar America, 1945–1968* (Philadelphia, 1981). On popular music, see Albert Goldman, *Elvis* (New York, 1981); the literature on Presley is vast; see the excellent essay by Mark

Crispin Miller, "The King," *New York Review of Books* 24, Dec. 8, 1977, 38–42; Dean is quoted in John Dos Passos, *Midcentury* (Boston, 1961), 479–86; and interpreted in Pauline Kael, *I Lost It at the Movies* (Boston, 1965), 55–57; on popular films, see Andy Rooney, *Movies Are Better than Ever: Wide-Screen Memories of the Fifties* (New York, 1973); the high-school teacher who suggested the Housman poem was Neil Postman, now a professor at New York University.

For a sympathetic view of young Americans in the fifties, see Edgar Z. Friedenberg, *The Vanishing Adolescent* (Boston, 1959); the exaggerated reports of the media are dealt with in James Gilbert, *A Cycle of Outrage: America's Reaction to the Juvenile Delinquent of the 1950s* (New York, 1985); J. D. Salinger deals sensitively with the complaints of the young in *The Catcher in the Rye* (Boston, 1951); on the confusion of generations, see Margaret Mead, *The School in American Culture* (Cambridge, 1950), quoted on p. 40; a much discussed criticism of students and teachers was Arthur Bestor's *Educational Wastelands: The Retreat From Learning in Our Public Schools* (Urbana, Ill., 1953); on parenting and peer influence, see Benjamin Spock, *Common Sense Book of Baby and Child Care* (New York, 1946); Philip Wylie, *Generation of Vipers* (New York, 1942); and Max Lerner, *America as a Civilization: Life and Thought in America Today* (New York, 1957). College students are studied in Kenneth Keniston, *The Uncommitted: Alienated Youth in American Society* (New York, 1965); Kinsey's wife is quoted in Stanley Elkin, "Alfred Kinsey: The Patron Saint of Sex," *Esquire* 100, Dec. 1983, 48–56; Salinger's character is quoted on sex in "A Perfect Day for Banana Fish," in *Nine Stories* (Boston, 1953); on the hesitancy about sex, see Benita Eisler, *Private Lives: Men and Women of the Fifties* (New York, 1986).

The fate of individualism and the spiritual shallowness of the era is explored in William H. Whyte, *The Organization Man* (New York, 1956); Will Herberg, *Protestant, Catholic, Jew: An Essay in American Religious Sociology* (Garden City, N.Y., 1956); Marshall Frady, *Billy Graham: A Parable of American Righteousness* (Boston, 1979); and David Riesman, *The Lonely Crowd: A Study of the Changing American Character* (New Haven, 1950).

On the status of women, see John Costello, *Virtue Under Fire: How World War II Changed Our Social and Sexual Attitudes* (Boston, 1985); Lois Banner, *Women in Modern America: A Brief History* (New York, 1974); William H. Chafe, *The American Woman: Her Changing Social, Economic and Political Roles, 1920–1970* (New York, 1974); and Betty Friedan, *The Feminine Mystique* (New York, 1963). Gloria Steinem is quoted in Marilyn French, "The Emancipation of Betty Friedan," *Esquire* 100, Dec. 1983, 518; several quotes on this subject are from Miller and Nowak, *The Fifties*, 147–56; Eisler, *Private Lives*, 209; Barbara Ehrenreich, *The Hearts of Men: American Dreams and the Flight From Commitment* (Garden City, N.Y., 1983). Presley on marriage is quoted in Manchester, *The Glory*, 759; for the historian's reaction, see Arthur Schlesinger, Jr., "The Crisis of Masculinity" (1958), in *The Politics of Hope* (Boston, 1963), 237–46. On gender relations in the films of the era, see Stanley Cavell, *Purists of Happiness: The Hollywood Comedy of Remarriage* (Cambridge, 1981). The two different evaluations of the fifties are given by Philip Catania and Michael DeStefano, quoted in Eisler, *Private Lives*, 20–21.

CHAPTER SEVEN

The negative description of the fifties comes from the title by Joseph Satin, ed., *The 1950s: America's "Placid" Decade* (Boston, 1960). Similar descriptions may be found in Miller and Nowak, *The Fifties.*

On music and ballet in the postwar era, see Joan Peyer, *The New Music: The Sense Beyond the Sound* (New York, 1971); Eric Salzman, *Twentieth-Century Music: An Introduction* (Englewood Cliffs, N.J., 1974); Leonard Bernstein, *The Unanswered Question: Six Talks at Harvard* (Cambridge, 1976); and Richard Poirier, "The American Genius of George Balanchine," *New Republic* 183, Oct. 11, 1983, 21–31.

Other artistic and scientific contributions of the refugees are discussed in William H. Jordy, "The Aftermath of the Bauhaus in America: Gropius, Mies, and Breuer," in *The Intellectual Migration: Europe and America, 1930–1960*, Donald H. Fleming and Bernard Bailyn, eds. (Charles Warren Center, Cambridge, Mass., 1968), vol. 2, *Perspectives in American History*, 485–543; Ada Louise Huxtable, *The Tall Building Artistically Considered: The Search for a Skyscraper Style* (New York, 1985); Tom Wolfe, *From Bauhaus to Our House* (New York, 1981). See too, the recollections of Leo Slizard, the collectively authored articles on John Von Neumann, Donald Fleming's study of refugee biologists, and Charles Weiner's of physicists, in *Intellectual Migration*, 94–269; Wolfgang Kohler, "The Scientists from Europe and Their New Environment," in *The Cultural Migration: The European Scholar in America*, ed. Franz Neumann et al. (Philadelphia, 1953), 112–137; and Laura Fermi, *The Illustrious Immigrants: The Intellectual Migration from Europe, 1930–1941* (Chicago, 1968). On European Gestalt psychology and Freudian analysis, see the articles by Jean and George Mandler and Marie Johoda in *Intellectual Migration*, 371–445; Lewis Coser, *The Refugee Scholars in America: Their Impact and Experiences* (New Haven, 1984); and Rudolph Arnheim, "Max Wertheim and Gestalt Psychology," in the special issue, "The Legacy of the German Refugee Intellectuals," *Salmagundi* 10–11 (Fall 1969–Winter 1970): 97–103. Two other important works are Anthony Heilbut, *Exiled in Paradise: German Refugee Artists and Intellectuals in America from the 1930s to the Present* (New York, 1983); and *The Muses Flee Hitler: Cultural Transfer and Adaptation, 1930–1945*, eds. Jarrell C. Jackman and Carla M. Borden (Washington, D.C., 1983). For a perceptive critical analysis of Erich Fromm, see John H. Schaar, *Escape From Authority: Perspectives on Erich Fromm* (New York, 1961).

On conservative economics, the classic text is Friedrich von Hayek, *The Road to Serfdom* (Chicago, 1946); see the responses by Herman Finer, *The Road to Reaction* (Boston, 1946); and Sidney Hook, *Political Power and Personal Freedom: Critical Studies in Democracy, Communism, and Civil Rights* (New York, 1959), 377–437, which includes the Hook-Eastman exchange over von Hayek and free-market economics. On the enduring influence of Austrian economics, see Mary Sennholz, ed., *On Freedom and Free Enterprise: Essays in Honor of Ludwig von Mises*, 2 vols. (Menlo Park, Calif., 1971).

For the Frankfurt School, see Theodor W. Adorno, "Scientific Experiences of a European Scholar in America," in *Intellectual Migration*, 338–370, and "Veblen's Attack on Culture," *Studies in Philosophy and Social Science* 9 (1941): 389–413. The literature on critical theory is enormous. The best place to begin is Martin Jay, *The Dialectical Imagination: A History of the Frankfurt School and the Institute of Social Research* (Cambridge, Mass., 1969); see also David Held, *Introduction to Critical Theory: Horkheimer to Habermas* (Berkeley, 1980). Hannah Arendt's most enduring work is *The Human Condition: A Study of the Central Dilemmas Facing Modern Man* (Chicago, 1958); a few years later

Arendt applied her classical predilections to the American Founders in *On Revolution* (New York, 1963); Leo Strauss's critical stance toward modern liberalism is articulated in *Natural Right and History* (Chicago, 1953).

The discussion of postwar American modern music and art was drawn from Leonard Bernstein, *The Joy of Music* (New York, 1954); David Schiff, *The Music of Elliot Carter* (New York, 1983); Ralph Ellison, *Shadow and Act* (New York, 1966), 187–240; Irving Sandler *The New York School: The Painters and Sculptors of the Fifties* (New York, 1978); Hilton Kramer, *The Age of the Avant-Garde* (New York, 1973); Robert Hughes, *The Shock of the New* (New York, 1982); Harold Rosenberg, *Anxious Object: Art Today and Its Audience* (New York, 1964); and *The Tradition and the New* (New York, 1959); Clement Greenberg, *Art and Culture: Critical Essays* (Boston, 1961); Tom Wolfe, *The Painted Word* (New York, 1975); a challenge to Wolfe's interpretation may be found in Edmund Burke, *A Philosophical Enquiry into the Origins of Our Ideas of the Sublime and the Beautiful* (1757; London: Routledge and Kegan Paul, 1958).

In *How New York Stole the Idea of Modern Art: Abstract Expressionism, Freedom, and the Cold War* (Chicago, 1983), Serge Guilbaut argues that the work of New York artists "came to coincide" with the image American liberalism was assuming vis-à-vis the Soviet Union: openness to experimentation, existential anxiety, and the like. For a less strained and more careful analysis of art and the cold war, see Jane deHart Matthews, "Art and Politics in Cold War America," *American Historical Review* 81 (Oct. 1976): 762–87.

On drama, see Catharine Hughes, *American Playwrights, 1945–1974* (London, 1976), 15–31; Arthur and Barbara Gelb, *O'Neill* (New York, 1962); John Henry Raleigh, "O'Neill's *Long Day's Journey into Night* and New England Catholicism," *Partisan Review* 26 (Fall 1959): 573–92; Arthur Miller, *Collected Plays* (New York, 1957); this valuable collection includes the author's fifty-page introduction. On literature, see William Van O'Connor and Edward Stone, *A Casebook on Ezra Pound* (New York, 1959); Warren French, ed., *The Fifties: Fiction, Poetry, Drama* (Deland, Florida, 1970); Robert von Hallberg, *American Poetry and Culture, 1945–1980* (Cambridge, 1985). Sylvia Plath, *Ariel* (New York, 1966); Edward Butscher, *Sylvia Plath: Method and Madness* (New York, 1976); also see Linda Wagner-Martin, *Sylvia Plath: A Biography* (New York, 1987), which appeared too late to use here. Carlos Baker, *Ernest Hemingway: A Life Story* (New York, 1969); Philip Young, "Ernest Hemingway," in *American Writers: A Collection of Literary Biographies*, ed. Leonard Unger (New York, 1974), vol. II, 247–70; Lowell's poem is "To Speak of the Woe that is in Marriage," in *Robert Lowell: Selected Poems* (London, 1965), 53.

The social philosopher who best conveyed the postwar mood of disenchantment was Daniel Bell and his controversial *The End of Ideology: On the Exhaustion of Political Ideas in the Fifties* (1960; rev. ed. New York: Free Press, 1965). See also Howard Brick, *Daniel Bell and the Decline of Intellectual Radicalism: Social Theory and Political Reconciliation in the 1940s* (Madison, Wis., 1986); Nathan Liebowitz, *Daniel Bell and the Agony of Modern Liberalism* (New York, 1985); Chaim I. Waxman, ed., *The End of Ideology Debate* (New York, 1968). Other social theorists are discussed in Guy Rocher, *Talcott Parsons and American Sociology* (London, 1974); John P. Diggins, "The Socialization of Authority and the Dilemmas of American Liberalism," *Social Research* 46 (Autumn 1979): 454–86; for an exceptional but important radical view, see C. Wright Mills, *The Power Elite* (New York, 1956); and the collection of essays in Richard Gillam, ed., *Power in Postwar America* (Boston, 1971).

On economic thought the representative figure was John Kenneth Galbraith and his

American Capitalism: The Theory of Countervailing Power (Boston, 1952), and *The Affluent Society* (1958; New York: Signet ed., 1963), quoted 199–200; and David Potter, *People of Plenty: Economic Abundance and the American Character* (Chicago, 1954). For political and historical thought, see Robert Dahl, *A Preface to Democratic Theory* (Chicago, 1956); Charles A. Beard, *The Republic: Conversations on Fundamentals* (New York, 1943); Carl Becker, *New Liberties for Old* (New Haven, 1941); Arthur Schlesinger, Jr., *The Age of Jackson* (Boston, 1945), quoted 523; Daniel J. Boorstin, *The Genius of American Politics* (Chicago, 1953); John P. Diggins, "Consciousness and Ideology in American History: The Burden of Daniel J. Boorstin," *American Historical Review* 76 (Feb. 1971): 99–118; Richard Hofstadter, *The American Political Tradition and the Men Who Made It* (New York, 1948); *The Age of Reform: From Bryan to FDR* (New York, 1955); and Louis Hartz, *The Liberal Tradition in America* (New York, 1955).

On philosophy and theology, see Mortimer J. Adler, "God and the Professors," in *Science, Philosophy and Religion: A Symposium*, vol. 1 (New York, 1941), 37–38, 121; William J. Kenealy, "The Majesty of the Law," *Loyola Law Review* (1950), reprinted in *American Ideas: Source Readings in the Intellectual History of the United States*, eds. Gerald N. Grob and Robert N. Beck (New York, 1963), 333–47; Sidney Hook, "The New Failure of Nerve," *Partisan Review* 10 (Jan.–Feb. 1943): 2–23 and John Dewey, "Antinaturalism in Extremis," ibid., 24–39; Yervant H. Krikorian, ed., *Naturalism and the Human Spirit* (New York, 1944); Henry Bamford Parkes, *The Pragmatic Test* (New York, 1941); William Barrett, *Irrational Man: A Study in Existential Philosophy* (Garden City, N.Y., 1958); Walter Kaufmann, "The Reception of Existentialism in the United States," *Salmagundi* 10–11 (Fall 1969–Winter 1970): 69–96; Paul Tillich, "The Conquest of Theological Provincialism," in *Intellectual Migration*, 138–56; *Religion and the Intellectuals: A Symposium* (New York, Partisan Review pamphlet, 1950); Thomas Merton, *The Seven Storey Mountain* (New York, 1948); and Will Herberg, *Judaism and Modern Man* (New York, 1951). On the great books debate, see James Sloan Allen, *The Romance of Commerce and Culture* (Chicago, 1983), 78–112; William F. Buckley, Jr., *God and Man at Yale* (Chicago, 1951); and Diggins, *Up From Communism*.

For the New York intellectuals and the San Francisco beatniks see Lionel Trilling, *The Liberal Imagination: Essays on Literature and Politics* (New York, 1950), Irving Howe, "The New York Intellectuals," in *Decline of the New* (New York, 1970), 211–68; William Barrett, *The Truants: Adventures Among the Intellectuals* (New York, 1983), quote on 37; Bell *End of Ideology*, 299–314; Alex Bloom, *Prodigal Sons: The New York Intellectuals and Their World* (New York, 1986); Alan M. Wald, *The New York Intellectuals: The Rise and Decline of the Anti-Stalinist Left* (Chapel Hill, N.C., 1987); Norman Podhoretz, *Making It* (New York, 1967); Alfred Kazin, *On Native Grounds: An Interpretation of Modern American Prose Fiction* (New York, 1942); Leslie Fiedler, *The End of American Innocence: Essays on Culture and Politics* (Boston, 1955); Paul Goodman, *Growing Up Absurd: Problems of Youth in the Organized Society* (New York, 1960). Norman Mailer's "The White Negro" first appeared in *Dissent* and is reprinted in his *Advertisements for Myself* (New York, 1959), 312–28. "Our Country and Our Culture: A Symposium" was published as a pamphlet under the title *America and the Intellectuals* (New York: Partisan Review, 1953). Two fine historical studies are Richard Pells, *The Liberal Mind in a Conservative Age* (New York, 1985); and Morris Dickstein, *Gates of Eden* (New York, 1977); Henry Miller is quoted in Kazin, 469; Allen Ginsberg, *Howl and Other Poems* (San Francisco, 1956), 9–26; Jack Kerouac, *On the Road* (New York, 1955); Kerouac is quoted in Bruce Cook, *The Beat Generation* (New York, 1971), 89. See also Barry Gifford and Lawrence Lee, *Jack's Book: An Oral Biography of Jack Kerouac* (New York, 1977); John Tytell, *Naked Angels: The Lives and Literature of the Beat Generation* (New York, 1976); and for a female perspective, Joyce Johnson, *Minor Characters* (Boston, 1983); Norman Podhoretz, "The Know-Nothing Bohemians," *Partisan Review* 25 (Spring 1958): 305–18; for Diana Trilling's views, see Dickstein, *Gates of Eden*, 3–5; Goodman's criticisms are cited in Irving Howe, "Mass Society and Postmodern Fiction," in *Decline of the New*, 205; his own quote on 206. The poem "The Goal of Intellectual Man" is Richard Eberhart's, in *Selected Poems, 1930–1965* (New York, 1965), 17.

CHAPTER EIGHT

On the politics and literature of black writers, see Richard Wright, "I Tried to be a Communist," *Atlantic Monthly* 174, Aug. 1944, 61–70 and 175, Sept. 1944, 48–56; Robert Bone, *Richard Wright* (Minneapolis, 1969); Irving Howe, "Black Boys and Native Sons, in *A World More Attractive* (New York, 1963), 98–122. Ralph Ellison, *Invisible Man* (New York, 1952); Ellison's remark on a Jim Crow army is quoted in Robert O'Meally, "Ralph Ellison," in *American Writers*, ed. A. Walton Litz (New York, 1980), supplement 2, part 4, 221–50; Franklin L. Broderick, *W. E. B. Du Bois: Negro Leader in a Time of Crisis* (Stanford, 1959); Langston Hughes's poem is in *Montage of a Dream Deferred* (New York, 1951); Baldwin's remark about his father is quoted in Perrett, *Dream of Greatness*, 358; Clayton R. Koppes and Gregory D. Black, "Blacks, Loyalty, and Motion-Picture Propaganda in World War II," *Journal of American History* 73 (Sept. 1986): 383–406; Gail Lumet Buckley, *The Hornes: An American Family* (New York, 1986); Winfred Lynn's letter to the draftboard is reprinted in Dwight Macdonald, "The Novel Case of Winfred Lynn," *The Nation* 156, Feb. 20, 1943, 268–70; Robert Allen, "The Port Chicago Disaster and Its Aftermath," *The Black Scholar* (Spring 1982): 3–29.

On the background to the Brown decision, see the revealing memoir, "The Solicitor General's Office, Justice Frankfurter, and Civil Rights Legislation, 1946–1960: An Oral History, Philip Elman interviewed by Norman Silber," *Harvard Law Review* (Feb. 1987): 817–52. The description of Warren's "middle-of-the-road" philosophy is in Eugene Gressman, "The Coming Trials of Justice Warren," *New Republic* 128, Oct. 12, 1953, 8–10. See also Bernard Schwartz and Stephen Lesker, *Inside the Warren Court, 1953–1969* (Garden City, N.Y., 1983), 68–102; Richard Kluger, *Simple Justice* (New York, 1975); J. H. Wilkinson, *From Brown to Bakke: The Supreme Court and School Integration, 1954–1978* (New York, 1979); for the controversy over the validity of sociological evidence, see I. A. Newby, *Challenge to the Court: Social Scientists and the Defense of Segregation* (Baton Rouge, La., 1969); two opposing views, one contemporary and supportive of Brown, the other retrospective and critical, are C. Vann Woodward, *The Strange Career of Jim Crow* (New York, 1955); and Raymond Wolters, *The Burden of Brown: Thirty Years of School Desegregation* (Knoxville, Tenn., 1984).

Eisenhower's statements warning against speedy integration are in Richard Polenberg, *One Nation Divisible: Class, Race, and Ethnicity in the United States Since 1938* (New York, 1980), 159–60; Ike's response to the question about equal rights for women is in Ambrose, *Eisenhower*, 412. For southern resistance to *Brown*, see Walter F. Murphy, "The South Counterattacks: The Anti-NAACP Laws," *Western Political Quarterly* 12 (June 1959): 371–90; the Little Rock confrontation is discussed in Perrett, *Dream of Greatness*, 428–30; Ambrose, *Eisenhower*, 2 (New York, 1984) 402–23; Robert Frederick Burk, *The Eisenhower Administration and Black Civil Rights* (Knoxville, Tenn., 1984);

Tony Freyer, *The Little Rock Crisis: A Constitutional Interpretation* (Westport, Conn., 1984); Stevenson's remarks are in Martin, *Adlai Stevenson*, 417–18.

On the Montgomery boycott and Martin Luther King, Jr., see Janet Stevenson, "Rosa Parks Wouldn't Budge," *American Heritage* 23, Feb. 1972, 56–64; Martin Luther King., Jr., *Stride Toward Freedom: The Montgomery Story* (New York, 1958) and *Letter From a Birmingham Jail* (pamphlet, Philadelphia: American Friends Service Committee, 1963); Stephen B. Oates, *Let the Trumpet Sound: The Life of Martin Luther King, Jr.* (New York, 1982); John J. Anshoro, *Martin Luther King., Jr., The Making of a Mind* (New York, 1982); Eisenhower and the black janitor are quoted in Oates, *Let the Trumpet Sound*, 112, 134; for a study of Gandhi and King, see Elliot M. Zashin, *Civil Disobedience and Democracy* (New York, 1971), 149–94; a recent thorough biography that appeared too late to use here is David J. Garrow, *Bearing the Cross: Martin Luther King, Jr., and the Southern Christian Leadership Conference* (New York, 1986).

CHAPTER NINE

On United States diplomacy in Asia under the Eisenhower administration, see Iriye, *Cold War in Asia*; Schaller, *US and China in the Twentieth Century*; and George and Smoke, *Deterrence*. Dulles is quoted in James Shepley, "How Dulles Averted War," *Life* 40, Jan. 16, 1956, 70–80. The position of the Republican party was critically analyzed in "Must We Fight in Indo-China?" *New Republic* 130, May 3, 1954, 7–8; on the Suez crisis, see "Sharing the Blame," *New Republic* 135, Nov. 19, 1956, 5–6; on the Hungarian crisis, Stephen Ambrose and Alonzo L. Hamby are among the many historians who have concluded that Eisenhower had no alternative but complete nonintervention (Ambrose, *Eisenhower*, 367–75; Hamby, *Imperial Years*, 202). The discussion about the possibility of negotiating a mutual withdrawal of forces is indebted to Richard Lowenthal's analysis in "Were We Helpless?" *New Republic* 135, Nov. 26, 1956, 9–15; see also Richard Lowenthal, *World Communism: The Disintegration of a Secular Faith* (New York, 1964).

On the election of 1956, see Lubell, *Revolt of the Moderates*; John Barlow Martin, *Adlai Stevenson*, 230–390, Arthur Larson, *A Republican Looks at His Party* (New York, 1956); Richard M. Nixon, *Six Crises* (Garden City, N.Y., 1962); Dwight D. Eisenhower, *Mandate for Change, 1953–1956* (New York, 1963).

Eisenhower's second inaugural and his comments on Quemoy and Ma-tsu are quoted in Ambrose, 484–85, as is Bridge's criticisms of foreign aid, 379; Dulles's denial of Soviets in the Mideast is in George and Smoke, *Deterrence*, 309–58; the growing rifts among Communist countries that the United States failed to appreciate are treated in Lowenthal, *World Communism*; Kennan's proposal for mutual withdrawal was first elaborated in a series of BBC lectures and then published as *Russia, the Atom and the West* (New York 1958); see also Michael Howard, *Disengagement in Europe* (Baltimore, 1958); and James E. King, Jr., "Kennan and Kennanism: The Case Against Disengagement," *New Republic* 138, April 7, 1958, 12–16.

The senator who proclaimed "a week of shame and danger" in response to Sputnik was Henry ("Scoop") Jackson of Washington, quoted in Manchester, *The Glory*, 788; the discussion of the space race is drawn from Walter A. McDougall, *The Heavens and the Earth: A Political History of the Space Age* (New York, 1985) and Khrushchev is quoted on 255–56. Tom Bower, *The Paperclip Conspiracy: The Hunt for the Nazi Scientists* (Boston, 1987) appeared too late for use here. See also Sir Bernard Lovell, "The

Great Competition in Space," *Foreign Affairs* 5 (Oct. 1971): 124–38; John Lear, "Ike and the Peaceful Atom," in *Eisenhower as President*, ed. Albertson, 87–101. On the armament race, see Henry A. Kissinger, *Nuclear Weapons and Foreign Policy* (New York, 1957); Bernard Brodie, *Strategy in the Missile Age* (Princeton, 1959); for Brodie's prescient views at the premissile dawn of the cold war, see his "Military Policy and the Atomic Bomb," in Wylie, *American Thought: 1947,* 271–89; three sophisticated works by Lawrence Freedman are crucial to an understanding of the armament race: *The Evolution of Nuclear Strategy* (New York, 1983); *US Intelligence and the Soviet Strategic Threat* (1977; 2nd ed., Princeton, 1986); and "The First Two Generations of Nuclear Strategists," in *Makers of Modern Strategy: From Machiavelli to the Nuclear Age*, ed. Peter Paret (Princeton, 1986), 735–78.

Chapter Ten

In addition to the Supreme Court upholding civil liberties after McCarthyism, the cold war also resulted in some shifting theoretical perspectives on the Constitution. See Herman Belz, "Changing Conceptions of Constitutionalism in the Era of World War II and the Cold War," *Journal of American History* 59 (Dec. 1972): 640–89; see also Martin Shapiro, "The Supreme Court: From Warren to Burger," *The New American Political System*, ed. Anthony Y. King, (Washington, D.C., 1979), 179–211. On labor, see Bell, *End of Ideology*, 175–209; Dos Passos, *Midcentury;* Herbert Hill, "The ILGWU Today— The Decay of a Labor Union," *New Politics*, 1 (1962): 6–17; Adlai Stevenson's remark on the Democrats and business is in "My Faith in Democratic Capitalism," *Fortune* 52, Oct. 1955, 126–27, 156–68; Paul H. Douglas, *In the Fullness of Time* (New York, 1972); on the Adams-Goldfine scandal, see Hughes, *Ordeal of Power*, 266–69, Manchester, *The Glory*, 834–43; the *Chicago Daily News* and other critical remarks on Eisenhower during the 1958 elections are in Manchester, *Glory*, 853, and Perrett, *Dream of Greatness*, 554.

On threats to the environment, see Rachel Carson, *The Silent Spring* (Boston, 1962); Richard L. Neuberger, "Unfinished Business Outdoors," *New Republic* 140, Mar. 9, 1959, 15–16; Tom Lehrer's songs and photos of bomb shelters are in Time-Life Books *This Fabulous Century: America, 1950–1960* (New York, 1970), 31, 72–73; much of discussion of radiation and critics of nuclear armament comes from Miller and Nowak, *The Fifties*, 43–83; Perrett, *A Dream*, 454–62; and H. Stuart Hughes, *An Essay for Our Times* (New York, 1950).

On the CIA and Batista, see Ambrose, *Eisenhower*, 504–7; the "new humanist socialism" image of Castro is described in Dennis H. Wrong, "The American Left and Cuba," *Commentary* 33, Feb. 1962, 93–103; Castro's "feeding on humanity" is quoted in Manchester, *The Glory*, 860–63; Eisenhower's preference for a "third force" is quoted in Ambrose, 505; The case for Castro was made by C. Wright Mills, *Listen Yankee: The Revolution in Cuba* (New York, 1960); Roca is quoted in Boris Rosenberg, "Latin America: Castro's Course," in *Polycentrism: The New Factor in International Communism*, eds. Walter Laquer and Leopold Labedz (New York, 1962), 252; Carlo Franqui, *Family Portrait with Fidel: A Memoir*, trans. Alfred MacAdam (New York, 1984), 78; see also Richard E. Welch, Jr., *Response to Revolution: The United States and the Cuban Revolution, 1959–1961* (Chapel Hill, 1985); Theodore Draper, *Castro's Revolution: Myth and Realities* (New York, 1961), and his "The Strange Case of Professor Williams," *New Leader* 46 (April 29, 1963), 13–20; and the recent Tad Szulc, *Fidel: A Critical Portrait* (New York, 1986).

Khrushchev's tour is described in Manchester, *The Glory*, 855–59; the U-2 episode in Michael R. Beschloss, *Mayday: Eisenhower, Khrushchev, and the U-2 Affair* (New York, 1986); and Ulam, *The Rivals*, 310–11.

The Gallup poll on the 1960 election is in "Political Notes," *Time* 75, June 20, 1960, 12; Nixon debating Khrushchev in Manchester, *The Glory*, 855–57; John F. Kennedy in West Virginia, in Theodore Sorensen, *Kennedy* (New York, 1965), 65–66; the choice of Lyndon Johnson in Perrett, *Dream of Greatness*, 564–65, and Theodore H. White, *The Making of the President: 1960* (New York, 1961), 172–79; Eisenhower's remark about Nixon in Nixon, *Six Crises*, 339; the exchange between Jacqueline and JFK in White, 18; the Kennedys and King in Arthur Schlesinger, Jr., *A Thousand Days: John F. Kennedy in the White House* (Boston, 1965), 74; for the involvement of the family in the campaign and an insightful portrait of its members, see Doris Kearns Goodwin, *The Fitzgeralds and the Kennedys: An American Saga* (New York, 1986).

CONCLUSION

The changing attitudes toward desegregation are discussed in Benjamin Muse, *Ten Years of Prelude: The Story of Integration Since the Supreme Court's 1954 Decision* (New York, 1964). On the legacy of the arms race, see Freedman, "The First Two Generations of Nuclear Strategists," *Makers of Modern Strategy*; his quote is from *Evolution of Nuclear Strategy*, 399; Kenneth S. Davis, "Ike and I," *American Scholar* 55 (Winter 1985–86): 55–74; *Fortune* magazine, *USA the Permanent Revolution* (New York, 1951), ix, xv, 30. All the quotes bewailing America are from Hans Meyerhoff, "The Case of the Missing Purpose," *The Nation* 191, Aug. 20, 1960, 85–89.

Photograph Credits

Page 4, AP/Wide World Photos; p. 5, National Archives; p. 11, AP/Wide World Photos; p. 24, Alfred Eisenstaedt, *Life* Magazine © Time Inc.; p. 25, The Library of Congress; p. 27, UPI/Bettmann Newsphotos; p. 28, The Library of Congress; p. 30, Wide World Photos; p. 33, National Archives; p. 40, UPI/Bettmann Photos; p. 44, Ralph Morse, *Life* Magazine © Time Inc.; p. 46, Wide World Photos; p. 49, UN Photo; p. 50, UN Photo; p. 51, Alfred Eisenstaedt, *Life* Magazine © 1945 Time Inc.; p. 52, AP/Wide World Photos; p. 60, US Army Photograph; p. 78, Wide World Photos; p. 82, The Library of Congress; p. 83, Alfred Eisenstaedt, *Life* Magazine © Time Inc.; p. 87, Eastfoto; p. 90, AP/Wide World Photos; p. 97, UPI/Bettmann Newsphotos; p. 106, Wide World Photos; p. 113, AP/Wide World Photos; p. 114, AP/Wide World Photos; p. 123, AP/Wide World Photos; p. 129, UPI/Bettmann Newsphotos; p. 140, UPI/Bettmann Newsphotos; p. 150, UPI/Bettmann Newsphotos; p. 160, Springer/Bettmann Film Archive; p. 162, Leonard McCombe, *Life* Magazine © 1947 Time Inc.; p. 164, UPI/Bettmann Newsphotos; p. 168, AP/Wide World Photos; p. 170, UPI/Bettmann Newsphotos; p. 172, AP/Wide World Photos; p. 174, AP/Wide World Photos; p. 176, Courtesy William F. Buckley, Jr.; p. 182, J. R. Eyerman, *Life* Magazine © 1953 Time Inc.; p. 184, Joe Steinmetz, courtesy The Carpenter Center, Harvard University; p. 189, Culver Pictures, Inc.; p. 190, The Bettmann Archive; p. 193, Wide World Photos; p. 195, Herb Gehr, *Life* Magazine © 1943 Time Inc.; p. 196, AP/Wide World Photos; p. 197, Billy Rose Theatre Collection, The New York Public Library at Lincoln Center, Astor, Lenox and Tilden Foundation; p. 199, Museum of Modern Art/Film Stills Archive; p. 200, Bruce Davidson/Magnum Photos, Inc.; p. 205, Museum of Modern Art/Film Stills Archive; p. 213, Joe Steinmetz, courtesy The Carpenter Center, Harvard University; p. 215, courtesy W. W. Norton & Co.; p. 218, courtesy Estevez; p. 222, courtesy G. D. Hackett; p. 223 © Martha Swope; p. 224, Seagram Building, 1957 (architects: Ludwig Mies van der Rohe and Philip Johnson; photographer: Ezra Stoller), lent by Joseph E. Seagram & Sons, Inc.; p. 225, Mitchell Valentine/Courtesy AIP Niels Bohr Library; p. 226, Alfred Eisenstaedt, *Life* Magazine © 1947 Time Inc.; p. 228, AP/Wide World Photos; p. 230, courtesy the New School for Social Research; p. 232, G. D. Hackett; p. 233, G. D. Hackett; p. 234, The Metropolitan Museum of Art, Anonymous Gift, 1965; p. 235, Hans Namuth © 1987; p. 238, The Warder Collection; p. 240, Eliot Elisofan, *Life* Magazine © 1947 Time Inc.; p. 241, Springer/Bettmann Film Archive; p. 244, AP/ Wide World Photos; p. 250, Columbiana Collection, Rare Book and Manuscript Library, Columbia University; p. 251, The Library of Congress; p. 264, Columbiana Collection, Rare Book and Manuscript Library, Columbia University; p.

Khrushchev's tour is described in Manchester, *The Glory*, 855–59; the U-2 episode in Michael R. Beschloss, *Mayday: Eisenhower, Khrushchev, and the U-2 Affair* (New York, 1986); and Ulam, *The Rivals*, 310–11.

The Gallup poll on the 1960 election is in "Political Notes," *Time* 75, June 20, 1960, 12; Nixon debating Khrushchev in Manchester, *The Glory*, 855–57; John F. Kennedy in West Virginia, in Theodore Sorensen, *Kennedy* (New York, 1965), 65–66; the choice of Lyndon Johnson in Perrett, *Dream of Greatness*, 564–65, and Theodore H. White, *The Making of the President: 1960* (New York, 1961), 172–79; Eisenhower's remark about Nixon in Nixon, *Six Crises*, 339; the exchange between Jacqueline and JFK in White, 18; the Kennedys and King in Arthur Schlesinger, Jr., *A Thousand Days: John F. Kennedy in the White House* (Boston, 1965), 74; for the involvement of the family in the campaign and an insightful portrait of its members, see Doris Kearns Goodwin, *The Fitzgeralds and the Kennedys: An American Saga* (New York, 1986).

Conclusion

The changing attitudes toward desegregation are discussed in Benjamin Muse, *Ten Years of Prelude: The Story of Integration Since the Supreme Court's 1954 Decision* (New York, 1964). On the legacy of the arms race, see Freedman, "The First Two Generations of Nuclear Strategists," *Makers of Modern Strategy*; his quote is from *Evolution of Nuclear Strategy*, 399; Kenneth S. Davis, "Ike and I," *American Scholar* 55 (Winter 1985–86): 55–74; *Fortune* magazine, *USA the Permanent Revolution* (New York, 1951), ix, xv, 30. All the quotes bewailing America are from Hans Meyerhoff, "The Case of the Missing Purpose," *The Nation* 191, Aug. 20, 1960, 85–89.

Photograph Credits

Index

italicized page numbers refer to photographs